CW01368080

PLANET HONG KONG

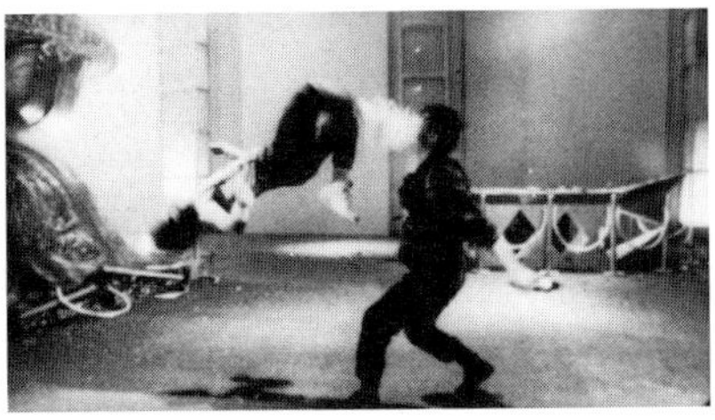
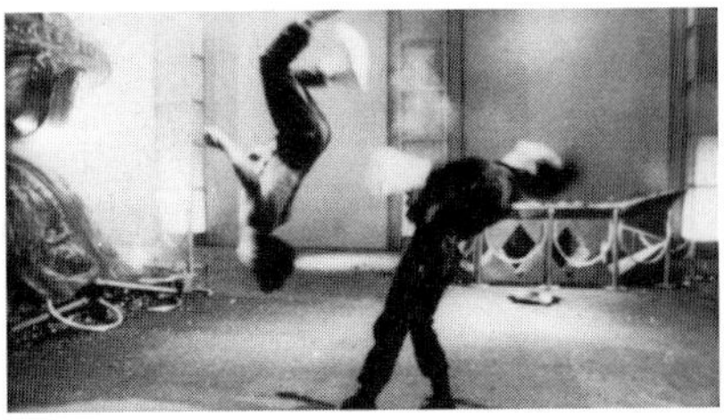
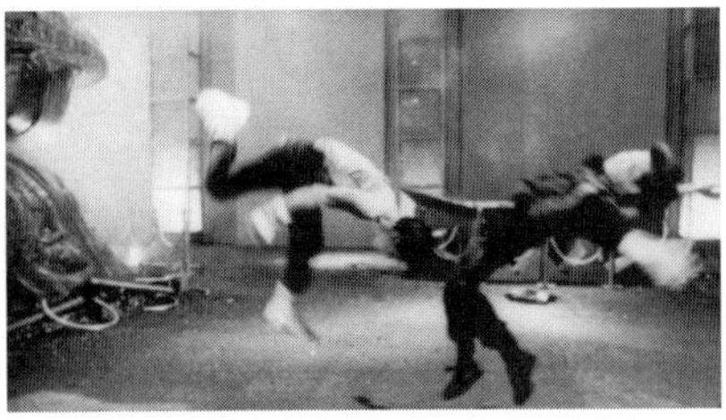

PLANET HONG KONG

POPULAR CINEMA AND THE ART OF ENTERTAINMENT

DAVID BORDWELL

HARVARD UNIVERSITY PRESS
CAMBRIDGE, MASSACHUSETTS, AND LONDON, ENGLAND

Copyright © 2000 by the President and Fellows of Harvard College
All rights reserved
Printed in the United States of America
Designed by Marianne Perlak

Second printing, 2000

Library of Congress Cataloging-in-Publication Data

Bordwell, David.
    Planet Hong Kong : popular cinema and the art of entertainment / David Bordwell.
        p. cm.
    Includes bibliographical references and index.
    ISBN 0-674-00213-X (alk. paper) — ISBN 0-674-00214-8 (pbk. : alk. paper)
    1. Motion pictures—China—Hong Kong—History. I. Title.

PN1993.5.H6 B63 2000
791.43′095125—dc21   99-047938

For Noël
Once more, the power of movies

CONTENTS

PREFACE *ix*

1 · · · **ALL TOO EXTRAVAGANT, TOO GRATUITOUSLY WILD** *1*
HONG KONG AND/AS/OR HOLLYWOOD *18*

2 · · · **LOCAL HEROES** *26*
TWO DRAGONS: BRUCE LEE AND JACKIE CHAN *49*

3 · · · **THE CHINESE CONNECTIONS** *61*

4 · · · **ONCE UPON A TIME IN THE WEST** *82*
ENOUGH TO MAKE STRONG MEN WEEP: JOHN WOO *98*

5 · · · **MADE IN HONG KONG** *115*
A CHINESE FEAST: TSUI HARK *135*

6 · · · **FORMULA, FORM, AND NORM** *149*
WHATEVER YOU WANT: WONG JING *171*

7 · · · **PLOTS, SLACK AND STRETCHED** *178*

8 · · · **MOTION EMOTION: THE ART OF THE ACTION MOVIE** *199*
THREE MARTIAL MASTERS: ZHANG CHE, LAU KAR-LEUNG, KING HU *248*

9 · · · **AVANT-POP CINEMA** *261*
ROMANCE ON YOUR MENU: CHUNGKING EXPRESS *282*

FURTHER READING *291*
NOTES *295*
ACKNOWLEDGMENTS *321*
INDEX *323*

PREFACE

Some of the best books on Hong Kong start with the author flying in to the old Kai Tak airport, the jumbo jet nearly scraping the rooftops of Kowloon City before wheeling around sharply to land. (An Australian pilot is supposed to have described the trip as eight hours of sheer boredom followed by eight minutes of sheer terror.) This magnificent arrival is impressed in my memory too, but the real thrill came later, when on a sultry March night I wandered along Nathan Road, staring up at a forest of towering neon. Columns of Chinese characters several stories high, blazing crimson or gold, stretched alongside more familiar names: Toshiba in silver and red, an aqua OK signaling karaoke.

Drifting with the crowd, I sauntered among old men walking gravely with hands clasped behind their back, executive men and women hollering into cell phones, matrons strolling four and five abreast, children trotting along in shorts and suspenders, slender boys in white shirts and blue trousers, auburn-haired girls with knapsack purses strapped to their backs. There were plenty of tourists: big German and Australian couples appraised cameras and Discmen in shop windows while American students rummaged through a cart of bootleg CDs. The noise was overwhelming: buses screeched to discharge their passengers, people shouted amiably at one another. Occasionally a man would try to pull me out of the commotion. "Copy watch?" "Sir! Where are you from, sir? Are you thinking of a suit?"

To cross from Nathan Road to Salisbury Road, the street that runs along the harbor, is to leave most of the turmoil behind. Among the cool columns of the Cultural Centre, at the tip of the peninsula, people shift gears. The Centre is less popular for its museums and theaters, I suspect, than for its tranquillity; later I would discover that every day families fresh from the Marriage Registry gathered in front of a fountain there for photographs, the bride dazzling in a white gown and perhaps clutching a Snoopy handbag. That first night, though, I was behind the Centre staring at the skyline of Hong Kong Island across the harbor.

As with all legendary views, the postcard version is too cramped. Here were skyscrapers spread out carefully, as if designed to lead your eye from the spiky profile of the Bank of China to the Neo-Deco Central Plaza and soon enough to the gigantic glowing signs for Citizen and San Miguel. Behind these, misty green hills rose to the Peak. Everything was reflected in the bay, not in perfect outline but in thousands of red, blue, and gold highlights broken by the ferries and barges that crisscrossed your line of sight. This view may be Hong Kong's greatest work of art. I picked up smells too—the pungent "fragrant harbor" that gave the colony its name, the odor of floor wax from the lobby of the Centre. On the esplanade, couples loitered and tourists snapped photos of the great contrivance shining across the water.

What had brought me here? In the fall of 1973, soon after I had started teaching at the University of Wisconsin, I went to see *Five Fingers of Death* paired with *The Chinese Connection* in the dilapidated Majestic Theatre. Not long afterward I saw *Enter the Dragon*. These movies shook me up. A few years later in Richmond, Virginia, I saw *Bruce Lee's Game of Death*, a film of such surpassing oddness that I screened it for my film theory class. At the same time, during trips to Europe, I caught up with King Hu's exhilarating masterworks.

During the 1980s, while writing about Hollywood cinema and film theory and the films of Yasujiro Ozu, I occasionally checked in on Hong Kong cinema. I caught a Jackie Chan here, a Tsui Hark there, and cable TV yielded up oddities like *Shaolin Kung-Fu Mystagogue*. The films appealed to me as "pure cinema," popular fare that, like American Westerns and gangster movies of the 1930s, seemed to have an intuitive understanding of the kinetics of movies. Over these years, my old friend Tony Rayns saw to it that I was sent the annual catalogues of the Hong Kong International Film Festival, and so I came to learn something of this cinema's history.

In the early 1990s I dived in, not least because these movies aroused my students' passion in a way that I had not seen for a long time. I began booking Hong Kong films for my courses, subscribing to the fanzines, picking up videotapes and laserdiscs. Soon I was convinced that this was a popular cinema of great vigor. When I gained a semester's leave in the spring of 1995, I decided that it was time to visit the Festival.

Through the Festival I met Li Cheuk-to, Athena Tsui, Stephen Teo, Shu Kei, Michael Campi, and many others who have become firm friends. I also saw a selection of recent films, a retrospective of postwar movies, and a sample of what was playing at the moment. At the first Hong Kong Critics Society award ceremony I met Ann Hui, Wong Kar-wai, and other filmmakers. I managed to slip into the Hong Kong Film Awards, where I snapped photos and got autographs of stars and directors I admired. During my three weeks' stay I lived in a fan's paradise. I even ate at Chungking Mansions.

I became addicted to visiting Hong Kong. Sometime after the third trip, at the urgings of my wife, Kristin Thompson, and my friend Noël Carroll, I decided to write a book. It was a difficult decision, not only because I don't speak or read Chinese. For one thing, there is already a lot written about this cinema, and there is going to be a lot more. Web pages are sprouting at this moment. Further, I have seen only about three hundred seventy Hong Kong movies. (If you think that's a lot, you are not yet a hardcore fan.) Still, perhaps out of stubborn naïveté, I thought that I had something original to say about the movies produced in this tiny corner of Asia. I thought that I could explore this cinema not as an expression of local society, nor as part of the history of Chinese culture, but as an example of how popular cinema can produce movies that are beautiful.

What follows, then, is an essayistic attempt to understand the interplay of art and entertainment in one popular cinema. Because I have felt free to choose what interests me, I have left to one side, for example, the Cantonese Opera films, the social realist tradition of the 1950s, the musicals and comedies and melodramas of the 1960s, and the films of Sadean violence. I have also not touched upon the work of certain directors whose work is unavailable in good film prints. Selective though it is, I hope that *Planet Hong Kong* will serve as both an introduction to Hong Kong film and an exploration of matters not addressed elsewhere—industry background, production practices, and above all filmic structure and style.

The book also delineates Hong Kong's significance for international popular filmmaking. How did cheap movies made in a distant outpost of the British Empire achieve broad international appeal, while European filmmakers bemoan their inability to reach even their own national audiences? How did Hong Kong filmmakers manage to create artful movies within the framework of modern entertainment? What can these films tell us about storytelling in a mass medium—its history and craft, its design features and emotional effects? Such questions inevitably lead us back to the unique achievements of Hong Kong cinema and to an assessment of the delights and the shortcomings of the films themselves.

Some might say that the book risks imposing an outsider's values on a cinema that exists in and through unique cultural circumstances. But despite many claims to the contrary in our multicultural milieu, there are more commonalities than differences in human cultures: universal physical, social, and psychological predispositions and the facial expressions of many emotions will be quickly understood in a film, whatever its country of origin. Many practices—such as acquiring shelter and caring for children—are similar in different societies. Cultures also converge historically, because when they come into contact, borrowing is inevitable. The traditions of Hollywood and Japanese cinema have powerfully influenced Hong Kong film.

Popular cinema, moreover, is deliberately designed to cross cultural boundaries. Reliance on pictures and music rather than on words, appeal to cross-cultural emotions, easily learned conventions of style and story, and redundancy at many levels all help films travel outside their immediate context. That audiences all over the world enjoy Hong Kong movies dramatically illustrates the transcultural power of popular cinema.

Today the Asian financial crisis has driven the crowds from Nathan Road, and the Hong Kong film industry is struggling to survive. This book portrays a vibrant moment in the history of popular film and shows how it participates in a vigorous tradition of mass entertainment. That tradition is nearly as old as the century that is now ending, and it is becoming, day by day, more powerful in every land. It is time we understood it better. These films can help us to do so, and along the way they can show us a splendid time.

Madison, Wisconsin
December 1999

PLANET HONG KONG

1

ALL TOO EXTRAVAGANT, TOO GRATUITOUSLY WILD

Hong Kong cinema is one of the success stories of film history. For about twenty years, this city-state of around six million people had one of the most robust cinema industries in the world. In number of films released, it regularly surpassed nearly all Western countries. In export it was second only to the United States. It ruled the East Asian market, eventually obliterating one neighboring country's film industry. Distributed in the West, Hong Kong films became a cult phenomenon on an unprecedented scale. Although a typical production cost about as much as a German or French one, the industry enjoyed no subsidies of the sort that keep European cinema alive. Hong Kong movies were made simply because millions of people wanted to watch them.

Over the last two decades American film has devoured the world market. In some countries Hollywood claims 90 percent of box office receipts. Yet over the same years Hollywood movies held a minority position in Hong Kong, with U.S. market share sometimes falling to less than 30 percent. Global blockbusters often failed in Hong Kong. *Raiders of the Lost Ark* (1981) ranked only sixteenth in local admissions, beaten by *The Dead and the Deadly*, *Legendary Weapons of China*, and *Boat People*. *Who Framed Roger Rabbit?* (1989) earned just one-third the grosses of *God of Gamblers*. Not until the fateful year 1997 did Hollywood edge out the local product, claiming slightly over half the admission receipts—and some would blame that outcome on local underproduction and elevated ticket prices for Western fare.

How did this tiny cinema come to be so successful? Some answers lie in history and culture, but many others are to be found in the films themselves. Hong Kong's film industry offered something audiences desired. Year in and year out it produced dozens of fresh, lively, and thrilling movies. Since the 1970s it has been arguably the world's most energetic, imaginative popular cinema.

Every fan has favorite examples; here are two of mine. At the climax of the first part of King Hu's *A Touch of Zen* (1971), a swordsman and swords-

1.1 Swordfighters clash in midair in *A Touch of Zen*.

woman confront enemy warriors in a bamboo grove. It is no ordinary combat. The fighters leap twenty feet in the air, pivoting and somersaulting, sometimes clashing with one another (Fig. 1.1). The woman strategically vaults up, caroms off one tree trunk, and alights on another, clinging there like a spider before swiveling and dive-bombing her prey. Apart from the aerobatics, the swordfight is filmed and cut in a daringly opaque way. Although each image is carefully composed, the editing makes the shots so brief that we merely glimpse the fighters' extraordinary feats. Eisenstein and Kurosawa might admire the precise force of this sequence.

In Tsui Hark's *Peking Opera Blues* (1986), a young woman has allowed several friends to sleep overnight in her room, but in the morning her father bustles in unexpectedly. The friends must hide anywhere they can—crouching under the blanket, scampering around behind the father's back, even clambering up to the rafters (Fig. 1.2). Each shot's dodges are choreographed in layers for maximal comic effect (Figs. 1.3–1.5). As in *A Touch of Zen*, an outlandish premise is subjected to a rousing exactitude of execution.

Hong Kong films can be sentimental, joyous, rip-roaring, silly, bloody, and bizarre. Their audacity, their slickness, and their unabashed appeal to emotion have won them audiences throughout the world. "It is all too extravagant, too gratuitously wild," a *New York Times* reviewer complained of an early kung-fu import; now the charge looks like a badge of honor.[1] These outrageous entertainments harbor remarkable inventiveness and careful craftsmanship. They are Hong Kong's most important contribution to global culture. The best of them are not only crowd-pleasing but also richly and delightfully artful.

How can mass-produced movies be artful? To answer this question, we must be willing to grant that the compromises of business do not prevent mass entertainment from achieving genuine artistry. We must also grant that there is a distinct aesthetic of popular film–a set of principles that shape its forms and effects. Finally, we must be willing to look closely at

1.2 *Peking Opera Blues:* Bedroom farce becomes silent slapstick.

1.3 *Peking Opera Blues:* A hanging basket is knocked away . . .

1.4 . . . and accidentally swings out at the viewer . . .

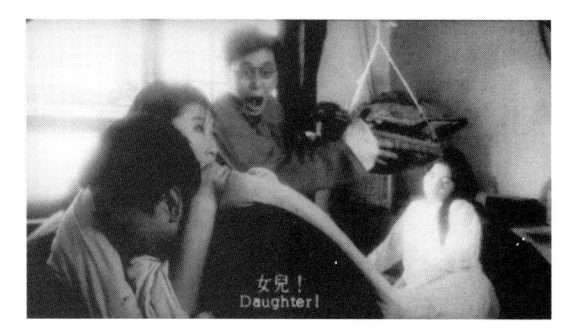

1.5 . . . but is caught on the return by a boy who pops into view.

popular movies, to study how they tell their stories and deploy film technique; we must be ready to analyze.

Hong Kong cinema has been an industry for more than sixty years. During the war-torn 1930s and 1940s Shanghai film companies fled to the relative tranquillity of the British colony. Soon after the triumph of Mao's 1949 revolution, Hong Kong began turning out scores of movies in well-tried genres: comedies, crime movies, family dramas, swordfight films, and Chinese operas. Films were made in both Mandarin and Cantonese. The highest output came from large companies, most notably that of the Shaw brothers, who ran their "Movietown" like an old-fashioned Hollywood studio (Fig. 1.6).

Until the 1970s, Hong Kong movies found distribution only in Asia and in émigré communities. Most westerners learned of this cinema through the kung-fu film, with its revenge-driven plots and flamboyant martial arts. The worldwide success of Bruce Lee's films guaranteed that Hong Kong would be forever identified with this genre. But the world market became glutted with kung-fu films, and locally other trends emerged, such as the Cantonese dialect comedy identified with Michael Hui, a former TV star. Soon afterward Jackie Chan cultivated comic kung-fu and became the biggest star in Asia.

1.6 Run Run Shaw with some of his 1960s stars.

By the early 1980s virtually all Hong Kong films were in Cantonese, and a new generation of directors came to the fore. Often trained in the West and in television, less tied to Mainland traditions than older hands, these young filmmakers turned away from the martial arts and toward gangster films, sword-and-sorcery fantasy, and dramas of contemporary life. Many of the films garnered acclaim in festivals and foreign exhibition, the most notable success being Ann Hui's *Boat People* (1982). Although this "new wave" did not overturn the mass-production ethos of the industry (most of the young directors wound up in the mainstream), its energy reshaped Hong Kong cinema into a modern and distinctive part of the territory's mass culture.

Just as Margaret Thatcher's government prepared to cede the colony back to China, the Hong Kong film industry was launched upon what many regard as its golden decade. A flood of lively films raised production standards while expanding the possibilities of established genres. The hugely successful *Aces Go Places* series, launched in 1982, streamlined Cantonese comedy in farcical pastiches of James Bond intrigue. Jackie Chan modernized the kung-fu film by recasting it as adventure saga (*Pro-

ject A, 1983) and urban police thriller (*Police Story*, 1985). In films like *Shanghai Blues* (1984), Tsui Hark updated older formulas through bold style and tongue-in-cheek humor. He also revived the historical kung-fu movie with his nationalistic epic *Once upon a Time in China* (1991). The gangster film returned with a hyperbolic romanticism in the "heroes" films of John Woo (*A Better Tomorrow*, 1986; *The Killer*, 1989), as well as in movies by Kirk Wong (*Gun Men*, 1988) and Ringo Lam (*Full Contact*, 1992). In the early 1990s the resurgent Hong Kong cinema finally came to public notice in the West. Jackie Chan and John Woo became American celebrities, and Tsui, Lam, Wong, and others finished films in Hollywood. Ironically, as local films gained respect, the industry went into a tailspin, losing its regional markets and falling prey to video piracy and the Asian financial crisis. Yet even as journalists were writing *finis* to this cinema, remarkable films continued to be made, and a new generation maintained Hong Kong's lively traditions.

How did such a frankly commercial filmmaking tradition manage to create the conditions for something we might recognize as artistry? Posing the question this way presumes that art suffers when it is bound up by commerce, yet many of the fine-art traditions we honor sprang from the market. Italian Renaissance painting was an intensely economic enterprise, responding to demands for portraits, frescoes, altarpieces, and decorated furniture. Artists were artisans, like the shoemaker, organizing their shops for efficiency and maximum profitability. Today, sculpture, painting, and orchestral music, along with virtually all architectural projects, result from commissions, in which market forces reveal themselves nakedly.

But in high art, some might argue, economic demand doesn't shape the specific outcome: whereas the elite artist expresses a singular vision, the popular artist must compromise in order to satisfy the audience. Yet this claim is an exaggeration. The Renaissance painter often had to fulfill a program laid down in the commission, which often specified subject, composition, materials, coloring, and iconography. In the nineteenth century the collapse of academic painting led to the rise of genre painting and the impressionist style, both shaped to the tastes of new customers, while composers were urged to court a comparatively untutored public by writing program music and overtly nationalistic pieces.

We need not go quite so far as Virgil Thomson, who once suggested that a composer's musical style changes in accord with the funding source.[2] It is just that in any art, form tends to follow format, and format is often shaped by business pressures. After Beethoven, composers increased the size and varied the instrumentation of the orchestra, partly in order to mount a massive sound that would fill the new, bigger auditoria built for general audiences. In eighteenth-century England, as writers lost their patrons, they came to depend upon booksellers, who demanded long pieces of prose fiction. Commercial demands mold styles and forms, in both elite art and popular art. That a work of art is financed and marketed does not make it any less a work of art.

In popular cinema, highly personal films may be produced for an entertainment industry—witness those of Buster Keaton, Alfred Hitchcock, John Ford, Howard Hawks, and other distinctive filmmakers. But "art films" are a business as well. Granted, many are not the products of profit-driven local industries or entrepreneurs; they receive public funding. (In the late 1990s, the average European film was 70 percent state-financed.) Few of these subsidized films attract a local audience or overseas distribution, so as purely economic investments they are disastrous.[3] Instead payback shifts to another level. The subsidized film competes to win places in the world's four hundred annual film festivals, which are hungry for non-mainstream fare of all kinds.[4] If a festival entry wins acclaim, perhaps an award, the sponsoring agency is confirmed in its decision to back the project, with honor flowing to national culture. For such reasons, the festival network has become a circuit of production, distribution, and exhibition parallel to that of mass-market cinema. Art cinema is not always profit-driven, but it remains market-oriented, and this pressure has affected its traditions, genres, and conventions.[5]

Hong Kong has a few "art films" that feed into festivals. Wong Kar-wai's *Chungking Express* (1994) became a cult hit, and his *Happy Together* (1997) won the Best Director prize at Cannes. Until very recently, though, local moviemaking has been unsubsidized, so internationally prestigious directors like Clara Law, Ann Hui, and Stanley Kwan depend upon mainstream styles, stars, and genres. In comparison to their contemporaries—say, the austere Taiwanese directors Hou Hsiao-Hsien and Edward Yang—Hong Kong's "festival" filmmakers look decidedly pop.

Popular cinema begins in business—the impulse to turn out pictures regularly to satisfy a mass audience's appetite. What, then, would an aesthetic of popular film look like? Unsurprisingly, it is founded on mass tastes, and these often favor force over finesse. A mass-market movie from any culture tends to highlight pratfalls, spills, bodily functions, ladder accidents, and other base constants of human life. Since the 1930s Hollywood has been constrained by some lower-middle-class canons of taste, so we often forget how the silent clowns (even Chaplin's romanticized Little Tramp) dwell on the ugly tactility of motor oil on spats, pie dripping from eyelashes, thumbtacks fished out of the soup. Abbott and Costello, Jerry Lewis, Rodney Dangerfield, John Belushi, and Jim Carrey have maintained this tradition.

The vulgarity of popular cinema reaches paroxysmic extremes in Hong Kong. Here a typical movie will feature spitting, vomiting, nose-picking, and vistas of toilets and people's mouths. In *Fight Back to School* (1991) Stephen Chiau pretends a condom is chewing gum and blows a bubble with it. In the farce *All's Well End's Well* (1992), offscreen a masseuse whacks a man's feet with a baseball bat while a school official squats on a toilet; as the bat cracks, the official groans with bowel strain. Later in a hospital the film's amnesiac protagonist begins his day by gargling with the urine from his bedpan. Gags like these indicate that the spectacle of kung-fu is only one side of a cinema thoroughly fascinated with bodies *in extremis*. Hong Kong film celebrates voluptuousness and grotesquerie; it savors cleavage and penises, comic warts and farts, mold-blotched vampires, greedy eaters smeared with sauce and fat, and creatures with gigantic tongues. Nothing gorgeous or hideous is alien to this cinema.

Vulgarity offers one kind of forcefulness; striking images yield another. Hong Kong director Ringo Lam speaks for many of his peers: "I like visuals and simple stories. I would prefer my movies to have very little dialogue."[6] When Robert Parrish asked how he could learn to direct actors, John Ford suggested he watch *Stagecoach*. Parrish returned from the screening protesting that John Wayne had scarcely a dozen lines. "That's the way to direct actors," Ford replied. "Don't let 'em talk." Intellectuals often quote lame dialogue to show the callowness of popular cinema, but they thereby miss what lies in the images. It's hard to find weighty significance in the bedroom feints of *Peking Opera Blues* and the aerobatics of *A Touch of Zen*. In many movies, the chief pleasures are pictorial.

Which is to say that popular filmmakers have refined techniques of vivid visual storytelling. The foundations of "film language" were laid by the entertainment cinema of the 1900s and 1910s, when directors had to get stories across fast and vividly. D. W. Griffith, Victor Sjöström, and Louis Feuillade, the three finest directors of the period before 1918, were all churning out films for mass audiences. Today's popular cinema preserves many devices from the medium's earliest years—the chase, the hairbreadth escape, the cliff-hanging hero, the struggle with storms or gravity or locomotives. Hong Kong cinema, in its drive for clarity and impact, has revitalized silent-film techniques. Slow- and fast-motion, dynamic editing, striking camera angles, and other devices that the avant-garde of the 1920s declared to be "purely cinematic" are stock in trade in this popular cinema. Its makers have intuitively rediscovered the short, sharp flashback that serves to remind the audience of an earlier scene, as well as the "symbolic insert" beloved of early filmic storytelling (Fig. 1.7).

But doesn't all cinema exploit the power of moving images? Again we come to the trade-off between fastidiousness and force. Since the late 1950s, much Western art cinema has dwelt on static compositions and ambivalent moods (Fig. 1.8). Antonioni, Tarkovsky, Fassbinder, Wenders, and other outstanding directors have created a cinema of suggestive atmosphere.[7] The mass-entertainment filmmaker, committed to storytelling, anxious to rivet the audience's attention, strives for clear and dynamic images rather than contemplative ones. Style will tend toward functional economy. It favors the graceful behavior of performers, such as John

1.7 *The Killer:* Jenny's memory of John, treated as an emblematic image of his trade.

1.8 A moment in the odyssey of two children in Theo Angelopoulos' *Landscape in the Mist* (1988).

Wayne's strides and pauses at the rocky stream at the close of *The Quiet Man* (1952) or Bruce Lee's soaring kicks in *Fist of Fury* (1971). Filmmakers will take pride in the subtle precision of certain camera movements, or in editing tactics that convey stupendous agility.

A few filmmakers will prolong certain grace notes, spinning stylistic cadenzas around the narrative core. King Hu, doyen of the Hong Kong swordplay film, realized early in his career that "if the plots are simple, the stylistic delivery will be even richer."[8] What Western fans consider "over the top" in Hong Kong movies is partly a richness of stylistic delivery—an effort to see how delightful or thrilling one can make the mix of dialogue, music, sound effects, light, color, and movement. Realism is less important than a bold expressiveness in every dimension. In particular, physical activity can achieve a real magnificence when it is sustained and embellished. This delight in expressive technique is a local elaboration of the sensuous abundance sought by popular filmmakers everywhere.

In the art of popular cinema, vivid visuals are shot through with emotion. In order to attract a mass audience, popular art deals in emotions like anger, disgust, fear, happiness, sadness, and indignation.[9] Since these feelings evidently operate in all cultures, a film that appeals to them travels well. Entertainment mobilizes playground passions, direct responses to blatant aggression, kindness, or selfishness. Cinema is particularly good at arousing emotions kinesthetically, through action and music. Bruce Lee asked his students to give their fighting techniques "emotional content," such as purposefully directed anger.[10] When this quality is captured in vigorous, strictly patterned movement, in nicely judged framings and crackling cutting, with overwhelming music and sound effects, you can feel yourself tensing and twitching to the rhythms of the fight. This is filmic emotion at its most sheerly physical.

1.9 The *Chinese Feast:* Ka-fai checks Sun's sincerity by seeing if her picture has the privileged place in his wallet.

We are told that mass entertainment favors simple, pure states of feeling, but plainly it works with mixed emotions too. One aim of mass art is to make you laugh through your tears, to give you a smile and a lump in your throat. In *The Chinese Feast* (1995), Ka-fai (Anita Yuen) has taken off her chef's hat, but her hair stays erect in a Woody Woodpecker topknot. This adds an exuberant zaniness to the romantic climax, when Sun (Leslie Cheung) confesses his love (Fig. 1.9). Still, popular plotting does exploit manichean opposites: self-sacrifice is sharpened by contrast with cruelty, generosity by contrast with greed. In *Task Force* (1997), the policewoman Shirley (Karen Mok) returns to the apartment she shares with her boyfriend, Kelvin. He has ignored her, dodged appointments, and skipped her father's funeral. Everything has aroused our indignation at Kelvin's callousness. Now Shirley has decided to leave him. She comes to claim her things while her partner, Rod, waits outside in the car. The scene dwells on Shirley drifting wistfully around the apartment. Suddenly, cut outside to show her returning to Rod, telling him she's decided to take away none of her things after all. The abruptness of the transition seems to mark her sharp decision to accept the breakup with Kelvin. The two drive off, and a tear trickles down from behind Shirley's sunglasses. But then we realize that the sudden cut to her entering the car omitted a piece of action. We now get a miniflashback showing her angrily pulling down bookshelves, knocking over the stereo, and generally laying waste to Kelvin's life. Shirley's surge of righteous anger stands out more strongly against the suggestion that she took his indifference passively, and we get to feel both pity for her and satisfaction at her retribution.

The opponent of mass culture objects that this tactic indulges the audience, letting it "have things both ways." But popular film strives for a wide-open emotional range, and having things both ways perfectly suits that purpose. Entertainment aims to chart the highest highs and the lowest lows. The tactic is seen most strikingly in the "double ending," which allows the characters' fortunes to sink abysmally before the plot swerves into a happy ending, sometimes one of stupendous implausibility. Mabel Cheung's *Autumn's Tale* (1987) centers on Jenny (Cherie Chung) and Piggy (Chow Yun-fat), both Hong Kong émigrés living in Manhattan. Jenny tries to reform Piggy, a happy-go-lucky wastrel working at menial jobs and overfond of drinking and brawling. When he seems to have fallen into his old ways again, Jenny accepts a job as an *au pair* on Long Island. As she prepares to leave her apartment, Piggy races to bring her a present, for which he has traded his beloved wreck of a car. He catches up with her just as her old boyfriend prepares to drive her to Long Island. They say an awkward good-bye and exchange gifts. As she drives off Piggy runs tentatively after her, arousing our hope that he will catch up with her for a happier resolution, but he gives up the chase.

The scene of separation fills nearly ten minutes. Yet the movie is not over. In an epilogue, Jenny and her charge, Anna, are strolling on a Long Island beach. Jenny says that she once had a friend who dreamed of owning a café on the pier. Suddenly they find that a café is there. "Table for two?" Piggy beams at them as the film ends. We have no idea how much time has elapsed since Jenny left Manhattan, no clue as to how Piggy has earned enough money to set up his business. In defiance of probability, an abrupt two-minute epilogue offers the audience a second ending, a casually miraculous reunion proving Piggy's reformation. Cheung has remarked: "I know that in real life the heroine and the hero are bound to go separate ways. But in the film, I am free to write the ending as I wish . . . I wanted [Piggy] still to have hope, so I added the fairytale element."[11]

Taken to the extreme, the switches in emotional register seen in *Task Force* and *An Autumn's Tale* can become a reckless mix of moods. Popular cinema delights in jamming together very diverse splendors.[12] One of the screenwriters for the *Lethal Weapon* series explains:

> A lot of it I recognize as pure sentimentality, but people love it. All of that bonding stuff between Mel and Danny is corny, but people love it—Mel kind of crying and spitting and telling Danny that he loves him and he's like a brother, Danny kind of cradling Mel in his arms. That stuff is so hokey and so corny, but it works. They make it work. Then you throw in, out of nowhere, the most unexpected kind of humor, whether it's the silly gags of Mel eating a dog biscuit or Joe Pesci's character. So you have this kind of Mulligan stew that never slows down: that keeps jumping from pathos to sentimentality to deep emotion to pure action.[13]

This urge for kaleidoscopic variety elevates momentary vividness above broad dramatic form. A Hong Kong film can dump a cornucopia at your feet. Forty-three seconds into Wong Jing's *Boys Are Easy* (1993) we get a gun battle and car chase, followed by a procession of beautiful young men and women entangled in a comedy of mistaken identity. We get a male striptease, a satire of triads, a farcical game of poker, an animated demon representing one character's weak side, a musical number in praise of bowling, LSD hallucinations, a necktie that pops upright à la Tex Avery, and a scene in which a woman records each night's orgasms by notching her bedroom wall. *Boys Are Easy* is an extreme case, but Hong Kong films do not generally aspire to the Hollywood tradition of tight plotting that runs from, say, Keaton's *Our Hospitality* (1923) and Lubitsch's *The Marriage Circle* (1924) to *Die Hard* (1988) and *Groundhog Day* (1993).[14] Hong Kong plots tend to be organized around vivid moments, fights or chases or comic turns or melodramatic catastrophes. The creators' skill lies in making each set piece powerful and in livening up the connecting passages.

An emphasis on striking moments leads naturally to a scavenger aesthetic. In today's Hong Kong thrillers you cannot escape scenes lifted from *Die Hard* and *Speed* (1994), complete with snatches of the original scores. For *The Chinese Feast* Tsui Hark swipes the plot from kung-fu movies, the theme of food from the Taiwanese movie *Eat Drink Man Woman* (1994), and the premise of a cooking contest from a Japanese TV show. For good measure Tsui recycles (and improves) ideas from a previous film of his own, *The Banquet* (1991). If popular cinema often seems shameless, it is partly because its commitment to vivacious moments encourages filmmakers to grab anything that has already proved alluring.

The same impulse governs the reliance on conventions, unkindly called formulas and clichés—all those laughable, taken-for-granted devices that communicate instantly. Conventions are the lifeblood of popular art. Cowboys can dodge bullets, boy and girl "meet cute," and endings are usually happy. Villains have bad aim, except when it comes to wounding the hero's friends. Hong Kong cinema relies shamelessly on the oldest contrivances of entertainment: eavesdropping, mistaken identity, confusion of twins or accidental lookalikes, wretchedly inadequate disguise, and coincidental encounters that complicate or resolve the plot. If a woman dresses as a man, everyone takes her as one; when she returns to woman's costume, no one recognizes her resemblance to the man. When you are angry with your lover, you tear up his or her photo. In Hong Kong night is not black but blue, and terribly bright. Caucasians usually look large and Australian, and they speak English with an accent known nowhere on the planet.

Hong Kong action films are rich in such artifice. Even the harmless-looking citizen knows kung-fu. A half-frozen man can suddenly recover and somersault over a car. Immediately after a stinging blow, the victim bruises horribly. If someone has a pistol, somebody else will become a hostage, with that pistol pointed to his or her head. During a gunfight, someone is sure to run out of ammunition at a crucial moment. A cop wounded in a firefight will show up later with a bit of gauze taped to his forehead. A man can have an arm hacked off and still fight, and win. During a kung-fu combat, if blood trickles from a character's mouth, death is usually at hand. Certain wounds heal miraculously: a bullet smacks into the hero's leg, and he cries in agony; a few shots later he is limping; a few shots later the leg is as good as new, though stained a bit red.

Vulgarity, pictorial storytelling, the pull of sensuous wonders and emotional intensity, the mélange of tonal switches and vivid moments and tested conventions: these are essential ingredients of popular cinema. But their power comes at a price. Because entertainment favors forcefulness, and because it strives to offer a grab-bag of attractions, we shouldn't be surprised that it harbors some questionable impulses. For example, Hong Kong cinema is very brutal. Women suffer terribly in most action films, a circumstance not offset by the woman-warrior tradition. Although one can argue that the territory's low crime rate suggests that viewers aren't imitating what they see, the casual acceptance of rapes, beatings, and bloodshed may have more pervasive social effects. The films also put prejudices on display. Non-Asians, particularly blacks, are almost always corrupt and rapacious, while some Asians, such as Hong Kong's ubiquitous Filipinas, become virtually invisible. Attitudes toward law and justice seem particularly blinkered: again and again, it is taken for granted that police—even our heroes—will torture suspects. In its search for powerful sensations, this cinema becomes sensationalistic.

At the same time, like much Asian popular culture, it can be blandly infantile. A cop in *Chungking Express* lives surrounded by big stuffed kitties. Anita Yuen, a reigning ingenue star, takes pride in her Mickey Mouse collectibles. Hong Kong film does not oscillate quite as startlingly between scalding violence and cloying cuteness as Japanese entertainment does, but both traditions often suggest that to be grown up is to be aggressive, and the only way to be gentle is to regress into childhood.[15]

Often, too, the films simply invoke conventions without vital commitment or revivification. There is too much facetious music during comic scenes. There is a lot of visual bombast, especially slow motion and exaggerated angles. The urge to grip the audience has created a cinema that is often overbusy, with little room for the contemplative moments that make other popular cinemas rich. Having mastered certain skills supremely, particularly the power to generate excitement through vigorous action, Hong Kong directors have not generally sought to stretch themselves in other directions. By training their audience to expect ever more rapid-fire gratification, they have too often cramped their craft.

But despite these faults, many Hong Kong films display qualities that we value in any art, high or low, modern or classic. They have structural ingenuity (echoic motifs, contrapuntal story parallels), functional beauty of style (for example, bold cutting and dynamic composition), expressive intensity (through the manipulation of tone, color, and rousing physicality), appeal to common feelings and experiences (loneliness, injustice, the loss that triggers revenge, the hunger for love), and originality (for example, the constant reworking of conventions in directors as various as King Hu, John Woo, Tsui Hark, and Wong Kar-wai). Most of these virtues are tied to the mass nature of the enterprise: they make it more likely that the film will provide an arresting experience for a wide range of viewers.[16] These qualities don't negate what is socially or morally objectionable in the films, but because of its need to capitalize on current trends, to repeat tried forms and turn them in fresh but not alienating directions, any popular cinema is unlikely to be wholly on the side of the angels.

To orchestrate an abundance of appeals you need craft. Intellectuals who expatiate on the cultural significance of a movie or pop song pay virtually no attention to the ways in which the artisan has used the medium. Perhaps they think it's simple to make amusing, exciting, tear-jerking movies. Let them try. Mass entertainment looks easy only to those who have not struggled to shoot a coherent scene, write a passable song, or draw a decent cartoon. The most minimal competence in filmmaking is an achievement to be prized; many of today's young directors could profitably study the Roy Del Ruths of the Golden Age. "A great director," Andrew Sarris once noted, "has to be at least a good director."[17] And more expert filmmaking cannot consist in merely following rules by rote, for no two situations are exactly the same. The old hand knows the routine practices, the standard solutions, and then adapts them to fresh situations—perhaps setting up technical problems to be ingeniously overcome. Craft demands flexibility, ingenuity, and no small amount of imagination. The direct, forceful effects prized by the popular aesthetic are often the product of subtle shaping.

In entertainment film, the artisan's imagination goes to work upon well-defined norms. "Polishing the jade," the Chinese call it. Seeking originality at all costs can lead to chaos, but quietly refining the tradition enriches the art and refines the perceiver's sensibility. Yet popular filmmakers innovate as well: King Hu cut *Touch of Zen*'s airborne combat in a way that eliminated normal cues for position and trajectory, and thereby recast the conventions he had inherited. Setting oneself a craft problem and solving it in a fresh, virtuosic, but absolutely comprehensible way may be one equivalent in popular cinema for the experimental daring we find in the avant-garde.

If we want to understand how a popular cinema's artisans mobilize a range of appeals, we cannot neglect form and style. We must learn to look closely. We must examine popular films as wholes, seeking out what makes them cohere (or not). We must probe their moment-by-moment texture. We should scrutinize climaxes, like Shirley's leaving Kelvin in *Task Force*, as well as low-key passages, always trying—though it's hard, especially in a kinetic cinema like Hong Kong's—to suggest through words and photos what a sequence looks like.[18]

Just as analyzing Beethoven involves acknowledging the formal traditions that developed within Viennese classicism, understanding popular art requires awareness of its craft practices. We can usefully trace out the proximate conditions of production—the filmmaking institutions, shaped by the customs that govern the filmmaker's tacit assumptions about everything from running times and character development to lighting patterns and the musical score. To become a proficient filmmaker is to learn a repertoire of skills, and often those skills are routinized in order to benefit the mode of production.

For example, in a typical Hollywood scene many shots simply repeat camera positions in ABAB alternation. (See Figs. 1.10–1.16.) Thanks to this technique, the viewer can take an already-seen view as read and concentrate on the slight changes that occur in the actor's performance—a shift of glance, a tiny movement (Figs. 1.11–1.14). In addition, after an ABABA series of repeated setups, a change to setup C can carry a greater emphasis than it would in a constantly varying string of setups (say, ABCDE). (See Figs. 1.15–1.16.) Alternating repeated setups has practical value too. The filmmaker can save time by filming all the shots from setup A—say, all the medium-shots of Neil McCauley—in succession. Then the camera can be shifted, and all the shots of Kelso from position B can be made. In the editing process, the shots from setups A and B are intercut. Or the filmmaker can use two cameras at once, as Michael Mann did in our scene from *Heat*.[19] Stylistic patterning meshes with craft practice: artistic economy has arisen from production economies.

Paying attention to craft also allows us to confront one last objection to popular film's mass-production origins. Bulk filmmaking is that System which screenwriters and critics have been railing against for eighty years; it is, we are told, what keeps movies meretricious and clichéd. Yet there is much to be said for it. At the least, mass-market filmmaking has imposed a discipline on its makers, fostering a commitment to professional responsibility. One motto of mass filmmaking might well be that of Steve Jobs hurrying his staff to finish the Macintosh: "Real artists ship." Industrialized

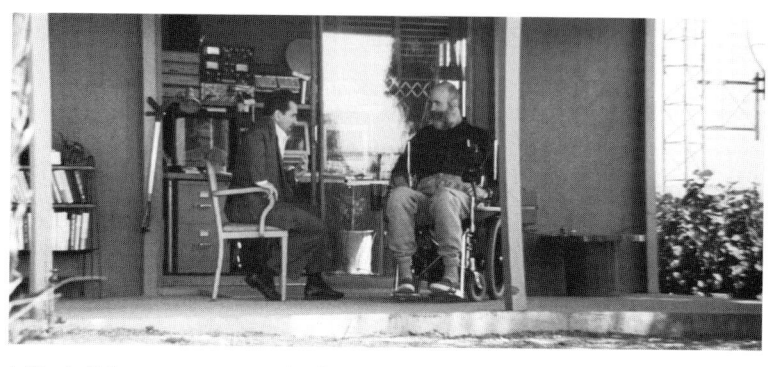

1.10 A dialogue scene in Michael Mann's *Heat* (1995) begins with a "master shot."

1.11 An analytical cut highlights McCauley.

1.12 A reverse-angle shot on Kelso allows us to see his reaction.

1.13 The cutting shifts back and forth across several shots, always presenting each man from the same camera position.

1.14 After several replays of the same camera setup on Kelso, the turning of his head becomes a significant action.

HONG KONG AND/AS/OR HOLLYWOOD

From the start Hong Kong film was indebted to America. In the silent era several Chinese filmmakers worked in Hollywood. Mon Kwan Man-ching, one of the founders of the Daguan (Grandview) company had been a consultant on Griffith's *Broken Blossoms* (1919).[1] Hollywood films played in Hong Kong from the 1920s on, and *The Love Parade* (1929) and *Camille* (1937) were adapted into Cantonese plays and operas, which in turn were filmed. American production methods and lighting styles strongly influenced Cantonese cinema for decades after World War II. Whereas the Japanese studios encouraged experimentation, Hong Kong filmmakers stuck fairly closely to those guidelines for shot design and continuity editing first formulated in Hollywood.

By studying foreign films, Hong Kong filmmakers have been able to produce work aspiring to an international standard. In trying to catch up, though, the films sometimes seem stuck in a time warp. The standard score for a chase, synthesizers cranking out a soft pop/rock/jazz pulse, evokes 1970s Hollywood. Stephen Chiau's *From Beijing with Love* (1994) can raise laughs with James Bond parodies. *Eastern Condors* (1987) lifts elements not only from *The Deer Hunter* (1978) and *Rambo* (1985) but also from *The Dirty Dozen* (1967).

The new cosmopolitan style of the 1980s was created by directors who took notice of what Hollywood was doing. Inspired by *Raiders of the Lost Ark* (1981) and *48 HRS* (1982), young filmmakers turned out action pictures bursting with pyrotechnics and gunplay. The 1980s crime cycle was launched by Leone's *Once upon a Time in America* (1984). Like their 1930s predecessors, directors swiped plots with abandon: *Top Gun* (1986) became *Proud and Confident* (1989), *Witness* (1985) was recast as *Wild Search* (1989). Today Hollywood remains the reference point. A cop in *The Big Bullet* (1996) is a gun collector, proudly showing off his Beretta, "same as Mel Gibson used in *Lethal Weapon.*" *All's Well End's Well* (1993) refers to *Ghost, Fatal Attraction, Terminator 2, Pretty Woman,* and *Wolf,* as well as *Casablanca* and *ET.* As Hong Kong cinema became part of world film culture, American filmmakers returned the compliment of plagiarism. *Tango and Cash* (1989) restages two sequences from Jackie Chan's *Police Story* (1985). Robert Rodriguez's *Desperado* (1995), Michael Bay's *Bad Boys* (1995), and Antoine Fuqua's *Replacement Killers* (1998) signal the Hongkongification of American cinema.

Yet Hong Kong is not Hollywood; local tastes are too idiosyncratic. Says producer Terence Chang: "A lot of Hong Kong films have things that I think American audiences can't accept."[2] As popular cinemas go, Hollywood is unusually fastidious about realism of detail, restraint of emotion, and plausibility of plot. By Hollywood standards, Piggy's fairytale success at the end of *An Autumn's Tale* (1987) is recklessly unmotivated. In Hong Kong movies any character, female or male, may cry, and in comedies the actors cross their eyes. Then there is the gore. Hong Kong's cinema is a deeply carnal one. Since the 1970s, local filmmakers capitalized on the rising international tolerance for mayhem by making thrashings, torture, and sudden, almost offhand death central ingredients. The gruesomeness is unredeemed by the solemn elegance of the Japanese *jidai-geki*, and even Hollywood is far more restrained in showing fights. When a Hong Kong filmmaker swipes from *Lethal Weapon 2* (1989) the notion that a carpenter's nail-gun makes a nifty weapon, prepare for the worst: a nail to the crotch (*Fight Back to School*, 1991), a nail through the brain (*Pom Pom and Hot Hot*, 1992). Hollywood pours its energies into endless script rewrites and lavish sets and costumes. Hong Kong filmmakers devote much of theirs to furious, prolonged, elaborate, often massively implausible violence.

Kirk Wong's *Gun Men* (1988) is a barefaced steal from Brian De Palma's *The Untouchables* (1987). In Shanghai during the late 1920s, Ding Chun-bee, an honest policeman working in the French Concession, becomes frustrated by the corruption in the force and recruits a team of scruffy war buddies to help him defeat Haye, a powerful gangster. The milieu corresponds to the Chicago of the American film, and opium smuggling stands in for bootlegging. Like Elliot Ness, Ding has a wife and daughter he strives to protect; he is misled into making raids that yield nothing; he cherishes a token from a friend killed in the line of duty (a scarf left behind by his captain). Even the score borrows from Ennio Morricone's *Untouchables* quick march. As in many crime films, alternating scenes underscore parallels between the protagonist and his adversary. While Haye vows vengeance for the death of his superior, Ding pays homage at the grave of the murdered captain. And in both films the hero's ideal of cleaning up corruption becomes intensified by the drive for revenge. Yet a closer look at the two films allows us to pick out some significant variations within two major traditions of popular cinema.

Gun Men squeezes its busy plot into about ninety minutes, while *The*

Untouchables takes two hours. *Gun Men*'s credits fly by in forty seconds, as opposed to about two and a half minutes in De Palma's film. *The Untouchables* has a four-minute epilogue that shows Ness leaving his office, bidding good-bye to his surviving partner, and heading home. *Gun Men* has virtually no epilogue, following the resolution of the climactic gun battle with a paltry seven-second montage of photographs before the final credits roll. *Gun Men* has far more physical action, whether you measure by screen time or by the number of scenes devoted to fights and chases. So *Gun Men* has sacrificed something. What?

Most obviously, characterization and psychological change. Contrary to what many critics believe, the plot of an American movie often centers upon character development. The Hollywood hero or heroine, far from being a perfect specimen, has faults—shyness *(While You Were Sleeping)*, manipulativeness *(Tootsie)*, lack of confidence *(Back to the Future, Sleepless in Seattle)*, rash overconfidence *(Speed)*, even selfishness and arrogance *(Groundhog Day)*. The plot arranges events so that the character improves, perhaps also coming to understand his or her frailty. *The Untouchables'* "character arc," as Hollywood screenwriters call it, traces Ness's development from a by-the-book crusader into a tough, resourceful warrior. Ness learns from the hardheaded cop Malone that he must raise the stakes ("Capone comes at you with a knife, you come at him with a gun") and break the rules—partly because "This is Chicago," partly because Ness is up against men who know no morality. At the climax Ness hesitates before shooting Frank Nitti, the murderer of his friends; duty to law wins out briefly and Ness arrests Nitti. But when Nitti assures him he will not be convicted and smirkingly adds that Malone died "squealing like a pig," Ness frogmarches Nitti across the rooftop and shoves him off, calling after the howling killer: "Did he sound anything like that?" At the end, as if purged, Ness can muse over the photo of his squad, murmuring, "So much violence," and declare that if indeed Prohibition is repealed—well, then he will have a drink. He has moved toward Malone's leathery pragmatism without forswearing his adherence to the law.

Wong's *Gun Men* traces no such arc. Ding is first seen as a frightened soldier during the civil war of 1926, about to undergo torture at the hands of Haye; he and his pals are saved only when a bombardment throws Haye's men into disarray. After Ding is reunited with his wife, Chu-chiao, and his daughter Sze-sze, the credits cover an ellipsis. Now he is in Shanghai and enlisting in the police. No reason is supplied for his decision. He is given no traits akin to Ness's stiff-necked idealism. Ding is simply a country-boy soldier who would naturally be repelled by urban corruption. When he invades a mahjong parlor thinking that it's an opium den, he suffers no public humiliation, and his failure does not lower his morale. (Compare the mockery that greets Ness's failed raid on the bootleggers' warehouse, and his despondency when he realizes the obstacles he faces.) Similarly, whereas *The Untouchables* devotes scenes to characterizing each member of the team as Ness recruits them, *Gun Men*'s prologue introduces Ding's pals en masse, and thereafter the three men remain largely indistinguishable.

As if to compensate for the thinner characterization, *Gun Men* piles up plot twists. A decision will immediately trigger a fight or pursuit. In Haye's first shootout with Ding, the captain is killed; Haye is next seen planning revenge on his rival gang; immediately that gang bursts into Haye's headquarters, and another gun battle ensues. The quick reversals give the film a breathless pace. Ding trails Haye's lieutenant, Tsou, and Mona to a hotel room, where he hides in a wardrobe. Then Tsou's other woman breaks in, Tsou flees, and the women fight. Ding steps in to protect Mona, and after her rival is gone she asks for his sympathy. When he offers it, she suddenly pulls away and leaves. The next thing we know, she has become Ding's informer in the underworld.

At the climax, Ding needs to make his wife and child flee Shanghai, so he announces that he plans to leave them and live with Mona. Crushed, Chu-chiao and Sze-sze set out for the station, and Ding runs after them in remorse (not unlike the futile chase of Piggy in *An Autumn's Tale*). This turn of events prolongs his moment of loss. En route to the station Chu-chiao finds a message Ding intended her to read much later, in which he pledges his love. She abruptly hurries back, and Ding races toward his family for a reconciliation—just as Haye's gang thunders in for an all-out assault. The scene's whole emotional zigzag takes less than four minutes. *Gun Men* may be significantly shorter than *The Untouchables*, but its abrupt reversals create a packed plot and rapid fluctuations of feeling.

In one respect, though, the character relations of *Gun Men* are more elaborate than those in *The Untouchables*. In De Palma's film, Ness is a chaste knight: he defends his family, the woman whose little girl was killed by a Capone bomb, and the mother with the baby carriage at the train station. Ness repeats that "It's nice to be married." (This sets him off from his nemesis Capone, who, contrary to most movie gangsters, seems to have no sex life.) When Capone threatens Ness's family, Ness spirits them out of town. By contrast, *Gun Men* embeds Ding in a romantic triangle. Out of sympathy he begins an affair with his informer Mona, and this puts both Mona and Chu-chiao in danger from Haye. Capone threatens to burn down Ness's house, but Haye does incinerate Ding's apartment building. In the climactic crossfire, Mona dies, not unlike the doomed prostitute of Hollywood tradition, and Ding becomes reconciled with his wife and child. *The Untouchables* starts with middle-class family stability, then presents Capone's forces as the threat to it, but *Gun Men* begins with the family already fractured. In the first scene Ding is writing a letter home from the battlefront, reassuring Chu-chiao and Sze-sze that he's fine, all the while facing torture and execution. When he returns from the war, Sze-sze will not call the stranger daddy.

The restabilizing of Ding's family takes place in a climax profoundly typi-

HKH.1 *Gun Men:* Sze-szu fires at Haye.

HKH.2 *Gun Men:* The final photo provides plot closure.

HKH.3 *The Untouchables:* The photo celebrating the team's first victory.

cal of Hong Kong—and virtually unthinkable in Hollywood. In the climactic street battle Haye blasts Ding to the ground. Sze-sze runs into the field of fire, crying, "Daddy!" for the first time. Both Ding and Haye are wounded and crawling in the dirt, but Haye reaches for a fallen pistol. Sze-sze grabs the pistol and shoots Haye point-blank (Fig. HKH.1). For good measure Ding struggles up and, embracing his daughter, helps her squeeze off two more shots. Father-daughter reconciliation through collaborative homicide is a characteristically audacious Hong Kong twist, and it knots together strands of family love and social warfare that were interwoven at the film's start. The film's last moments show the family reintegrated: Sze-sze's worn photograph of her father gives way to a new shot of her in his arms, and then to a photograph of the family surrounded by Ding's friends and supervising officer (Fig. HKH.2). Given *The Untouchables'* parallel photograph, which projects all-male comradeship (Fig. HKH.3), one can argue that *Gun Men* takes the protagonist's family life more seriously.

An all-out sequence like the climax is perhaps the most glaring mark of the difference between Hollywood and Hong Kong cinemas, but there are

HKH.4 *The Untouchables:* A wide-angle reconstruction of 1920s Chicago.

HKH.5 *Gun Men:* A telephoto lens makes a narrow street seem even more cramped.

subtler ones as well. All of *Gun Men*'s scenes, expository or action-filled, are shot close to the characters, and even distant shots are densely packed, thanks to long lenses. The film has none of the spaciousness of *The Untouchables*; Chicago is roomy (Fig. HKH.4), but Shanghai is suffocating. *Gun Men*'s budget, which obliges Wong to sketch the period through costume and furnishings, doesn't permit him to stage his action scenes in the breadth that De Palma can. Whereas the rooftop climax of *The Untouchables* can exploit the Chicago skyline, the final fight of *Gun Men* takes place in a narrow street (Fig. HKH.5). De Palma's massive budget permits some striking widescreen effects (Fig. HKH.6), but it can also vitiate the action sequences, which tend to emphasize scenery. *Gun Men*'s action scenes, like most Hong Kong ones, keep to a more human scale, with medium shots and close-ups predominating.

This approach tends to make the violence more visceral. Although most viewers would consider *The Untouchables* a pretty violent movie, *Gun Men* goes much further. In the opening, a man is stabbed in the buttock (in close-up); soon a hand grenade sends soldiers flying. Shortly thereafter a woman tries to splash acid on another woman, she gets boiling water

HKH.6 *The Untouchables:* A typical De Palma shot: a striking overhead composition shows Nitti's body after his fall.

tossed in her own face, and several men catch fire. In a frantic fight around a pier one man's head is impaled on a boat hook (close-up), another man is shot through the ankle (close-up), and a third man's hand is hacked by a fish spear. Dozens of bodies are hit by bullets, flung out of windows, dunked in water; a truck smashes a rickshaw against a fence; in the final scene Ding and Sze-sze dispatch Haye. Some moments in the fights are intelligible only in detail shots (Figs. HKH.7, HKH.8).

The Untouchables' nearest analogue to the frenzied combats of *Gun Men* is the ten-minute sequence in which Ness and Stone close in on Capone's fleeing bookkeeper at the steps of the train station. Apart from a quasi–Hong Kong touch—Stone scooting under the descending baby carriage to brace it while he draws a bead on a thug—De Palma stages the scene as a self-congratulatory set-piece, an overblown homage to *Potemkin*'s Odessa Steps massacre. Underlining its revisionism through an orgy of slow motion, it is a display of directorial prowess, not an effort to seize the audience through rapid-fire action. The train-station scene looks especially clumsy when compared with a moment in *Gun Men* probably inspired by it. Ding is at the pier trying to arrest Haye and his men, who are wheeling what Ding assumes is a cart of opium. The scene is tersely cut, with silhouettes thrusting to and from the camera and a tight, fluid topography: first Ding and the gang on the pier, then Ding dodging underneath while the gang fires at him through the planks, then Ding returning fire and hauling men down to the water.

W. S. Van Dyke, director of *The Thin Man* (1934) and other adroit studio products, advised a beginner: "Just keep it close and keep it moving."[3] Watching *Gun Men* in this light, you notice that Hong Kong's debt to Hollywood goes beyond borrowing from post-1960 movies. Local directors have intuitively preserved the swift pacing, the precise staging and economical cutting, the proliferating plot twists, and the trust in genre roles

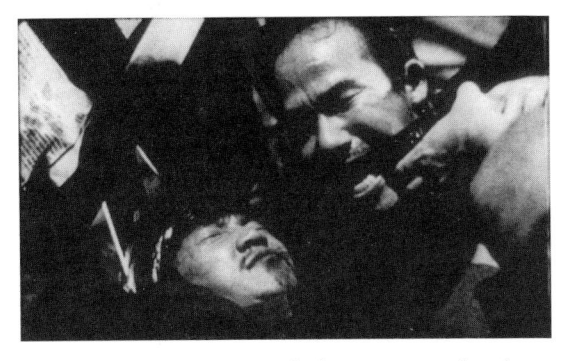

HKH.7 *Gun Men:* Mona and Ching are pinned to the ground by an adversary, who has locked Ding's gun hand; Ching must clamp the barrel in his teeth . . .

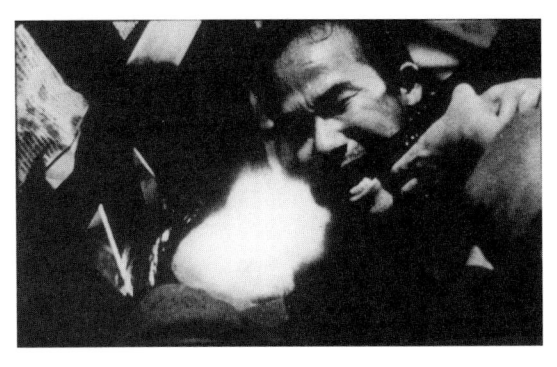

HKH.8 . . . and aim it at the villain, allowing Ding to fire.

(dutiful cop-father, whore with a heart of gold) that one finds in classic American studio cinema. The result is a film that, though not as slick as *The Untouchables*, achieves a nervous vigor and, particularly in the finale, a genuine sense of life at risk, down to the bare bones, everything reduced to the settling of scores. We never think that Elliot Ness will die, but Ding might; at the start of *The Untouchables* a little girl is killed by the gangsters, but in a Hong Kong movie a little girl can blast the villain.

To call this a more innocent cinema than the New Hollywood would smack of condescension. And of course *Gun Men*'s gore quotient and its technical polish owe a good deal to standards governing a lot of world cinema. Nonetheless Hong Kong filmmakers remain willing, for the sake of kinetic and emotional force, to put together a movie that has the sheer narrative drive and the unfussy professionalism of *Girl Shy* (1924) or *Footlight Parade* (1933) or *The Roaring Twenties* (1939). Movie Brats like De Palma, assuming that the classical cinema is dead, render homage to their mentors. Hong Kong directors, less concerned with paying tribute, simply plow ahead. In the process they maintain unpretentious, craft-centered cinema as a living tradition.

2

LOCAL HEROES

At ten-thirty on one of those sticky nights that typify spring in Hong Kong, the crowd was already packing the sidewalk and spilling into traffic. My friend waved me over. "You just missed the lions," she said.

Although admission to the Majestic Theatre was by special pass, this was no celebrity preview. In the crowd stood the same young people you find in the video shops, on the subway, in McDonald's. When the doors finally opened, a postmodern-Piranesian zigzag of escalators carried us to the top floor of the multiplex. I seemed to be the only *gweilo* in the auditorium, and I was probably the only person over forty (except maybe for the film's producer, who gave a little speech). We settled down to watch the first public screening of *Young and Dangerous 4*.

The *Young and Dangerous* series centers on twentysomethings who have all the normal problems—finding good jobs, surviving love affairs, quarreling and reconciling with their elders. They are a charming, cinegenic lot (Fig. 2.1). They wear black jeans and glossy jackets. They sport shoulder-length or buzz-cut hair in Kool-Aid colors. They are also triads. Resplendent in dragon tattoos, they run loan-sharking and car-parking rackets, scrap with other youngsters, stand loyally by their superiors, avenge their slain lovers, and commit murder on orders. They are upwardly mobile members of Hong Kong's most enduring service sector.[1]

When the first film proved a hit in 1996, it was followed by two sequels just months apart, as well as by a raft of copies. (There was, for instance, *Sexy and Dangerous*, in which girl gangs run roughshod over the posturing but ineffectual boys.) The success of the cycle triggered an outcry from parents, teachers, and film-industry figures. But some critics found the "young rascals" (the literal Cantonese title) praiseworthy. They suggested that in a largely moribund Hong Kong cinema, the *Young and Dangerous* phenomenon expressed authentic passions—and fairly affirmative ones at that, stressing young people's devotion to their surrogate family. Even the

2.1 Rock star Ekin Chan and popular actor Jordan Chan in *Young and Dangerous 4*.

secret societies were not shy about showing their support. The lion dancers I just missed seeing outside the theater were almost certainly kung-fu students, probably associated with triad gangs.

The audience—mostly young people, wearing fashionable clothes and sporting hair colors from auburn to grape to taffy pink—followed the movie intently. They laughed at the ritual humiliations suffered by figures of civic authority. The old priest, a series character usually satirized, aroused the loudest amusement. A vulpine young thug kills one of the boys' mentors and unleashes a gang war. (The actor, Roy Cheung, who had played this sort of character in triad movies since the 1980s, was brought back for a new role after portraying the villain in the previous *Young and Dangerous* entry. He has also starred in some of the series' clones.) The most charming, virtuous, and unfairly judged characters were our protagonists: the leader, played by darkly handsome pop singer Ekin Chan; his sidekick, Chicken, a scowling lump with a Sluggo cut (Jordan Chan); and Chicken's tough, foul-mouthed girlfriend (Karen Mok).

Later I learned that the *Young and Dangerous* films were addressed to an audience living in the characters' world; perhaps half of the audience were themselves more or less attached to triad gangs. I learned that the stars did not have the aura of the big names of the 1980s, instead selling themselves as the person next door. And I learned that for many critics the series expressed a certain pragmatic optimism about facing 1997.

At the show's end, the audience poured out to the street and surrounded one of the stars, Anthony Wong. Wong not only specializes in flamboyantly repulsive roles but also writes a newspaper column and sings his own rock songs like "Let Thunder-God Dash All the Manic Bullies." He signed autographs and posed for snapshots. Other stars were inside the multiplex, awaiting the end of the second screening. They would be greeting their fans at around two in the morning.

Not all new releases generated the anticipation of *Young and Dangerous 4*, but seeing this response to any film reminds you of the power of even average movies to hold an audience. Asked to define a typical Hong Kong film, director Kirk Wong replied: "A film that tries very hard to please the audience all the time."[2] The next day *Young and Dangerous 4* would move into more than twenty theaters and become the spring's second most lucrative Hong Kong film. Within five months it would be released on video. Of course bootleg copies were already for sale the night I zigzagged through a jammed Nathan Road to the Majestic Theatre.

Perched on the South China coast, Hong Kong consists of Hong Kong Island, Lantau Island, a scatter of smaller islands, the Kowloon Peninsula, and the New Territories abutting the Chinese mainland. Hong Kong has about six and a half million people, most of them crammed into forty of the territory's 415 square miles. Mongkok, in Kowloon, is four times more densely populated than Calcutta; even the "new towns" of the New Territories consist largely of towerblocks of tiny apartments. From their cramped household space people escape to public entertainments—parks, playgrounds, restaurants, festivals, karaoke, and cinemas.

The things achieved on this postage stamp of land have made it one of the triumphs of the industrialized world. By the early 1990s it had become the third wealthiest Asian territory (after Japan and Singapore) and the world's eighth commercial power. It had the third highest gross domestic product per capita, just behind the United States and Switzerland and well ahead of Canada, Germany, France, Italy, and Britain. Its citizens' average income surpassed that of its colonizing nation, and by 1990 more investment flowed to Britain from Hong Kong than in the opposite direction. The biggests, firsts, and mosts are endless. Hong Kong exports more goods than Mainland China or India. It boasts the world's largest container port. It is the top exporter of garments, toys, watches, and candles. It leads the world in per-capita consumption of brandy and Rolls-Royces.[3]

Guidebook statistics distort the picture somewhat, though, for the gap between rich and poor is wide. The top 10 percent of households earns 42 percent of all income, while the lower half of households earns only 19 percent. Thanks to government intervention, most people live in public housing at low rents. But property speculation has driven the purchase price of apartments to unreasonable heights. Those who are paying off their homes spend an average two-thirds of their household income on mortgages. The social services are among the best in Asia, but a mere 2 percent of the territory's revenues go toward them, and there is no unemployment insurance or pension system. Only domestic workers, principally the maids and nannies brought in from the Philippines, are guaranteed a minimum wage. No legislation limits working hours.[4]

Hong Kong achieved its success under colonial rule. It was run by a British governor, advised by the influential businessmen and lawyers whom he appointed to an executive council and a legislative council. Paternalistic though it was, the arrangement gave Hong Kong a degree of freedom unknown on the Mainland. There was rule of law (a tradition not well-rooted in Chinese history), citizens' individual rights were protected, and people enjoyed freedom of speech, of the press, and of association. Still, there were no political parties, and until 1985 citizens could not vote for any representatives on the Legislative Council.[5] Neither Britain nor China wanted Hong Kong to be self-governing. The British feared that creating a true electoral democracy would allow Communists to establish opposition parties. The Chinese feared that Hong Kongers, most of whose families had fled the Mainland, might set up a government opposed to Communism.[6] Only in 1995, when the British were about to depart, did Governor Chris Patten, to Beijing's profound annoyance, hold elections that created more democratic representation on the Legislative Council.

Britain had got its foothold in the region early in the nineteenth century. To pay for precious tea and silk, British companies shipped vast quantities of opium into China, ignoring the Chinese government's ban on the drug. After the first Opium War, China was forced to cede Hong Kong island to Britain in 1842. The second Opium War won Kowloon for the empire in 1860, and in 1898 Britain leased the New Territories for ninety-nine years. Throughout this period Hong Kong's excellent deep-water port made it a major entrepôt. The local economy was dominated by "hongs," the trading companies owned by Swires, Jardine, and other entrepreneurial families. Hong Kong became a regional center of banking, shipping, shipbuilding, cargo services, and insurance.[7]

It was a city of immigrants and expatriates. The dissolution of the Chinese empire in 1911, the struggles between the Communists and the Nationalist Party, and the Japanese invasion during the 1930s drove many Mainland Chinese to the colony. When the Japanese occupied Hong Kong between 1941 and 1945, some refugees returned to the Mainland, but soon after the war the struggles between the forces of Mao Zedong and Chiang Kai-shek sent thousands of immigrants back to Hong Kong. In 1941 Hong Kong had a population of 1.6 million; in 1945 it had only 600,000; by 1949, it was a refugee camp of more than 2 million. Shantytowns ringed the harbor, and families slept on rooftops. Mao's victory over Chiang and successive phases of Communist repression, particularly the Cultural Revolution of 1965–1976, drove more people out.

Although Hong Kong came to be known as Asia's transit lounge, many emigrants stayed. The great majority were Cantonese, pouring in from farming communities throughout Guangdong Province. Chiuchow and Hakka people came as well, along with Russians, Eurasians, and Indochinese. Particularly important were the emigrants from Shanghai, many of them entrepreneurs, professionals, and white-collar workers. With their ability to raise capital, the Shanghai businessmen helped Hong Kong launch rapid industrial growth during the 1950s. Although they accounted for only 4 percent of the population, Shanghainese became industrial leaders, making fortunes in textiles, shipping, and plastics.[8]

With a constant supply of enterprising arrivals, the British let Hong Kong develop a massive experiment in free marketeering. "If you want to see capitalism at work," Milton Friedman famously remarked, "go to Hong Kong."[9] The colony recovered from the war swiftly. Overseas Chinese money poured in, and local lenders proved accommodating. During the Korean War, the United Nations' embargo on trade with China drastically cut Hong Kong's role as a shipping center. In response, the colony transformed itself into an export-based manufacturing economy, specializing in textiles and clothing, then toys and timepieces, then quality printing and metal products, and finally electronics, from circuit boards to video games. Public transportation and utilities were privatized, creating a reliable infrastructure. Apart from building public housing and regulating the sale of land, the government intervened little in the whirl of moneymaking. During the 1970s Hong Kong's economy grew at the rate of 10 percent a year.[10]

Soon the colony became an important financial center, with banks eager to participate in global markets. Deng Xiaoping opened China after 1978, and Hong Kong businessmen began shifting their plants across the border, where land was more plentiful and wages were lower. By 1996, less than 10 percent of the colony's labor force worked in industry. Hong Kong became service-oriented, concentrating on banking, trading, investment, and tourism. Chinese millionaires began to buy out old British firms, and local companies invested heavily in the emerging Mainland market. Hong Kong became a center of world commerce, playing host to U.S., European, and Asian companies. Despite financial crises during the 1980s, Hong Kong continued to prosper.[11]

The colony was always closely bound to the Mainland. Hong Kong cannot feed itself, so since the end of World War II, China had controlled the colony's supply of water and food. As the saying went, "A Chinese takeover is only a telephone call away." The Cultural Revolution spilled over into Hong Kong, and strikes and protests sparked riots. During the 1980s boom, the colony became indispensable to a China trying to live up to Deng's new edict, "To get rich is glorious." Hong Kong's holdings in China were estimated at two-thirds of all foreign investment there, while Mainland entrepreneurs eagerly sank money into Hong Kong enterprises. Hong Kong residents frequently visited their families across the border, and tourists and dealmakers flowed into Hong Kong from the People's Republic.

Two major events complicated this rosy relationship. Seeing the lease on the New Territories about to expire, and worried that Deng Xiaoping might be succeeded by someone more hard-line, Britain raised the matter of renewing the leases. The government sent preliminary feelers to Beijing in the early 1980s, claiming that businessmen and bankers could not confidently write mortgages and loans past 1997. Although China had always signaled its intentions to retake Hong Kong someday, the British policymakers seem to have believed that China had benefited so greatly from the status quo that it might renew the leases. It was a miscalculation. Merely raising the matter may have forced Beijing to stand by the original deadlines. After two years of talks, Margaret Thatcher's government agreed to cede all claims to the colony.[12] When Britain announced the terms of the Joint Declaration in April of 1984, business decisions, family plans, and career choices came to be ruled by the deadline. Many of the educated and well-off fled. When the handover arrived, over half a million of the colony's most talented had gone.

A second crucial event occurred in Beijing in the spring of 1989, when students occupied Tiananmen Square to protest corruption and the lack of civil liberties. The action galvanized Hong Kong. Millions marched and rallied in support of the students, and local citizens donated over US$3 million to help their cause. The outpouring of feeling surprised outside observers, who had long claimed that Hong Kong people were uninterested in politics. On 4 June, China's leaders ordered the People's Liberation Army to attack the demonstrators in Tiananmen Square. Hundreds of people were killed, and in the months that followed many more were executed and imprisoned. The news struck Hong Kong like a thunderbolt.[13] What would life be like under this regime?

The question was still being asked, if more softly, when on 1 July 1997 British authorities transferred authority to the People's Republic.[14] A year later, there were few signs that the Mainland intended to rule heavy-handedly. Far more worrisome was the financial catastrophe that struck Asia in the autumn. Hong Kong property values tumbled to half their former levels, tourism dropped disastrously, and unemployment climbed. By early 1999 Hong Kong was suffering its first serious recession in decades.

The shock of the Tiananmen crackdown had been intensified by the fact that many Hong Kongers believed they had forged a unique cultural identity. Certainly most accepted Confucian values, took the family as the model for social organization, and recognized "face" as a sign of mutual respect. But over the decades, Hong Kong's roots in Cantonese society, the influences from Shanghai and from Britain, and a business-driven openness to the West had shaped a unique version of Chinese culture.

During the 1970s, as the economy began its long boom, there appeared a new generation—comparatively affluent young people born after the war, lacking memories of the Mainland, taught largely in the colonists' English and often graduates of a university in England, Australia, or North America.[15] The urbanized and cosmopolitan young, though often proud to be Chinese, were less interested in traditional Cantonese entertainments such as opera and the moralizing melodrama of "social education." They were drawn to foreign mass media. Local bands played tunes by Elvis and the Beatles. Perry Mason and Columbo were on television. For several years, *The Sound of Music* remained the top-grossing film. To many citizens, Hong Kong now represented a pragmatic blend of Chinese traditions and Western tastes.

Broadcast television, introduced in 1967, intensified the modernization of Hong Kong culture.[16] By 1973 the Cantonese-language channel dominated prime-time viewing, offering, among its soap-opera serials, several episodic dramas centering on current social problems. The channel launched a generation of directors, including Tsui Hark, Ann Hui, and Ringo Lam.[17] Cantonese television also popularized the waspish, deadpan comedian Michael Hui, whose nightly program (based on *Laugh-In*) established him and his brother Sam as a team. The Hui brothers' hugely successful film comedies *Games Gamblers Play* (1974), *The Private Eyes* (1976), and *The Contract* (1978) spearheaded the resurgence of Cantonese-language cinema. At the same time, television provided a showcase for Sam Hui's rock band Lotus, which led the music industry toward "Cantopop," that mix of Hong Kong vernacular and Western-style middle-of-the-road pop.[18] A song by Sam often played under the opening credits of a Hui film, and the lyrics usually vented a complaint about the strains of trying to make it in an unfeeling city.

> We're all poor employees
> Getting ulcers running around for a buck.
> The money we make won't even last a month.
> What a rough deal!...
> Nothing ever happens, we just slave till we drop.
> Nothing ever changes, things just keep going wrong.
> If things don't change, we'll go rob a bank.
> We've worked so hard we want a just reward.
> With things so hard we can't hope for a fair go.
> (The Private Eyes)

The success of the Hui brothers in film, television, and the music business was part of a wider shift in taste, as Hong Kongers began to stake out a distinctive popular culture. There emerged the new *gang-chan-pian* (Hong Kong–made films), characterized by swift pace, Cantonese slang, and the absence of Confucian moralizing. "For the first time," writes historian Choi Po-king, "the makers of cultural products for the local market were people with primary allegiance to Hong Kong itself."[19] After 1984, discussions of local identity were intensified by the impending handover to China. The closer 1997 came, the more aggressively distinctive Hong Kong's lifestyle seemed to become, as if to assert a cultural liberation from the Mainland even as economic and political ties were tightening. By 1988, over 80 percent of respondents to a poll claimed that they felt themselves primarily neither British nor Chinese but Hong Kongers.[20]

The 1970s was also the decade when midnight shows became a ritual.

Producers started to promote films by premiering them at eleven-thirty or so at ten to twenty theaters on the same Friday or Saturday. The midnight show generated word-of-mouth opinion—important in an industry with small advertising budgets. It was also a social ritual for students, young couples, and the slightly shady street people who frequented late-night bars and mahjong parlors. By the time of my visit to *Young and Dangerous 4*, the late show was purely a marketing device, but in its heyday the midnight screening gave filmmakers feedback. Producers began to force directors to attend. Kirk Wong has vivid memories of crowd reactions:

> If they see something they don't like, they'll boo and scream at you knowing that you're the director. I mean, I've been to shows where people would be pissed off, standing up and shouting, "Who the hell is the director? I want him out here," or "Who the hell wrote the script? Go get that stupid asshole!" But at the same time, if they go to a good show, they'll be cheering, clapping, it's like a riot. So once you're a director, you've got to get through this experience. You get nervous, man. You know you're gonna face that crowd eventually.[21]

If a gag didn't work or a sequence proved unsuspenseful, the director would recut scenes or even reshoot them and then rush to fix every print before the official opening a few days later.

Midnight screenings toughened filmmakers, giving the survivors an ability to criticize their work with unusual detachment. The ritual of attending the midnight show also nurtured a local film culture; cinéphiles could rendezvous at a show and then debate the film over tea and snacks until dawn. And the midnight screenings influenced the creative process itself. How many filmmakers made their choices on the set with the hardened late-night audience peering over their shoulders? Some directors have said that the ritual pushed them to make hyperactive films, movies that tried to glue the viewer to the screen every second. It forced them to try very hard to please the audience all the time.

"I don't think this happens anywhere else in the world," Kirk Wong says of the midnight show. "The Hong Kong audience has such an instant reaction, like instant coffee or instant noodles! It's a very typical Hong Kong thing."[22] That instantaneity will not surprise the visitor, who finds some parts of Hong Kong moving at an even faster pace than New York or Tokyo. In Central, the business district of the island, everyone seems in a frantic hurry. As soon as you step into an elevator, you push the button to close the door; on the subway you can place a quick call. People must capitalize on every instant if they are to succeed in a city whose chief religion is purportedly "moneytheism." An advertisement for a textile company appeared in the first issue of the *South China Morning Post* at the end of World War II: "Reopening soon. Sooner if possible."[23]

Hong Kong filmmakers participate in a quick-moving dialogue with one another and with their public. Cinema is woven into the city's life. Part of the interest of the *Young and Dangerous 4* preview lay in the fact that the audience could look forward to two or three new movies every week. Hong Kong is one of the few local cinemas ever to achieve the critical mass that underpins a full-blown film industry—a systematic mesh of production, distribution, and exhibition that sustains and satisfies the public's demand for entertainment.

For decades Hong Kongers were among the world's most frequent moviegoers. In 1959, when the city had around three million people, the average attendance per capita was twenty-two visits per year—by far the highest in the world and about twice that of the United States. At its peak, in 1967, attendance stood at an astonishing twenty-seven annual visits per capita. As television became available, business declined somewhat, but throughout the 1970s per capita attendance remained far ahead of that in other Asian countries.[24] This is all the more remarkable in that most Hong Kongers have traditionally worked six-day weeks, with only evenings and Sundays free for moviegoing.

The arrival of home video seems to have sharpened viewers' appetites. By the mid-1980s, half a million Hong Kongers owned VCRs, with over 250 videotape rental outlets serving them.[25] The laserdisc format, a high-end taste in the West, flourished. Karaoke helped popularize discs, and film viewers found discs' sharp image and uncropped widescreen a good source for their own tape copies. A movie that was successful in its theatrical run was often released on two cassettes or discs, thus doubling rental fees.

Despite the frenzy for video, viewers did not abandon the theaters. From 1977 to 1988 attendance was stable at about 65 million per year. And the audience preferred Hong Kong films. Up to the late 1960s, Hollywood held sway, but thereafter the local product ruled the box office. Eleven of the top twenty films of the 1970s were Hong Kong movies, and the top four were far ahead of the first Hollywood import to make the list *(The Towering Inferno)*. In some years no foreign film even ranked in the top ten. European bureaucrats rail against Hollywood imports, but it was European audiences who made global hits of *The Lion King, Forrest Gump, Batman, Home Alone, Ghostbusters, Aladdin, Mrs. Doubtfire, Beverly Hills Cop,* and *Back to the Future*. All failed in Hong Kong.

How could this happen? A Hong Kong film was typically released on a circuit of twenty to thirty large houses, while most foreign features played fewer than ten "mini-theatres."[26] In effect, the industry created a screen quota that limited Hollywood's earnings. As venues available for the U.S. product grew in the 1990s, so did box office returns. When *Jurassic Park* rolled out on about twenty screens, it was able to become the top-grossing film of the year, far outstripping the local favorites. The same thing happened with *Speed* (1994) and *Titanic* (1997).

Still, the quota could not have worked if Hong Kong had not offered a fairly competitive product. For one thing, it had quantity. After World War II it became one of Asia's most consistently prolific film industries. In 1965 the colony turned out 235 pictures, more than France and Germany put together. When most Western and many Asian film industries retrenched during the 1970s, Hong Kong's production never fell below 100. In the boom year of 1993, local producers churned out nearly 250 titles, equal to the domestic output of Japan—a country with twenty times Hong Kong's population. In most years the tiny territory's film output even outstripped that of the People's Republic of China.

Producers also maintained a competitive degree of quality. Granted, Hong Kong films were always cheaply made, and in the 1940s and 1950s they usually looked it. A rich family's walls would be stapled canvas, while the lighting would scatter shadows in all directions. But the emergence of big studios standardized a higher-gloss surface. Films from the Shaw Brothers company and its rivals boasted large casts and sets, as well as impressive camera movements and colorful costume design. Though not as sumptuous as Hollywood or Japanese productions, they made other Asian products look downmarket. After the rather tawdry kung-fu films of the 1970s began to falter, filmmakers deliberately aimed for Western-style production values. By the mid-1980s Hong Kong could compete with Hollywood by offering familiar genres and stars in a dazzling modern package.

Just as important, the movies spoke local languages. The demand for a southern-dialect cinema had helped create the Hong Kong industry back in the 1930s. Over 90 percent of the population spoke Cantonese, but films in Mandarin, the language of Beijing and much of northern China, also flourished. For a time they even obliterated films in the local language. But since the late 1970s, nearly all films have been in Cantonese. In the 1980s they became distinctly colloquial, and even subtitles began to use expressions that Chinese outside Hong Kong find hard to follow.[27]

The public has also been rather provincial. The flow of immigrants through Hong Kong, chiefly from China, created an audience that found local films more accessible than imports. Until very recently, a newcomer from Shanghai or Guangzhou would not recognize Arnold Schwarzenegger or Julia Roberts, but Andy Lau's movies and music videos are seen all over China. The audience consists mostly of students, lower-end white collar and clerical workers, and people with a high-school education or less. Middle-class people tend to prefer Hollywood, European, or Japanese cinema. Just as American intellectuals often loathe American movies, many cultivated Hong Kongers consider their own films trash.

The film industry adjusted to the rhythms of local life. Around the world, a holiday means moviegoing, and in Hong Kong the "golden slots" for a release became late summer, when students are out of school; the Christmas season; and above all the Lunar New Year, which falls between late January and late February. The top five films of the year almost invariably open in these playdates. Christmas and Lunar New Year bring out people who seldom go to the movies, so theaters offer family-friendly comedies and lighthearted action pictures. During the 1980s and early 1990s, Michael Hui, Jackie Chan, Chow Yun-fat, Stephen Chiau, Jet Li, and other big stars ruled the golden slots.

Accommodating to their clientele, theaters became neighborhood centers in the 1950s, hosting Cantonese Opera, variety shows, amateur theatricals, graduation ceremonies, and religious assemblies.[28] Today concession stands offer snack favorites like shrimp chips and dried squid. In this capital of commerce, an announcement runs before every film asking viewers to turn off their pagers and cellular phones, yet viewers freely answer their beepers, and occasionally they call friends to describe the film they're watching.

Beyond quantity and production values, beyond linguistic accessibility and user-friendliness, the movies evoke a comfortable milieu. Like New Yorkers or Parisians, Hong Kong viewers are used to seeing their neighborhoods on the screen. There are probably few thoroughfares in Kowloon or Hong Kong Island that have not been filmed; numberless jewel heists and chases have been staged along Nathan Road and its tributaries. The geography can get very specific. Wong Kar-wai built *Chungking Express* (1994) around Kowloon's Chungking Mansions and the island's California Café, while Ann Hui's *Summer Snow* (1995) is set in an old-fashioned neighborhood of Tai Po. Less prestigious productions such as Cha Chuen-yee's *The Rapist* (1994) and *Once upon a Time in Triad Society 2* (1996) base their sensational action upon the layouts of particular neighborhoods.

The films include familiar faces and voices too. From the start, local stars have commanded immense followings. The industry meshes easily with the pop music business, as singing stars move inevitably into films and film actors (like Anthony Wong, but also Andy Lau, Sally Yeh, and even Chow Yun-fat) take up singing. The multimedia mix known as *ge-ying-shi* (music—film—TV) obliges the most successful stars to cross over constantly.[29] *Ge-ying-shi* is geared to promoting the star first and the vehicles—movies, CDs, concerts, and the like—secondarily. While Hollywood publicizes the particular film through tie-ins with toys, souvenirs, and fast-food chains, a Hong Kong producer builds everything around the star, who will have strong fan clubs and sell a film through personal appearances and stories in the fan magazines.

Many critics will go on to claim that local films do more than adjust to popular tastes. Don't they actually reflect the audience's attitudes? We ought, I think, to be skeptical of relying too much on the reflection metaphor. An ingenious critic can make virtually any film reflect anything; a great many views, even contradictory ones, can be attributed to a diverse public. More concretely, not every member of a society goes to the cinema, and not all who go approve of everything they see. Producers try to create trends as well as reflect them, and films may drastically reshape their sources in everyday life. And even vociferous approval doesn't demonstrate that a movie mirrors mass attitudes. On 6 May 1998 Hong Kong theaters premiered *Casino*, a biography of the Macau gangster Wan Kok-koi, familiarly known as "Broken-Tooth" Koi. Broken-Tooth, given to large shirts depicting tropical landscapes, also financed the film. Although he was arrested shortly before the premiere, the opening-night audience applauded fiercely when Broken-Tooth's name appeared in the credits.[30] Does the applause for *Casino* mean that Hong Kongers admire gangsters? That they secretly want to rebel against the vestiges of colonial law and order? Or is it just that any premiere is likely to be packed with friends of the filmmakers? Broken-Tooth's friends might go to considerable lengths to make sure that the initial response was enthusiastic.

Instead of reflecting the mood of the moment, popular cinema is better considered as part of an open-ended dialogue with its culture. People with different points of view contribute, and the result never freezes into a snapshot of a zeitgeist or a national character. Filmmakers, critics, and audiences—or rather, diverse segments of audiences—participate in a vernacular conversation in which familiar subjects, both topical and traditional, are reworked according to various agendas.

Producers know, for example, that Hong Kongers' passion for mahjong and betting on horse races will furnish material for both serious characterizations and comic mishaps. One company found its biggest success with a long-running cycle of movies about high-stakes poker. Likewise, a city that treats eating as the principal social recreation—there are 20,000 restaurants—has created a culinary cinema. Virtually every film shows people dining, and a whole subgenre of movies centers on machinations around food (*Chicken and Duck Talk*, 1988; *The Chinese Feast*, 1995; *God of Cookery*, 1996). Gags involve overspiced dishes, misfired recipes, and noisy defecation and regurgitation. Utensils are standard comic props, particularly in kung-fu movies, where cups, teakettles, and chopsticks become weapons.

Films press every aspect of local color into service. Fight scenes are staged on the lashed-bamboo scaffolds that cling like giant spiderwebs to construction projects. (In *God of Gamblers*, 1989, the scaffolding permits a cross-reference to the urban choreography of *West Side Story*.) A shootout may take place in the Hong Lok Street bird market, while the local custom of taking caged birds out for a walk and into tea shops provides the premise for the opening firefight in *Hard Boiled* (1992). Goldfish bring good luck, so movie homes display aquariums. In this vertical city, elevators are part of daily life, so their closing doors are handy for claustrophobic horror scenes

(*Thou Shalt Not Swear*, 1993), last-minute reconciliations (*He's a Woman, She's a Man*, 1994), and images of plot closure (*Casino Raiders*, 1989). There are many jokes on video culture too; in *Don't Give a Damn* (1995) a police superintendent complains that when he asks an officer to return some rented laserdiscs for him, the officer takes them home to watch, running up late fees.

Passing fads become iconography. In the heroic triad cycle of the late 1980s the protagonists smoked Marlboros, enhancing their rebellious cowboy image. By the end of the 1990s, Salems were a preferred brand among young triads, and when *Young and Dangerous* heroes smoked them, Salems became associated with obedient young people. In *To Be No. 1* (1996), the protagonist smokes Marlboro Lights, as if the filmmakers wanted to present him as a throwback to the 1980s who has not yet achieved true heroism.[31]

As we would expect, Hong Kong's ubiquitous pagers and cellular phones become plot devices. A little girl swipes her mother's cell phone to call her father, a mad bomber (*In the Heat of Summer*, 1994). In a restaurant, two rival gangs and a police squad all face off at gunpoint; the scene explodes into a gun battle when someone's phone suddenly beeps (*Private Eye Blues*, 1994). An unmarried mother dining with a prospective husband is phoned by her gay friend from another table; when she sees him pick up a youth in the men's toilet, she phones him there to express her anger (*He and She*, 1994).

Moviemakers draw on low-riding currents of the culture—slang, recent scandals or catastrophes, bestselling comic books (the source of the *Young and Dangerous* series). In-jokes cite old movies and ephemeral TV shows, while retro films remake and update old material. Like *Back to the Future*, Peter Chan's *He Ain't Heavy, He's My Father* (1993) returns a young man to the 1950s. There he meets his father, a poor but virtuous man living in a neighborhood that is a glossier version of that in such Cantonese classics as *In the Face of Demolition* (1953) and *The Great Devotion* (1961). The result is at once a nostalgia film, an affectionate parody of old movies, and a celebration of the intermixing of Western and Chinese popular culture. (The father courts a rich girl by dancing with her to the tune of "Tell Laura I Love Her.") Chan's *Comrades, Almost a Love Story* (1996) activates local memories of popular-culture milestones from the 1950s (William Holden's visit to shoot *Love Is a Many-Splendored Thing*), the 1960s and 1970s (the Mandarin songs of Teresa Tang), and the 1980s and 1990s (McDonald's, ATMs, and the lure of emigration; Fig. 2.2). A more ambitious, or pretentious, citation of popular memory can be seen in Wong Kar-wai's *Days of Being Wild* (1990); its Cantonese title, "The Story of Rebellious Youth," uses the 1960s slang for young rebels, *ah fei*.[32]

"The Story of Rebellious Youth" is also the Cantonese title for *Rebel without a Cause* (1954), allowing Wong to indulge in another habit of local

2.2 *Comrades:* Two Mainland émigrés seen through an automatic teller machine.

cinema, a dialogue among films, filmmakers, and audiences. Critique is the most obvious riposte; Wong's *Days of Being Wild* is brought low in *Days of Being Dumb* (1992), and his other films have been widely parodied. Similarly, a theater short promoting the 1998 Hong Kong Film Awards gives us star Andy Lau in a kitchen, complaining to Anthony Wong that "There must be a conspiracy," an allusion to the fact that Andy has never won an award. Wong hands him a piece of bamboo to hold as a substitute, and Andy suddenly glows and prepares to give an acceptance speech.

The cultural crosstalk can be bruising, but the audience delights in it. Wong Jing makes *City Hunter* (1993), a comic-book spoof starring Jackie Chan. Chan complains that the movie is bad. Wong Jing responds with *High Risk* (1995), which mocks Chan in the form of the cowardly, drunken movie star Frankie Lone and brutally kills off his craven agent, a dead ringer for Jackie's manager. The glorification of gang life in *Young and Dangerous* has aroused at least one brace of replies, the *Once upon a Time in Triad Society* films, which turn hoodlums into petty fumblers.

Still, many aspects of local life seldom show up in the films—the poverty in which many residents live, or the Filipina maids who every Sunday spread their food, boomboxes, and knitting under the awnings of Cartier's and Chanel. Above all, as local critics often point out, the films offer virtually no explicit political commentary.[33] Only one film so far has dealt directly with the Tiananmen Square massacre: Shu Kei's *Sunless Days* (1990), a documentary diary of local reactions. In fact, television dramas have dealt more directly with political issues than films have.[34]

Partly because of censorship, partly because of the scale of investment at stake, Hong Kong filmmakers, like their peers in other popular cinemas, address politics in oblique ways. Again and again filmmakers have mocked the colony's rulers. Try to find a Britisher in these movies who is not a brute, a bumbling timeserver, or a vain and dense boss. In *Righting Wrongs* (1986), a policewoman says, "Shit!" Cut directly to the lion-and-unicorn insignia of the police force. The films are also full of references to Mainland China and "the 1997 syndrome," and the various treatments signal the range of the vernacular conversation. Some movies seem quite reconciled to future reunion. In Ringo Lam's *Undeclared War* (1990) a Hong Kong cop picks up a suspect in Guangzhou, where the police chief mouths policy: "We would like to see Hong Kong stable and prosperous." At the end of Kirk Wong's *Rock n' Roll Cop* (1994), detectives from Hong Kong and China, both harassed by bureaucratic constraints as they try to capture a maniacal killer, unite in weary professional amity: "We cops don't give a shit about politics. We just know how to arrest criminals."

Other films have adopted more complex attitudes to the colony's relations with China. Stephen Teo argues that from the 1970s Hong Kong cinema has often endorsed an "abstract nationalism" based upon *tian xia*, the moral and cultural traditions of the motherland, an attitude very different from allegiance to a particular political regime *(guo)*. Any form of government—Mainland, Taiwanese, British colonialist—is likely to be corrupt. Hence Hong Kong films signal local allegiance to Mainland history and tradition while displaying skepticism, even cynicism, about institutions.[35] Teo's point is supported by the critical viewpoint implicit in several crime thrillers, in which the villains are veterans of the People's Liberation Army, many of them having fought in the 1979 border war with Vietnam. Gangster leaders often carry the name Li Peng, the Party leader usually held responsible for the PLA's attack on the students at Tiananmen.[36] John Woo's *Bullet in the Head* (1990) and Tsui Hark's *A Better Tomorrow III: Love and Death in Saigon* (1989) are widely taken as despairing "aftershock" reactions to the massacre. Political points are often carried through allusion. "If you want to talk about current political anxieties," said producer Nansun Shi in 1988, "you make it an allegory, put it in the time of the warlords in China."[37]

The cultural dialogue is carried on more overtly in comedies, which have developed some stinging political satire. In Michael Hui's *The Front Page* (1990), the hero mulling over plastic surgery asks for Mao's chin and Deng Xiaoping's eyes. Movies often portray the cousins to the north as hayseeds or martinets. In *All for the Winner* (1990) Stephen Chiau plays a nose-picking hick from Beijing, complete with plaid suit, shrill tie, and straw suitcase. The *Her Fatal Ways* series (1990–1994) centers on a prim, officious woman cop from the PRC dispatched to Hong Kong, where she and her easily tempted partner encounter the fleshpots of rampant capitalism.

These jabs at authority may seem trivial by Oliver Stone standards, but we should expect them in a less pretentious filmmaking tradition. Sidelong references and moments of mockery attract less controversy than would an explicit and thoroughgoing political critique. Indeed, the *Young and Dangerous* franchise may have won some street credibility because of its edgy disrespect of China. In the third installment, when a Taiwanese

2.3 Mark and Ho enjoy their success in *A Better Tomorrow*.

triad leader arrives at a funeral, he taunts the local bosses: "Such poor Mandarin! How can you survive after 1997?" In the series' next offering a triad banquet is regaled with a karaoke version of the Maoist anthem "The East Is Red." Later the triads hold a gang election parodying the appointment of Tung Chee-hwa as Hong Kong's Chief Executive.

Such scenes, like the triads' lion dance outside the Majestic Theatre the night I visited, point up another area of fascination for local audiences: the underworld. "I won't go to the movies," a cabdriver curtly told me. "It's a business run by triads. The movies make them good guys." Hong Kong is the world capital of the *heishehui* ("black societies"). Since the end of World War II triad gangs have controlled extortion, gambling, heroin smuggling, and prostitution. Their networks stretch through Asia and into Europe and North America. Triad members, many of them martial artists, have long been involved in filmmaking.[38]

During the 1980s Hong Kong's mass media began glamorizing triad culture, notably in films like *A Better Tomorrow* (1986), with Armani-clad racketeers professing sentimental brotherhood (Fig. 2.3). At the same time, the societies began investing in the booming film industry and used productions to launder money. Stars and directors were bullied into working for triad companies. There were thefts, at least one firebombing, beatings, and murders.[39] Win's, a major company founded in 1984, is widely assumed to be a triad-related enterprise. It is currently operated by Charles Heung, brother of an alleged "Grand Dragon" of one of the top societies. In a wink typical of Hong Kong film, Charles Heung plays the unsmiling triad bodyguard Lone Ng in Win's *God of Gamblers* series. His scorpion tattoo, an icon signifying a Vietnamese Chinese, adds to the character's (and the producer's) mystique.

A Better Tomorrow's Cantonese title is "True Colors of a Hero." When Tsui Hark proposed the project to John Woo, Tsui recalled, "We talked a lot about heroes. The trend at the time was comedy. It was difficult to invest in a violent and romantic film."[40] The film's success touched off a string of gangster films known as the "heroes" cycle. Nowhere is the cultural conversation taking place in and around local movies more evident than in the ongoing reappraisals of what counts as heroism.

The Chinese heroic tale can be found in written and oral forms as early as the ninth century, but the conventions most pertinent for film came into focus in popular serial novels during the nineteenth century.[41] The martial hero, or *wuxia,* is, like all folk heroes, strong and skillful in combat. He operates, Ma Ka-fai points out, by exercising righteousness *(yi)* for the sake of particular people, not for the society as a whole or in service to an abstract ideal.[42] Chinese history is full of corrupt and rapacious rulers, and there is no strong tradition of appeal to an impersonal principle of justice. Popular storytelling therefore made the hero a loner outside the law and opposed to the ruling elite. Contrary to the Western chivalric tradition, the Chinese wandering knight does not serve a woman or even fall in love (although a female warrior may assist him). The hero is supremely governed by loyalty—to his family, particularly his father, and to his friends, or "brothers."[43]

Chinese films based on this heroic tradition were made as early as the 1920s, and it formed the basis of many chivalric tales and supernatural-swordplay fantasies in later decades. The swordplay novels continue to flourish as a form of mass fiction. Ma Ka-fai has shown in a fascinating study that the swordplay films of the 1960s, the kung-fu films of the 1970s, and the 1980s gangster sagas all tend to adhere to the chivalric conception of heroism.[44] There is no appeal to the law; the hero must wreak punishment on those who have wronged him; he must rely on his friends and his master, an overt father-figure. If his friend or his boss betrays him, he is plunged into despair, but his vengeance will be fearsome.

Powerful though it is, this conception of heroism doesn't seem to have obliterated all others; the cultural dialogue generated variants. Athena Tsui points out that there are tragic heroes, such as those played by Chow Yun-fat, and comic, even antiheroic figures, such as Stephen Chiau.[45] In some classic swordplay films, heroism depends upon fighting skills, but the hero might have a flaw that needs correcting, as the protagonist in *The New One-Armed Swordsman* (1971) learns humility by being bettered in a match with the treacherous master. A conception of "group heroism" was also somewhat common, from the warrior women of *Fourteen Amazons* (1972) to the fighting teams of *Crippled Avengers* (1978) and *Avenging Warriors* (1979), with each hero cultivating a specific weapon or skill. In the kung-fu comedies, heroism was redefined to include both frenzied endurance (the films of Jackie Chan) and petty craftiness (the hero of Sammo Hung's *The Dead and the Deadly,* 1982).

By the early 1990s, partly because of the charge that the heroic triad films had led youngsters to admire the gangs, more filmmakers played up the self-sacrificing heroism displayed by peace officers (*Hard Boiled,* 1992; *The Final Option,* 1994; *The Log,* 1996; *The Big Bullet,* 1996). An outstand-

2.4 The firefighting team after the climax of *Lifeline*.

ing example is *Lifeline* (1997), which appeared two months after a fire in a decrepit Kowloon office block killed nearly forty sweatshop workers. At first glance *Lifeline* might seem merely a ripoff of *Backdraft*, but unlike the Hollywood film it centers on a team of ordinary people trying to be responsible firefighters. The plot is episodic, alternating between dramatic rescue situations and moments of crisis in the team members' personal lives. Although there is one inflexible authority figure, the film—remarkably for a Hong Kong movie—has no real villain. A major conflict comes from the attitude of one insubordinate hero toward authority, since he is considered reckless for admitting that he would violate procedures if it would save lives. The action scenes, particularly the overwhelming final set-piece in a burning office block, display the squad's solidarity and devotion to duty. When the firefighters manage to survive and face their superior (Fig. 2.4), it is hard not to see them as both an updated version of the warrior team and a bid for a different conception of heroism: one that roots loyalty to the immediate group within a larger frame of civic responsibility. A 1980s hero would sacrifice himself for his friend or his gang, but not for an abstraction like the community. The tagline on *Lifeline*'s poster reads: "Save as Many as You Can."

It is tempting to see *Lifeline* as reflecting a pervasive trust in local institutions, standing stalwart against the arrival of rulers appointed by Beijing. But as usual the cultural dialogue sounded several registers. In the fraught year of 1997, *Lifeline* was countered by *Downtown Torpedoes* (released in August), which centered on adventurous young thieves, experts in burglary and computer hacking who want only to make money and retire to the Caribbean. By contrast *Young and Dangerous 4*, released a few months earlier than *Downtown Torpedoes*, celebrated youths standing by one another in loyalty to family, neighborhood, and Hong Kong. October brought the very different *Made in Hong Kong*, a cry of adolescent despair from life lived on society's margins. Then there was *Task Force* (November), which seems a less melodramatic version of *Lifeline*, praising those who do their duty and refuse violence—a theme, in turn, at odds with updated kung-fu revenge tales like *Hero* and *Legend of the Wolf* (both released in May). Even in the months before and after China's reclamation of sovereignty, the movies' vernacular conversation about heroism was constantly divided, dispersed, and mediated by the conventions of popular entertainment.

> *I want to make a film that reflects our time. If not, no one will know that we ever existed.*
> THE ÉMIGRÉ FILM DIRECTOR IN *AH YING* (1983)

Hong Kong critics are closely tied to the film industry. Although the city boasts a large popular press, there are no "quality" venues like *The Nation* or *The New Yorker*. Most film critics write for daily newspapers, some for weekly or biweekly popular magazines. A piece longer than a thousand words will seldom get published. As a result, no one survives simply by writing film criticism.[46] A few critics get jobs at the festival, and some work in the film industry, typically as screenwriters. Manfred Wong is both a film critic and a successful screenwriter-producer; he also runs a restaurant.

Proximity to a fast-paced industry promotes a rapid dialogue. The midnight public responds to a film "like instant noodles," the films try to latch on to fads and new tastes, and many critics address a piece less to the public than to the filmmakers or other critics. In this close-knit community, what one writes is noticed by all.

Significant positions emerge from the conversation. For example, many critics hold that Hong Kong cinema has been in a postmodern phase, but they disagree about the timing and the consequences. For Jimmy Ngai, local postmodernism began around 1984, with the rise of the Cinema City studio and the signing of the Basic Agreement between Britain and China; it marked a turn to shamelessly commercial entertainment. For Li Cheuk-to, the postmodern moment came after the Tiananmen Square massacre of 1989, and it expressed the public's urge to escape into nostalgia and nonsense, emblematized in a series of parodic retro films and Stephen Chiau's *mo-lei-tau* ("gibberish") comedy.[47] Readers in the know will consider even a short piece in the light of each author's position. In turn, filmmakers respond by slipping references, not always flattering, to postmodernism into their films.

Most of the critics I have been describing are twenty to forty years old and belong to the Hong Kong Film Critics Society, an ambitious group formed in 1994 to promote serious discussion of cinema. Few members of the society were trained in film schools, so what was shown locally became their window on film history. Hong Kong distributors seldom import European and American independent work; a single screening of a Tarkovsky or a Godard can become a reference point for months. The younger critics formed their tastes around the New Hollywood (*The Godfather* remains a landmark), European masters from neorealism to the present, postwar Japanese cinema, Americans like Lynch and Tarantino, and the Hong Kong cinema of the 1980s. Spielberg, Tarkovsky, Scorsese, and Kieślowski are major presences. These critics do not usually look back to silent cinema or to Hong Kong's postwar realist tradition. Many work in production and see corners cut and compromises made, so they cast a jaundiced eye on current local films.[48]

There is also an older generation of critics who speak for more traditional cinema. These critics came out of the late 1960s, when the student press and campus film societies sought to build a cosmopolitan film culture.[49] Studio One, a ciné-club for expatriates, had already been created in 1962, but venues for locals opened in the following decade, such as the Phoenix Cine-Club (1973) and the Hong Kong Arts Centre (1976).[50] Several filmmakers and critics founded the Film Culture Centre of Hong Kong in 1978, offering lectures and filmmaking workshops as well as screenings of films not available theatrically. The first decade of the Hong Kong Film Festival (1977–1986) was central to this effort, exposing young critics to trends from abroad and providing a showcase for their writings. Another forum was the serious journal–first, *Close-Up,* founded by the film director Shu Shuen in 1975; and then, when that ceased, *Film Biweekly,* founded in 1979 and allied with the New Wave.

This generation, which includes senior figures like Law Kar and Sek Kei, greeted the early New Wave efforts as the start of an "alternative cinema."[51] The critics have seen their hopes dashed as Hong Kong cinema has become more flagrantly mercantile. The ciné-clubs folded, and the Film Culture Centre closed. By late 1990 *Film Biweekly* had turned into the more mainstream *City Entertainment.* A handful of arthouse screens and the annual festival are the only sources of prestigious international films.

On the whole, the older writers are more critical of 1980s and 1990s Hong Kong cinema than are the younger ones. They tend to find the genuine traditions of Hong Kong cinema in the realist postwar films and in the New Wave of the early 1980s. In many respects, though, the two generations are not far apart. They share, for instance, a fairly firm canon. In any national film culture, establishing a canon serves not only to guide viewers' tastes; it also serves to mark out a tradition, to set agendas, and to make the present intelligible. In the West, critical consensus on the great silent films enabled scholars to ask how these films might be linked into a coherent history.[52] A canon can define a local cinema around a specific set of values, something that is particularly important for a community emerging from colonialism.

Naturally not all critics will agree on the finest Hong Kong films, but tastes converge surprisingly often. A 1995 poll asked the twenty-five members of the Critics Society to name the best Hong Kong films ever made. Some heavily favored 1950s and 1960s critical realism, but even young critics included at least two films from before 1970 on their lists. And all agreed on the eminence of the leading New Wave directors, with films by Yim Ho, Allen Fong, Tsui Hark, Stanley Kwan, and Ann Hui receiving very high scores. The most-cited film was Wong Kar-wai's *Days of Being Wild* (fourteen votes), and Wong was also the most-cited director (eighteen votes).[53] In sum, critics with contemporary tastes seem to respect Hong Kong's traditions, while those favoring older films tend to exempt Wong from their disapproval of recent work. More broadly, the splits in tastes have become part of the critics' dialogue with contemporary cinema; every faction will be looking for aspects of recent releases that resonate with the virtues they find in the canon.

The two generations also agree that filmmakers must address the community on matters of moral consequence. Chinese intellectuals have traditionally been committed to public education, and this attitude has shaped Hong Kong film criticism. During the first postwar years critics and filmmakers debated how to make cinema a vehicle for progressive ideas, and a series of "clean-up campaigns" sought to gain filmmakers a measure of cultural respectability. *Film Tribute,* a journal launched in 1947, offered analyses of cinema and politics, while most daily newspapers began film pages soon thereafter.[54] Many critics were liberals or Communists, and their call for a socially critical cinema tallied with the emergence of left-wing studios.

Critics of the 1960s generation pushed the commitment to social commentary in new directions. In a careful historical study, Hector Rodriguez has shown that these young writers promoted a fresh cultural agenda.[55] The new cinema, they argued, would explore contemporary life in the colony. It would no longer portray Hong Kong as an ersatz Shanghai, as the Mainland exiles of the late 1940s and 1950s had, or retreat into Shaw Brothers' mythical, generic Chinese past. The ideal film auteur would struggle to present a serious inquiry into the colony's neglected history and its current concerns.

The critics' contribution to the cultural dialogue helped prepare for the New Wave. When Ann Hui's *The Secret* (1979) and Tsui Hark's *Dangerous Encounter—First Kind* (1980) stirred controversy, many critics defended the rising generation. They claimed that sincere and cosmopolitan filmmakers like Hui, Tsui, Yim Ho, Patrick Tam, and Allen Fong could grasp modern Hong Kong in a way that the studio filmmakers could not. These young artists combined an understanding of up-to-date film technique with what Rodriguez calls "a realist commitment to the specificity of a local identity."[56] They fought the pressures of the industry, producing personal films from within an impersonal system. The emergence of the New Wave was a defining moment not only for Hong Kong filmmaking but also for film criticism. New Wave directors rank so highly in the 1995 poll because they showed that local filmmaking could present serious artistic treatments of contemporary life.

If the auteur thoughtfully meditates upon local culture, mass-produced cinema blindly reproduces it. Rodriguez suggests that many 1960s writers saw Hong Kong's commercial films as erasing local history in favor of an immediate appeal to the audience's whims. Today many critics still find that entertainment cinema usually fails in its moral responsibility, but even so it remains an index of the audience's beliefs, desires, and attitudes. Like American commentators who seek traces of cultural problems in Hollywood movies, Hong Kong critics treat the industry's output as reflecting social trends. This is the most powerful and pervasive assumption in Hong Kong film criticism, uniting writers of all ages and tastes.

Reflectionism is a useful journalistic strategy in a fast-turnaround community. When you have limited space to make an argument, you can lure a reader by linking an unremarkable new release to something manifestly important, the temper of the moment. Like the critics who turn out Sunday "think pieces" for U.S. newspapers, Hong Kong critics use this form of reflectionism as an occasion to explore a film's relation to current social trends. The tactic poses the sort of conceptual difficulties I've mentioned, but in a close-knit community, reflectionism can serve as a rhetorical strategy to sharpen the ongoing dialogue with the filmmakers. It urges directors and scriptwriters to think about their role as public educators, suggesting that if they do not take explicit stands they will be parroting popular tastes.

This view has considerable resonance in a tradition that requires not only the intellectual but also the artist to be a teacher. The Cantonese film classics of the 1950s and 1960s often had a didactic Confucian streak, and the New Wave proved that entertainment could be infused with social criticism. Many younger critics believe strongly with their elders that a good filmmaker presents personal reflections upon the immediate cultural moment, even when their candidates for auteurs might not be attractive to older writers. To defend a film, the critic will often argue that the director is sending a message to the public, expressing her or his feelings about matters of current concern. For example, Li Cheuk-to, a pivotal figure between the older and younger generation of critics, has suggested that in the face of the Mainland takeover Gordon Chan's *First Option* (1996) presents a heroic image of team spirit and professional discipline, qualities reflected in the film's style: "The heroism of the Special Duties Unit and their sense of professional confidence are seen as common traits of Hong Kong people, thus showing how Hong Kong in general could deal with any situation under adverse circumstances. The film's own sense of professionalism is a mark of this confidence . . . Put heads together and face the challenge and you can turn defeat into victory."[57] For most critics anywhere, the best *of Death* was released in 1978, incorporating some of the footage Lee had shot but adding a storyline that required three doubles to take his place.

Bruce Lee was the first Hong Kong star to achieve worldwide renown, and he remains the territory's most famous citizen. He helped popularize Chinese martial arts; many a black or Hispanic youth was inspired by Lee's fearless confrontations with white power. Lee's films changed popular cinema forever, giving screen combat a new force and grace. When in *Lethal Weapon 3* (1992) Mel Gibson and Rene Russo match combat skills, we take it for granted they will fight as much with their feet as with their fists. No film hero has been so widely and illegally appropriated, in the dozens of pseudo–Bruce Lee films made not only in Asia but even in Canada *(Sexy Ilsa Meets Bruce Lee in the Devil's Triangle)* and Brazil *(Bruce Lee versus the Gay Power)*.[3] And where would video games and superhero comics be without the martial arts conventions Lee introduced to the West?

Raised on Nathan Road, Lee was a child of crowded Kowloon. As a young star he played orphans and street urchins, then teen rebels. In his last film of this period, *The Orphan* (1960), he portrayed an anguished youth in the James Dean mold, confusedly lashing out at all who want to help him. In real life he enjoyed roaming the streets picking fights. He learned to dance and eventually became Hong Kong's cha-cha champion. Everyone knew that he had been turned down for the starring role in the *Kung Fu* TV series, and the fact that he launched a colossal career from Hong Kong rather than Hollywood made the public love him. Golden Harvest provided him a modest flat in the Waterloo Hill area of Kowloon, and many mornings Lee could be seen on his run through the neighborhood. After his death more than twenty thousand people filled the streets in tribute.

Lee remains the reference point for local action cinema. Producers have reassembled and reissued every frame of film in which he appeared. One of the most peculiar releases to come from a major motion picture company, *Game of Death* mixes authentic footage of Lee with scenes whose main purpose is the concealment of the Lee stand-in's face. There was a crowd of imitators, from Bruce Li to Tarzen [sic] Lee, and scores of films that claimed his imprimatur. Every Hong Kong comedian has parodied him, and current action star Jet Li has paid tribute by remaking *Fist of Fury* (*Fist of Legend*, 1994). In *City Hunter* (1993), when Jackie Chan is fighting in a movie theater, he gets some tips from Lee's moves against Kareem Abdul Jabbar in *Game of Death.*

Lee was determined to prove the excellence of Chinese martial arts. During his stay in the United States he held tournament demonstrations that astounded audiences. With a punch or kick he could break eight two-inch-thick boards taped together. He could kick through boards dangling in the air. He demonstrated a "one-inch" punch that knocked fighters several feet back. With *Fist of Fury,* set in 1909 Shanghai, he became vigorously nationalistic, celebrating Chinese dignity in the face of colonial oppression. He

TD.1 *Fist of Fury:* Lee smashes the sign "No Dogs or Chinese Allowed."

TD.2 The opening of *The Way of the Dragon:* Lee tries to ignore a dowager's disapproving stare.

thrashes an entire dojo of karate students, and with a stupendous leap and kick he shatters a sign barring Chinese entrance to an English-only compound (Fig. TD.1).

In *The Way of the Dragon*, the only finished project over which Lee had control, he becomes a good-natured bumpkin scorned by the West. Setting the film in Rome allows him to express the anxiety of the emigrant, who may at any moment lose face through a faux pas (Fig. TD.2). He moves uneasily through the '60s-mod apartment of a Westernized Chinese woman, afraid to cross his legs or set down his glass. Of course the bumpkin is actually a splendid fighter, and at the end he turns the West's emblem of combat, the Coliseum, into an arena for Eastern gladiators. *The Way of the Dragon*, which Lee aimed at the local audience, celebrates Hong Kong identity: his hero is from the New Territories, he tells the girl that the food is better at home than in Italy, and, shown a garden, he remarks that if it were in Hong Kong he'd build on it and make some money.

Lee's fighting style deliberately projects this sense of local identity, but in complex ways. *Fist of Fury* retells the legend of the death of He Yun-jia, founder of the Jing Wu School of Chinese martial arts, and in playing He's disciple Chen, Lee self-consciously continues the noble tradition. But the Jing Wu tradition was a northern one, and Lee identified passionately with the southern schools. He called his art by its Cantonese name, *kung-fu*. At age thirteen he began to study Wing Chun with the master Yip Man. Wing Chun is a southern Chinese technique emphasizing rapid punches, as opposed to the virtuosic leg work of northern styles. According to some reports, Yip taught a modified version of Wing Chun that emphasized a leaned-back, shuffling gait—features that Lee revised into a flowing, edgy strut.[4] Lee was very familiar with the dozens of films devoted to kung-fu master Huang Feihong, starring the legendary Kwan Tak-hing. In *Enter the Dragon*, Lee defeats the criminal mastermind Han in a bloody bout; the fact that Han was played by Shek Kin, the recurring villain in the old Huang Feihong series, made Lee the heir of Kwan, a 1970s update of a classic hero.

Yet Lee was an eclectic and an iconoclast. Kung-fu training rests upon a Confucian conception of fidelity: the master is the father, the pupil the obedient child. Such is the lesson of *Fist of Fury*, in which Chen must avenge his *sifu*'s death. But in *The Big Boss*, the master exploits his workers, and in *The Way of the Dragon* Uncle Wing betrays and kills the young men who have defended him against the racketeers. In *Enter the Dragon*, Lee must slay Han, a potent figure of paternal authority. Nothing shows Lee's nonconformity—and his address to Hong Kong's 1970s youth culture—more starkly than his insistence that the young warrior must often unseat the older man whom society has venerated.

In keeping with this attitude, Lee embraced a purely pragmatic conception of the martial arts. You learn kung fu in order to win real fights. "It isn't ritual and it isn't sport. It's self-defense."[5] He wrote a friend in 1969: "I've lost faith in the Chinese classical arts—though I still call mine Chinese—because, basically, all styles are a product of 'land swimming,' even the wing chun school. So my line of training is more toward efficient streetfighting with everything goes."[6] In his youth, before he took up Wing Chun, he joined a boxing team and learned to fence. He also mastered some northern forms, and in the United States he learned judo, Filipino martial arts, wrestling, karate, and Thai boxing. He trained in the Western manner, using a punching bag and devoting hours to rope skipping, which enhanced his fluid, bantamweight style. He amassed a library of books on all forms of combat, and he studied footage of Muhammed Ali's bouts, convinced that someday he and Ali would have to fight.

Lee called his approach Jeet Kune Do, "the way of the intercepting fist." It is an aggressive strategy that achieves maximum efficiency by making each parry a powerful attacking blow in itself. Jeet Kune Do is not a distinct style but a synthesis based on the premise that a real fight is not conducted according to sacred rules. The climax of *The Way of the Dragon* is a clash between a free-limbed, resourceful warrior (Lee) and a master (Chuck Norris) who cannot adjust to mercurial changes in attack. The original *Game of Death* was to conclude in a multistoried pagoda, each floor guarded by an expert in one martial art. The hero was to defeat them one by one, revealing every school as fatally frozen in tradition.

Whereas the ordinary martial arts master strove to keep his own version of kung-fu inviolate, Lee advocated mixing techniques to suit one's individuality. Instead of memorizing a narrow set of traditional styles and forms, the student had to learn tactics drawn from all traditions. For Lee, the spiritual dimension of kung-fu lay not in secret lore but in its ability to manifest each practitioner's personality. "If you have only two hands and two legs nationalities don't mean anything. We must approach it as an expression of oneself."[7] Lee's respectful but flexible attitude toward fighting traditions offers a martial version of what many saw as Hong Kong's growing sense of pragmatic individualism.

In adapting his style to film, Lee ranged still farther. Although he preferred the low kicks favored in the wing chun tradition, the high kick was so powerful onscreen that he cultivated it and made it central to his star image. From Japanese karate came Lee's battle cry, the *kiai* so reminiscent of a bird's shriek, which not only helped him "grip" his body for maximal energy but also raised the dramatic pitch of a fight. Lee was also preternaturally fast; he enjoyed plucking a coin from a man's palm before the victim could close his fingers. Onscreen, Lee's punch and withdrawal often take a mere six frames, a quarter of a second.

Jeet Kune Do was "simply the direct expression of one's feelings with the minimum of movements and energy."[8] In every film fight, Lee boldly expresses his changing emotions and his unique personality. Of course he is capable of ferocious rage, although usually it is compressed into a fierce glare and a stabbing forefinger. For unworthy opponents he shows undisguised contempt, cocking his head, strolling around them, rolling his eyes. Yet even when dispatching the lesser fighters, he seldom loses that brooding scowl suggesting a strange mixture of detachment and self-absorption. Sometimes his eyes turn from his enemy to fasten on something offscreen, and his blows seem merely to play out a pure pattern of elegant movement, largely indifferent to their devastation of the opponent. At other moments, after he delivers a punch his brows knit, his head swivels, and his mouth opens in astonishment at the damage he has done or draws into a grimace mixing strain, anger, and anguish.

The camera loved Lee only slightly more than he loved himself. From film to film his self-mythologization grew: frozen in a leap as he faces a hail of bullets in *Fist of Fury* (Fig. TD.3), fighting in the Coliseum in *The Way of the Dragon*, surrounded by reflections of himself in Han's mirrored museum (Fig. TD.4). After his death Lee's image multiplied endlessly, weirdly split and resplit in *Game of Death* (with its plot motif of doubles,

TD.3 The closing image of *Fist of Fury*.

TD.4 *Enter the Dragon:* Lee in Han's hall of mirrors.

photographs, and wax effigies) and exploited as an icon in spinoffs, as in *Exit the Dragon, Enter the Tiger* (1976), in which Lee senses that death is near and prepares a pupil to avenge him (Fig. TD.5). What critics have called his narcissism can be seen as a natural extension of his determination to achieve success by defining himself as an utterly singular individual. Lee obsessively pursued stardom, living out a plan that he committed to paper in 1969 as "My Definite Chief Aim": "I, Bruce Lee, will be the highest paid Oriental superstar in the United States. In return I will give the most exciting performances and render the best of quality in the capacity of an actor. Starting in 1970, I will achieve world fame and from then onward till the end of 1980 I will have in my possession $10,000,000. Then I will live the way I please and achieve inner harmony and happiness."[9] Many would say that the ideal of expressing one's distinct identity, becoming a multimillionaire, and then having the leisure to achieve spiritual harmony is one version of a powerful local dream.

It is tempting to trace aspects of Lee's career through his many names. When he was born in 1940 (in Chinese astrology, a year of the Dragon), a

TD.5 Homage to Lee and exploitation of his image (*Exit the Dragon, Enter the Tiger*).

nurse supposedly suggested the name Bruce, under which he would be known in America. His given name, Lee Chun-fan, translates as "gaining fame overseas" (literally, "shaking foreign countries"). At home his mother called him Mo Si-ting, "never sits still," and his sister nicknamed him Siu-lung, "little dragon," which became his film name early in his career as a child actor.

At birth, Jackie Chan was named Chan Kong Sang, meaning simply "born in Hong Kong."[10] At age six he began living at Yu Jim Yuen's Chinese Opera Research Institute in Hong Kong while his parents worked abroad. Under a harsh regimen he learned singing, dancing, martial arts, and acrobatics. Bruce Lee attended college in America and was an avid reader and book collector, but Chan never properly learned to read or write. When Yuen's institute was disbanded, Jackie and several of his fellow students found work in the film industry. Several of them, including Chan, worked on Bruce Lee projects. Chan rose through the ranks at Golden Harvest to become a stunt player, then an assistant to the fight director, and finally one of the Bruce Lee clones. Not until the enterprising producer Ng Seeyuen borrowed him for *Snake in the Eagle's Shadow* (1978), a kung-fu comedy, did Chan's career take off. In a short time he established himself as Hong Kong's top box-office star, graduating to directing in *Fearless Hyena* (1979).

Chan's film name, Sing Lung, means "to become a dragon," and this defined his problem: how to be the next Lee without becoming a Lee clone? Chan decided to invert Lee's heroic image. He has endlessly explained: "Instead of kicking high like Bruce Lee, I kick low. He plays the invincible hero, I'm the underdog. His movies are intense, mine are light."[11]

Bruce Lee's movies assume that he is the best fighter around. The plot therefore consists of finding ways to delay his confrontation with the main villain. So Lee is reluctant to fight, or he is ignorant of the villain's activity, or secondary villains step in. By contrast, Jackie Chan's typical kung-fu film starts with him as a talented but raw and naïve fighter. His are appren-

TD.6 Jackie's tortuous apprenticeship in *Snake in the Eagle's Shadow*, with Simon Yuen as his demanding sifu.

tice plots; he must learn discipline, stamina, and special techniques that will allow him to win—often very narrowly—against seasoned foes. In the course of *Snake in the Eagle's Shadow*, *Drunken Master* (1978), and other films, Chan must literally "become a dragon"—learn to endure pain and to perfect his skill (Fig. TD.6). He began to define another version of heroism, one stressing boundless determination and a good-humored willingness to suffer.

Aiming at winning real fights, Bruce Lee saw no reason to learn acrobatics. When a scene demanded leaps and tumbles, he used a double. By contrast, Chan and his school "brothers" Yuen Biao and Sammo Hung were brilliant acrobats. They and other graduates of the Opera Institute sparked a trend toward flashy stunts in the kung-fu films of the late 1970s. Hung became one of the industry's top fight choreographers and began to give Golden Harvest's kung-fu films swift fighting, hairbreadth timing, and bursts of comedy. Yuen Woo-ping, son of an expert fight choreographer, developed a comparable style in directing *Snake* and *Drunken Master*, and it suited Chan perfectly.

Like Lee, Chan mastered many styles—southern and northern kung-fu, Korean hapkido, and Japanese judo—but he never sought to found a style of his own, calling his approach "chop-suey": "After I started doing movies, I just mixed it all in together."[12] Lee the streetfighter had consciously reacted against the Peking Opera tradition, the main model for martial-arts films since the 1930s. He called for a "broken rhythm," which he took to be more realistic. By contrast, Chan and his contemporaries drew on the Peking Opera influence. Indeed, they intensified it, partly by absorbing Lee's lesson that the action should be filled with emotion, partly by creating long routines displaying varied techniques and presenting a smoothly accented rhythm. Chan's combat scenes showcased his instant reflexes and rubbery contortions. Training scenes became intricate exercises in footwork; Chan's hopping from bowl to bowl in *Fearless Hyena* sparkles with skittering energy (Figs. TD.7–TD.9). Like Keaton, he can turn any lo-

PLANET HONG KONG

TD.7 A training exercise from *Fearless Hyena*.

TD.8 *Fearless Hyena*.

TD.9 *Fearless Hyena*.

cale into an obstacle course, as when in *Young Master* (1980) Shek Kin's pursuit of Chan through a living room uses up all props to hand. Stunning exercises in pacing, his fights and chases avoid looking mechanical by their propulsive emotion—usually Chan's comically exaggerated panic.

At the end of *Young Master*, Chan must fight Master Kim, and the sequence brings out another aspect of Chan's comic persona: tireless tenacity. In a seventeen-minute battle that can push an audience to exhaustion, Chan is punched, slapped, kicked, kneed, bounced, stomped, dragged, flipped, flung into the air, and pounded into the ground. In desperation he swallows some tobacco juice, and only then does he summon up the manic energy to defeat Kim, in the process kicking him across the breadth of the CinemaScope screen. As so often, Chan wins largely by refusing to lose. Throughout he suffers mightily, bellowing and moaning as he takes blow after blow. Against the stoic Lee, Chan defined his genius as an infinite capacity for taking pain—a knack acquired, he has told interviewers, from the brutal training at the Opera Institute. If Bruce Lee is a flagrant narcissist, Jackie Chan is a passionate masochist. "I live for pain. Even when I was young I loved pain."[13]

Ever ambitious, Chan left period kung-fu behind and developed his own version of Hollywood action movies. He experimented with the fights/chases/stunts formula, first in the historical adventure *Project A* (1983); then in a series of contemporary action comedies such as *Wheels on Meals* (1984) and *Dragons Forever* (1986); in a string of cop films such as *Police Story* (1985); and in the freebooting sagas in which he plays the "Asian Hawk," *Armour of God* (1987) and *Operation Condor* (1991). Typically the film centers on a sweet-natured, fairly innocent, not-too-bright ordinary guy. The villains assail him mercilessly, and his superiors treat him unjustly, but his fighting skills are magnified by his untiring dedication to his goal and his seraphic luck. He is Hong Kong's Harold Lloyd, with Buster Keaton's and Douglas Fairbanks' gift for tailoring punishing stunts to his star persona.

Chan experimented with that persona in the early 1990s, veering from nonsensical comedy (*City Hunter*, 1992) to grim drama (*Crime Story*, 1993), but he usually portrayed himself as a Hong Kong everyman. He has said that *Project A*, set at the turn of the century, was an oblique comment on the news that Britain would hand its colony over to the Chinese. Chan plays a Coast Guard officer who learns that the corrupt British consular official is willing to pay off pirates to ransom a governor, and Chan forces the official to assume some backbone. The implication is that Hong Kong people can handle their affairs better than the British. At the film's end, the rescued British hostages must swim behind the heroes' raft. Later, Chan felt that the revived kung-fu films of the early 1990s, with their wire-borne special effects, had lost the true spirit of martial arts.[14] He made *Drunken Master II* (1994) to show what old-fashioned kung-fu could still do.

The star's innocent, indomitable urge to overcome all obstacles seems designed to project one modern image of Hong Kong. Another aspect of this image emerges in Chan's calculated cosmopolitanism. Lee had set *The Way of the Dragon* in Rome, but Chan really globe-hopped. He extended his playing field to Japan *(Thunderbolt)*, Russia and Australia (*First Strike*, 1996), North America (*Rumble in the Bronx*, 1995), and even South Africa

TD.10 Jackie in splints at end of *Young Master*; the replaying of key scenes in surrounding frames anticipates the "blooper credits" of Chan's later films.

(*Who Am I?* 1998). *Supercop* (1992) moves from Hong Kong to Mainland China to Malaysia, while *Operation Condor* showcases Asia, Europe, and the Sahara Desert. Similarly, Chan had a confident sense of what an "international" film should look like. Bruce Lee is virtually the only classy thing in the Bruce Lee films, which typically have shabby production values and fairly inept connecting scenes. Chan's box-office strength enabled him to insist on a high level of production design, shooting, and special effects. His awareness of the importance of packaging manifests not only Hong Kong culture's rising sense of world standards of quality but also the film industry's efforts to create more professional-looking products.

Young Master concludes with Chan cocooned in splints and bandages, smiling at the camera and painfully waving two fingers as previous scenes play out around him (Fig. TD.10). In the films that follow, star and character fold together; the hero's indefatigable dedication to his goal becomes the performer's dedication to entertaining his audience, especially in the face of death. So he falls head-first from a clock tower *(Project A)*, leaps from a hillside onto the top of a hot-air balloon *(Armour of God)*, slides several stories down a mall lighting fixture *(Police Story)*, roller-skates under a truck *(Winners and Sinners*, 1983), and dangles from a helicopter high above a city *(Supercop)*. Having decided that his audience wants him to suffer, he insists on delivering, however hard to watch the result may be—as when we see him writhing in a bed of hot coals in *Drunken Master II*. The filmmaker cheerfully counts up the number of times he has broken his nose and obligingly lets reporters feel his cranial fracture. The outtakes rolling under the film's final credits record the brushes with disaster, and prove how dangerous it is to please the public.

By the 1990s Jackie Chan had become an emblem of Hong Kong itself. Arrivals at Kai Tak airport were greeted by a Tourist Bureau poster of a smiling Jackie curling hand over fist in the traditional martial-arts greeting. The credits for the police force's public affairs TV program used the musical theme from *Police Story*. Chan was everywhere, exhorting people to give blood, stay in school, use condoms. He was selling his own line of teas, hawking cars for Mitsubishi, and for a time offering customized Jackie rulers, schoolbags, and notebooks through his merchandising outlet, the Star Shop. Signing the celebrity board at the 1995 Hong Kong Film Awards, he shamelessly wrote his name higher than anyone else's. His cheerful selling of himself, bolstered by the sense that he ought to enjoy his well-earned success, did not alienate his audience.

Two very different dragons, then: one glowering menacingly, the other comically cute. Both sought to symbolize aspects of the contemporary Hong Kong spirit, and they held their community's affection from the 1970s to the end of the century. Like the midnight screenings, the topical references and ephemeral in-jokes, and the converging concerns of critics and filmmakers, the two dragons epitomize the energies of their local cinema.

3

THE CHINESE CONNECTIONS

The movies were central to local life, but the kung-fu masters, the pistol-happy triads, the *Young and Dangerous* gang, and the other heroes played to a broader public as well. Throughout Asia, Hong Kong competed vigorously with the better-funded Japanese cinema. How did this small local cinema leap so successfully beyond its boundaries?

Before we fall back on the intuition—almost a reflex nowadays—that Hong Kong film travels so well because it is somehow suited to an age of cultural globalization, we should reflect on some concrete historical forces. We need at least to consider a middle zone between the local and the global—the region, a second concentric circle in the spread of films and their influence. Hong Kong's is the regional cinema par excellence. We also need to consider diaspora culture, the ethnic and social affinities that marble nations and communities. Finally, we need to hold cultural matters in suspension for a moment and follow the money. As it turns out, this profoundly local cinema depended on audiences far away for its financial survival.

Hong Kong is, after all, a big Chinatown on a Sunday.
FILM DIRECTOR EVANS CHAN

All the silent fiction films made in Hong Kong have apparently disappeared, so we shall probably never see the first two, *Right a Wrong with Earthenware Dish* and *Stealing the Roasted Duck*, both made in 1909. Local production was minuscule over the next two decades, since the market was dominated by U.S. films.[1] Not until the arrival of talkies did the industry take off. The 1933 Shanghai production *White Gold Dragon* proved that there was a market for films in Cantonese, a minority language on the continent. Soon the Kuomintang government demanded that all Chinese films be made in Mandarin, and Hong Kong became a center of emigrant Cantonese-language production. When Japan invaded the mainland, still more Shanghai filmmakers flocked to the colony. By 1939, Hong Kong studios were making over a hundred films per year, in Mandarin as well as Cantonese. The Japanese occupation of Hong Kong in 1941 halted local production, but companies revived after the war. Soon film professionals fled the civil war on the mainland and established themselves in Hong Kong. During the 1950s, Mao's nationalization of the PRC's film industry brought in still more refugees.[2]

The cinema, like the colony as a whole, was nurtured by emigrant energies. Virtually all the first generation of directors and stars emigrated from China, as did many members of the New Wave, like Ann Hui and Alex Cheung. Even creators whose films have a "typical" Hong Kong flavor have come from Vietnam (Tsui Hark), Thailand (Peter Chan), and South Africa (Lawrence Ah Mon). Shanghai producers and personnel were particularly important in helping local filmmaking mature.

At the end of the war, émigré film workers began to debate how Hong Kong cinema should develop. Many filmmakers' sympathies lay on the left, and their ties to the Mainland inclined them to social criticism. Some groups argued that to reach the people films had to be in the southern dialect. Others pressed for "clean-up campaigns" that pledged Cantonese filmmakers to make patriotic and progressive films. It was the age when filmmakers dreamed of collectives that paid all members of the troupe equally. The Zhonglian studio was founded in response to a clean-up campaign and turned out forty-four films under the collective system, including the classic *In the Face of Demolition* (1953). It is this era of socially engaged cinema that is so much admired by many Hong Kong critics.

Several production companies were founded, some with ties to China, others funded from local and regional sources. The cinema remained bilingual, but Cantonese films formed the bulk of production. Even left-wing firms did not concentrate solely on tendentious pictures, so there was a great deal of mass entertainment—musicals, melodramas, comedies, and martial-arts movies. By far the dominant genre was the Cantonese Opera picture, often shot in a week or so right on the opera stage. Budgets were paltry; a Mandarin picture would cost only US$20,000–30,000, a Cantonese picture half that.[3] Technique was often ragged. Tracking shots might be made by handholding the bulky studio camera, with an assistant bracing the cameraman. "Not unlike kung-fu practice," a director recalled.[4]

Most of these films were made by small companies. Soon two large enterprises emerged to dominate the market. The Motion Picture and General Investment Company was run from Singapore by the Malaysian mogul Loke Wan Tho. Loke owned theaters and distribution outlets throughout Asia, and he acquired local productions to feed them. MP & GI started producing Cantonese films in Hong Kong in 1953 and acquired a studio facility two years later. After Loke's sudden death in 1964, the firm would be renamed, somewhat awkwardly, "Cathay Film Company (1965)."[5]

3.1 Shaw Brothers' Movietown studio, complete with standing sets and staff apartment blocks.

MP & GI's rival was the formidable Shaw organization. The four Shaw brothers were Shanghai theater owners who expanded into production in the 1930s. Around 1933, Runde Shaw (Shao Cunren) transplanted the family studio to Hong Kong and made Cantonese movies there. After the war, the company turned to Mandarin production in order to supply the growing chain of Shaw theaters dotting Southeast Asia. In 1958 Run Run Shaw (Shao Yifu) came from the company headquarters in Singapore to head Shaw Brothers (Hong Kong) Ltd. A firm believer in integrating production, distribution, and exhibition ("Just as in the golden age of Hollywood," he explained), Run Run left another brother (Renmei, or Runme) to handle the local theater chain while he took over moviemaking.[6]

Run Run modernized production on a massive scale. In 1961 he finished building Movietown, a studio complex on Clearwater Bay in the then sparsely developed New Territories (Fig. 3.1). By 1970, according to the company's promotion, Movietown held thirty outdoor stages (including a lake), twelve sound stages, a color laboratory, a dubbing studio, a training school, three canteens, four dormitories for workers, and blocks of apartments housing performers and directors. Shaw plunged into color and widescreen production. He introduced exclusive contracts for personnel, usually in the neighborhood of US$50 per week. The studio ran twenty-four hours a day, working 1,200 employees in ten-hour shifts. Run Run explained that allowing his workers to form unions would hurt them, since the best way for them to earn raises was to work harder. Over its first twelve years Movietown ground out 300 pictures.[7]

Chinese funding was central to government and industry throughout Asia; in many countries, the Chinese have long been the most financially powerful ethnic group. Money from overseas made Hong Kong's postwar cinema possible; the Singapore-based Shaws and MP & GI are only the most visible instances. Xin Lian, the biggest of the 1950s Cantonese companies, was created by overseas Chinese. The Guangyi ("Bright Art") company was formed by yet another Singapore firm, this one owned by four brothers named He. Guangyi owned studios, distribution outlets, and theaters throughout Southeast Asia.

What attracted investors? Not, by and large, the money to be made locally. Even with a population keen on moviegoing, the colony was too small to yield profits. Like textile and toy manufacturers, film producers had to aim for export.

After World War II, Hong Kong displaced Shanghai as what Ezra Vogel has called "the region's de facto capital for industry, finance, commerce, education, and culture."[8] It was a plausible site for a regional cinema. Hong Kong had craftsmen willing to put in long hours at low wages. As the center of prewar Cantonese filmmaking, it had studio facilities in place. As a British colony, it could obtain Western film stock and up-to-date equipment. The government assured a stable legal and political system, friendly tax policies, and minimal regulation. The banking system was expert in handling foreign investments, and the port could efficiently ship films throughout the region.

In the 1950s rich opportunities offered themselves. Despite Asia's having over half the world's population, it was not overrun by Hollywood product. Low ticket prices, a drastic shortage of theaters, and protectionist measures like quotas and import licenses prevented Hollywood from saturating the market. U.S. firms concentrated on Europe and Latin America, which had higher ticket prices and far more screens per capita. Nor did Japan dominate the region. Although swordplay films did circulate throughout Asia, Japan could live comfortably on its vast national market. So Hong Kong survived by filling the cracks. Compared to Hollywood or Japan, it was a bottom-feeder; its profit margins were slim. Yet Chinese entrepreneurs have long preferred fast nickels to slow dollars. They have built successful enterprises upon narrow margins by borrowing for investment, keeping down wages and overhead, dealing in quantity, and working tirelessly. These are the principles by which Hong Kong cinema has operated for sixty years.

Foreign sales drove local production. During the 1950s the smaller studios financed their films by preselling rights to distributors abroad. In this manner, a producer could assemble up to 60 percent of a film's budget before shooting started.[9] Two companies, Great Wall and Phoenix, were financed by China and distributed their films there. The colony's three major studios—Shaws, MP & GI, and Guangyi—all served as production branches of regional entertainment empires. Ian Jarvie has suggested that if we think of Hong Kong as Hollywood (the glamorous moviemaking mecca), Singapore has to be New York, the real seat of financial power.[10] By making films in Hong Kong and buying pictures from smaller companies, the Singapore multinationals could ensure a steady flow of product to their theaters.

Thanks to Shaws and MP & GI, Hong Kong movies were guaranteed bookings in the best venues in Pacific Rim cities. Films were locked into playdates well before shooting, a process that guaranteed that production costs would be covered. Presales in turn permitted economies of scale. Shaws and MP & GI could invest in big and well-appointed sets, large casts, eye-catching costumes, elaborate musical numbers, and well-choreographed fight scenes. One way to keep Hollywood from taking over the market was to offer a Chinese equivalent of those production values in which U.S. firms set the standard. Throughout the decades to come, Hong Kong would strive to keep abreast of Hollywood production values, and this would allow it to beat less well-endowed rivals.

Cultural factors are important as well. After the 1911 revolution, touring theater troupes and recordings of popular songs kept emigrant Chinese in touch with home. The millions of Chinese dispersed throughout Southeast Asia formed a loyal audience for Hong Kong pictures. The immigrants came mostly from southern and eastern China, and so the world portrayed in these movies was familiar to them. Usually prosperous and sociable, they were inclined to take the whole family out for a meal and a movie. From the early 1950s onward, Hong Kong movies flourished in Taiwan and Thailand, homes to the biggest concentrations of Chinese outside the Mainland. The movies also did robust business in Singapore, Malaysia, and Indonesia, where Chinese formed large and affluent minorities. Even the small enclaves in Cambodia, Laos, and Vietnam could support distribution there.

Cantonese-language movies had an audience of eight to ten million viewers dotted throughout the Pacific region, principally Hong Kong and Malaysia. The Mandarin audience, even with China closed, was significantly larger. Mandarin was spoken in Singapore and Indonesia, and by the 1970s it had become Taiwan's official language. Hence the peculiar fact that each year Hong Kong made dozens of films in a tongue spoken by less than 5 percent of its population. Mandarin films boasted higher production values than Cantonese items because the overseas market supported bigger budgets. In order to maximize export possibilities, the major firms avoided specializing in any dialect. (Apart from Mandarin and Cantonese, many films were made in the Amoy and Chiu Chow dialects as well.) Of course films in one language could be dubbed into another, a practice that helped Cantonese companies crack the Taiwanese market.

The Chinese diaspora stretched well beyond Asia. Mainlanders had begun moving to Australia, Europe, and North America in the nineteenth century. By the mid-1980s, there were over one million Chinese immigrants living in the United States. There were movie theaters in the

Chinatowns of Melbourne, Sydney, Paris, London, Toronto, Montreal, New York, Chicago, Los Angeles, and San Francisco. Although most immigrants were Cantonese, they were not above enjoying Mandarin movies and the occasional Mainland item. Chinatown entrepreneurs brought over prints after their Asian runs, sometimes keeping hit titles on hand for revivals.

For the overseas audience, the films confirmed Hong Kong as the center of the diaspora's imagination. Lynn Pan has written movingly of the colony as "the place where flotsam and jetsam Chinese, many of them migrants twice or even three times over, fetch up in escapes from inhospitality elsewhere."[11] One might have left one's home in China, and one might harbor vague thoughts of returning; but the experience of fleeing to Hong Kong and sojourning there became the reference point for postwar generations. Asia's transit lounge became an object of nostalgia, and many films made there recorded the vibrant sights and sounds of life in this city of refugees.

Hong Kong businesses have long been willing to shape their product to the tastes of different national cultures, and the cinema was no exception. Filmmakers tailored the product to diverse tastes. Shaws, MP & GI, and other studios sent preproduction synopses to regional distributors, and if feedback was positive they would go ahead with the project. Mandarin films of the 1950s often included songs, not only because Shanghai filmmakers had relied on this convention but also because Southeast Asian audiences expected them. Films were drawn from Taiwanese swordplay novels and love stories. In the 1960s, producers initiated coproductions with neighboring countries, and Shaws set up a Taiwanese production facility. During the same period companies began adding bilingual subtitles: Chinese for those audiences who didn't know the dialect on the soundtrack, and English for everyone else.

By the early 1960s, Hong Kong had East Asia's most powerful export-based cinema. As competition for the offshore market intensified, smaller companies began to fold. Shaws and MP & GI kept production at a smart pace, and personnel found themselves on a treadmill. Between 1960 and 1967 Hong Kong's output exceeded Hollywood's.

In 1967 local attendance hit an all-time high of nearly 100 million. But soon the colony's exhibitors faced competition from the newly established Cantonese-language television, and attendance at Cantonese films began to fall. At the same moment the Southeast Asian demand for Mandarin titles grew. By the end of the decade Cantonese production was waning, and Mandarin production, under the aegis of Shaws and Cathay, won the market. In 1972 no Cantonese films were made. The curious result was that Bruce Lee and other Cantonese-speaking stars were dubbed into Mandarin and their films subtitled for the local audience.[12]

The rise of Mandarin cinema also owed a great deal to the dazzling production values that Cathay and Shaws had pumped into their films. The

3.2 Bravura fighting from King Hu's *Dragon Gate Inn*.

most banal Mandarin movie displayed sets and costumes of a richness that few Cantonese films, indeed no East Asian product outside Japan, could match. No longer a B cinema—rather, B-plus—Hong Kong offered Southeast Asia the next-best thing to Hollywood.

Still, the Mandarin cinema would probably not have achieved supremacy had not the big studios decided to back new trends in action filmmaking. Under the influence of Japanese *jidai-geki* pictures, producers launched a cycle of splendid and gruesome swordplay movies. Shaws initiated it with several films, the most famous of which are King Hu's *Come Drink with Me* (1966) and Zhang Cheh's *The One-Armed Swordsman* (1966). Hu consolidated the new approach with his Taiwan-based production *Dragon Gate Inn* (1967), which became the year's top film and conquered the region (Fig. 3.2). The new style led to dozens of swordplay films *(wuxia pian)*, soon to be followed by the kung-fu films of Jimmy Wang Yu *(Chinese Boxer,* 1970) and Bruce Lee *(The Big Boss,* 1971). These grueling sagas dominated the local box office, cemented the Asian market, and allowed Hong Kong to penetrate Western theaters.

Through the martial-arts films, Mandarin cinema achieved what historian Stephen Teo has called "a kind of pan-Chinese internationalism within the region."[13] Swordplay films might be shot in Korea or Taiwan, while kung-fu movies might take place in Malaysia or Thailand (the locale of Lee's *Big Boss*). Martial artists and actors from Southeast Asia and even Japan became stars in Hong Kong productions. By the early 1970s the Japanese had begun to cut back production and had fewer low-budget action pictures to export, so Hong Kong martial-arts movies faced little competition. To satisfy censorship regulations, kung-fu films circulated in three versions: the tamest cut went to Malaysia, Thailand, and Taiwan; a stronger one was made for Hong Kong; and the bloodiest version went to Europe and North America, where censorship was lenient.[14]

Despite the flourishing international market, Cathay began to fade: its stars were defecting to Shaws, and no strong manager replaced Loke Wan Tho. Cathay closed down film production in 1970. It remained a powerful leisure conglomerate while maintaining a film distribution company and a regional theater chain. Cathay's departure from production cleared the way for a new company, Golden Harvest.

Golden Harvest was founded in 1970 when Raymond Chow and Leonard Ho, two of Run Run Shaw's managers, struck out on their own. In their new firm, Chow became president, and Ho oversaw day-to-day production. Bankrolled by Thai and Taiwanese investors, Golden Harvest bought the Cathay studio in Diamond Hill and arranged for overseas distribution through Cathay.[15] Chow lured away King Hu, Wang Yu, director Lo Wei, and other Shaws talent, but his biggest coup was signing Bruce Lee. *The Big Boss* (1971) grossed an unprecedented HK$3.2 million (US$600,000) in the colony and millions more throughout the world. In terms of percentage returns on investment, this and the three other Lee/Chow vehicles are among the most profitable films ever made. Thanks to the charismatic Little Dragon, Chow was able to compete with the Shaws combine. By 1975 he controlled the largest Hong Kong theater circuit along with scores of screens throughout Asia.[16]

At first the demand for kung-fu seemed insatiable, and small companies sprang up. At a time when the average Hollywood film cost about a million dollars, Lee's second feature had a budget of about $120,000; an ordinary kung-fu item would cost only half that. With overseas markets ready to take virtually anything, Hong Kong cinema was for once a high-return industry. Even the flimsiest offering was guaranteed profits of about 20 percent.[17]

In the mid-1970s Western demand for kung-fu wound down, but the genre lived on for many years. Some companies turned out martial-arts films that would never play in Hong Kong at all, aiming at outlets in the U.S., Africa, Europe, India, and the Middle East. On Hong Kong screens, the continued popularity of higher-grade swordplay and kung-fu films allowed a few directors to push the genre to new heights of inventiveness. At the same time, producers developed other bulk-output genres—urban crime thrillers, comedies, and erotic films with titles like *Crazy Sex* (1976) and *Girls at the Gynecologist* (1977). All helped maintain the regional market.

It was in comedy that Cantonese-dialect cinema revived, first in Shaws' *House of 72 Tenants,* which tied with Bruce Lee's *Way of the Dragon* as 1973's top local attraction, and then in the social satires of Michael Hui, which won a large Japanese audience (who knew him as "Mr. Boo"; Fig. 3.3). Soon kung-fu returned to international success, but now as a comic genre, at the hands (and feet) of Sammo Hung and Jackie Chan. Holding contracts with these successful stars assured Golden Harvest the central role in the local industry, and Shaws began to slide down the box-office

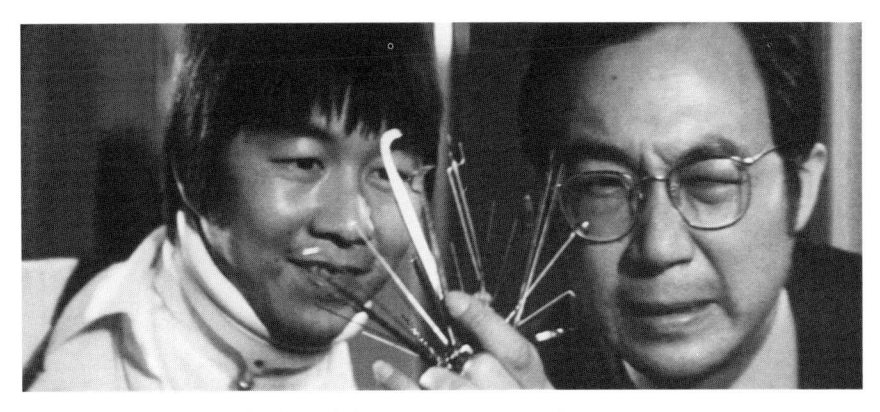

3.3 Ricky Hui and Michael Hui (*The Private Eyes*, 1976).

charts. In contrast to Shaws' centralized system, Chow delegated power to a circle of managers and developed a subcontracting system, whereby Golden Harvest financed companies headed by proven talent. Hui, Chan, and Hung had their own imprimaturs and enjoyed a fair amount of creative freedom, but the parent company still oversaw scripts, budgets, and schedules.[18]

The revival of Cantonese cinema coincided with public conversations about local identity. A film culture began to emerge, centering on magazines, ciné-clubs, and informal workshops teaching 16mm production. The Hong Kong International Film Festival, launched in 1977, not only broadened local access to foreign cinema but also began to investigate the colony's film history. The first in a series of invaluable festival catalogues chronicled Cantonese production.

The Hong Kong "New Wave" emerged from all these circumstances. Many New Wavers attended college in North America and England, and, since the film studios required a lengthy apprenticeship, most moved into television drama, where they could start directing immediately. Ann Hui, Patrick Tam, Tsui Hark, Ringo Lam, Kirk Wong, and many others learned to shoot on location and to turn out footage quickly. Their first theatrical features were often supported by backers from outside the studio setup. Unlike earlier generations, they took Hong Kong, not traditional China, as their subject, and many tackled contemporary social and psychological problems. Some made edgy, mildly experimental works, perhaps best exemplified by Ann Hui's *The Secret* (1979) and Tsui Hark's *Dangerous Encounter—First Kind* (1980). Most early New Wave films did moderately well at the box office, with Ann Hui's *Boat People* (1982) scoring the biggest popular success.[19]

Allen Fong, Yim Ho, and a few other New Wave directors became purveyors of "festival cinema" for European tastes, but most moved into mainstream filmmaking, preserving their individuality by giving estab-

THE CHINESE CONNECTIONS   ′ ′ ′ ′ ′   69

lished genres a personal twist. By bringing Western standards to the industry, the New Wavers rejuvenated Hong Kong's production framework. In this they paralleled their far less cosmopolitan contemporaries, studio-trained directors like Yuen Woo-ping, Sammo Hung, and Yuen Kuei, all of whom began long careers in the late 1970s by reviving the martial-arts film.

The rebirth of Cantonese cinema also brought back the local audience. In the mid-1970s annual attendance stabilized at around 65 million, and as Hong Kongers became more affluent, they patiently endured steep rises in admission prices.[20] Producers could, it seemed, take the local audience for granted. Yet the picture was not uniformly rosy. The Hong Kong market was becoming split between a few blockbuster films, which raked in most of the receipts, and all the rest, which barely broke even. The historian Law Kar has estimated that from the late 1970s on, up to 40 percent of all box-office returns came from the top ten films.[21] These "megapictures" helped attract audiences across Southeast Asia, where Hong Kong was going head-to-head with Hollywood.

By the early 1980s Golden Harvest led the box office. The Shaw studio was in decline; in 1986 it focused on turning out programs for TVB, Run Run's powerful powerful local television station.[22] But the market was not sewn up, as was proved by the breakthroughs made by a newer company, Cinema City.

Cinema City & Films Co., the name carried on its rather tacky yellow-red-blue credits logo, was founded in 1980 by three enterprising comedians, Raymond Wong, Karl Maka, and Dean Shek, who obtained funding from a theater chain seeking product. Cinema City avoided martial arts and aimed at wrapping Cantonese comedy in shiny Western production values. The breakthrough was the series launched by *Aces Go Places* (1982), a spy spoof brimming with chases, stunts, and outlandish gadgets. After a decade of grimy kung-fu films, shot in forest clearings and shabby standing sets, *Aces Go Places* offered polished set design and ambitious special effects (Fig. 3.4). Stunt experts were brought in from Hollywood and Australia; the cinematographer was American.[23] *Aces* was enlivened by European locations, rapid-fire gags, and a whistled theme song whose cheekiness seemed to embody the new cocksure Hong Kong. By featuring Sam Hui, the producers also exploited the growing regional taste for Canto-pop music. Costing about HK$8 million (US$1.5 million), the film earned over three times that in the local market alone. *Aces* and its first two sequels, always scheduled in the Lunar New Year slot, were the highest-grossing films to play in Hong Kong in the 1970s and 1980s. Cinema City's producers proved that investing in what they frankly called "packaging" would pay off; a B-plus cinema could become an A-minus one.[24]

3.4 A rocket chase among skyscrapers in *Aces Go Places*.

At the same time, action filmmaking left period kung-fu behind in such projects as Sammo Hung's contemporary comedy *Winners and Sinners* (1983) and Jackie Chan's historical adventure *Project A* (1983). Already Hong Kong's steadiest moneyspinner and Asia's biggest star, Chan was guaranteed prime playdates throughout the region. He confidently pushed his budgets higher in his quest for action sequences on the Hollywood scale.

The urge to upgrade the product was just as visible in the young director Tsui Hark. A slender workaholic with a forbidding goatee, Tsui made three controversial New Wave films before concentrating on raising the local product to international standards. He imported Hollywood effects experts to spruce up the swordplay fantasy *Zu: Warriors from the Magic Mountain* (1983); it became the prototype for the flying-swordsmen cycle Tsui would develop in the early 1990s. His first vehicle for his own company, Film Workshop, was the sprightly *Shanghai Blues* (1984), which conjured up a glamorous, bustling 1947 Shanghai on a minuscule budget. Tsui's most influential productions were *A Better Tomorrow* (1986), directed by John Woo, and *A Chinese Ghost Story* (1987), signed by Ching Siu-tung. Following Spielberg, Tsui borrowed plots from older hits. But he allowed Woo to imbue his triad drama with a masochistic romanticism out of the 1960s swordplay tradition, and he helped Ching dress up the ghost-story plot with low-tech but imaginative atmospheric effects. The films boasted sophisticated lighting and powerful original music. *A Better Tomorrow* and *A Chinese Ghost Story* marked the triumph of self-conscious modernization, what producer-director Wong Jing has called "an Eastern spirit in a Western package."[25]

Both movies galvanized the local audience and solidified the regional markets. *A Better Tomorrow* spawned scores of *policiers* and triad gun-fests, while *A Chinese Ghost Story* led to a massive revival of fantasy swordplay. A new generation of stars, led by Chow Yun-fat, Joey Wang,

Brigitte Lin, and Jet Li, built their careers on these resuscitated genres. And as the films became more lavish and outrageous, they began to command attention in Europe and the United States. The Western craze for Hong Kong cinema is largely due to production trends launched by Tsui's Film Workshop.

Filmmakers today look back on 1986–1993 as the last golden age. The local audience remained loyal, and the increasing number of theaters stepped up the demand for films.[26] The foreign markets were blossoming; South Korea joined the lineup when it liberalized its import policies in 1988.[27] Film workers hustled to make as much money as possible: who could say what opportunities would remain after 1997? A cameraman might shoot two or three films at once, and an actor might give one production a few hours, then be driven to another location.

Film critic Li Cheuk-to has pointed out that modern Hong Kong cinema has had a "classical" period, running from 1946 to 1970, dominated by studio-based production modeled on Hollywood and Japan; a transitional period (1971–1978), marked by the emergence of kung-fu and the fall and return of Cantonese-language cinema; and a "modern" period, starting in 1979 with the New Wave and the self-consciously upscale Cinema City look.[28] It can be argued that the production boom of the late 1980s launched a fourth phase. For one thing, it attracted triads, who now saw film production as not only a money-laundering device but also a reliable source of income.[29] Triad-funded companies sprang up, and although they intimidated stars and producers, they often allowed directors considerable freedom. The production surge also launched new filmmakers. Most were not much younger than the New Wave baby boomers, but they had languished as scriptwriters and assistant directors. Wong Kar-wai, who was born in 1958, worked for a decade as a TV and movie scriptwriter until his debut feature, *As Tears Go By* (1988). Others debuting at about this time were Eddie Fong, Lawrence Ah Mon, Mabel Cheung, Stanley Kwan, Derek Yee, Gordon Chan, Jeff Lau, Alex Law, and Clara Law. This cohort was able to consolidate and refine tendencies brought to the fore by the New Wave.[30] Just as important, their emergence illustrates one of the advantages of bulk production in popular cinema: when most films were making money, investors could afford to take chances on risky projects like Stanley Kwan's *Rouge* (1988, produced by Jackie Chan's company) and Wong Kai-wai's *Days of Being Wild* (1990, financed by actor Alan Tang).

Producers wooed the regional audience in all the standard ways. In *Supercop* (1992) Jackie Chan hops from China to Kuala Lumpur, while *Thunderbolt* (1995) has him brawling in a Tokyo pachinko parlor. Producers cast Cantopop idols in main roles, and if the singer performed the film's theme song, the movie could be promoted in album collections and overseas concerts. Stars were recruited from Malaysia (Michelle Yeoh), Taiwan (Brigitte Lin, Joey Wang), and Japan (the female martial artist

Oshima Yukari). In virtually a parody of multinational appeals, *Chungking Express* (1994) shrewdly makes the Taiwan-born Japanese pop singer Kaneshiro Takeshi a Hong Kong cop who claims he learned Japanese while living in Taiwan.

Just as Hollywood shoots racier versions of scenes for European screens, Hong Kong filmmakers provided extra material to suit foreign tastes. Korean and Taiwanese distributors insisted on plenty of action, even measuring the number and length of the fights, and kung-fu was added to as many films as possible. When the Japanese wanted more mayhem for *Heart of Dragon* (1985), Sammo Hung obligingly created it.[31] The Taiwanese print of *Ashes of Time* (1994) opens and closes with sword duels absent from the Hong Kong version.[32] Censors in Singapore and Malaysia frowned on glorifying gangsters, so in the *Young and Dangerous* series extra footage explained that the twentysomething triads were actually undercover police.

The regional market swelled still further thanks to new media. Just as Hong Kong movies could dominate theatrical distribution, video could carry them into shops and pushcarts and onto any blanket on any sidewalk. In the Chinese markets of Kuala Lumpur, bootleg tapes sold for the equivalent of US$8 ("high-grade" copies), $6 (middling quality), and $4 (poor quality). Grainy dubs popped up in Chinatown grocery stores and novelty shops. The Hong Kong video trade in North America has been sustained partly by the huge influx of Chinese students into universities there. Lynn Pan has argued that video definitively made Hong Kong the center of overseas Chinese popular culture. Sitting at home with their friends, both the *hua ch'iao*, those immigrants resisting assimilation to their new culture, and the *hua-i*, those with more Western tastes, could revel in the language, music, celebrities, and sights they had left behind.[33]

As usual, however, cultural dynamics owe something to the maneuverings of the film industry. The 1986–1993 boom was spurred only partly by the need to supply local theaters. It was also a response to an apparently inexhaustible regional audience. The key to success—and, ultimately, collapse—turned out to be Taiwan.

Home to twenty million Chinese, Taiwan had long been Hong Kong's major external market. Kuomintang government policies gave imported Mandarin movies subsidies and preferential taxation.[34] In the 1960s two important Hong Kong directors, King Hu and Li Hanxiang, moved to the island and stimulated domestic production. When kung-fu, Michael Hui, and Jackie Chan won over Taiwanese audiences, Taiwanese investors began to back Hong Kong movies. In the early 1980s videotapes of Hong Kong television shows poured into Taiwan and opened the market still further, familiarizing the audience with Andy Lau, Chow Yun-fat, and other TV stars who would rule the cinema.[35]

Taiwan's government responded by supporting a "New Wave" of local directors who won renown at festivals around the world. But the Taiwanese had little taste for the leisurely, demanding works of Edward Yang and Hou Hsiao-Hsien. They preferred Hong Kong pictures. By the mid-1980s over half of a Hong Kong movie's budget could be covered by presales to Taiwan.[36] Moreover, Hong Kong films were officially considered "domestic productions" and so escaped the quota restrictions that shut out many Hollywood films.[37]

To be assured of their share of the action, the top Taiwanese distributors shifted their investments from local projects to Hong Kong ones. In the early 1990s between 130 and 200 Hong Kong films were being released in Taiwan every year. Heroic triad sagas, big-budget costume pictures (the *Once upon a Time in China* series), swordplay fantasies (the *Swordsman* series), and revived kung-fu tales—most of the fanboy favorites owe their existence to the tastes of this lucrative foreign market. Meanwhile Taiwanese filmmaking virtually disappeared. In 1988 about 190 domestically made films were released; by 1994 there were only 18. Humiliatingly, Hong Kong imports almost always beat the local product in Taiwan's annual movie awards.

The late 1980s surge in production values—the glossy spectacles of Jackie Chan, Tsui Hark, and John Woo—stemmed principally from a confidence that a properly mounted Hong Kong film could not lose money in Taiwan. Gordon Chan recalls his chagrin at hearing the inevitable objection, "But the Taiwanese won't like it."[38] At the peak of the frenzy, a project could be presold to Taiwan for HK$20 million (US$2.6 million).[39] A film would sometimes premiere in Taiwan before opening in Hong Kong (partly to get the jump on video pirates), and stars would be flown in to greet their fans. The filmmakers did not stint. Their urge to put the money on the screen has left us the aerial combats of *Swordsman II* (1992), the outscaled hospital finale of *Hard Boiled* (1992), and the phantasmic landscapes of *Ashes of Time* (1994).

Budgets soared. Ching Siu-tung's *Terracotta Warrior* (1990) was said to cost HK$50 million, or about US$6.4 million—risibly low by contemporary U.S. standards, but steep in relation to likely return.[40] As in Hollywood today, guaranteed overseas markets pushed up stars' prices. A 1992 Jet Li movie could eat up HK$35 million (US$4.5 million), with a third or more devoted to the actor's salary. Worried about recouping production costs, Hong Kong producers began block-selling to Taiwan. In order to get the next sure-fire hit, a Taiwanese buyer would have to take some less desirable items as well.[41]

The problem was that not all big productions were recouping their investments. Audiences grew tired of swooping swordswomen. Taiwanese investors and distributors formed a cartel, forcing rental costs down by half. The crisis came in 1993, the Year of the Dinosaur. Throughout Asia *Jurassic Park* crushed the Hong Kong product at the box office. In the same year Taiwan logged on to cable and satellite television, and more people stayed home to watch movies. Now few stars could open or sustain a film. Brigitte Lin, once a guaranteed Taiwan draw, retired. From 1993 through 1995, twenty-five of the thirty top-grossing films in the Taiwanese market came from Hollywood, and only four from Hong Kong. Hong Kong films had destroyed Taiwanese cinema, but they in turn fell before the Western onslaught.

America's Taiwanese triumph reflected its growing power in the region. In the 1980s, as the international market came to represent over half of Hollywood's theatrical revenues, firms began to realize that a large part of their future lay in Asia. The region furnished a third to a half of all foreign film income. Hits like *Jurassic Park*, *The Fugitive* (1993), *True Lies* (1994), and *Speed* (1994) encouraged U.S. studios to distribute their pictures more aggressively. Hollywood companies began to invest in theaters in Japan, South Korea, and other major markets. As in Europe, the key to expansion lay in multiplex theaters. Ideal for the shopping malls springing up all over Asia, the multiplex normalized Western methods of presentation, reduced overhead per screen, and demonstrated the profitability of popcorn and candy.

By the end of 1996 the American initiative was paying off. Production throughout the region began to slump. Despite the economic crisis that began in 1997, Asian film revenues actually increased—chiefly because of the higher ticket prices charged by multiplexes, the showcases for the Hollywood product. Hong Kong films had little hope of recapturing their overseas market.[42]

For decades Hong Kong had counted on an expanding regional audience. By the mid-1990s the traditional markets had shrunk frighteningly: Taiwan was virtually dead, Korea and Thailand were buying just action films, and only Singapore and Malaysia still welcomed the Hong Kong product. Once again the local market assumed paramount importance, bringing in half to two-thirds of a film's total income. Unfortunately, after a decade of holding steady, attendance started to plummet: whereas 1988 saw ticket sales of 66 million, in 1993 sales were only 44 million. Total box office receipts increased over the period, but only because of the now customary rise in ticket prices. Things quickly got worse; in 1996 there were only 22 million admissions. One screenwriter traces the decline to a demographic change: the recent Mainland immigrants who formed a large part of the 1980s audience found the formulas novel, but by the early 1990s everyone knew all the gimmicks.[43] Some triad movies brought in crowds, but most of the swordplay fantasies so popular abroad failed. As a result the bulk of receipts came from a handful of hits—the usual vehicles for Chow Yun-fat, Jackie Chan, and Stephen Chiau, along with the occasional star-packed comedy.

The local audience also rediscovered Hollywood. With more access to screens, American blockbusters became competitive. The ten highest-grossing pictures of 1996 included five U.S. films, and overall the foreign product (principally U.S.) increased its takings to a record 45 percent of all receipts.[44] Hong Kong became a valuable market for Hollywood films, more lucrative than some European countries and considerably more important than the Mainland.[45]

Local distribution companies and theater chains had a powerful incentive to share in Hollywood's earnings. Golden Harvest began to invest heavily in exhibition, buying and building screens throughout Asia for the American product.[46] But Hong Kong's production sector was squeezed. In 1996 there were only 115 releases, less than half the 1993 total. Although many of the cutbacks came in marginal softcore pornography, there was no blinking the essential lesson: producers had to slash their costs. Most mid-1990s budgets ran between HK$4 million and HK$8 million (between half a million and a million U.S. dollars). Remarkably, the cost of a Hong Kong movie relative to an average Hollywood production was even lower than it had been twenty-five years before, at the beginning of the Bruce Lee craze. That such cheaply made films got finished and looked reasonably attractive is a continuing testament to the ingenuity, enterprise, and low wages of local moviemakers.

Filmmakers began to target the higher end of the public. The trend developed out of a cycle of "relationship" movies, low-key yuppie romances (*Heart to Hearts,* 1988) and wistful melodramas. Derek Yee's small-budget *C'est la vie, mon cheri* (1993), about a dying girl who redeems a self-destructive saxophonist, astonished critics by pulling in HK$30 million dollars (US$3.8 million), rivaling Jackie Chan's *City Hunter.* The relationship films, as flagrantly local in flavor as the swordplay films had been generically "pan-Chinese," had less-pricy stars, sentimental scripts devoid of special effects, and lyrical scores that could be marketed as CDs. When the nostalgia comedy *92 Legendary La Rose Noire* had an unprecedented run (from July to December 1992) and garnered as much as a Stephen Chaiu farce, it became evident that films with a decidedly Hong Kong flavor could succeed. In 1996 Gordon Chan, director of *The Yuppie Fantasia* (1989) and *The Final Option* (1994), summed it up: "I make my films for the local audience."[47]

Chan belongs to that fresh wave of directors launched during the production boom of the late 1980s. Many turned away from the *echt*-Chinese swordplay and gunplay spectaculars and tried to create something like a "cinema of quality." They presented a modern Hong Kong inhabited by educated young men and women, working in business or the media, living in comfort and sometimes bouncing between Hong Kong and the West. Whether or not these films actually tore many affluent people away from their laserdisc players, their portrayal of contemporary foibles and fashions attracted enough students and white-collar workers to repay their modest costs.

The pathbreaker was D&B, the company founded by jewelry magnate Dickson Poon. When D&B folded, United Filmmakers Organization, formed by a group of young directors, emerged to sustain the trend. UFO targeted films at upscale twentysomething sensibilities. Confined to low budgets, UFO followed Cinema City's precedent and concentrated on comedies, producing slightly racy, feel-good pictures like *Tom, Dick, and Hairy* (1993) and *Yesteryou, Yesterme, Yesterday* (1993), a trip back to the early 1980s modeled on the American television series *The Wonder Years.* Self-consciously up-to-date, UFO films raised issues of emigration (*Lost and Found*, 1996), date rape (*Happy Hour*, 1995), and the conflicts between the postwar generation and today's selfish yuppies (*He Ain't Heavy, He's My Father*, 1993). The most successful UFO director was Peter Chan, whose *He's a Woman, She's a Man*, an adept satire of gender relations and the pop music industry, became one of 1994's top grossers. Chan's émigré drama *Comrades, Almost a Love Story* (1996) did excellent business and won an unprecedented nine prizes at Hong Kong's annual film awards.[48]

At the same time some directors began to cultivate what can only be called local exploitation movies. Typical is Herman Yau, who directed a string of cheerfully savage thrillers. In *Taxi Hunter* (1993), a cross between *Death Wish* (1974) and *Falling Down* (1993), Anthony Wong plays a man whose pregnant wife is killed by a callous taxi driver and who declares guerrilla war on the trade. Yau's most notorious effort is *The Untold Story* (1993), which sensationalizes an incident of rape, murder, and cannibalism in Macau. Anthony Wong, playing a twitchy restaurateur who serves his victims up as pork buns, was named best actor of the year at the Hong Kong Film Awards. A long-haired rock-and-roll guitarist and a director of music videos, Yau enjoys watching his films hit the public at midnight screenings. "I definitely want that experience."[49]

Later cycles fell somewhere between UFO's sensitivity and Yau's shock tactics. The *Young and Dangerous* series, featuring pop idols indulging in brotherly self-sacrifice, was a low-end version of the 1980s "heroes" films, shot in rough-edged style on seedy locations. The *Y&D* movies remained aggressively local products, delighting the audience with their bad manners. Andrew Lau reports regretfully that the censors demanded that he remove from *Young and Dangerous 4* a joke centering on Tung Chee-hwa, the newly appointed chief executive. More decorous was another comic-book spinoff, the *Feel 100%* series. Working with Bob & Partners, the *Young and Dangerous* company, writer-director-producer Joe Ma packaged *Feel 100%* (1996) and its sequels (*Feel 100% . . . Once More*, 1996; *Love Amoeba Style*, 1997) as wholesome counterparts of the young-triad saga. Ekin Chan, star of the *Y&D* films, played the romantic lead, surrounded by scrubbed newer stars like songstress Sammi Cheng and comedian Eric

Kot. Curiously cut off from their families, these roommates become surrogate brothers and sisters. They face job problems, class snobbery, crisscrossed love affairs, all the while eating Italian food, surfing the Net, following the adventures of Sailor Moon, and shopping for DKNY fashions.[50]

Many of these trends had some export appeal as well. Pseudo-B-films like Yau's and Lau's could succeed in regional markets, largely because they were made on tiny budgets at lightning speed. Overseas Yau's *Untold Story* grossed ten times its cost (HK$2 million, about US$255,000). Even the UFO product, for all its local texture, could appeal to a cosmopolitan tier of the Chinese diaspora, middle-class success stories who feel at home in both East and West.[51]

But yuppie romances and B-movies could not rescue the entire industry. The local market was eroding very fast, not least because video piracy was reaching epidemic proportions. Piracy had been a problem since the early 1980s, but it intensified just before the handover. Gray-market malls all over the city were filled with copies of current hits. Sometimes a projectionist or lab staffer would smuggle out a print to be duplicated, but more and more the video copies were "auditorium versions" taped during an ordinary screening, complete with audience noise and chancy framing. (The spread of auditorium versions helped end the ritual of the midnight preview.) Worse, a new digital format called Video Compact Disc allowed cheap and fast reproduction in bulk. Legal VCDs retailed for about US$10–12, but anyone could find a pirated copy for as little as US$3—about half the cost of a movie ticket. By 1998 the VCD had wiped out the laserdisc format and marginalized videotape. Manfred Wong, producer of the *Young and Dangerous* series, bought a bootleg VCD of the fourth installment on the day the movie premiered. "Piracy," he points out, "is the best distribution system."[52]

When both overseas and domestic markets began to shrivel in the mid-1990s, many had asked an obvious question. What about China, the biggest market of all? Might that rescue the film industry?

At first, China seemed to need Hong Kong movies. In 1979, thanks to Deng Xiaoping's economic reform, the doors opened to foreign trade. As bootleg videotapes became available, Mainland film attendance went into a free-fall. The studios, mired in endless bureaucratic maneuverings, could not meet the exhibitors' demands for popular fare. Hong Kong films attracted audiences—not through theatrical releases but via television broadcast and bootleg video copies, many of which were openly shown in theaters or "video parlors."[53]

Even in legal distribution Hong Kong companies could not benefit from their films' popularity. China imposed a strict ten-film limit on foreign imports, and Hong Kong pictures counted as foreign. There was a loophole, though: some coproductions could be considered domestic films and escape import restrictions. So, like the Hong Kong manufacturers who were moving their factories across the border to tap a cheaper labor pool, producers started making movies on the Mainland. A coproduction often amounted to little more than using China as a vast backlot and labor pool, but some of these films did squeeze into Chinese theaters—usually through exhibitors' outright purchase at rock-bottom prices. The Chinese locations added impressive visual values for the overseas market as well.

The few major pictures allowed to play in China, notably Jackie Chan's, did well. By 1994 and 1995 some films were playing on a revenue-sharing basis with Hong Kong companies. To many observers the handover in 1997 seemed likely to open the market fully. After reunification, Hong Kong might become the Hollywood of China.

At the end of 1999, however, prospects looked murky at best. China was still a very poor country; its most affluent consumers accounted for no more than 30 million people, and they were not well-off by Western standards.[54] China's strict quota still barred Hong Kong films. Censorship was becoming stricter, targeting "spiritual pollution"—a charge vague enough to apply to virtually any Hong Kong film. Access to exhibition was not coordinated by any central agency, so producers had to dicker with theater managers city by city.[55] And sources of financing were frightened off by China's formidable censorship bureaucracy. Taiwanese film companies had for several years used Hong Kong as a conduit for funding Mainland-shot films like *Farewell My Concubine* (1993) and the work of Zhang Yimou. These films won acclaim at international festivals and found eager distributors in Europe and North America. In 1995, however, China began to set up new conditions for coproductions, demanding that editing and sound work be completed on the Mainland and that the negative remain there.[56] *Temptress Moon* (1996), a Taiwan-backed project budgeted high in the expectation of receiving a Mainland release, was judged unacceptable by government censors.

In the meantime, China's exhibitors had developed an affection for Hollywood blockbusters, which the quota count favored over Hong Kong fare. By 1998, while the major cities were dominated by Western movies, Hong Kong films were playing in smaller cities and the countryside. In the People's Republic, as in the rest of Asia, Hong Kong movies created a taste that Hollywood proved better at satisfying.[57]

True, even Hollywood has not had an easy time of it. Like the imperialist adventurers of the nineteenth century, the U.S. movie moguls of the 1920s saw China as a market ripe for exploitation. Yet China has always resisted. Although its own film business is on the verge of extinction, policymakers have taken a tough line on imports, refusing to admit American films unless U.S. companies would agree to distribute Chinese films internationally.[58] Offended by Disney's *Kundun* (1997) and Columbia's *Seven Years in Tibet* (1997), China banned imports from these studios for more than a year.[59] When festivals have programmed unauthorized independent Mainland films, China has retaliated by withholding "legal" titles.[60] Hong Kong companies have little leverage with Beijing, especially since their titles are already available throughout the Mainland on pirated VCDs.

Part of China's bargaining strength comes from the likelihood that it will become the region's core state, the center of the "bamboo network" that binds the PRC, Taiwan, and the wealthy emigrant Chinese. As Japan's economic woes intensified during the late 1990s, China looked more and more to be East Asia's anchor. The Mainland movie market will be a target for Hollywood for years, and Hong Kong's films may not prevail there.

Mainland resistance, fading overseas markets, the growing taste for Hollywood movies, and video piracy all combined to foster a fear that the Hong Kong industry was about to collapse. Since the mid-1990s pan-Asian coproductions and a shift to a local accent have been filmmakers' chief survival strategies, but they have not done the trick. In 1997 fewer than a hundred new films were released, and admissions dropped another 8 percent. For the first time in decades the total box-office grosses of foreign imports surpassed those of local products, 53 percent to 47 percent. While most countries would be happy to confine Hollywood to a little more than half the takings,[61] the symbolic shift in power demoralized the film community. In October 1997 Tung Chee-hwa, the Special Administrative Region's new chief executive, pledged to establish a film office that would coordinate local productions and allocate land for a studio complex.[62] In the meantime, players looked elsewhere for action. Producers began to invest in Taiwanese features, reversing the trend of the boom years.

The Asian financial crisis of 1997–98 plunged the industry into still more turmoil. Although Asians flocked to new, comfortable multiplexes, those exhibitors and distributors in Malaysia, Indonesia, South Korea, and Thailand still buying Hong Kong films were dealing in devalued currencies. Exhibitors dared not raise admission prices to make up the difference, so Hong Kong suppliers were asked to wait for payment or cut their prices. By the spring of 1998, regional companies were buying fewer titles, which tended to shrink Hong Kong's output even more.[63]

One measure of sagging local fortunes was the cascade of disasters befalling Golden Harvest. Golden Harvest Entertainment, the company's publicly listed distribution and exhibition wing, was still expanding into multiplexes when it posted a US$6 million loss in the first half of 1998. To save the unit, Raymond Chow agreed to share controlling interest in GHE with Village Roadshow, a powerful Australian exhibition chain. At the same time, Chow's partner, Leonard Ho, died, and Jackie Chan resigned from GHE's board of directors. When the government auctioned off a tract of land as a site for a state-of-the-art production facility, the winning bid was put together by a consortium from which Golden Harvest was conspicuously absent.[64] In autumn Golden Harvest moved out of its Diamond

Hill studio facility, and Chow announced that he was considering relocating to Singapore.[65]

In the summer of 1998, a year or so after my visit to the Majestic Theater and *Young and Dangerous 4,* a writer for the *New York Times* dropped in at the opening of *Young and Dangerous: The Prequel.* Only thirty-five people showed up. You could buy the film on VCD across the street for US$2.50. The industry had nearly hit bottom: slashed budgets, sparse output, and disenchanted workers. Gordon Chan, one of the most successful directors, had to take a pay cut of 75 percent. Local critic Paul Fonoroff pronounced the epitaph: "I think the film industry is over as we know it."[66]

Sustained for fifty years as a regional enterprise, Hong Kong film came to depend on its immediate audience, and that audience was virtually gone. Yet many of Hong Kong's most accomplished films were made in the years after the 1993 downturn. Directors had become more sophisticated, and perhaps financial desperation freed them to experiment. At the same time, the keener compctition and the momentum of craft tradition spurred them to find something fresh and stimulating. The golden age is over; like most local cinemas, Hong Kong's will probably consist of a small annual output and a handful of films of artistic interest. Nonetheless, the films that stand out will probably display an unswerving appeal to the norms and forms of popular cinema.

4

ONCE UPON A TIME
IN THE WEST

You know, I am rather tired of people saying, "Are you trying to challenge Hollywood?" I really feel we have something quite different and equally as good as Hollywood has to offer.

RUN RUN SHAW

A local cinema definitely, but with fast-diminishing resources. A regional cinema for decades, but retreating before Hollywood's imperial advance. A diasporan cinema, chiefly on video. To what extent, we might now ask, has Hong Kong created a "global" popular cinema?

Few countries can support domestic moviemaking solely on the basis of their national market. A country must export, as American cinema does, or receive substantial government aid, as in Europe.[1] But a global cinema is not simply one that might win outside markets. Thanks to videotape, any film can slip across any border. A truly global cinema is one that claims significant space on theater screens throughout developed and developing countries. By this definition, 1980s–1990s Hong Kong films did not constitute a global cinema. Nor does any European cinema; only one in five European films is ever seen outside its country of origin.[2] The only global cinema comes from America. Blockbusters like *Independence Day* (1996) and *Titanic* (1997) are international media events. Dubbed versions of midrange pictures and TV movies saturate the world's television screens. Cheap action and horror movies fill in the cracks from Eastern Europe to Latin America and Africa. Any video shop plainly reveals what people are willing to pay for—U.S. movies from *Star Wars* to low-grade exploitation.

It is true that until the 1990s industry crisis Hong Kong was second to Hollywood in total overseas exports of its films. But it was not a close second. Its exports went almost completely to the regional market, and in 1995 they earned about US$130 million. By contrast American films are currently grossing over US$5 billion abroad.[3] Moreover, Hong Kong's media firms scarcely compare to the multinational conglomerates of North

America, Europe, and Japan. Golden Harvest, one of the strongest regional forces, was never among the world's top fifty media companies.[4] Time-Warner, MCA-Universal, Sony, Bertelsmann, and Disney operate with international financing, especially bank investment, and this assures them entry into global markets. In Hong Kong, production is driven by small companies, and films are made on a one-off basis. The total 1995 investment for all films in Hong Kong was US$150 million, with $12 million of that going into one Jackie Chan production. By the bleak summer of 1998, the budget of one major Hollywood release could have financed the territory's entire output. And Hong Kong films were never disseminated on the scale of the most widely popular form of Asian film, Japanese animation *(anime)*. The Hollywood of the East is Hollywood.

To be sure, this cottage industry has long tried to break into Western markets. In the 1960s Run Run Shaw aimed to place his films in international festivals, and many Hong Kong companies still try to sell their films in the West's most lucrative markets. But local producers face chronic problems. European and North American audiences have never been particularly interested in Asian cinema, apart from the occasional exotic import and *anime* (whose characters don't "look Japanese"). In addition, Hollywood's major firms have distribution offices throughout the world, regulating a continuous flow of product to local exhibitors. Non-U.S. companies have seldom had this on-the-spot representation. Hong Kong producers have had to license their films country by country, striking one-off deals with local distributors at slim profit margins. Hong Kong companies owned no theaters outside East Asia and a few Chinatowns, so they had no Western showcases for their product.

Hong Kong made only one substantial breakthrough to the West, and its economic rewards, though substantial, were fleeting. Apparently neither Shaws nor Golden Harvest expected that kung-fu—a typical product tailored to local and regional audiences—would travel globally. Shaws' *Chinese Boxer* (1970) initiated the genre, but the world was oblivious until 1972, when Raymond Chow brought his first two Bruce Lee pictures to the film market at the Cannes Film Festival. They sold well, even to Middle Eastern markets. In the winter of 1972–73 the Shaws picture *King Boxer* (aka *Invincible Boxer,* 1972) found a huge success in London. During the first half of 1973 seven kung-fu films played in Paris, and twenty-six appeared in Italy. In the spring of 1973, Bruce Lee's second film, known in the West as both *Fist of Fury* and *The Chinese Connection* (1972), broke box-office records in London. By the end of 1973, many European theaters were showing kung-fu every week.[5]

Most important, kung-fu cracked the huge, lucrative American market. As in Britain, the key release was *King Boxer,* known in the United States as *Five Fingers of Death,* in March 1973. Bruce Lee's films followed quickly. By the end of the year, thirty-eight Hong Kong films had been purchased for U.S. distribution, and at the end of 1974 *Variety* was reporting that these had grossed over $11 million.[6] American filmgoers were prepared for the onslaught, since interest in Chinese food, religion, and martial arts had been on the rise. The television series *Kung Fu* (in which Bruce Lee had hoped to star) premiered in the fall of 1972 and introduced this exotic fighting style to the mass audience. The films rejected the quietist message of the television show and benefited from the rising thresholds of screen violence created by *Bonnie and Clyde* (1967), *The Wild Bunch* (1969), and the spaghetti Westerns.

Once the novelty wore off, however, kung-fu became a bad joke. Hollywood studios had distributed a few of the first imports, but after a couple of years the product was being sold cheaply by marginal distributors. Kung-fu became a downtown genre, playing in neighborhoods abandoned by white flight. Audiences of Asian, African, and Hispanic heritage kept the genre alive into the early 1980s before video wiped out the local movie house. Still, for about a decade, and for the only time in history, Asian films were staples of many theaters in the United States.

Run Run Shaw and Raymond Chow used the kung-fu boom to launch coproductions with the West. Shaw allied with Italian companies, with the U.K. company Hammer on a string of horror pictures such as *The Legend of the Seven Golden Vampires* (1974), and with Warners to produce *Cleopatra Jones* (1973) and other "blaxploitation." Shaw joked that if his partners demanded it, he would trim his employees' work week from seven days to six.[7] Such largesse was unnecessary, since the coproductions quickly proved to be dead ends. Chow was more ambitious, underwriting English-language films for the international market, but the only success Golden Harvest had in this vein came much later, with the hugely profitable *Teenage Mutant Ninja Turtles* (1990).

If Hong Kong could not coproduce hits, why not try to sell its stars to the West? When Jackie Chan won over Asian audiences, Chow determined to make him as widely known as Bruce Lee. Chan had to conquer America in an English-language movie. Chow produced *The Big Brawl* (aka *Battle Creek Brawl*, 1980), a period comedy; the *Cannonball Run* farces (1981, 1984); and *The Protector* (1985), a cop-buddy movie, but all failed to ignite interest in Chan.[8] Nonetheless, over the next ten years a cult audience grew up around him, thanks to video, screenings at campuses and repertory cinemas, and tastemakers like Quentin Tarantino. In 1995 Miramax and New Line Cinema struck deals with Golden Harvest to distribute some Chan titles, and, at Tarantino's insistence, Chan received the MTV Lifetime Achievement Award. He declared his ambition to attract a U.S. audience: "That's what I want! That kind of people coming to see me is better. Then it makes me like Stallone, big American star, like Schwarzenegger, big American star. In China, there are one billion people. When I walk anywhere, people recognize me, go 'Aaah! It's him!' It's me—big star! You say to me, 'You're a big star in United States!' I say 'No.' Here, I'm very small star. Maybe I walk on the street, somebody once in a while go, 'You Jackie Chan?' But most people just passing by."[9]

The 1996 U.S. theatrical release of *Rumble in the Bronx* (1994), in a dubbed, recut, and rescored version, proved to be Chan's American breakthrough. With a $32 million box-office gross, it was New Line's most profitable film of the year.[10] Chan visited the Sundance Film Festival, clowned on talk shows, and raced through a hectic soft-drink commercial. He pressed his feet, hands, and prominent nose into cement at Mann's Chinese(!) Theater. It was rumored that his American success encouraged him to expand his budgets further.

Four more Chan pictures were released in American versions between 1996 and 1998, but to weakening business. Chan finally secured a mass Western audience in *Rush Hour* (1998), an American action comedy that garnered $130 million in the United States alone. While in the English-language market his Hong Kong imports were little more than novelties for the young male audience, *Rush Hour* showed that Chan, without losing his sunny good humor, could reinvent himself as a mainstream Hollywood actor.

Golden Harvest's "international" films came to little, but Jackie Chan's notoriety paved the way for other Asian talent. America's studios have long attracted a flow of foreign talent, and once Hollywood decisionmakers got a glimpse of Hong Kong cinema, it was likely that some directors would be emigrating—especially when producers realized the growing significance of the Asian market.[11] It was significant, then, when John Woo's modest Jean-Claude Van Damme picture *Hard Target* (1993) did decent business. With a bigger budget and greater star power Woo made *Broken Arrow,* one of the most successful films of 1996. His summer 1997 offering, *Face/Off,* achieved $225 million receipts worldwide, about as much as Disney's *Hercules.*[12] Woo's success convinced producers to import other Hong Kong action directors—Ringo Lam (*Maximum Risk,* 1996; Van Damme again), Tsui Hark (*Double Team,* 1997; Van Damme yet again), Stanley Tong (*Mr. Magoo,* 1997), Kirk Wong (*The Big Hit,* 1998), and Ronnie Yu (*Bride of Chucky,* 1998). U.S. critics, many of them Hong Kong aficionados, were surprisingly kind to some of these efforts, but no film measured up to any director's best Hong Kong work. A cynic might suggest that Hong Kong has served as a cheap source of directorial labor for second-rate productions. Yet Woo's emergence as an A-list director suggests that Hollywood is prepared to invest heavily in creators who can play according to its rules and who might attract audiences in Asia.

One force behind Woo's rise was Terence Chang, a new kind of local producer. A graduate of NYU's film school, Chang became general manager of Tsui Hark's Film Workshop when Woo was directing there. He served as production executive on *The Killer,* and when Woo broke away to form his own company, Chang went with him, producing *Bullet in the Head* (1990), *Once a Thief* (1991), and *Hard Boiled* (1992). Chang explained: "I want to help as many people as possible to make international films. I mean films that are liable to find a world audience."¹³ That meant, as ever, aiming for America.

Detecting U.S. cult interest in Woo's work, Chang shuttled between Hong Kong and North America to build up Woo's reputation. He emphasized Woo's alliance with the charismatic Chow Yun-fat, arranging Chow retrospectives and personal appearances. Soon he was Chow's talent manager. With Woo and a third partner, Chang founded a production company in 1994 and became producer on all of Woo's American projects. He encouraged Woo to keep working to achieve creative control, a strategy that paid off when *Face/Off* became a top-grossing film. Chang guided Chow to *Replacement Killers* (1998) and eased his other client, Michelle Yeoh, into the James Bond film *Tomorrow Never Dies* (1997). He began to be a gatekeeper. "People are saying [to me], 'If we cannot get John Woo, who's the next one?'"¹⁴

Run Run Shaw oversaw a bustling studio of contract labor. Raymond Chow's subcontracting system allowed him to finance independent projects and keep overhead low. Each man's policy suited the opportunities available locally and regionally. As an independent producer, Terence Chang became Hong Kong's first significant liaison with the United States, able to sign deals, deliver completed projects, and open American doors for his clients. Through cosmopolitan people like him, Hong Kong filmmakers began to go global—by joining the only truly global film industry.

In *True Romance* (1993), the heroes get trapped in the middle of a three-way pistol standoff reminiscent of countless Hong Kong movies. Quentin Tarantino, *True Romance*'s screenwriter, stages a similar scene in *Reservoir Dogs* (1992) while also borrowing a plotline from Ringo Lam's *City on Fire* (1987). In a swordfight in *The Mask of Zorro* (1998), the caped hero somersaults over his opponents. *The Matrix* (1999) plays out kung-fu and Woo-like gun battles in a dystopian cyberworld. Video games and comic books feature Jackie Chan, and role-playing games invite players to be an anti-Triad cop or a kung-fu warrior.¹⁵ The lyrics of hip-hop groups like the Wu-Tang Clan sample martial-arts movies.¹⁶ On television the fighters in *Xena, Warrior Princess* deploy kung-fu, while Sammo Hung shows off his skills in *Martial Law*.

A glance at almost any popular medium shows that the Asian cinema exercising most influence on Western culture is Hong Kong's. The trend started in the early 1970s, when kung-fu films influenced blaxploitation and set new standards of fighting for Hollywood. Bruce Lee has proven a timeless symbol of rebellious youth and ethnic pride. In the biopic *Dragon* (1993), Lee is driven almost to hysteria by racial prejudice and his mission to be a mythic warrior. Lee's poster image is itself an icon. He frowns down

4.1 *Irma Vep* recasts Feuillade's silent-film intrigues with Maggie Cheung; at the end, her image undergoes Lettrist defacement.

on John Travolta preening in *Saturday Night Fever* (1977), and he inspires the naive porn star Dirk Diggler in *Boogie Nights* (1997).

More experimental films have also fallen under the Hong Kong spell. At the very start of the kung-fu craze came *La dialectique peut-elle casser des briques? (Can Dialectics Break Bricks?* 1973), the product of a Situationist splinter group who subjected the kung-fu movie *The Crush* (aka *Crush Karate*, 1972) to a radical swerve *(détournement)* by adding new subtitles. A flirtatious interlude between a fighter and a maid becomes a discussion of commodity fetishism, and the head bureaucrat threatens to quell a rebellion by sending in his sociologists, psychiatrists, and structuralists, even "My Foucaults! My Lacans!"[17] Two decades later came *Irma Vep* (1996), which links Hong Kong to French popular and avant-garde traditions (Fig. 4.1).

Respectable Western critics have long been at a loss to explain why audiences and filmmakers are fascinated by Hong Kong film. From the start, these movies offended guardians of taste. Yet by the early 1990s, despite having been almost completely ignored by the mainstream press, Hong Kong cinema attracted a cult following. Undeterred by complaints of crudeness, fans plunged in. They produced fanzines and Web pages celebrating the movies with a mixture of awe, aggressiveness, and proselytizing zeal. A popular cinema gave birth to a populist fan culture. Subterranean tastes helped push Hong Kong cinema into the mainstream, and by the mid-1990s *Time* and *Newsweek* were praising John Woo's and Tsui Hark's Hollywood debuts. How could this happen?

After World War II, for Europe and North America, the dignified Asian cinema was Japan's; Hong Kong film was virtually unknown until the kung-fu cycle of the early 1970s. At the start of the boom Hong Kong proved foolproof copy. Reporters rushed to Clearwater Bay, where Run Run Shaw regaled them with yarns, ushered them through Movietown, and invited them to meet his family.[18] But the coverage was almost always condescending, starting with jokes on the boss's name. ("What," asked one article, "Makes Run Run Run?") Then as now, most Western journalists treated Hong Kong productions as vulgar and stupid. After watching two of the early "karate" imports, Vincent Canby of the New York Times confidently condemned the entire genre. Kung-fu was amusingly awful: the English dubbing "was obviously meant to be funny," the fighting was overblown, and Bruce Lee looked "like Alain Delon with a lot of bee stings."[19] Compared to the high-budget swordplay spectacles of Kurosawa, the raucous kung-fu movie could only look jejeune.

A few critics were more sympathetic. In a French film journal Guy Braucourt mounted a structural analysis of martial-arts plots.[20] The gifted critic Tony Rayns began to review Chinatown releases for the British Film Institute's Monthly Film Bulletin.[21] In 1974 another London-based journalist, Verina Glaessner, published Kung Fu: Cinema of Vengeance, an astute account of the genre.[22] Meanwhile in Hong Kong philosopher and sociologist Ian Jarvie produced an incisive assessment of the cinema's place in local culture.[23]

The new awareness of Hong Kong cinema led critics to recognize King Hu, a major director whose Touch of Zen won a special technical award at Cannes in 1975, four years after its Asian release. A Hu retrospective at London's National Film Theater followed, but this did not lead to a wider circulation of Hong Kong's prestige products. With a few exceptions like Father and Son (1981) and Boat People (1982), the New Wave went largely unnoticed. Although the Hong Kong International Film Festival published its informative catalogues in bilingual editions, these were largely ignored by Western film culture.

Throughout the early 1980s martial-arts sagas lingered in neighborhood theaters and on late-night television. Hong Kong films poured into America's growing Chinatowns. Then the festival circuit discovered this explosive cinema. For the 1983 Pesaro Film Festival, Marco Müller mounted "Cinemasia," a panorama giving special attention to Hong Kong. The Pesaro screenings, accompanied by a two-volume collection of essays on Asian cinemas,[24] spurred the editors of Cahiers du cinéma to publish a splendid survey issue, "Made in Hong-Kong," in 1984. At that time, when Cahiers spoke, Western film culture listened. Hong Kong films began to appear at festivals, often as midnight attractions. In 1988 David Chute, another devotee, assembled for the New York journal Film Comment a string of eloquent essays by critics and programmers, centering on Tsui Hark, Jackie Chan, and horror movies.[25] Soon Barbara Scharres of Chicago's Film Center of the Art Institute began mounting annual programs of the best of recent Hong Kong releases.

Momentum built. In the spring of 1991 Once upon a Time in China had a one-month run in Manhattan. That fall Asian CineVision, a nonprofit distributor, assembled a Hong Kong package, called it "Cinema of Blazing

Passions," and circulated it to campuses and cultural venues. The response was enthusiastic. The *New York Review of Books* ran Geoffrey O'Brien's thoughtful review of the Asian CineVision programs.[26] A new niche market opened, and by the mid-1990s it was flourishing. Film programmers had found that in the age of videotape they could no longer attract audiences with Buñuel and Resnais. Hong Kong movies filled theaters, not only with Asians but with the young and the hip. "This stuff and *anime* are the only things that sell," one told me regretfully.

Cinéphile culture merged with other currents. Ever since the 1970s vogue for martial arts, kung-fu magazines had included information on Hong Kong cinema. The word of a new kind of action cinema spread to video aficionados. In 1985 there appeared *Martial Arts Movies: From Bruce Lee to the Ninjas*, a true fan's guide, supplying extensive historical background, many photographs, and lists of the best and worst films in the genre. "At its worst," the authors noted, "the martial arts movie is laughable, totally deserving of derision. But at its best, it can supply an audience exhilaration that cannot be found in any other cinema . . . These are great action movies. These are great superhero movies. They deliver where other unimaginative, overblown, and campy superhero movies fail."[27]

By this time the action film had moved to the center of Hollywood's genre system, and Hong Kong filmmakers had begun to turn out comparatively cheap, location-shot urban thrillers. Many Western viewers, primed by Indiana Jones and *Lethal Weapon* (1987), found Hong Kong cop and adventure films easier to swallow than kung-fu. In 1988, the same year as the *Film Comment* supplement, the British television series *The Incredibly Strange Film Show* devoted an episode to the action pictures of Jackie Chan and Tsui Hark, and it became a staple rerun on U.S. cable channels. The 1991 Asian CineVision touring package highlighted gunplay pictures like *City on Fire, A Better Tomorrow,* and *God of Gamblers* (1989). Soon the Western canon crystallized around Woo's heroic triad sagas, Tsui's revival of kung-fu and swordplay adventures, and the *policiers* featuring beautiful women cops in hair-raising stunts.

Unlike other foreign films, Hong Kong movies were subtitled in English upon local release. Just as important, they were readily available on videotape. Fans who lived near a Chinatown could boast of seeing the latest hits on the big screen, but most loyalists depended on cassettes, sniffing out rarities in tiny video shops and Asian food stores. In our town you could rent Hong Kong tapes from Chinese restaurants, food stores, and even a beauty parlor. Since the tapes were often poor copies, some students routinely drove to Chicago, rented a batch of laser discs, and spent days in motel rooms making clean dubs.

As video drove the Hong Kong craze, competing versions proliferated. Bootleggers clipped out scenes or picked up versions tailored to specific Asian markets. Even legitimate video releases sometimes varied from the original, since Hong Kong companies gave foreign distributors carte blanche to recut their films. Nearly twenty-five minutes were eliminated from the U.S. video version of Jackie Chan's *Police Story* (1985); the final credits even included a different set of outtakes. By contrast, the video version of Tsui Hark's *Once upon a Time in China* (1991) is longer than the original Hong Kong release, which had to be trimmed to fit theater schedules.[28]

Hong Kong fever took firm hold in the early 1990s. Cult interest grew in Europe, and in Japan one could buy tourist guides highlighting famous movie locations.[29] Self-published fanzines proliferated: in England, *Eastern Heroes* and *Film Extremes*; in Canada, Colin Geddes' discerning *Asian Eye* and later the bilingual *Screen Machine*; in the United States *Hong Kong Film Connection*, *Hong Kong Film Magazine*, *Asian Trash Cinema* (later *Asian Cult Cinema*), and *Skam* (later *Cineraider*). By 1998 most of the zines had folded, but for a few years they created a lively fan culture. Their pages were open to young men and women who apparently lived solely to watch Hong Kong movies and write breathless appreciations of them. The fans joyously retold the plots, appraised the action scenes, caught in-jokes, spotted a bit player, pledged fealty to a star, registered amazement at moments of bizarre sex and violence, and ranked every film according to a refined calculus of excellence. Apparently unaware of the Hong Kong Festival volumes, zine writers boldly set out to provide reference tools.[30] The fans had to know what tapes to rent, how to distinguish an early (and probably bad) Jackie Chan from a later tour de force, why *In the Line of Duty 3* is also known as *Yes Madam 2*.

The zines and the tape market fed one another, with publishers often starting video sales companies. By the end of the 1990s, with the fanzines largely gone, authorized distributors like the U.S.-based Tai Seng began to exploit the market systematically. Today hundreds of Hong Kong titles crowd my campus video store; the dominant language in the foreign section is Cantonese.

What led a younger generation to embrace the gratuitously wild cinema that had so irked the *New York Times*? At first glance, the appeals seem obvious. There is the girls-and-guns factor, typified by *Yes, Madam!* (1985) and *Heroic Trio* (1993). Jonathan Ross wrote: "The whole idea of sexy Chinese girls wearing tight superhero type costumes, fighting and then having sex, is possibly the finest development in the hundred years of cinema history a man could possibly hope for."[31] There is also the flamboyant action of hand-to-hand combat on flimsy ladders or flaming posts, inexhaustibly gymnastic gunfights, and soaring and somersaulting swordplay. Moreover, the most "mainstream" Hong Kong film casually shows violence that Hollywood would not. In *Angel* (1987), one female fighter sets a live grenade on the floor and folds a man over it like dry cleaning. Later the villainess slams a nail-studded board into another woman's shoulder, where it sticks a while. There is also the sheer sensationalism of the horror films, in which people are perfunctorily raped, tortured, flayed, and burnt to a crisp. And there are subtitles straight out of Raymond Roussel, passed happily around the world through e-mail:

I am damn unsatisfied to be killed in this way.
Same old rules: no eyes, no groin.
I have been scared shitless too much lately.
How can you use my intestines as a gift?
You always use violence. I should've ordered glutinous rice chicken.[32]

Violence, exploitation, and nuttiness always have a potential audience, but the broad American public was not (and probably never will be) ready for the shocks and peculiarities on display in these films. Hong Kong's Western audience is composed largely of subcultures, a state of affairs that owes as much to the vagaries of the viewers as it does to the charms of the movies.

For many programmers and critics who brought the films into festival culture, Hong Kong evoked American silent cinema. "It reminds me a lot of Hollywood," David Overbey remarked, "before the great split between commerce and art."[33] Dave Kehr declared Jackie Chan a modern Keaton: "He is one of the very few contemporary figures who could have had a career in silent movies."[34] American action movies of the 1980s had promised a return to the visually dynamic pleasures associated with the silent era, but many critics found the blockbusters increasingly inflated and heartless. Hong Kong films still believed in the exalted possibilities of physical grace.

For younger admirers, however, the films offered downmarket pleasures. Since the 1940s, some critics had defended marginal and low-budget films as a source of unpretentious craft. By the 1970s one could find critics prepared to defend exploitation—minuscule-budgeted science fiction, horror, crime, and sex films. Russ Meyer's *Faster, Pussycat, Kill, Kill!* (1965), George Romero's *Night of the Living Dead* (1968), and *The Last House on the Left* (1972) were being taken seriously. As censorship broke down and mainstream films like *The Exorcist* (1973) began to incorporate exploitation elements, David Cronenberg, Wes Craven, Joe Dante, and other marginal filmmakers pushed further into sadistic violence and outrageous sexuality, eventually pulling the downmarket attitude into the mainstream. Video nourished a more transgressive cinema, both through straight-to-video releases and through American dubs of grotesque esoterica, like Italian *giallo* horror and Japanese rape movies.

Apart from B-film connoisseurs and the "splatterheads" who savored erotic gore, another strain of downmarket tastes was key to the success of Hong Kong movies. In the early 1970s young people turned Camp to new ends, reveling in a self-congratulatory superiority to ineptly made movies.

College film societies hosted pot-hazed screenings of *Marijuana: Weed with Roots in Hell* (1931), and in 1978 Harry and Michael Medved launched careers by celebrating the worst films of all time, announcing, "It's more enjoyable for people to laugh together over absurdities and disasters than it is to praise the all-time movie greats."[35] The weekly rituals of *Rocky Horror Picture Show* (1976), the canonization of Edward D. Wood (*Plan Nine from Outer Space*, 1959) as the world's worst director, and midnight screenings of *Beyond the Valley of the Dolls* (1970) and *The Wizard of Oz* (1939) all intensified the atmosphere of knowing mockery, an attitude sustained today in *Mystery Science Theater 3000*.

As the Asian product most widely seen in the West, Hong Kong films delivered all these downmarket pleasures. The tough urban action films echo the glories of B noir. Geoffrey O'Brien calls Hong Kong cinema "one of the last outposts of the kind of efficaciously formulaic medium-to-low-budget filmmaking that in America faded along with the studios."[36] Likewise, the films' visceral effects—spouting blood, exotic tortures, bizarre sexuality—have exploitation elements in abundance. America fanguides recommend films like *The Holy Virgin versus the Evil Dead* (1991): "Lots of martial action and witchy-nudie stuff, but a dearth of (needed) bugs and slime."[37] And from the first years, the florid acting and outrageous plot twists made Hong Kong products into "bad movies we love." "It is entirely possible," wrote the *Times* reviewer of *King Boxer*, "to take the film as a joke."[38] Run Run Shaw recognized that whereas local audiences took kung-fu seriously, "Americans see it as comedy."[39] Run Run proved prophetic. In Europe and North America young people come to screenings of *The Killer* determined to ridicule its excesses.[40]

Still, hardcore Hong Kong fans do not come to mock. For them, as for the Camp followers Susan Sontag described in the 1960s, the wilder regions of popular culture harbor emotional directness and imaginative sincerity. Rather than reveling in the irony that postmodernists claim is our universal fate, many admirers of exploitation films, trash movies, sick and twisted films, midnight movies, cult movies, and all the rest find there a naive, nonconformist honesty missing from the mass-marketed product. Just as they praise the Incredibly Strange Music of Esquivel and Les Baxter, they value eccentric films that cast off poise and measure. Here is a young cartoon artist, Daniel Clowes, on roughneck filmmakers of an earlier generation: "They play everything to such a degree that it's got this electricity through it . . . The thing about a guy like Sam Fuller or Jack Webb is that they might do something really awful, but they mean it, they're dead serious, and there is something really powerful about that conviction."[41] The ragged expression of post-Punk music, grunge and thrash and speed metal, may have cultivated a taste for art that was at once histrionic and authentic. For many fans, films relentlessly committed to emotional expression, no matter how hyperbolic or rough-hewn, carried a jolt of honesty.

In the case of Hong Kong, the emotions are very hyperbolic, but filmmakers have expressed them with fluency and polish. These films won over a larger fraction of cultists than the grossout esoterica did, partly because Hong Kong movies respect most rules of craft. Their imaginative excesses can be realized appealingly, thanks to glossy production values and performers who are athletic, versatile, and charming in a way the denizens of splatter films can never be. Big-budget films with low-budget audacity, Hong Kong movies can be outrageous in splendid ways. They can dress up an exploitation idea in brilliant, sharply paced visuals, as when during a warehouse shootout in *The Outlaw Brothers* (1990), a hanging cage bursts and sends a rain of frightened chickens into the crossfire.

Such scenes are playfully outrageous without being paralyzingly knowing. Most young connoisseurs did not see in Hong Kong a retrieval of the innocence of the silent era. Instead they found a rapturous, unpredictable energy that made contemporary popular entertainment look pallid. Hong Kong satisfied a yearning for zany, well-crafted, and unironic enjoyment. These films defied canons of Western taste and plausibility while remaining familiar in genre and enticing in technique. Their bold twists on comfortable conventions reenchanted mass entertainment.

Hong Kong's own critics have tended to measure current releases against two baselines, the socially critical films of the 1950s and the New Wave works of the early 1980s. Western fans and critics have judged Hong Kong chiefly in relation to Hollywood, either old or new. Writing of *A Chinese Ghost Story 2* (1990), a fan notes that "The Lucas/Spielberg Corporations can only WISH they could create such genuine flights of fantasy as this."[42] Yet the fans are not really anti-Hollywood; most would not sit through *L'avventura,* let alone *Wavelength.* What the fan wants is Hollywood done right, all stops out and with an unpredictable spin. One of the most articulate columnists testifies: "Most HK fans were converted by the unique experience, the 'Whoa, where did *this* come from?' feel of that first film, which was not so much an encounter with a foreign culture as the twisting of something vaguely familiar into a new universe."[43]

Accordingly, the Western fan canon is weighted toward Hongkongified Hollywood and refracted through the lens of downmarket pleasures. The favorites tend to be action films by John Woo, Tsui Hark, Jackie Chan, Ching Siu-tung, and Sammo Hung.[44] Hong Kong's own critics, by contrast, scarcely mention Jackie Chan and Sammo Hung and instead canonize arthouse items like *Centre Stage* (1992), *Days of Being Wild* (1990), *Rouge* (1988), and *Ashes of Time* (1994). Western fans idolize Woo's *The Killer,* while for most Hong Kong critics *A Better Tomorrow* remains his best work. Fans favor Tsui's *Peking Opera Blues* (1987), but local writers tend to prefer his *Dangerous Encounters—First Kind* (1980) and *Shanghai Blues* (1984).[45] Many fan favorites, like *Naked Killer* (1992) and *Don't Stop My Crazy Love for You* (1993), will arouse only disdain in a Hong Kong critic.

Hardcore Western fans form an authentic subculture. The exchange of precious tapes and the delighted recital of favorite moments constitute core rituals. In the zines and on the Net, fans launch queries and rants. Plot synopses initiate newcomers. Sacred scenes are commemorated in print or in the instant replay. "This sequence always warrants a rewind! If either one of those gags had gone wrong, Jackie could easily have been killed."[46] The ultimate ritual may be the List: the ten best films, the ten best action sequences, the ten cutest women.

As with any community, fandom can be divisive. There is some bitterness between admirers of the classic martial-arts films of the 1970s and those gunplay aficionados for whom the great days of Hong Kong cinema began when Tsui Hark and John Woo launched heroic bloodshed. Wirework, the use of nearly invisible cables to make performers soar, is a perennial source of debate; purists hold out for the genuine acrobatics of the 1970s. And fandom can be cruel. You get ethos the hard way. Were you there at the beginning, before the wannabes moved in? Do you know plot details, actors' Chinese names, obscure lines? Do you hold a big collection of magazines or autographs or tapes? Have you seen all the versions of *Bullet in the Head* (1990)? If not, prepare to defend yourself. Damon Foster, scourge of the Asian fan scene, castigates the "fat slobs who consider themselves cool for laughing out loud," other fans too young to have grown up watching 1970s kung-fu movies, and those "Johnny-come-lately" critics who admired *Hard Boiled:* "American critics and the mainstream had *finally* discovered a good thing, that incomparable teaming of John Woo and Chow Yun-fat. Few of these asskissing critics were into the genre back when a true masterpiece like *A Better Tomorrow* originally came out, so the next best thing, the way to seem hip, was to praise *Hard Boiled* mercilessly."[47] When Tarantino lifted a plotline from *City on Fire* for *Reservoir Dogs*, fans pounced. They delightedly dissected the similarities, and one made a ten-minute video, *Who's Fooling Who*, which compared the films shot by shot.[48] The episode exposed a certain ambivalence: Tarantino was a fellow fan, and he made a movie that had a Hong Kong edge; but he thought that no one would notice, and so needed to be chastised.

If taste is made of a thousand distastes, rants add fun to fandom; here inventive insult plays out a ceremonial clash of bias and expertise. But most fan writing is breathlessly affirmative. The distinguishing mark is the hyperbolic adjective (incredible, amazing, delirious, insane), preferably hyphenated. A scene is jaw-dropping, eye-popping, super-charged, high-octane, whiplash-edited, over-the-edge, edge-of-your-seat, balls-to-the-wall, and, invariably, over-the-top. In the fanzines these phrases recur like Homeric epithets, soldered into prose that is often apostrophically challenged and scattered across pages laid out like ransom notes. Yet the enthusiasm is infectious, and there are bursts of heartfelt bombast:

> Media god Tsui Hark and his team yank both yin and yang to display the craggiest dragon "ladies," the butchiest blade-wielding babes, the most ag-

ile, most flexible, wildest transsexuals in all of cinema! Glen, or Glenda for that matter, would quake in their size 11 pumps at the full-on drag strip of high-speed action Tsui's bevy of cross-dressing hero/ines inspire.[49]

Zines may have been a transitional phenomenon; Hong Kong fandom blooms more beautifully on the Net. An international cinema packaged in VHS came naturally to a generation who grew up time-shifting, and it perfectly suited the digital culture the kids mastered. There was another advantage: this cinema, like arcane software, video games, and Webculture itself, was something adults just didn't get. So fan covens spread through the Net to bulletin boards, chatrooms, fan-club sites, databases, and personal pages. Your Webpage immortalizes your preferences: Tauna the Black favors Shaw Brothers, while Girls on Film offer a Drool Page full of male stars who represent "chunks of tasty eye candy." To backtrack through the gossip, opinion (a sequence is OTT, over-the-top), and trivia (name all the tongue jokes in Stephen Chiau movies) is to discover a sanctuary where literally anything about these films can be discussed. If a teacher required fans to learn as much about anything else, they would cry tyranny.[50]

Still, newsweeklies would not be running stories about the Asian Invasion if only tapeheads and Web mavens were promoting these movies. As Hong Kong cinema passed into general awareness from both the festival culture and the fan subculture, the chief gatekeepers were fan aesthetes. These were film journalists who celebrated and proselytized. Most were cinéphiles first and Hong Kong fans second, but their writing had some of the amphetamine pulse of rock reviewing. In *Film Comment*, the *Village Voice*, and free weeklies all over the country they took the outlandishness of this cinema as an occasion for turbocharged prose and ricochet cultural citations. Here references to high and low culture are whipped into a phantasmagoria reminiscent of the films themselves.

> In Tsui [Hark]'s *Double Team*, the basic vacuity of the nonplot has been taken to the point of almost pure formalization. Shooting the sub-mannequin triumvirate of Van Damme, Dennis Rodman, and Mickey Rourke (looking and acting like an advertisement for the Steroid Club for Men) as beefcake sculpture, in spots Tsui hints at a Mapplethorpe photo session slipped into a mildly outré Sixties spy film. (The surefire ad quote that never was: "The best edge-of-your-seat thrillride since Ken Russell's *Billion Dollar Brain!*")[51]

Starting from the tenets of pop journalism (and its proliferating parentheses), the writer weaves in the conventions of fan discourse—the hyphenate adjectives, the cross-referencing of films—while avoiding geekiness with a casual urbanity, mixing references to gallery art and old spy thrillers, jumping registers ("outré" and "beefcake"), and evoking the high-art conceit that a plot might be the occasion for "pure formalization."

Hardcore fans display innocent mania, but aesthetes are the dandies of fandom. They relish not merely chases and fights; they treasure peculiar spectacle and piquant ruptures of tone. Steeped in Camp and other alternative pleasures, they often subscribe to J. Hoberman's notion of "vulgar modernism," the possibility that mass cinema's off-center products parallel the avant-garde in the high arts. The good things in popular art, according to this postsurrealist view, are the moments of radical *dépaysement*, absurdly farfetched plot twists, violations of taste and logic.[52] The fan's spontaneous "Whoa, where did *this* come from?" becomes a self-conscious principle, a connoisseurship of radical weirdness.

The journalist-aesthetes were crucial in bringing Hong Kong cinema to the attention of mass-media tastemakers. Critics must sniff what's stirring on the margins. It did not hurt at all that Hong Kong films were in recognizable genres and had many qualities in common with Hollywood—vulgarity, sensuous pleasures, violent action, keen emotion—but with a harder edge. Reviewers for *Newsweek* and *Entertainment Weekly* could genuinely applaud Hong Kong cinema: its outrageousness appealed to the self-assured nonconformity that now defines one way of consuming mass entertainment.

So there is another way in which a popular cinema can go global. The analogy might be to World Music, a loose constellation of African, Asian, and ethnic European traditions defined against a bland mainstream. To some degree the advent of video has brought us a World Film. It is composed of Japanese *anime*, Indian melodramas, Italian horror, Mexican masked-wrestler films, Indonesian fantasies, and other off-center media materials from various countries. In all these cases, a local cinema has achieved international reach by becoming a subcultural cinema.[53] From this standpoint, Hong Kong becomes the leading edge of World Film, its salsa or reggae, so powerful that it can seize Hollywood's attention. When Jet Li was slighted on Warners' *Lethal Weapon 4* Webpage, the howls of protest from fans forced Warners to redesign its advertising campaign.[54]

Hong Kong's Western admirers have been excellent drumbeaters for a cinema that might otherwise have been ignored. As fact-finders and zestful appreciators, they have served their gods faithfully. But fans and the journalist aesthetes tend to offer rhapsody rather than analysis; they favor exclamation over explanation. How, we might ask them, do Hong Kong movies achieve their infectious force and grace? Some fans will dismiss the question as academic. "Film-school polemics," one fanguide starts by assuring us, fail with Hong Kong cinema "because over-intellectualizing film denies the primary purpose of moviegoing: entertainment."[55]

The professor's reply is that we can legitimately ask what makes these films so vivid, gripping, thrilling, moving—in sum, entertaining. Even when it becomes defensive, however, the fans' zealotry makes a point that professors often forget. Everywhere, and especially in academe, we are asked to acknowledge the specificity of different cultures. When media cross borders, intellectuals are likely to emphasize the variations in how a film is "read." A famous example is the way in which Australian aboriginal viewers watching a TV western are reported to cheer for the Indians rather than for the cowboys.[56] Surely this sort of "resistant reading" could take place; but before attaching their sympathies to the Indians the aboriginal viewers have understood that all those shapes on the screen represent people, that the conflicts line up in a certain way, that particular genre conventions are in force. That is, differences in interpretation build upon convergences in comprehension.

We can usefully treat a work of popular art as a bundle of appeals, some quite narrow in range, others quite broad. Where detractors see mass culture as aimed at the "lowest common denominator," we can identify a power to cross borders. In the case of Hong Kong film the fan subculture has celebrated aspects of the films which travel well. If the films did not find a mainstream audience in the West, that was not because they were difficult to understand but because they ran afoul of certain canons of taste (too gory, too sentimental, too much slapstick and overacting). For an audience less committed to Hollywood's standards of value, the barriers came down easily. Fans primed to enjoy downmarket pleasures were able to embrace the movies' transcultural force.

Of course many aspects of Hong Kong films go unnoticed by overseas viewers. But international audiences, fans or not, respond to some core appeals—how the story is told, how images and music are combined, how widely-shared human feelings are aroused and shaped. These transcultural appeals are matters of artistry, the artistry of entertainment.

ENOUGH TO MAKE STRONG MEN WEEP: JOHN WOO

Festival cinema trades on a director's distinctive style and worldview; a film by Angelopoulos, Kitano, or Kiarostami is taken as a personal statement. But mass-market filmmaking also has auteurs, directors such as Griffith, Hitchcock, and Welles who display a consistency of theme and technique from film to film. Most Hong Kong films look like most other Hong Kong films, but John Woo has made his movies exaggeratedly distinctive, caricaturally personal. In a highly obvious cinema, he is a very obvious auteur.

Like many auteurs, Woo has given himself a "biographical legend," a version of his life that shapes our attitude toward the films. Born in 1948 in Guangdong, he came to Hong Kong with his family soon after the Communist revolution. He has told of a harrowing childhood: the family homeless, the father tubercular, a neighborhood of gang warfare and wretched poverty. Thanks to American donations to the Lutheran church, Woo was able to go to high school and college. By presenting his youth as torn between violence and faith, Woo has positioned both as central to his movies. "I am a Christian, influenced by religious beliefs about love, sin, and redemption. The spirit of chivalry that existed in ancient warriors was destroyed, so now we have to face evil alone."[1]

Woo is a child of the studio system, starting out as a production assistant at Cathay, then moving to Shaw Brothers in 1971. There he was assistant director to Zhang Che, the master of violent swordplay and kung-fu, and Woo has talked of learning from Zhang how to manage action scenes. (His swordplay drama *Last Hurrah for Chivalry*, 1979, can be considered an homage to the Zhang tradition of bloody brotherhood.) In 1973 a private investor financed Woo's first project, *Young Dragons*; because of its excessive violence a cut version was released in 1975, but Golden Harvest took Woo on the payroll. He proved versatile, directing kung-fu movies and learning comedy by assisting Michael Hui. In 1976 his Cantonese Opera film *Princess Chang Ping* succeeded despite its antiquated genre, and the following year his farce *Money Crazy* (aka *Pilferer's Progress*), starring Michael Hui's brother Ricky, was a huge hit. Woo went on to direct eight more comedies for Golden Harvest and Cinema City from 1977 through 1986. He confessed himself torn between genres. "I like to amuse or make people laugh," he told an interviewer, but he also wanted to depict violence. "A lot of people get relief by seeing somebody beaten up."[2]

When his films began to fail, Woo was exiled to Taiwan, where he supervised second-line Cinema City product and turned out two slight comedies. In 1983 he also made a grim film about Hong Kong mercenaries in Vietnam, *Heroes Shed No Tears* (aka *Sunset Warrior*), which was not released until 1986. At his lowest point, he and Tsui Hark decided to remake Lung Kong's 1967 classic *Story of a Discharged Prisoner* (originally called *True Colors of a Hero*). It became *A Better Tomorrow* (1986), the story of a triad member who tries to go straight. It won colossal success and established a cycle of gangster movies known as "heroes" films. The film also revived the career of Ti Lung, star of many Zhang Che swordplay films, and made Chow Yun-fat one of the colony's most popular actors. *A Better Tomorrow* did very well overseas, and all over Asia young men copied Chow's look: long topcoat, dark glasses, matchstick between sullen lips. In Hong Kong the slangy dialogue, particularly the partners' musings on the nighttime skyline, entered everyday conversation.

A Better Tomorrow was followed by the profitable but lesser *A Better Tomorrow II* (1987). *The Killer* (1989), a more stylized effort, won local acclaim and good box office; in the early 1990s it become Woo's breakthrough to Western audiences. *Bullet in the Head* (1990) proved a financial disaster but a critical favorite; *Once a Thief* (1991) was a money-spinning New Year's film; and *Hard Boiled* (1992) was greeted by disappointing box office and critical indifference but proved quite successful overseas in the wake of *The Killer*.[3]

In all these, Woo's unrestrained approach—not just the airily choreographed gun battles but the moist, soulful exchanges between urban warriors bound together in duty and friendship—was atypical of the local industry. "His stuff is more heroic," noted Ringo Lam, "and mine is more realistic . . . My characters never do any flipping while they shoot!"[4] Western viewers, embarrassed by the films' excesses, ask if Hong Kong viewers laugh at them. They don't, but they know hyperstylization when they see it. They know that Woo's self-sacrificing knights are far removed from reality (even if triads began to imitate Chow's dazzling fashions). As for the violence and tearful male bonding, critic Law Kar declares, "The emotions are too narrow and too often overplayed," while Li Cheuk-to suggests that "a lot of times we cannot take the passionate action films of John Woo, but Western genre film fans love them precisely because such uninhibited wildness is almost impossible to find in Western genre films."[5]

Local critics saw Woo as updating the romantic, violent martial-arts tradition of the 1960s. *The Killer*, Peter Tsi has suggested, borrows heavily from swordplay fiction; and others have pointed out that Woo's heroes resemble those seen in Chor Yuan's 1970s film adaptations of Gu Long novels.[6] Most important was Woo's mentor Zhang Che. "I use some of his techniques in the gun battle scenes," Woo admits.[7] Woo seems to acknowledge this tradition in *A Better Tomorrow II*, when during an apocalyptic assault on a gangster's mansion Ti Lung grabs a sword and slashes his way through his enemies. *A Better Tomorrow* was also influenced by Zhang's "unrestrained way of writing emotions and chivalry," Woo said after completing it. "Chinese cinema has always been too low-keyed. We should be more expressive, put more of ourselves into our films."[8]

Woo found inspiration in more far-flung sources as well. As a young man he admired Kurosawa and Japanese gangster films.[9] He claimed a range of Western influences: the slow-motion violence of Sam Peckinpah and the somber performance of Alain Delon in Jean-Pierre Melville's *Le Samourai*, as well as Coppola, Ford, Truffaut, Fellini, Bergman, Kubrick, and Scorsese ("my long-time idol").[10] Although Woo was not part of the New Wave, his alertness to what he could borrow helped make Hong Kong film more cosmopolitan. *Plain Jane to the Rescue* (1982), with its graceful tracking shots and clever cutting, has a technical finish rare in local comedy of the time. Many of Woo's visual tics, like freeze-frames and slow-motion walks and glances, were already passé in the West, but the "heroes" cycle allowed him to integrate them with MTV dissolving musical segues, an endlessly arcing camera, wistful silhouettes against saturated landscapes, and glamorous, anguished players. The result was a glossy synthesis of Italian Westerns, swordplay, film noir, and romantic melodrama new to both Hong Kong and the West.

One might have expected that New Wave directors, many of whom had studied in film schools in the West, would be the first Hong Kong directors to build a career in the United States. Instead it was Woo, climbing up through the local studio system, who slipped into Hollywood and patiently began his climb again, reaching A-list status with *Face/Off* (1997). His ascent does not surprise Hong Kong critics, who have long considered him the most adaptable of their directors. Told to turn out kung-fu, then opera, then comedy, he became known as accommodating. On *A Better Tomorrow*, he worked closely with Chow Yun-fat, whose part grew as shooting proceeded, and with producer Tsui Hark, who dictated the film's final cut. Reluctantly, Woo made *A Better Tomorrow II*, which is said to have been drastically recut by Tsui. After the failure of *Bullet in the Head*, produced by Woo's own company, he recovered with *Once a Thief*, an audience-pleasing caper comedy. *Hard Boiled* was frankly designed as a portfolio film for Hollywood.

Once in America, he was prepared to tailor *Hard Target* (1993) to local tastes. After a disastrous preview in which adolescents snickered at all the dissolves and freeze-frames, "I realized that in the American action film the technique and the story are very straightforward."[11] *Hard Target* was recut seven times in order to placate U.S. censorship, a fact shrewdly played up in publicity. Woo occasionally complained about the strictness ("The American hero shouldn't take so many bullets . . . and he never dies . . . It's so square!") but he shrugged: "Now I know the system. Next time, I will avoid some things."[12] He played safe by making *Broken Arrow* (1996); if it succeeded, his producer and business partner Terence Chang explained, "then John will have a chance to do whatever he wants to do."[13] That included not only *Face/Off* but the perfunctory TV pilots *Once a Thief* (1996) and *Blackjack* (1998). Woo was hired to direct the Brazilian soccer team in Nike's "Airport '98" TV commercials, and he was slated for *Mission: Impossible 2*.[14] The director who called for more self-expression in Chinese cinema began explaining that he left Hong Kong because "I'm not very Chinese. My techniques, my themes, my film language are not traditionally Chinese."[15]

It is rare for a director to find his métier after a string of fairly impersonal films over a dozen years, yet with *A Better Tomorrow* Woo hit upon his definitive world and his authoritative tone. Ho (Ti Lung) and his young friend Mark (Chow Yun-fat) are smooth triads working for a counterfeiting ring. Ho's brother Kit (Leslie Cheung) is an ambitious police officer who is unaware of Ho's criminal life. In Taiwan Ho is lured into an ambush while back in Hong Kong the same gang kills his father. Ho surrenders to the police, covering the escape of his subordinate Shing. Mark kills the gang leader responsible for Ho's fate but is himself wounded in the knee. Years later, when Ho is released, he finds Mark a limping vassal of Shing, who is now the gang's boss. Kit blames Ho for their father's death and is resolved to bring down Shing. Ho tries to go straight, but Shing wants him back in the gang and threatens both Mark and Kit. Ho and Mark steal Shing's counterfeiting tapes to help Kit's investigation. In a fiery climax at a wharf, Ho and Mark fight off Shing's men until Kit comes to join them. When Mark is killed in a shattering fusillade, Kit helps Ho eliminate Shing. The film ends with Kit leading his brother away in handcuffs.

Woo has often said that seeing "lost" young people of the mid-1980s moved him to make a film about the traditional values of family and friendship.[16] The result is a plot that includes only one woman (Kit's wife) and hinges on a male ethos of loyalty, face, and shared suffering. Ho and Mark are at ease only in all-male societies: the gang, or the taxi company in which Ho finds work. In defiance of family ties, Kit rejects his criminal brother, so Mark becomes Ho's Kit-substitute. Ho tries to convince Kit he has reformed, but only sacrifice will redeem him—or indeed any man in the film. The father dies to protect Ho, Ho surrenders to save Shing, Mark is crippled while avenging Ho ("How can I thank you? I can never make it

EM.1 *A Better Tomorrow:* Boyish brotherhood among triads.

EM.2 Limping from his wound, Mark has sunk to the bottom of the gang hierarchy.

up to you"), Mark and Ho risk their lives to steal the computer tapes for Kit. In the final gun battle, Kit still hesitates to aid the fallen Ho, so Mark must shout: "Hasn't he paid you back yet?" One of the film's most powerful moments comes when Mark, sent by Ho in a powerboat away from the fight, bares his teeth and ferociously wheels the boat back to the wharf. In returning to help his friend, Mark will lose his life. "A typical Asian hero," says Woo.[17]

Woo underscores the pathos of these cascading loyalties by sharp contrasts. In the opening Ho and Mark swagger into the counterfeiting headquarters, respected by all. But after Ho is captured and Mark is wounded, they are brought pitiably low. Here Woo exploits one of his favorite devices, exaggerated parallels between scenes. In the opening, Ho picks Mark up on the street in a cab, both all smiles and unstructured suits. Mark is pure boyishness, waggling his eyebrows and letting Ho lick his finger for a taste of fish (Fig. EM.1). When Ho returns from prison, they meet on the street again. Ho is now a cabdriver in gray denim, and Mark limps along the curb, scrubbing windshields with a rag (Fig. EM.2). He has soured, and his impishness is gone. This is the shabbiness of dishonor.

The parallels come to a pitch of intensity, as often in Woo, during a facedown. An early nightclub scene had shown Mark and Ho at the height of success, with Shing fawning on them. Now Shing is the boss, condescending to his old friends, and Mark bitterly accepts Shing's toast by hauling his bum leg onto the table and dashing a glass of whiskey over it. (Payback will come later: during the final shootout Shing's own leg will be blasted.) The two men's world has turned upside down; all they have left is their self-respect and their devotion to each other.

For *A Better Tomorrow*, Woo says, "I shot in the American way."[18] Most scenes alternate camera setups in the Hollywood manner (Figs. 1.10–1.16), and Woo borrows Peckinpah's slow-motion cutaways, which stretch out time during a firefight. When Mark invades the Taipei gangsters' party, he fires rapidly, but his victims go down with excruciating slowness (Figs. EM.3–EM.7). Woo's preference for alternating camera positions, rather

EM.3 *A Better Tomorrow:* Mark launches the restaurant assassination.

EM.4 His target is hit.

EM.5 Mark dispatches a bodyguard to his left.

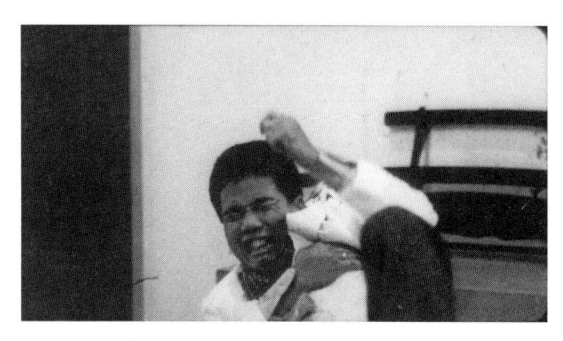

EM.6 Cut back to the camera position of Fig. EM.4: the victim still falling.

EM.7 Cut back to the camera position of Fig. EM.5: the victim still falling.

than for changing setups to accommodate each bit of action, led naturally to shooting gunplay with several cameras at once, some mounted on tracks zigzagging through the fight.[19]

Woo's sources aren't only American. His action style is anticipated in the floating fights of Chor Yuan (Figs. EM.8–EM.11), the gas station robbery in Danny Lee's *Law with Two Phases* (1984), and the climax of Johnny Mak's *Long Arm of the Law* (1984; Fig. EM.12). Still, *A Better Tomorrow* develops its visual ideas with unprecedented smoothness and emotional force. The film has most of Woo's authorial fingerprints. There is the lan-

ENOUGH TO MAKE STRONG MEN WEEP 103

EM.8 Midair gunplay in Chor Yuan's *The Killer* (aka *Sacred Knives of Vengeance,* 1972): The hero leaps up . . .

EM.9 . . . and is hit in midair.

EM.10 The villain fires again.

EM.11 Still floating, the hero takes the bullet.

EM.12 A Woo-like standoff in *Long Arm of the Law*.

EM.13 *A Better Tomorrow*: Kit on the firing range.

EM.14 Kit's target . . .

EM.15 . . . standing in for his convict brother Ho.

guid slow motion that magnifies expressions or bits of gesture. There is a fondness for tight, deep compositions shot with a circling camera racking focus constantly. There are those frozen moments during combat when the gunfire unaccountably halts to permit men to confide in one another. There is Woo's remarkably concise handling of exposition. In the prologue Ho dreams of Kit's death, then sits bolt upright, his sweat-soaked shirt sticking to the triad tattoos on his back. Later, Kit's festering rage toward his brother is handled in crisply cut imagery: convicts on parade are intercut with targets on a shooting range, which are then juxtaposed with sorrowful close-ups of Ho in prison (Figs. EM.13–EM.15).

Pressed by Tsui Hark, Woo made a sequel. Perhaps the most striking feature of *A Better Tomorrow II* is its display of popular entertainment's shameless ingenuity. Chow Yun-fat's portrayal of Mark was a crowd-pleaser, but Mark got killed in Part I. So Tsui and Woo brought Chow back as Mark's twin brother Ken, summoned to Hong Kong from his New York restaurant by a vendetta against a revered gang leader. A scene in an artist's studio unabashedly acknowledges the audience's desire to have more of Mark; the camera coasts past paintings of him in characteristic poses and ends by revealing his revered bullet-riddled coat. Eventually Ken grows into Mark, complete with sunglasses, duster, matchstick, and massive firepower.

ENOUGH TO MAKE STRONG MEN WEEP

The climax of *A Better Tomorrow II*, an all-out assault on a gangster's mansion, is one of the most incendiary gun battles in cinema. It also reveals Woo's tendency to rerun earlier ideas, only louder. (His resort to escalating explosions would come to a climax in the use of a nuclear blast as a turning point in *Broken Arrow*.) Again we find proliferating symmetries. The opening of *A Better Tomorrow II* works as both parallel and echo: once more Ho dreams of a death, but it is now Mark's, reprised from the first installment. Correspondingly, it is Kit who gets killed—by the sinister Japanese assassin who is made analogous, through fighting style and a courtly exchange of guns, with Mark's brother Ken. The drinking motif of the first film becomes a food motif, linked to Ken's insistence in his restaurant that "rice is my father and mother." And there are the usual spikes of sheer melodrama. Kit is shot while his wife Jacky gives birth, and he dies in a phone booth as she joyously tells him of the baby. Revenge for Kit's death propels the furious onslaught that closes the film.

Of *The Killer* Woo has remarked: "Only in the Western world did people appreciate what I did in this film."[20] It remains his best-known Hong Kong effort, carrying to mannered extremes the themes and techniques of *A Better Tomorrow*, now backed by a bigger budget. There is again an overindulgence in ordnance, and the plot lacks the tight thrust-and-parry of *A Better Tomorrow*'s. But *The Killer* offers unique delights of both pattern and passion.

John is a paid assassin who kills only those who he is convinced deserve to die. Sidney, a retired hitman, is his agent. During a routine killing in a nightclub, John accidentally blinds Jenny, a nightclub singer, and her suffering brings home to him the immorality of his way of life. He falls in love with her and vows to finance the surgery that will restore her sight. So he takes on one last job, assassinating Weng, a crime boss. But now John becomes the target of the boss's nephew, Johnny, who had secretly hired John for the killing and had persuaded Sidney to betray him. At the same time, "Eagle" Li, a detective, is trying to track John down. Li comes to respect his quarry, especially after John risks his life to rescue a little girl. When John discovers Sidney's treachery, he agonizingly decides to forgive him, and Sidney vows to retrieve the money Weng owes John. John shifts his affection to detective Li, and in the film's last stretch they become allies, fighting off Weng's army of assassins. John is killed. Li stalks vengefully to Weng, already in custody, and shoots him in front of the other officers. Li collapses to his knees sobbing, "John."

The Killer is a triumph of sheer romanticism, recycling clichés with unabashed conviction: the blinded beloved who needs an operation, the innocents wounded in crossfire, the crook who must pull one last job, the cop who becomes fascinated with his quarry, the aging professional who recovers his dignity in a final act of courage. Each element is pushed to a limit, steeped in sentiment, swathed in dreamy hyperbole. Woo links his three beautiful principals by sinuous camera movements, languid superimpositions, and Jenny's love ballads. When John sets out on a hit, his first step falls on the downbeat of a piano melody, and to Jenny's song he floats into the nightclub through slow motion, freeze-frames, and luxurious tracking shots. Eagle Li muses over police sketches of his suspect: "There's something heroic about him. He doesn't look like a killer. He comes across so calm; he acts like he has a dream, his eyes full of passion." Dissolve to John, distraught, waiting for the man who has betrayed him. At another point the camera, coasting across a street, catches red neon reflections and turns trickling rainwater into a stream of blood.

During the climactic siege on the church, John asks Li to promise that if he should die, Jenny will get her operation and John's corneas will be used for the transplants. But even this pledge can't be honored: when John is killed, he is shot in the eyes. He and Jenny crawl toward and past one another, crying out each other's name. They never connect. John dies on his belly, gripping the dust fiercely before sagging with a sigh; impossible to say if it is slow motion or Chow's performance, languorous to the end. As Luc Moullet once remarked of Samuel Fuller: you may like the film, you may hate it, but let him who is not a ghost dare say that he has felt nothing.

There is method to the manic stylization. The kaleidoscopic technique and flamboyant melodrama are supported by firm character parallels. In the opening, John's attack on the nightclub and the scorching of Jenny's eyes are followed by John being tended in the church, staring in agony at the cross. The cross dissolves to Jenny, a link between Christian and romantic love, as bandages are stripped off her eyes. Then she's back singing, but in a café. John haunts it, watching her perform. He goes to visit her in her apartment, and she puts on a tape: what else but the song she sang in the nightclub as he drifted in? His guilt-stricken face is intercut with a quick reprise of the accident, soaking the moment in his pity and self-pity, and then the scene shifts gently to Li, waiting for his partner Chang as John had waited at the church for Sidney; Jenny's music brings him into the plot.

These opening scenes, like the Cantonese title of the film ("Two Blood-Spattered Heroes"), signal that *The Killer* will present Woo's beloved character symmetries with a new explicitness. Instead of the parallel brothers of *A Better Tomorrow* we have parallel father-son relations. For the elders, the retired killer Sidney and the old cop Chang, tradition is dying: "Our nostalgia is our saving grace," Sidney says. But young John and Li try to sustain the heroic ideal, however futile the effort may prove. Sidney's betrayal of John and the death of Chang lead to the union of killer and cop, a fusion as well of Christianity (John's drop point is the Catholic church, where he finds tranquillity among fluttering doves and statues of the Virgin) and Chinese tradition (Li is associated with the statue of General Kwan in the police station's shrine). But the link between the two younger

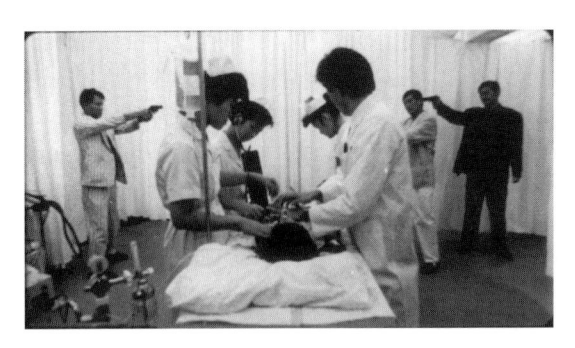

EM.16 *The Killer:* Li and John in a standoff at the hospital.

men has already been established, not just by Jenny's ballad but also by the two costly attacks that open the film: John's wounding of Jenny when he kills his target, and Li's killing of the thug Eddie on the tram, which gives an innocent woman a heart attack.

Thereafter John and Li are compared by every stylistic means Woo can find: crosscutting, echoing lines of dialogue, and visual parallels. One would think that a shot like Fig. EM.16 goes about as far as one could in stressing affinities between the men, but our auteur is just getting started. He intercuts tracking shots in John's apartment to make Li literally replace John, and he will have them face off again and again, in a dizzying series of variant framings, while telling the blind Jenny they're childhood friends. Woo violates Hollywood's 180-degree cutting rule in order to underscore graphic similarities between the two men (Figs. EM.17, EM.18). On top of this Woo just tells us: "It's a very simple idea. They are in the same situation and they've got the same feeling and they've got the same position. It's like looking in a mirror."[21] Admittedly, the techniques aren't perfectly redundant, since each Doppelgänger encounter also marks a new stage in the men's growing friendship. Nonetheless, *The Killer*'s florid style magnifies the sort of points that were made more quietly in *A Better Tomorrow*.

There is an audacious exhilaration in Woo's freedom of narration. As in silent films, scenes are interrupted by short flashbacks to action we've already seen, so that certain images—Jenny's streaming mascara as she clutches her eyes, John's agony before the cross—are driven home as obsessively as a motif in Griffith. As Li's superior describes the Dragon Boat race that will take place that afternoon, Woo gives us thrusting illustrative shots of the race in progress, a technique straight out of *M*. John's white scarf becomes a visual token: at first a sign of his wealth and stylishness (and an echo of the white knights of Zhang Che), it is used to bandage Jenny's bleeding eyes. Thereafter it becomes a souvenir of John's mistaken way of life, but it can still serve as a sling or tourniquet. Woo is willing to top himself as things proceed. Blind Jenny serves tea while the men press

EM.17 As John and Li remark on their affinities . . .

EM.18 . . . Woo cuts across the axis of action to make them pictorially parallel.

EM.19 Jenny serves tea while killer and cop keep each other occupied.

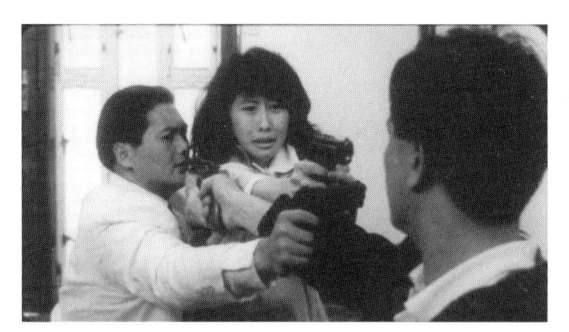

EM.20 Jenny joins the face-off.

pistols to each other's heads (Fig. EM.19). "When we made this scene," Woo reports, "we feel so much joy."[22] In a later scene the standoff duet becomes a trio when Jenny, trying to protect John from Li, grabs a pistol herself (Fig. EM.20). When John phones Jenny from the harbor's edge at dawn, she says she can imagine the deep blue sky; the dissolves and silhouettes turn the scene into a melancholic TV commercial. As Li and John discuss honor ("It's going out of style"), cut to Sidney being beaten for refusing to inform on John; but that is not enough, so the beating is shot in slow motion and backed by a choir out of Morricone. In the late 1980s critics, particularly in Paris, were beginning to wonder if cinema was finished. *The Killer*, flaunting a pre-postmodern freedom from cool irony, seemed at a stroke to reinvent sincere, bravura storytelling.

Woo conceived *Bullet in the Head* as a vehicle for his despair at the 1989 massacre in Tiananmen Square. Three young friends growing up in late 1960s Hong Kong flee to Vietnam. They plunge into an inferno—U.S. rapacity, corruption, terrorist attacks, Vietcong torture—and their friendship dissolves. It is Woo's most anguished movie. Paul turns greedy, risking the lives of his friends for a trunkful of stolen gold leaf. The childish Frank, forced to shoot prisoners for the Vietcong soldiers' amusement, is himself shot in the head by Paul. He survives but becomes a gibbering madman, a hitman and heroin addict. Ben, the most balanced, survives to settle accounts in the only way the men have learned. He kills his friends: Frank, to put him out of his misery; Paul, as revenge for the sufferings of Frank. Hong Kong cinema knows no more excruciating passage than the prolonged sequence of Frank, wailing with fear, executing American soldiers as Ben urges him to kill for sheer survival, unless it is the film's final scene, in which Ben and Paul duel in a fiery arena on the dock where they had played as boys. Frank's skull, lovingly preserved by Ben, rests among the flames as Ben sends a bullet into Paul's head. The symmetrical woundings of which Woo is so fond have reached a nightmarish climax.

Political points are scored throughout. *Bullet in the Head* starts during the 1967 riots, when Hong Kong police attack demonstrating students; the sympathy seems all with the protesters until Woo shows a British officer blasted by a terrorist bomb. Soon Vietnam stands in for China, as it did in Ann Hui's *Boat People* (1982). Seeing all the killing in Saigon, Paul adopts a version of Maoist pragmatism: "If you have guns you have everything." South Vietnamese demonstrate to stop the war, and a student stands patiently in front of a tank, as at Tiananmen. Back in Hong Kong, Paul's stolen gold has enabled him to enter big business, and the brief scene in which Ben strides in and sets Frank's bloodstained skull on the boardroom table presents a galvanizing image of all that Hong Kong capitalism would like to forget. No distinctions are drawn among colonizing British, imperialistic Americans, sadistic Vietcong, corrupt Hong Kong businessmen, and (implicitly) Beijing's hard-liners. Taken as a whole, the film seems not so much a consistent indictment of totalitarian violence as a hallucinatory vision of sheer chaos, the collapse of all social and personal ideals in the face of aggression and naked greed.

Not even the longest version of the film develops either the social or personal contexts. There is always another ambush, another costly escape. Character development is shorthand: Paul gets more greedy, Frank more childlike, Ben tries to stay steady.[23] They pick up the singer Sally and start to take her back to Hong Kong, but she is killed soon afterward, so that her entire rescue seems little more than padding. The alternation of brief scenes of intimacy with prolonged battles points again to Woo's weakness for overlong set-pieces. Never using one shot where three will do, he indulges a tic already emerging in *The Killer:* images of an anonymous gunman going down, seen from many angles and stressed through aching slow motion. The field of fire also expands; *Bullet in the Head* revels in impersonal, Hollywood-blockbuster combats that look forward to Woo's American films.

Bullet in the Head was the first film from Woo's own company, and it proved a commercial disaster. He has claimed that audiences dispirited by

Tiananmen did not want to see such a horrifying world. Ever adroit, Woo transposed his characteristic preoccupations into a brighter key. *A Better Tomorrow II, The Killer,* and *Bullet in the Head* sustain an unusually consistent tone by Hong Kong standards, but *Once a Thief* is much more typical of the local product. It mixes drama, frantic action, and zany vulgarity. Joe (Chow Yun-fat), James (Leslie Cheung), and Cherie (Cherie Chung) are street orphans raised by a tyrannical pickpocket. They grow up to be suave art thieves, living in a chaste *ménage à trois:* Joe and James (echoing Woo's fondness for *Jules et Jim*) romp with each other boyishly, while Cherie looks after them. Another gang tries to cut in on their theft of a painting, leading Joe to sacrifice himself for his friends in a fiery crash. He disappears. James and Cherie fall guiltily in love, both haunted by memories of Joe. Joe reappears handicapped, like Mark in *A Better Tomorrow,* and they join forces for another heist. In a bristling shootout they discover that they have been targeted by their estranged stepfather, and we discover, when Joe vaults out of his wheelchair, that his infirmity is faked. The three partners reunite, and a coda shows them settled in America, with Joe babysitting and watching football on TV.

From the opening scene, with Joe strolling around a museum and trying to make sense of a Modigliani, to the climax, in which he roasts a card-flinging assassin by spitting out flaming cleaning fluid, *Once a Thief* abounds with little and big pleasures. It is the sort of unpretentious caper sendup that Hollywood can no longer produce: what *Hudson Hawk* (1991) wanted to be. There are comically suspenseful heists, acrobatic gunplay, a joyous scene with Cherie and Joe in his wheelchair on a dance floor, and a string of sight gags and in-jokes. Joe and James slither under burglar-detection laser rays, and the soundtrack obliges with some limbo music. Later they team up for a robbery, despite Joe's being wheelchair-bound, and they blow the safe by tricking a hapless gangster into falling on a detonator.

All the things that matter in the other films—loyalty, friendship, hand grenades—are milked for gags, and parallels seem piled on sheerly for amusement. The trio's domestic horseplay recalls their thieving childhood days, Cherie's attraction to Joe is given in *Killer* cuts-and-tracks that replace James with Joe, and the policeman pursuing them becomes a benevolent alternative father-figure. Christian references are limited to a snatch from the *Messiah* describing resurrection—exactly what will happen to the supposedly dead Joe. The reference points are now secular, usually satiric jabs at Western art. Paintings glow like the gold leaf of *Bullet in the Head,* and Cherie, often dressed in gold, becomes the incarnation of Caillebot's *Harem Servant,* the painting that fascinates all the men (Fig. EM.21). The shut-in Joe paints a mural of Rousseau's *Snake Charmer,* perhaps another reference to Cherie's mesmerizing charms. A shootout at a French pier becomes a riot of impressionist pastels as flowers, striped awnings, and tricolor balloons are blown to bits by the rival gang.

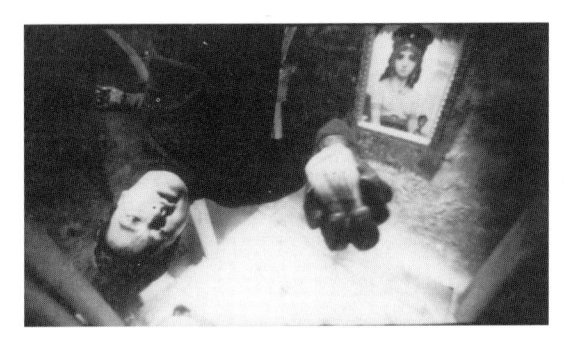

EM.21 *Once a Thief:* Acrobatic Joe prepares to steal the *Harem Servant*.

EM.22 Virtuoso staging for the hospital battle in *Hard Boiled*.

Once a Thief reportedly grossed HK$33 million, four times the receipts of *Bullet in the Head*. By now *The Killer* had become known abroad, and Woo could design *Hard Boiled* as much for Western tastes as for his local and regional audiences. His last Hong Kong film is an anthology of action sequences (brilliantly staged by Philip Kwok Chun-fung, one of the greatest of Shaws' kung-fu performers). The opening is a titanic gun battle in a teahouse, with the cop Tequila (Chow Yun-fat) ducking, diving, and drifting through the cordite haze, pistols blazing. As usual, Woo makes ingenious use of site-specific props, when Tequila tilts a birdcage mirror in order to watch the gang and when he grabs a teakettle to slam into an attacker. The film concludes with a forty-five-minute siege of a hospital in which the gang have stored their arms. Woo and Kwok display inexhaustible (if exhausting) ingenuity in this climax (Fig. EM.22). They mix in somber drama when Tequila's undercover man Tony (Tony Leung Chiu-wai) accidentally shoots a policeman. There is relaxed comedy as well, as when Tequila quiets the baby he is trying to rescue: after plugging a thug, he goes into a calming nonsense lullaby. The baby saves him too, for when Tequila catches fire, the baby dampens the flames by wetting Tequila's pants.

The story is unusually slim for a late Woo, paralleling Tequila with Tony the undercover man. The affinities are merely sketched, and their growing mutual regard is never given the luscious definition and restatement we find in *The Killer*. Starting out focused on Tequila and his slain partner, the plot settles on Tony, perpetually tormented by an undercover assignment that obliges him to watch innocents murdered. Here, Stephen Teo has remarked, Woo recognizes the limits of a code of loyalty governing the closed world of crooks and cops; eventually brotherhood must answer to the higher claims of law and morality.[24] As something of a demo reel for Woo's move to America, *Hard Boiled* remains chiefly an exhilarating exercise in amplified genre conventions.

By this time Woo had become "Woo"; his signature style and themes had won him admirers all over the world. His fans rejoiced when *Face/Off*

112 **PLANET HONG KONG**

seemed at last to confirm that the master could make a Woo film, or at least a "Woo" film, in Hollywood. Here the authorial marks are reiterated in nearly caricatural degree. The psychopathic villains are devoted brothers, Castor and Pollux Troy; the hero is Scan (read John) Archer (another sign in the Zodiac). Castor has a woman, Sasha, and a son, Michael; he has killed Sean's son and left Sean and his wife (Eve!) with only a daughter. Woo gives up rendering heroic masculine communion in favor of portraying men's allegiances to their families, presumably an attitude more appealing to the American audience.

The parallel identities embedded in the plot of *A Better Tomorrow*, embroidered by the style of *The Killer*, and tossed off in *Once a Thief* now become a high-concept gimmick, the surgical switching of faces and bodies. Woo's repeated face-offs get literalized, Sean becoming Castor and Castor becoming Sean. And Castor mordantly comments on the artifice of the plot he's caught up in: "Ah, the eternal battle of good and evil." The more carefully judged scenes, such as the mirror/window confrontation of Sean-as-Castor and Castor-as-Sean, exemplify the literalness of the entire enterprise. The problem is that the plot has not justified any psychological likeness between them. Sean is obsessed with revenge, but he has none of Castor's sadism, egotism, or gonzo wit, and he does not ease himself into Castor's feelings, as Li does with John in *The Killer*. The visual parallels of *The Killer* are built upon genuine affinities between the protagonists, but here we have only the pictorial symmetries.

Everything in *Face/Off* becomes a self-conscious inflation of Wooness. Woo's religious imagery comes to a hyperbolic climax in yet another church scene, with the doves from *The Killer* flapping through in slow motion and the villain laying a pistol at Jesus' feet. And how to top action you've already taken over the top? Bigger explosions, more hurricane gunfights, thousands of rounds of ammunition, a speedboat chase left over from *Hard Target*, and lots of two-fisted firing as your men leap and soar. By now there are so many cameras trained on every actor that the capture of Pollux or Sean's prison break can be as elaborately disorganized as anything produced in Hollywood. What should have been a nerve-wracking facedown between Sean and his daughter, who takes him for Castor, serves only to launch a villain's quip ("No daughter of mine would shoot so wide"). Woo tells interviewers that he borrowed the water chase and the Virgin Mary from *The Killer*, the child amid violence from *Hard Boiled*, and the symmetrical cutting of the antagonists from *The Killer* to show "how good and evil function as if in a mirror."[25]

Hong Kong authorship, like everything else about this cinema, can outsize the norm: flamboyantly eclectic, aggressively distinctive. Woo is the ultimate Hong Kong auteur, fully aware of his directorial personality, adapting his themes and techniques to the needs of the moment, eager to make them his international calling card, ready to turn them into trademarks. "John Woo is God," my students tell me. The remark puts you in mind of two moments. The first occurs in *Plain Jane to the Rescue:* the heroine is working at an unemployment office, and John Woo comes up to her explaining that he's a movie director. Jane: "What does a director do?" Woo: "He's a god!" As he flings up his arms he is bathed in a beam of light. In *A Better Tomorrow,* Ho asks Mark: "Do you believe there is a God?" "Sure," Mark answers. "I am one . . . A god is someone who controls his own destiny."

5

MADE IN HONG KONG

Hong Kong's industry flourished for so long because of its power in regional markets. Income from overseas enabled companies to raise production values, which in turn kept the industry's neighboring rivals provincial. Until the early 1990s, it competed vigorously with Hollywood throughout East Asia, and even as it was flagging there, it was penetrating some niches of Western markets. Hong Kong filmmakers dedicated themselves to supplying mass-produced entertainment, and the concrete choices they made gave this form of entertainment its particular identity. Here the craft of moviemaking has ingeniously adapted to the demands of mass production.[1]

No money, no time: just do it.
RINGO LAM

In any cinema industry, films are produced in bulk so that theaters may regularly screen new product. During the 1900s and 1910s, the rapid success of U.S. film exhibition encouraged filmmakers to routinize production, thus creating a division of labor characteristic of the studio system. Some scholars have argued that around 1906 fiction films won the privileged place on our screens they have enjoyed ever since, because *actualités*, the brief documentaries showing parades, fires, and scenic views, could not be produced with the dependable regularity of scripted and staged movies.[2] The major film industries of Europe, Latin America, and Asia followed the principles of mass production.

One way to assure a flow of product is to create vertical integration, that situation in which each major company controls production, distribution, and exhibition. Historically, vertical integration has often come about when exhibitors acquire distribution outlets and production companies; this was the general trend in the United States (creating Fox, Universal, MGM, and Paramount) and in Japan. A vertically integrated industry is not a prerequisite for mass-market filmmaking, but it does provide great stability, making it likely that most films that are started get finished and shown.[3]

Hong Kong achieved robust vertical integration. In the 1960s Shaws and MP & GI (later Cathay) dominated Mandarin-language production, distribution, and exhibition, supported by their circuits of Southeast Asian screens. Integration of the Cantonese companies came somewhat later. In the early 1970s, when Golden Harvest began to take off as a production house, Raymond Chow moved quickly to lease theaters. In 1980 the Golden Princess theater chain underwrote Cinema City in order to have a supply of product. When jewelry retailer Dickson Poon launched D & B Films in 1984, he secured screen space by taking over the Shaws chain.[4]

Typically a Hong Kong chain has consisted of twenty to thirty screens, dotted throughout Hong Kong island, Kowloon peninsula, and the New Territories. In 1997 there were three Chinese circuits, each holding around twenty-five screens and needing thirty to forty local films per year. Because the production company gets no more than a third of the receipts, a movie can recoup its costs only by opening on the same day over an entire circuit. And a film's life is almost always brief. Many movies play only a week, a success plays two or three weeks, and a big success plays a month. The Hong Kong film world was amazed when *A Better Tomorrow* (1986) ran for sixty-one days. Second runs are virtually unknown; the film goes to video very quickly.

With most films having such quick playoffs, big profits have mattered less than rapid turnover. The golden slots at Lunar New Year, July, August, and Christmas have been reserved for vehicles for Jackie Chan, Stephen Chiau, and other superstars, along with feel-good family pictures. At other times exhibitors open mid-range star-based comedies or action pictures. In the early 1990s the weakest playdates were given to "break-even" films. Made for as little as HK$3 million (US$385,000), these movies earned skimpy theatrical returns, but, at least until the 1997–98 nosedive, producers could be fairly sure that broadcast and video sales would eventually cover costs. Just as Shaws and MP & GI formerly turned out program filler, Golden Harvest and other firms now invest in small projects chiefly to complete their release schedule and to keep cash flowing through the box office.[5]

From blockbusters to break-even items, Hong Kong achieved an enviably high and steady output for two decades.[6] Between 1977 and 1997, Hong Kong companies released between 90 and 135 mainstream films per year. (There were also a great many pornographic movies, which sometimes rivaled the number of mainstream releases.)[7] A parcel of two or three films per week gave the chains great flexibility. An exhibitor could keep the most successful films in several theaters while playing losers on a handful of screens during a second week. With so many films available, exhibitors could maintain the traditional segregation between local and imported product, reserving certain screens for Hong Kong films and others for Hollywood items.[8] One problem created by the 1997–98 crisis in output was that when a Hong Kong film failed in its first week, many exhibitors had no replacement handy and were forced to bring in an American film.

Regularized production demands routinized filmmaking. There must be budgets, schedules, and all the paperwork of tracking dozens of people through a complex work process. These routines require an efficiency and speed born of craft. Tsui Hark, whose *Chinese Feast* went from script to release in two months, points out: "Making a movie doesn't take a lot of time if everybody knows what to do."[9] Global income permits Hollywood filmmaking to be wasteful, but Hong Kong filmmakers have always placed a premium on calmly professional adherence to cost and schedule. Craft shows up onscreen in the film worker's hard-won, largely intuitive knowledge of the ways in which to accomplish the task—how to depict character in crisp, concise strokes; how to lay out a plot, intensify drama, spring a surprise; how to stage and shoot and cut a sequence to arouse excitement or sadness. A tradition gives the artisan some practical knowledge of the tried and true while also allowing room for innovation.

Whereas Hollywood directors count themselves lucky to make a film every three years, until quite recently Hong Kong filmmakers got to practice their trade constantly. Prodigality is a noble tradition here. Wang Tianlin started directing in 1950 and by 1973 had made more than 120 films; some 1950s and 1960s Cantonese directors are reputed to have finished more than 200. No one today can rival the output of the studio years, but directors still try to work fast and often. When Andrew Lau, director of the *Young and Dangerous* series, started his career, he was shooting one film in the morning and another in the afternoon.[10] In the late 1990s Lau was directing as many as 4 films per year.

In all domains, Hong Kong business has built its success on cheap labor. Unions, Run Run Shaw's nightmare, are still absent from the film scene. Even the major players are not getting rich by Beverly Hills standards. Only the top directors can obtain profit participation in a project; most are paid a flat salary and waive any rights to earnings downstream. Some increase their earnings by becoming producers, handling their own work or that of other directors. In the mid-1990s the salaries of director, producer, and screenwriter usually added up to around HK$1 million (US$128,000). Stars claimed bigger paychecks. The top female performers received HK$1–2 million per picture, the top males between HK$2.5 million (Jacky Cheung) and HK$5 million (Leslie Cheung's minimum).[11] So if a major male star made three films a year—a plausible schedule—he took home US$1–$2 million. This is very good pay compared to Europe and the rest of Asia but unacceptably low for the United States.

Costs stay low partly because of an ideology of professionalism. The industry depends on people who are willing to plunge into a project for a fixed wage and no benefits. Part of the Hong Kong spirit is a pride in knowing that through sheer dint of effort, one has turned meager resources into something worthy. The belief that you give your all for the production—from Jackie Chan's "I risk my life for my audience" to the production assistant combing the city for a prop—instills in film workers a cool self-sufficiency and a devotion to craft.

Tsui Hark, who needs little sleep and pushes his crews to the limit, acknowledges that during production he gets no real rest: "Every night you lie down and start the movie in your head."[12] The ones who survive learn to endure the pace. Many film workers come from television, which accustomed them to short schedules and unforgiving deadlines. As in most film industries, Hong Kong companies recruit young people, who tend to work very hard for little money. Clifton Ko started straight out of high school; Shu Kei began writing scripts when he was a college student. Most directors finish their first features before they turn thirty. Jackie Chan, Eric Tsang, John Woo, Danny Lee, and many others debuted as directors at twenty-five. In 1996 no working director was over fifty.

Most films made anywhere today are less elegantly designed than the American studio pictures of the 1950s. Location filming, a necessity in most film industries, has leveled out many differences between the big-budget product and the small picture. European and American technology, designed to trim costs and save time, has proved a godsend to marginal cinemas, and Hong Kong filmmakers have exploited the opportunities better than most of their rivals. The local supply house, Salon Films, has given them access to up-to-date equipment, such as lightweight cameras and portable lighting fixtures that make any setting filmable. Gyroscopically balanced camera braces have enabled low-budget filmmakers to get a professional look quite cheaply (especially now that audiences have come to tolerate shaky shots in big Hollywood productions). Local directors have used the great latitude of modern film stocks not to create muddy chiaroscuro, as in Hollywood, but to generate crisp, bright images. You can easily come to prefer Hong Kong films' brilliant images to the murky monochromatic look in fashion among U.S. cinematographers. Who would not find the luminous colors of Tsui Hark's *Peking Opera Blues* (1987) more attractive than the drab period palette of Woody Allen's film about theater, *Bullets over Broadway* (1994)? In addition, the worldwide availability of music synthesizers has allowed regional composers to create rich scores on tiny budgets, and Hong Kong has seized this opportunity. Some of the swordplay fantasies throb with wall-to-wall music.

Production efficiency is enhanced by the density of population. Meetings can be scheduled on short notice, and ideas get diffused rapidly. Compactness favors not only networking but also nepotism. Just as in Hollywood, where "the son-in-law also rises," family ties matter. One of Sammo Hung's brothers is a cameraman, another is an assistant director; his cousin is an editor. Tsui Hark's wife, Nansun Shi, was a producer and art director at Cinema City before she became Tsui's partner in Film Workshop. Like the Warners, Hong Kong brothers bond. The studios Guangyi and Shaws were run by brothers; Charles and Jimmy Heung oversaw Win's Entertainment. Ringo Lam's brother Nam Yin has been his principal scriptwriter. The productions of martial-arts director Lau Kar-leung often featured his brothers Lau Kar-fai and Lau Kar-wing, and when they took up directing he assisted them. Without this web of relations, friends, and friends of relations, production could probably not proceed so smoothly. And as in Hollywood, even rivals and ex-friends must collaborate for mutual benefit.

Exhibition sets the tempo for production, since playdates are often established well before shooting begins. Until the late 1990s the locomotives for the year's schedule were the Jackie Chan, Stephen Chiau, and Jet Li pictures, massively budgeted by local standards and likely to attract audiences overseas. Next comes the upscale comedy, drama, or action picture featuring currently bankable stars; examples would be *He's a Woman, She's a Man* (1994) and *The Big Bullet* (1996). Paralleling and overlapping this type is the prestige picture, often made with significant stars but on a moderate budget and unlikely to make money locally or regionally. The film is aimed at festivals with the hope of Western theatrical or television distribution. Many of the films of Yim Ho (*Kitchen*, 1997) and Stanley Kwan (*Red Rose, White Rose*, 1994) are prestige pictures. Below these lie the program pictures, mostly break-even propositions, although some, like the *Young and Dangerous* series, become top-grossers. A few films, notably those of Wong Kar-wai, cut across these tiers. Thanks to Wong's European and Japanese presales, he can use major stars and gain festival exposure for what remain, by Hong Kong standards, offbeat genre films.

With the exception of Jackie Chan's projects, in the mid-1990s a blockbuster might cost up to HK$50 million (US$6.4 million). At the other extreme, in 1997 the cheapest break-even production would cost HK$3–5 million (US$385,000–640,000). An upscale feature would run about twice that, around US$1 million. The cast, including at least one big star, would consume at least a third of the budget, with salaries for other personnel taking about a quarter. Production and postproduction costs would consume about another quarter. Add the cost of prints (twenty-five to thirty copies at HK$10,000 each) and advertising (HK$1 million maximum), and the typical bottom line would be HK$9–10 million (about US$1.2 million). Most American studio films cost twenty times this amount, but it is close to Europe's average.[13] With the 1997–98 dropoff, budgets were slashed drastically; the average film cost HK$4 million (US$500,000), and some were made for as little as HK$1.5 million (US$200,000).[14]

In Hollywood and Europe, financing comes from media conglomerates, banks, television companies, or government subsidy. Hong Kong films are typically bankrolled by individual investors and distribution/exhibition firms. During the 1989–1993 boom, for example, the two major Taiwanese distributors Long Shong and Scholar funded Hong Kong productions through presale of rights. Golden Harvest supplied two-thirds of its theaters' product by funding directors' companies with which they had a long relationship, buying the rest (mostly break-even fillers) from independents.[15] The distributor and investment company Media Asia contracted a few directors on a multifilm basis, to be supported by a pool of funds drawn from banks and private investors across Southeast Asia.[16]

A Hollywood project is almost always launched on the basis of a screenplay circulated by an agent. The script becomes the core of a package—a producer, a director, and stars interested in the script—at which point a studio invests in script rewrites. One purchased script in ten gets filmed, and it takes several years to get to the screen. Hong Kong makes things much simpler. The project usually starts as the director's idea. The director hires a scriptwriter to help create a synopsis, and then meets with potential investors. Some powerful producer-directors, like Tsui Hark, Sammo Hung, and Wong Jing, have financing more or less in place because they have contracted with Win's, Golden Harvest, Media Asia, or similar companies to provide a certain number of films per year.[17] They need only to propose a specific project.

In either case, the director can get funding and start production with only a synopsis, a budget, and a cast list. This system avoids the development hell of Hollywood's script-centered process. In Los Angeles, Terence Chang became frustrated at the number of petty meetings he had to take: "[In Hong Kong] I just went to my boss and said, 'Hey, I've got this director, this star, and I've got this budget, I can guarantee you'll have so much money in return if you make this movie,' and within half a day they would have given the green light to the picture."[18] Yet basing the funding decision solely on the pitch makes the script the vaguest part of the package. If Hollywood film scripts are overmanicured, Hong Kong ones often seem slapdash, and this is because the script is usually ill-defined throughout production.

A script is very unlikely to be an adaptation from literature or drama; Clifton Ko's *I Have a Date with Spring* (1994) and Shu Kei's *Hu-Du-Men* (1996) are exceptional in deriving from plays. The chief literary source is martial-arts fiction, notably the work of Jin Yong, which has provided situations for many swordplay movies. Recently Japanese *anime* and local comic books have become sources; if the *Young and Dangerous* comic sells 40,000 copies each week, a film adaptation can tap a preexisting audience.[19] Occasionally a current event makes it onscreen in fictionalized form; a sensational kidnapping involving both the triads and the People's Republic inspired *Operation Billionaires* (1998), and the case was still in the headlines when the film opened. Most often, a script's source is a genre premise, a successful Hong Kong movie, or a Hollywood movie.

Script writing has long been a fairly casual process. MP & GI (Cathay) and Shaws maintained a staff to work up scripts for the boss's approval; Wong Jing recalls that one Shaws writer turned out a script in three days.[20] Bruce Lee was furious that his first two films for Lo Wei had no screenplay of the sort he had used in Hollywood. The typical film was shot according to a rough story outline, with little indication of dialogue. Many directors, including the kung-fu master Lau Kar-leung, simply asked their players to recite numbers during takes and dubbed in lines later.[21] The New Wave generation developed somewhat more detailed scripts, but even then a script was seldom the product of a single hand. Since the early 1980s the most common screenwriting method has been "collective creation," or "brainstorming," and it is the source of some of the distinctive flavors of Hong Kong movies.

Whereas Hollywood typically passes the script from writer to writer, each one revising it until the decisionmakers think it jells, Hong Kong filmmakers do not spare the time for slow development. Instead, once funding has been secured, the director calls several screenwriters to a meeting and explains the project. An open discussion ensues, with everyone tossing in ideas for scenes, character traits, and dialogue. One writer takes notes. After five or six such brainstorming sessions, a writer is charged with synthesizing the ideas and preparing a draft script. This the director reviews before launching into production.[22] Cinema City refined this procedure, which became standard at Golden Harvest, Win's, and other companies. At first the companies employed a team of full-time scriptwriters; today directors fill their meetings with free-lancers.

The brainstorming process is not unknown in Hollywood—Spielberg and Lucas used it with screenwriter Lawrence Kasdan on *Raiders of the Lost Ark* (1981)—but gathering together several "idea men" to hash out situations and gags is something of a throwback to animation studios of the 1930s. The method puts a premium on imagination and quick-wittedness, and it swiftly initiates newcomers. Sandy Shaw, a senior scriptwriter at Win's, has mixed beginners and old hands in her sessions.[23] A policeman provided the idea for Kirk Wong's *Organized Crime and Triad Bureau* (1994), and by sitting in on brainstorming meetings he learned enough to become a professional scriptwriter. The Hollywood writer works in solitude and weaves a script line by line (only to see it unpicked by other hands), but Hong Kong encourages its writers to become gregarious founts of story ideas, for whom considerations of fine texture are secondary. Striking situations or gimmicks are most important, connective tissue comes next, and dialogue runs a distant third. Here is one source of the delirious and outlandish scenes that so appeal to Western fans: a group of writers, usually quite young, trying to outdo other filmmakers (and one another) in coming up with arresting incidents that must somehow be hooked up into a plot.

Aspiring Hollywood scriptwriters are usually taught to create a "three-act" script, planting the key "plot points" at one-quarter and three-quarters of the film's length. This schema is virtually unknown in Hong Kong. Instead, director and scenarists work within the ineluctable constraints of exhibition. Hong Kong movies must be 90–100 minutes long because theaters seek to maximize the number of shows. If the film runs around an hour and a half, six screenings can be squeezed in between noon and midnight.[24] This limitation on running time has provided a template for plot construction.

A movie running around ninety-five minutes consists of nine or ten reels of film, and in the mid-1970s Hong Kong filmmakers began to structure the action reel by reel. They outlined the plot so that the film would have a vigorous first reel, a major climax in the fourth reel, another climax in the sixth or seventh, and an overwhelming dénouement in the last reel or two.[25] Then, to keep things lively between the high points, they made sure that each reel was packed with gags, chases, and fights, however tangentially related to the main action. This strategy became second nature to scriptwriters; as Clifton Ko puts it, "It's virtually in our blood."[26]

At first glance, this compulsion to flood the audience with attractions seems to betray excessive anxiety. According to Ko, the fourth and seventh reel had to "keep them in their seats."[27] We might object that once people have spent half an hour in the theater, they are unlikely to leave. Perhaps the specter of indifferent or hostile midnight audiences compelled filmmakers to pump up interest at every moment.

Today many creators do not plot the film reel by reel, but there is still little pressure for complete and detailed scripting. Most films begin shooting without detailed screenplays; key dialogue is not fully written, and plot resolutions may remain to be worked out.[28] The blueprint for production is the story line, fleshed out during filming. Peter Chan put off solving major script problems on *Who's the Woman, Who's the Man?* (1996) until the very last day of shooting.[29]

The Hollywood ideal for a mid-range picture is 80 to 100 days of shooting, ten hours a day, but most shoots run over schedule. Needless to say, Hong Kong production is more pressurized. Each workday runs twelve to fifteen hours. During the high times of the late 1980s and early 1990s, the average shoot consumed up to 80 days, and elaborate martial-arts films needed up to 110 shooting days (still very brief by high-end U.S. standards). Producers mounting a coproduction in China had to plan on a lengthy stay, since the crews on loan from regional studios tended to work more slowly than Hong Kong staff.[30]

After the belt-tightening of the mid-1990s, shooting a midrange picture consumed only twenty to thirty days.[31] (Interestingly, this is about the production schedule of the high-end Cantonese studio pictures of the 1950s and 1960s.)[32] A more elaborate action picture or a big-budget star vehicle would take up to forty shooting days, while the lowest-budget movie would be filmed in sixteen days or less. Shu Kei, scrambling to fill a golden-slot playdate, took only eleven days to film the 106-minute *Love Amoeba Style* (1997). Armed with an unusually complete script, Cha Chuen-yee filmed *Once upon a Time in Triad Society 1* (1996) in ten days, which included location work in Japan.[33]

Most productions, even break-even ones, use a crew of thirty or more people, with a few assistants for the lighting supervisor and the cinematographer (who usually operates the camera). Until very recently all dialogue was dubbed in after editing, so there was no sound unit on the set. But since the dialogue might be finalized during shooting, with the director feeding the actors their lines, the dubbers needed a "guide track" recording what the performers actually said. So the staff member in charge of keeping track of what had been shot—the "script supervisor," in American parlance—would tape the actors' lines with a microcassette recorder. Sometimes the actors taped themselves, hiding the recorder in their laps. Chow Yun-fat is remembered as being very skillful at switching on the recorder while driving a car and firing a pistol at the same time.[34] Now many films use direct ("sync") sound, although some dialogue stretches are post-dubbed.

Regardless of the budget, all productions cut certain corners. There is no time to prepare storyboards, those comic-strip sketches that help Hollywood crews execute complex scenes. There is very little rehearsal; each actor goes into makeup with that day's dialogue pages and comes out with the lines memorized. The director will have to explain the scene's overall shape just before the shots are taken.

During the 1980s and early 1990s directors prepared action scenes in considerable detail. The trampolines and wires that allow characters to hurtle through space require a degree of attention that was seldom devoted to characterization and line delivery. Whereas a dialogue scene might be shot perfunctorily, a gunfight or kung-fu bout would need several days. The stunning combat on the ladders in *Once upon a Time in China* was filmed over two weeks. It was broken into segments and shot chronologically, with the martial-arts choreographers and Tsui Hark checking each day's footage and planning the next day's action on the basis of the best takes.[35] In recent years, financial pressures have forced directors to work faster, but they still lavish most of their time on action scenes. The climax of *Rock n' Roll Cop* (1994) takes place near the villages on the Mainland border. The chase shows men handcuffed together hurling themselves down hillsides, dodging bullets in marshlands, fistfighting in boats, and slashing at each other with cleavers in dusty streets. To film the scene, Kirk Wong's crew worked three days, ten to twelve hours each day.

Location shooting has long been a necessity. A few productions have the budget to build sets, but most scenes will be set in actual offices, apartments, streets, and bars. To cope with the vagaries of locations, the crew relies on well-tried craft habits. Short focal-length lenses are favored for interiors, since they cover a wide field of view. Bounce lighting supplies a serviceable if often flat illumination, although atmospheric shots will be streaked with transparent shadow, courtesy of fast filmstocks from Fuji and Eastman. Night scenes are often saturated in blue light or filmed through blue gels, then brightened by a splash of orange or ruby red. Location shooting puts a premium on shooting fast and getting out, so handheld camerawork, which saves time in shifting around the set, has become very popular. A handheld approach can yield thirty to fifty setups a day.[36]

Filming on location is riddled with problems. If neighbors complain, the police will order the filmmakers out, and triad gangs interrupt filming with demands for protection money. So filmmakers favor out-of-the-way sites. Since the early 1980s, action scenes have often been shot in vacant lots, construction sites, and inconspicuous alleyways. Setting off fires and explosions is illegal in Hong Kong, so pyrotechnic scenes are often staged in remote areas or on deserted stretches of highway.

Often, however, the plot requires a crowded location. Suppose the plot calls for a car chase down a busy Kowloon street. Until recently, the police would grant a permit, although the filming period would be restricted to two hours at most. For *The Final Option* (1994) Gordon Chan had only fifteen minutes to film a 7:30 A.M. chase, but he was allowed to return to the location a week later and repeat the scene—over another fifteen minutes.[37]

Well before shooting, the director and assistants will visit the scene and map out the action. On the day of the shoot, cast and crew will rehearse their moves for several hours before the area has filled with civilians. At the moment of filming, streets will be blocked off, traffic rerouted, and banners hung to warn people that shooting is in progress. Several cameras will probably be used, largely because the scene will probably not be played out more than twice. How much time would a crew have to shoot a ten-minute urban action scene? "Twenty minutes," grins low-budget director and cinematographer Herman Yau.[38] Facing ever-tightening budgets, directors are driven to guerrilla tactics. For *Full Alert* (1997), Ringo Lam filmed a tense pursuit through the arterials of Hong Kong island during five days of traffic; without blocking off roads or obtaining official permission, he managed to film cars whizzing between trams and flipping fatally over.[39]

Actors may perform in some action scenes, but doing so is risky; filming *Dragon Inn* (1992) in China, Brigitte Lin was struck by an arrow and had to return to Hong Kong for surgery.[40] Not even Jackie Chan executes all his own stunts. Crews include stunt doubles as well as "movement doubles," who handle special tasks like flying and wielding weaponry.[41] Stunt experts not only substitute for the stars but also play all the hapless triads, swordsmen, and Shaolin disciples mown down. Most have training in martial arts and Peking Opera techniques, so they can embellish their falls with somersaults and corkscrew spins. Hollywood stunt people break their landings with airbags and high-technology cushions, but Hong Kong filmmakers make do with mattresses piled on top of cardboard boxes—a technique learned, everyone will tell you, from watching Robert Wise film *The Sand Pebbles* (1965) in Hong Kong. Stuntman-turned-director Stanley Tong, who has broken his shoulder, ribs, knees, and elbow, ruefully recalls: "I've had my whole body set on fire and gone through a windshield, I've been hit by cars going thirty miles an hour, jumped from a helicopter onto a moving train in *Supercop* and off a bridge 90 feet high, driven a moving car that exploded while I was inside, and I jumped from shore onto a speedboat in *A Better Tomorrow 2*."[42] The stunt actor who gets injured usually has no contract and can expect little compensation.

The action choreographer is one of the most important members of the team and may well display more cinematic creativity than the official director. In an expansion of Hollywood's "second-unit" practices, the named director often supervises only the dialogue scenes and leaves the staging and filming of fights to the choreographer. Without storyboards or a shot-by-shot script, often without any shot lists, the action choreographer and the supervising director have become resourceful craftsmen who plan how to use the location and then move quickly through the scene. There is little time to try out a dozen angles or alternative ways of shooting a sequence. The director walks onto the site, confirms the best setups for different phases of the action, and with the help of the script supervisor keeps track of how the bits will cut together.

The *Young and Dangerous* series offers a clear instance of some ways in which recent belt-tightening has shaped craft practice and visual style. The films are shot very fast; *Young and Dangerous 4* was finished, from shooting through postproduction, in twenty-five days. Andrew Lau serves as both director and cinematographer. He rehearses his actors before they go to location, and he films in flowing handheld takes that can be cut together easily. As a result he can finish a lengthy scene in three to six hours, a brief dialogue in thirty minutes. Exploiting direct sound, he uses wireless microphone booms. He relies on wide-angle lenses to make composition easier, and he uses handheld lighting fixtures that can move with his camera. Sometimes offscreen actors will hold the lights.

Postproduction, the assembly and polishing phase, proceeds as swiftly as one would expect. Hollywood's ideal postproduction schedule is five to six months (now sometimes compressed to three for summer blockbusters), but Hong Kong filmmakers can assemble their films in two or three weeks, and never need more than two months. Computer-based editing systems, which can greatly speed up assembly, are seldom used here because of their expense, and because, one suspects, filmmakers are so used to cutting in their minds that they don't need them.

Once cut, the film is dubbed. Dubbed sound became entrenched during the late 1960s, giving birth to a cadre of "voice doublers" who sang or spoke for famous stars. The tradition continued when Jackie Chan, Sammo Hung, and Andy Lau hired professional doublers to deliver their dialogue, thus saving time and giving more polished line readings. Dubbing also allowed filmmakers to make last-minute changes. Tsui Hark taught younger directors that dialogue could be radically altered in postproduction; he sometimes gives new lines to actors whose lips aren't moving.

Since dialogue is not recorded during shooting (and often not written in advance), Hong Kong filmmakers have relied on conveying information visually. Directors can hustle actors around a set with no worry that they will move out of microphone range, and the editor can freely insert shots without regard for continuous dialogue. Shu Kei suggests that the fast cutting tempo of the 1980s sprang partly from the lack of direct sound.[43] Today, with audiences starting to regard direct sound as a mark of quality, some filmmakers are using longer takes for dialogue scenes. Long takes are also a production economy, since if they are carefully rehearsed they can yield more footage per shooting day.

When the first cut is ready the director sends a videotape of it to the composer. Well into the 1980s Hong Kong films were lifting music from records or other films. With the advent of electronic synthesizers and sequencers, composers have written, orchestrated, and recorded their own scores. The composer may have less than a week to come up with the film's entire music track. After the director has made suggestions for changes, the composer mixes the final score onto digital audio tape or a music CD.

The films are usually released with subtitles in Chinese and English, so cinematographers try to avoid putting important information too low in the frame. Hong Kong subtitles, as we've seen, provide great pleasure to the Western fan, but they were not always so clumsy. Shaw Brothers and Golden Harvest had their own subtitling departments, whose results were checked by native English-speakers. In the mid-1970s, with the revival of Cantonese-language film and a burst of independent production, there appeared tiny companies, often family businesses, to which filmmakers could farm out the task of making subtitles. The same routine is followed today. The firm receives an audiocassette of the film's dialogue. Employees—often high-school students in the family—transcribe the Cantonese and translate it into English. The firm typesets and shoots the titles and sends them back to be spliced into the film.[44] The whole process takes no more than two or three days and costs the equivalent of a few hundred U.S. dollars. No wonder that there are recurring grammatical howlers (using the negative for the affirmative, as in "Don't you have AIDS?") and a reluctance to translate song lyrics. And no wonder that in one film "Heil Hitler" becomes "Hi, Hitler." Since the subtitler doesn't see the film, signs, intertitles, and written messages tend not to be captioned. The subtitler also may have to guess from the soundtrack whether to use "he," "she," "you," and "I," because the subject of a sentence is often elided in Chinese. So even if a woman is holding a pistol, the subtitle may translate an onlooker's warning as "He's got a gun."

The same indifference to niceties of translation is revealed in the fact that the English-language title of a Hong Kong film is almost never equivalent to the Cantonese one. *The Tyrant Flowers of the Godly Courageous Flying Tigers* (1989) becomes *The Inspector Wears Skirts 2*. Sometimes the original title would carry little meaning in English, rooted as it is in traditional symbolism. The title *The Chinese Feast* (1995) is more significant to a Westerner than is *Gold Jade Full Hall* (the film's two stars had already been associated with jade and gold in an earlier title). Some English titles are drawn from American pop songs (*Always on My Mind*, 1993; *I've Got You Babe*, 1994). The difference between the Cantonese and the English titles may alter the way we approach the film. Call a movie *Two Blood-Spattered Heroes* (1989) and you weight Chow Yun-fat and Danny Lee equally, but by giving it the English title *The Killer* John Woo put Chow at the center. The English title can be concocted by anyone—producer, director, distributor, flunky—and nobody cares much about the result, as can be seen from inadvertently Dadaist titles like *Kung Fu vs. Acrobatic* (1990), *Burning Sensation* (1989), *Killing Me Hardly* (1997), *Temptation Summary* (1990), *Raped by an Angel 2: The Uniform Fan* (1998), and *Double Fattiness* (1988).

Before theater prints are struck, the film must be submitted to censorship. A government censorship body was established in 1953 and proved quite liberal with respect to sex and violence. Even so, during 1980–81 the authorities demanded excisions in a batch of particularly bloody films, most notably Tsui Hark's anarchic *Dangerous Encounter—First Kind* (1980). Ringo Lam's *On Fire* action pictures were significantly cut, as was Woo's *Hard Boiled* (1992).[45] Politics was a much more sensitive area. Censors banned Shu Shuen's *China Behind* (1974) for showing the depredations of the Cultural Revolution. After 1977, the Television and Entertainment Licensing Authority operated with a policy that no film could be shown which damaged "good relations with other territories." This effectively outlawed films critical of China; the Taiwanese import *The Coldest Winter in Peking* (1981) was withdrawn after a few screenings. As a result, Hong Kong filmmakers either steered away from criticizing China or did so in oblique ways (as in Clara Law's *Farewell China*, 1989). After the *Asian Wall Street Journal* disclosed that banning films was probably illegal, a film-censorship law was passed in 1988 reserving the right to excise footage that might offend other nations.[46]

5.1 *Young and Dangerous 4:* Chicken is in the foreground, and a young triad offscreen right is boastfully saying he'll free a captive woman if Chicken begs and calls him Daddy.

5.2 Chicken's pal leans over as the camera pans: "You can't do that. Let's go."

5.3 The camera shifts slightly to center and rack focus to Shuk-fan, who says only, "Chicken," reminding him of his duty.

5.4 Rack focus and pan slightly back to Chicken. He asks the thug to let the girl go.

5.5 Pan slightly to pick up the thug: "Call me Daddy."

5.6 Chicken accedes, and as the thug laughs in victory the camera moves back slightly to show the reactions of Chicken's friends.

routine. Hours spent polishing a script did not yield the tangible benefits of hours spent practicing and shooting vigorous combat. Of course, segment shooting is labor-intensive, but labor was something the Hong Kong studios had in abundance. Segment shooting also paid artistic dividends, yielding both variety and visual exactness. Whereas the master shot/coverage method tends to alternate between similar setups, segment shooting presents a rich range of camera positions, each one highlighting a certain piece of action, as in the scramble around the bedroom in *Peking Opera Blues* (Figs. 1.2–1.5). Segment shooting soon became a common procedure in comedies and dramas.

Craft routines born of economic pressures, then, can yield stylistic rewards.[51] But don't those pressures limit the film's value in the long run? Doesn't quantity inevitably drive down quality? Actually, rapid-turnover, high-output cinema tends to provide not *low* quality but a *range* of quality. Most films will be negligible, and many will be just fair. Yet some will probably be good, and a few may be excellent. How can this happen?

For one thing, a mass-output industry can give the most talented personnel a chance to work steadily and become masters. Yasujiro Ozu made more than forty films before he directed *Tokyo Story* (1953), John Ford more than eighty before tackling *Stagecoach* (1939). Middling talents also benefit from practicing their trade frequently, exploring different avenues and perhaps hitting upon genres or subjects that call forth their best. Even the hacks, the ones Hollywood calls traffic cops, must acquire the bare rudiments of craft. And apprentices learn from working with all. One reason today's Hollywood films look so unimaginative, sometimes barely competent, is that there are too many directors for hire and too many first-time directors anxious to work cheaply. A director has little chance to improve through constant practice.

In addition, a high-output industry encourages a prodigality of ideas. Hong Kong has no Stanley Kubricks, fiddling with a project for a decade. This system selects for the likes of Tsui Hark or Wong Jing, who come up with so many ideas for movies that they must farm directing chores out to others. Most of these ideas are likely to be bad ones, but simply having many balls in the air stimulates the community, and some of the ideas turn out well.

For this interchange to work, filmmakers must swipe from each other. Make a film called *01:00 a.m.* (1995), and someone is sure to make *02:00 a.m.* (January 1997) and *03:00 a.m.* (November 1997). The locals see Ralph Nelson's *Once a Thief* (1965), starring Alain Delon, and knock the plot off for *Story of a Discharged Prisoner* (1967). This version becomes the basis of *A Better Tomorrow* (1986), which yields two sequels. Soon the director of *A Better Tomorrow* makes a caper comedy he calls . . . *Once a Thief* (1991). He likes the title so much that he uses it again on a Canadian TV series he produces.

The rapid recycling of ideas can create its own form of competitive achievement. Hong Kong is famous for running a genre or fad into the ground, but before burnout takes place intriguing things can happen. Take the cycle launched by Wong Jing in 1989 with *God of Gamblers*. Other filmmakers pastiched and parodied it, and Wong Jing himself provided sequels, a prequel, and send-ups. What emerged was less a string of individual movies than a free-floating bank of images, characters, themes, tunes, and gimmicks—a method of cheating, a physical tic—on which any entry could draw. Each movie, in striving to outdo its predecessors, was forced to revamp the basic *données.* The *God of Gamblers* cycle exemplifies the sort of competition-driven ingenuity we find in the 1930s British detective story, where Marjorie Allingham and John Dickson Carr cheerfully tried to surpass Christie or Sayers in finding least-likely killers and new ways to commit locked-room murders.

Such variations on a hit also remind us that it is misleading to call movie companies film factories and assembly lines. The film industry trades on prototypes, not on replicas. Not even the *God of Gamblers* ripoffs are true clones. Because movies are made by serial manufacture, each one is a distinct challenge, to be met with all the skills the makers can muster. A better analogy than the factory might be the acting troupe obliged to open a new play every month, or the Renaissance workshop, with artisans commissioned to paint murals (even very banal ones). In a film studio, the production process is highly rationalized and depends upon sophisticated technology, but it remains genuine creation, not the mindless minting of copies.

Likewise, film workers are not mere automatons carrying out others' will. Sometimes directors take suggestions from their staff. Powerful workers, those with track records and clout, can affect the production process. And division of labor can foster graceful collaborative effort. For example, a director often builds up a trusted team, usually a small cadre of writers, cinematographers, composers, editors, and performers. Ford, Renoir, Ozu, Kurosawa, Hitchcock, Hawks, Sirk, and many other directors created such teams. Reliable collaborators need not be puppets; they bring unique gifts to the process and make contributions the director could not have anticipated. A studio-based system can be hospitable to the director's cadre, if only because administrators can plan that X, Y, and Z will be routinely assigned to certain projects. Some film industries, such as Japan's in the 1930s, put the production process securely in the hands of the director's team, with the producer okaying the project initially and then passing judgment on it at the end. This decentralized approach to production is one common way in which popular filmmaking can get the best out of its talents while also meeting its fiscal responsibilities.

Hong Kong has long balanced collective creation with business demands in just this way. Although Run Run Shaw claimed to oversee every production personally, his directors Zhang Cheh and Lau Kar-leung were able to assemble creative teams and push the martial-arts film in fresh directions. Once production became more decentralized during the kung-fu boom of the 1970s, the demand for rapid output discouraged producers' interference. Today, the speed with which a project can be started gives the director a great deal of control over the film—partly because the investment levels are fairly low, but also because the director has established a record for turning in acceptable work on time and within budget. Granted, most directors have not pushed their opportunities as far as they might, but the latitude yielded by Hong Kong's cadre system has produced King Hu, Tsui Hark, Wong Kar-wai, Johnnie To, and other innovative filmmakers.

Perhaps more vividly than Hollywood, Hong Kong films illustrate a dialectic between constraint and freedom that is characteristic of popular cinema. At the outset, demands of genre, casting, financing, and cost-cutting set stringent limits. Within those limits, however, and exactly because the industry is so small-scale, there is a stimulating looseness—plotting by brainstorming and improvisation on the set; incorporating last-minute ideas during cutting and dubbing; an openness to accident yielded by location filming; chances to push conventions of staging and shooting in fresh directions; provocative revisions of plot and genre; ever more elaborate manipulations of the human body created by challenging the performers to outdo themselves.

We now have a better sense where the films of the 1980s and 1990s got that audacious brio that wins fans' hearts. The makers could concentrate on becoming proficient in a very restricted batch of genres, and a vein of local talent could execute risky and picturesque stunts suitable for them. Exports supported rising budgets, and filmmakers concentrated on prolonged and spectacular set-pieces in the hope that something new and outrageous might impress midnight audiences. Perhaps most important, there was keen competition. With so many films on the market, creators had to offer many twists on familiar material. The variorum nature of popular tradition pushed them to copy, amplify, and invert every rival innovation. At brainstorming sessions, collaborators were goaded to push an idea further; on the set, actors and martial artists had to surpass what they and their peers had already done. Hence gratuitously wild scenes—a little girl and her dad shooting an enemy *(Gun Men)*, chickens raining down during a firefight *(The Outlaw Brothers)*, or a martial combat on ladders *(Once upon a Time in China)* or on the heads of the onlookers *(Fong Sai-yuk, 1993)*.

The profusion of ideas also suggests that here popular cinema flourished because many of its creators became addicted to the rush of making it. Steady, high-speed production originates in purely economic need, but it can quickly become a game pursued for its own sake, a competition/cooperation among professionals who want to excel. The result is a product for the market, but the creative reward, and perhaps the greatest value, comes from honing a craft one loves. No other cinema—certainly not Hollywood or most European filmmaking—conveys so well the pure nervous exhilaration of making a movie. A Hollywood producer says that he now turns out films "to keep the library fresh, to build an asset base, so when you sell your company you can sell it for more."⁵² Hong Kong filmmakers, with no asset base to speak of, tend to be in the business as much for love as for money. They take keen pleasure in creating films, talking about films, speculating about films. The bravura onscreen comes partly from filmmakers who strive to work at the top of their game.

This guilt-free zest is visible in that quaint convention whereby the final credits unroll over outtakes and bloopers from the shooting. No modernist reflexivity here. Anachronistic by international standards (they recall the tiresome blooper credits of 1970s Burt Reynolds movies), these montages announce the films' eagerness to please, trading on the performers' endearing embarrassment when gags or stunts or solemn moments fail to come off. The credits celebrate the strenuous effort and cheerful informality of Hong Kong showmanship.

Mass-output filming demands regularized production, but this need not lower quality. Speed, efficiency, tight budgets, shameless commercialism, networking, commitment to tradition (even cliché), ingenuity in working variations on familiar material, and a contagious enthusiasm for the very act of putting together a piece of entertainment—all can sustain filmmakers in their dedication to craft. And in popular filmmaking, craft is the source of a great deal that is good.

A CHINESE FEAST: TSUI HARK

In a cement-block complex smelling of deep-frying and cigarette smoke, Film Workshop has its quarters. The offices are spacious but spartan: no mahogany executive suite, no plush screening rooms. One room is all gray cubicles. In a large loft next door several young men, surrounded by Post-Its and pinned-up character drawings, hunch over computers tweaking the animated feature *A Chinese Ghost Story*. The flashiest spot is the reception area, with its gleaming Film Workshop logo, a blowup from *Once upon a Time in China*, and a cartoon mural of the Workshop staff, with its leader sitting at the center, frowning behind dark glasses and a long cigar.

Tsui Hark (pronounced *chui haak*) moves swiftly from meeting to meeting before settling down for an interview. He is slender, with glowing eyes, a famous goatee, and a forbidding demeanor. He gives the impression of a coiled spring. This is the man who can shoot for thirty-six hours straight, who can cut, dub, mix, subtitle, and print a film in five days and still be making "small revisions" four hours before a midnight show.[1] He responds to questions courteously and at length, but seldom directly; thoughts spin off in a dozen directions. Tsui is an intense talker who conveys both the pragmatism of a producer and the energy of a director.

There are two versions of what happened to Hong Kong film during the 1980s, and he is central to both. In the optimistic version, Tsui was the key innovator and modernizer. His first feature, *The Butterfly Murders* (1979), was a revisionist martial-arts film; *We're Going to Eat You* (1980) brought something of the wildness of 1970s American exploitation to a tale of cannibalism; and even the censored version of *Dangerous Encounter—First Kind* (1980) offered blistering criticism of social inequities in the colony. According to Li Cheuk-to, *All the Wrong Clues (For the Right Solution)* (1981) "made modern, streamlined comedies about high life a staple of the Hong Kong cinema."[2] *Zu: Warriors from the Magic Mountain* (1983) brought Hollywood special effects to a quasi-mystical swordplay fantasy.

After forming his independent company Film Workshop, Tsui launched a firecracker string of films that were frantic, colorful, and triumphantly new. As producer and director, he pioneered heroic gunplay (*A Better Tomorrow*, 1986), historical adventure (*Peking Opera Blues*, 1986; *Gun Men*, 1988; *The Raid*, 1991), and futuristic fantasy (*Roboforce*, 1988; *Wicked City*, 1992). He revived and updated the Shanghai comedy (*Shanghai Blues*, 1984), the ghost romance (*A Chinese Ghost Story*, 1987), the swordplay fantasy (the *Swordsman* series, 1990–1993; *Green Snake*, 1993), and the kung-fu drama (the *Once upon a Time in China* series, 1991–1997; *Iron Monkey*, 1993). In 1997 he remade *A Chinese Ghost Story* as Hong Kong's first animated feature.

Tsui consolidated the slick look and the vulgar, freewheeling imagination that became the hallmarks of Hong Kong cinema for world film culture. From Film Workshop came bloodbaths of male honor and sacrifice, kung-fu duels on flaming posts and oil-slicked floors, cross-dressing swordfighters and bisexual lords of the underworld, giant tongues and rampaging oversize clocks and shotgun-blasting women in trench coats—all the outrageous splendors that regaled Western fans and, on many occasions, won big box office throughout East Asia. By this reckoning, Tsui has been the most farsighted creative force of the past twenty years.

According to the other version of 1980s history, Tsui epitomizes the lost promise of the New Wave. His first three films flung down challenges to mainstream cinema, but all were box-office disasters. So, the story goes, Tsui lost interest in social provocation and channeled his volcanic energy into noisy lowbrow entertainment. He recycled old movies and tired genres while shamelessly copying Hollywood trends; not for nothing is he called the Stephen Spielberg of Hong Kong. Worse, say his critics, having created Film Workshop as a haven for independents, he turned into a meddlesome producer. He recut Woo's *A Better Tomorrow* and took over Yim Ho's *King of Chess* (1992); some say he tried to overhaul *The Killer* (1989). Ching Siu-tung was credited as director of *A Chinese Ghost Story*, but Tsui shot and edited many of the dramatic scenes. He arranged for King Hu's comeback project *The Swordsman*, but the two disagreed so strongly that Hu left the production. In this version of history, Tsui pulled the New Wave into the mainstream, dumbing down local cinema and leaving no niche for personal filmmaking. Ambitious directors stifled their own inclinations and obediently stamped out Tsui Hark product. No surprise that he would keep trying to make movies in Hollywood, from *The Master* (belatedly released in 1992) to *Double Team* (1997) and *Knock Off* (1998).[3]

It is true that Tsui was never one to work modestly and patiently. His output—as of late 1998, he had directed twenty-six features and produced another two dozen—certainly stems from a temperament that needs to move at full throttle. It seems that he finds the act of making the film more satisfying than the product. He prefers Hong Kong to Hollywood, he says, because here while he's shooting one film he can be planning his next. He also likes to act in films directed by others. He has made "benefit films," like *Twin Dragons* (1993), a Jackie Chan vehicle he codirected to aid the Directors' Guild, and *The Banquet* (1991), a comedy that raised money for Chinese flood victims.

It is also true that Tsui sees his collaborators as assistants. "Ideas come easy to me": so easy that he can't direct all the films he dreams up. Once he has got financing for a project, he controls his productions by overseeing brainstorming sessions and creating a "production diary" detailing how the ideas should be carried out. Although some Film Workshop projects have explored offbeat styles, such as Daniel Lee's *Black Mask* (1996), most look very close to the Tsui prototype.

Tsui's pragmatism and hands-on approach guarantee a marketable product. He believes that in the Hong Kong industry anyone who doesn't churn out new work will fall by the wayside. He noticed in the 1970s that television was constantly threatening cinema, because it was offering freer creative circumstances to young talent like himself. Tsui recognized that only constant innovation could keep the industry healthy. The sort of innovation he had in mind was probably not too radical; he has criticized the New Wave for having technical expertise but little commercial sense.[4] *Dangerous Encounter*, still in many ways his most experimental film, was something of an exception. *The Butterfly Murders* and *We're Going to Eat You* were flamboyant genre revisions, closer to the mainstream than the more veristic exercises of Allen Fong and Ann Hui. Though nonconformist in certain ways, Tsui's earliest efforts display his eternal penchant for grotesquerie and vulgar comedy, both solid Hong Kong traditions. He would have been unlikely to lead the New Wave toward radical avant-gardism.

Tsui is one of the few Hong Kong directors to be a true film brat. "I am a crazy movie freak."[5] He was born in Vietnam in 1951 and started making super-8mm films at age thirteen. When he got out of high school he spent two years at loose ends, watching three or four movies a day. After graduating from the film program at Southern Methodist University in Dallas, he worked briefly in New York before returning to Hong Kong in 1977. He quickly began directing for television, and the success of his *Gold Dagger Romance* series led to *The Butterfly Murders*. Tsui called the film "a futuristic costume drama," cannily aiming at both fans of martial arts and young people wanting something more modern.[6] Tsui set himself some severe technical problems, like evoking thousands of swarming butterflies and lighting lengthy scenes in caverns. Shot in Taiwan, *The Butterfly Murders* is far more polished than most late 1970s Hong Kong films.

After two more commercial failures, Tsui made *All the Wrong Clues* for Cinema City. It was a tame spoof, but it showed great technical bravado. Avoiding the flat lighting and casual set design of Cantonese comedies, Tsui experimented with saturated comic-book colors and amusingly exaggerated chiaroscuro. *All the Wrong Clues* was one of 1981's top-grossing films and earned Tsui the chance to make *Zu: Warriors from the Magic*

Mountain. Golden Harvest gave him an unprecedented HK$30 million budget to import special-effects experts from the United States. The result, however, was quite un-Hollywood in its strident color design. The film attracted less than HK$2 million at the box office and sent Tsui diving for safety, directing the third installment of Cinema City's *Aces Go Places* series, *Our Man from Bond Street* (1984). Tsui brought a Pop-Art sensibility to the sets and played with ambitious robot effects. He pledged himself to entertainment. "We can't make mature films all the time. Sometimes it's fun to be stupid."[7]

Our Man from Bond Street was the top hit of 1984 and gave Tsui the power to set up Film Workshop. His wife, Nansun Shi, a Cinema City executive who also designed the sets for *Our Man from Bond Street,* joined him as a producer. *Shanghai Blues* (1984) was the first Film Workshop release, but the firm's major successes came two years later, with *A Better Tomorrow* and *Peking Opera Blues.* Both placed in the year's top ten pictures, and they proved hugely popular in Japan, Taiwan, and Korea. Film Workshop was now able to obtain financing from overseas, boosting budgets to between HK$7 million and $30 million.

In a 1988 interview Tsui defined what Film Workshop asked of its directors:

1. You must develop your own style.
2. There must be content—even if it's kung-fu, there must be a point to it.
3. You have to "go the way of the masses" . . . A commercial film must be entertaining, cathartic, and make a person feel better. Film is a mass medium. Hopefully we will become one with the audience . . . The masses go to feel, not to understand.[8]

Tsui and Shi declared that Film Workshop had to keep up with viewers' tastes. When the audience tired of comedies, Film Workshop established a new trend with *A Better Tomorrow.* It set off another one in 1987 by reviving the costume fantasy in *A Chinese Ghost Story.* Film Workshop milked its hits. Although Woo virtually disowned *A Better Tomorrow II* (1987), it did very well, and Tsui took over directing *A Better Tomorrow III: Love and Death in Saigon* (1990).

After a surge of success, Film Workshop ran into problems. *The Swordsman* was in production from 1988 to 1991, employed six directors in all, and wound up costing twice its initial budget of HK$15 million. Over the same years Film Workshop had several box-office failures. Tsui amply redeemed himself with *Once upon a Time in China* (1991), which starred the new Mainland import Jet Li as a revered Cantonese folk hero. It was a hit both domestically and abroad, especially in the large Korean market. Buoyed by its success, Film Workshop released twelve features in 1992 and 1993, many of them sequels to *Swordsman* and *Once upon a Time in China,* along with genre variants like *Magic Crane* (1993) and *Green Snake* (1993). Only two placed in the local top ten, and most of them failed in the

CF.3 *Once upon a Time in China:* Huang Feihong balances his adversary on a ladder.

CF.4 Later in the scene, the two battle on upright ladders.

more shot from a different spot. The astounding final combat of *Once upon a Time in China* takes place in a warehouse. Huang Feihong fights the old sifu on the ground, on catwalks, and on ladders, and, with scarcely any repeated setups, the nearly three hundred shots render the action utterly intelligible and maximally forceful (Figs. CF.3–CF.4).

As in the fluid sound/image interchanges of *Shanghai Blues, Peking Opera Blues* showcases Tsui's inventive use of music. The opera scenes are cut to James Wong's throbbing score, and the spectacular rooftop battle employs a carefully modulated ostinato, broken by stings that accentuate key action. From the start Tsui explored speech as well. *The Butterfly Murders* anticipates Wong Kar-wai's experiments with voice-over narration by beginning with the scholar's recollection and then *nearly* ending it with his final ruminations—except that he walks out of the action, declaring in voice-over, "I never found out what happened." Tsui goes on to show us how things turned out. It is a device he will pick up nearly twenty years later in *The Blade,* where a secondary character's running commentary yields an inadequate understanding of the action. Tsui even goes so far as to mock local films' error-prone English subtitles. One scene of *Working*

A CHINESE FEAST   143

Class (1985) translates Cantonese Opera lyrics into nonsense Italian: "La scala, mama mia . . . Machismo si si pronto."

Some argue that Tsui's best years were the 1980s, and it is true that many of his latest films have been mechanical exercises. Nonetheless, the three movies he released in 1995 showed that his versatile talents could still work at full stretch.

Love in the Time of Twilight showcased Nicky Wu and Charlie Young, two pop singers who had been successful in Tsui's costume romance *The Lovers* (1994). Instead of making a carbon copy, he set himself new problems in storytelling and special effects. Again the context is popular theater, this time in 1930s Shanghai. Yan Yan works in her father's vaudeville troupe and, during a visit to a matchmaking temple, bumps into the bank clerk Kong. They quarrel so energetically that we know they are destined to fall in love. Kong is seduced by another woman, who secretly fills his briefcase with pistols. Kong unwittingly carries the pistols past security guards into the bank, where the woman's gangster boyfriend uses the guns for a robbery. He then strangles Kong. Kong's ghost visits the theater and explains to Yan Yan what has happened. He asks Yan Yan to go back in time with him to thwart the robbery and save his life.

Like Marty in *Back to the Future 2*, Kong the ghost and the transported Yan Yan encounter themselves in the past; and like *Groundhog Day*, the film delights in replaying earlier scenes. (Tsui the film freak slightly changes camera angles in the replayed scenes so that the doubles are forever ducking out of the frame.) To complicate things further, the gangster also finds a way to revisit the past and tries to thwart the couple's efforts to change history. The special effects are handled adroitly, but Tsui is chiefly interested in piling up misunderstandings to a height unattempted in Hollywood movies. His lovers from the future quarrel with their earlier selves and adopt disguises that confuse each other. In a fit of anger the gangster, heedless of the consequences, tries to kill his past self. The confusion culminates in a hide-and-seek chase in the theater involving all three pairs of doubles, each one ignorant of the whole situation. Folding in upon itself again and again, *Love in the Time of Twilight* is Tsui's effort to beat Hollywood time-travel comedy at its own game.

The Blade looks back further for inspiration, to Zhang Che's *One-Armed Swordsman* (1967), but it tries out a female point of view. Siu-lung, daughter of a swordmaker, fantasizes that the blacksmiths Ding On and Iron Head are competing for her. Ding On loses his sword arm in an effort to protect Siu-lung from an outlaw gang, and she is carried off by Iron Head. Ding On is nursed back to health by an orphaned, nearly feral tomboy, and he sets about retraining with his father's broken sword and a charred combat manual. He finally tracks down Fei Lung, the tattooed outlaw who killed his father, and while the women and Iron Head watch, he engages Fei in a furious duel.

Well aware that what he calls the "software generation" has particular

CF.5 *The Blade:* The hero launches a dazzling spin as his target waits implacably in the foreground.

CF.6 *The Blade:* The hero attacked by his father's murderer.

tastes, Tsui gives us his version of MTV—which is, needless to say, like nothing you have seen on MTV. Everything in *The Blade* is bent toward heightening one emotion: ferocity. It is nightmarishly raw not just in its incidents (it begins with a dog caught in a wolf trap) but also in its style. Swords are banged into shape on anvils; tom-toms pound out a frenzied rhythm. The world is in flames. Charged dialogues are filmed in firelit close-ups. The combats were shot from a crane, but they still rattle the camera: through a walkie-talkie Tsui instructed his operator to swivel against the grain of a character's movement, to zoom abruptly to a distant detail, or to struggle to reframe the action. In many films such a rough-edged style is just distracting, but here it presents a phantasmagoric world ruled by agony and aggression. Blades become an obsessive motif, each character defined in relation to them; at one point, the Christian cross becomes yet another sword. The climax, one of the most visceral swordfights in Hong Kong cinema, is all silhouettes in billowing dust, twisting and spinning attacks, clashing chains and sawteeth and snapping traps (Figs. CF.5–CF.6). Few films leave the viewer so physically drained.

Neither *Love in the Time of Twilight* nor *The Blade* was a box-office success, but *The Chinese Feast*, Tsui's film for the 1995 Lunar New Year, did very well. One of Hong Kong's zestiest comedies, it stages a cooking contest as a martial-arts tournament, complete with challenge, training sessions, flamboyant rival styles, and secret winning techniques. Yet this makes the movie sound too straightforward, for here we find Tsui in his goofy mood. Sun is a triad debt collector trying to learn cooking in order to emigrate to Canada and join his girlfriend. He apprentices to a restaurant where Ka-wai, also trying to evade responsibility, dyes her hair punkily and acts like a lunatic, hoping to shock her father into kicking her out. Wong, a rival entrepreneur, challenges Ka-wai's father to cook Qing and Han Imperial Feast, the supreme test of skill. Upon accepting the challenge the father promptly has a heart attack. Sun and Ka-wai must coax a retired Mainland chef out of his drunken torpor to help them.

On this promising plotline Tsui hangs wonderful nonsense. Sun's min-

CF.7 *The Chinese Feast:* High angles in the opening credits . . .

CF.8 . . . announce that camera angles will link people and food.

ions are not triad thugs but MBA yes-men. In a karaoke bar, Ka-fai screeches out Carmen's *habañera*, hoping to win Sun's attention. The tune becomes a soundtrack motif and permits Tsui to weave concertina, harp, and castanets into a crazily eclectic score. When Ka-fai learns that Sun's girlfriend is Japanese, she imagines herself in a Puccinian farewell waving tearfully as he sails off. The entrepreneur Wong, played with leering swagger by kung-fu master (and main villain of *The Blade*) Hung Yan-yan, plans to devour all of Hong Kong's restaurants; explaining that many successful men love shark fin, he strips a strand off with his teeth. There is satire of Shenzhen's efforts to go capitalist, and hugger-mugger with a giant flopping fish that invades the restaurant. The sodden master chef, Kit, must have all his five senses reawakened, which encourages Tsui to mount gags on acupuncture, aerobics, and, inevitably, farting. The Qing and Han banquet concludes with orders to find new ways to cook bear paw, elephant trunk, and monkey brain. To prepare "Golden Eyes and Burning Brain," our heroes apparently saw open a live monkey's skull and, while Sun cheerfully explains, "We don't need to cook fresh food," pour hot oil on the brain, letting the poor creature squeak in agony.

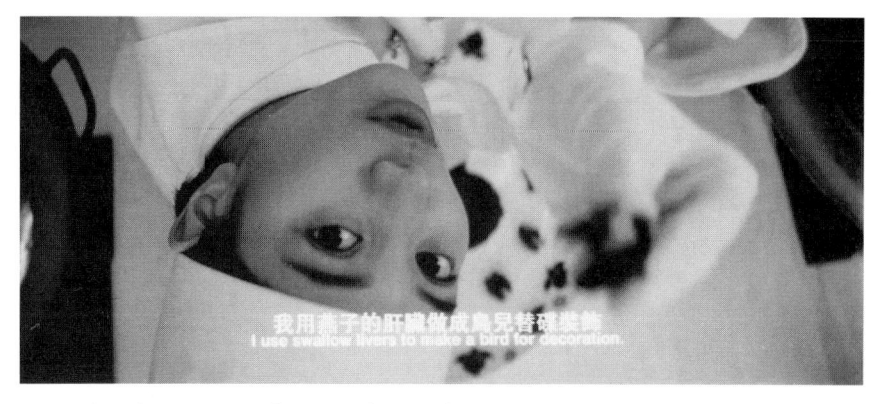

CF.9 *The Chinese Feast:* the crane shot neatly inverting Ka-wai as she decorates a plate.

CF.10 Making a monkey of Master Wong.

What *Shanghai Blues* does for popular music, what *Peking Opera Blues* does for opera, what the *Once upon a Time in China* series does for herbal medicine and the lion dance, this movie does for Chinese cuisine. Cooking becomes a lively, endlessly inventive popular tradition. A chef's genius is sensuously creative, coaxing new tastes from common ingredients. (Here is one retort to Tsui's critics: Like a filmmaker, a chef must adjust his art to his customers' tastes.) Since the preparations are part of the pleasure, the camerawork here is as fluent as it is disconcerting in *The Blade,* and the cooking scenes are shot with the bristling panache of kung-fu exercises.

Food, as one serving in the credits reminds us (Fig. CF.7), is at once yin and yang, the center of social life. Tsui's straight-down crane shots not only give us the best view of the dishes, as in the mouth-watering first image, coasting over course after course, but also turns people into food (Figs. CF.8–CF.9). The camera angles prophesy the bald Wong's defeat by likening him to the climactic night's entrée (Fig. CF.10). Above all, the film insists, real food comes from the heart. Most of the characters start by treating food as a pretext or a nuisance or a means to a selfish end: Sun needs to get to Canada, Ka-wai wants to break free of her father, Wong wants to rule the

A CHINESE FEAST

CF.11 The final shot of *The Chinese Feast:* Tsui leads cast and crew in a New Year's toast.

Hong Kong restaurant business. The master chef, Kit, still wields a mean chopper, but he no longer feels the food. The contest reawakens everyone to food's role in love and community. At the very end, Ka-wai has become her father's kitchen boss and is casually decorating a barbecued pig with birthday candles. Earlier, when Kit begins to recover his skill, his lover starts to cook for him. Her business life has taken away her taste for food, and she hopes that his recovery will make her enjoy it again. In response he sets a morsel of pork on her rice. "I've become a vegetarian," she says thoughtfully, and eats it.

Since this is a New Year's comedy, expect none of the bittersweet partings that conclude *Shanghai Blues* and *Peking Opera Blues.* Food brings all Chinese together. Master Kit's ally hails from Beijing; Kit lives in the new "economic zone" of Shenzhen; Ka-wai and Sun are thoroughly of Hong Kong, and by the end Sun decides not to emigrate. The banquet, or as the Cantonese title has it, "Gold Jade Full Hall," makes room for everyone. Appropriate, then, that in the epilogue all the wedding guests wind up squeezed into the kitchen cooking (this is a *Chinese* feast). And when they eventually settle down in the dining room, Sun's toast expands to include the entire crew, who turn and toast us (Fig. CF.11). In Tsui's best films, Hong Kong cinema becomes a Chinese feast, spiced by indigenous entertainment traditions, replenished by an artist's pragmatic energy and restless imagination.

6

FORMULA, FORM, AND NORM

We tend to think of the conventions of popular cinema as constraints, but I suspect that they are truly limiting only to the artists who don't see the opportunities they offer. Conventions are enabling. They attract an audience by their familiarity, and they give the artist a structure within which to exercise his or her talents. When certain choices are imposed by tradition—write a thirty-two-bar song, a sonnet, a three-act play with strong curtain lines—then the remaining choices become all-important. Since no popular artwork is an exact duplicate of another, even the strictest conventions afford a zone of creative freedom.

Workers in popular entertainment face problems of mastering a standard and differentiating each work, achieving familiarity and yet introducing novelty. Through trial and error, filmmakers have forged several norms capable of wide-ranging variation. This chapter focuses on three sets of norms central to Hong Kong cinema: genre conventions, the star system, and visual style. The next chapter looks at broad principles of storytelling. All of these norms and forms offer filmmakers both enabling frameworks and occasions to stretch their craft.

How do you get overseas sales before the shooting even begins? You have to sell relying on either the actors or the genre—anything that is tried and proven.
WONG KAR-WAI

Since mass-output cinema requires a steady flow of releases, there are always pressures toward predictability. And in an industry of prototypes rather than replicas, producers of entertainment take a substantial risk with every project: a new movie is hardly as sure to succeed as Windows 98.™ Those who condemn popular art as hamstrung by repetition often forget that a record company or movie studio exists by virtue of financial investment, and producers are always under the obligation to make that investment as safe as possible. Genres and stars can reduce risk and promote predictable output. The average viewer's taste is made up principally of favorite genres and stars, and fan magazines are built around them. American distributors selling foreign rights base the prices on these ingredients.[1] In Hong Kong, retro exercises like *Days of Tomorrow* (1993), *The Golden Girls* (1995), and *The Umbrella Story* (1995), which celebrate the genres and stars of earlier eras, attest that these remain strong appeals.

At the center of any genre is an interplay between familiarity and novelty, convention and innovation. Genres cross media, so it comes as no surprise that a film genre typically arises from conventions ruling literature and drama. In Hong Kong, Cantonese Opera films dominated 1950s and 1960s production. Erotic romances filmed by Li Hanxiang during the 1970s were based on literature and folktales.[2] Chivalric love stories, detective stories, stories of flying swordfighters, and tales of amazing martial feats were all literary genres before they made their way into cinema. Ghosts and zombies drift into film from folk culture and Chinese opera.

Foreign imports also inspired new genres. James Bond was hugely popular in the colony, so by 1967 20 out of about 150 Cantonese titles involved spies.[3] Hollywood's surge of big-budget cop films, starting with *Dirty Harry* (1971) and *The French Connection* (1971), eventually created one of the most popular and long-lasting Hong Kong genres, from *Jumping Ash* (1976) onward. It is likely that 1970s Hong Kong farcical comedy was influenced by Mel Brooks and Blake Edwards.[4]

In any national cinema, genres coalesce into a rough hierarchy. In Hong Kong, the musical comedy has been box-office poison for years (surprising, given the pervasive presence of pop stars onscreen). *Hong Kong Graffiti* (1995), Teddy Robin Kwan's effort to make a 1960s retro musical, and *Whatever Will Be, Will Be* (1995), a children's choir movie, were resounding failures. The comparative success of *Phantom Lover* (1995) is usually attributed to the fact that this remake of a Shanghai classic had unusually high production values and star power.

Since the mid-1970s comedy and action pictures (including kung-fu, crime thrillers, and swordplay) have remained the leading genres.[5] The modernization of Hong Kong film in the 1980s drove out some traditional genres, like the costume drama centering on romantic entanglements of rulers. One Shaws director, Li Hanxiang, made his reputation with these "palace-chamber" *(gongwei)* movies during the 1960s, but they were too costly to produce once the big studios closed. Although Ann Hui's sumptuous and elegant *Romance of Book and Sword* (1987) arguably comes close to being a *gongwei* drama, the genre has not flourished.

Some genres gained new popularity with the rise in production values. Boosted by new special effects, Tsui Hark's *Zu: Warriors of the Magic Mountain* (1983) upgraded the chivalric fantasy, producing images with comic-book flair. Tsui's experiments would underwrite his revival of fan-

6.1 *Mr. Vampire:* The ghost princess sends a glowing dagger flying to Kau, but he returns it to her.

tasy swordplay in *A Chinese Ghost Story* (1987) and come to digital maturity in Andrew Lau's *StormRiders* (1998). Another genre that benefited from Hong Kong's modernization was the film of supernatural fantasy. Because Chinese tradition holds that nature is alive with unseen powers, there is a fear of evil spirits and the dead, who can return to disturb the living.[6] During the mid-1970s, Hong Kong directors upgraded local horror by borrowing from Hollywood; *The Exorcist* (1973) was copied in *The Devil in Her* (1974). Still, it was not until the ever-creative Sammo Hung came up with a mix of comic kung-fu and ghost story in *Encounter of the Spooky Kind* (1980) and *The Dead and the Deadly* (1982) that the supernatural film became part of the 1980s upgrading of technique.

Hung also produced *Mr. Vampire* (1985) for Golden Harvest, a bonanza that yielded three sequels, as well as trading cards and comic books. It remains one of the most amusing exercises in the genre. A *fat si*, or Taoist master of things supernatural, assigns his clumsy assistants to shift an unluckily buried corpse, but they allow the body to escape, and it becomes a vampire. In Chinese lore vampires suffer from an imbalance of yin and yang and must feed on the living. Unlike debonair Western vampires, they are simply rotting corpses, hopping stiff-legged after their prey. How do you halt a movie vampire's attack? By slapping a yellow Taoist scroll to its forehead, by holding your breath, by dipping a string in ink; best of all, as in Western movies, by driving a stake through its heart.[7] Such elements serve as comic devices in *Mr. Vampire,* which also made use of some Tsui-style special effects (Fig. 6.1).

The genre hierarchy changed in another way during the early 1980s. Because of the need to satisfy a broad audience at home and overseas, producers developed the "multigenre" movie. An influential model was the action comedy *Aces Go Places* (1982). Sek Kei argues that Stephen Chiau's *All for the Winner* (1990) succeeded so spectacularly because it combined action, comedy, gambling, romance, and the theme of China.[8] Virtually no Hong Kong movie would become a "pure" genre piece; at the least, there would be dashes of comedy, and even an intimate drama might throw in a fight or chase for the export market.

The history of local production and regional distribution is largely a history of the emergence and eclipse of certain genres. As kung-fu declined and the softcore import *Emmanuelle* (1974) proved successful, many producers switched to low-budget eroticism.[9] In the rapid-copy frenzy of the 1990s, Hong Kong was particularly prone to cycles. There were, for instance, the "big-timer" films. These *Godfather*-like movies traced the rise of powerful criminals over the last two decades—gangsters in *To Be Number One* (1991), corrupt police in *Lee Rock* (1991) and *Powerful Four* (1992). Heavy on period detail, the big-timer films betrayed a fascination with wealth and a nostalgia for the 1950s and 1960s. Local critics saw them as glorifying Hong Kong greed and evading the 1997 issue by a fraudulent immersion in local history.[10]

Because Hong Kong movies are conceived and shot so quickly, a cycle has a brief shelf life. There had been gambling cycles before the one touched off by *God of Gamblers* (1989), but the rapidity of its spinoffs is impressive. Besides the authorized series (which included 1990 and 1991 installments) there were:

In 1990: *All for the Winner, King of Gambler* (sic)
In 1991: *All for the Gamblers, The Top Bet, Queen of Gamble* (sic), *Money Maker, Gambling Ghost*
In 1992: *Casino Tycoon, Casino Tycoon 2, The Mighty Gambler*

Turnover was even quicker in another cycle, the historical kung-fu movie as revived by Tsui Hark in *Once upon a Time in China* (1991) and *Once upon a Time in China II* (1992). In 1993 kung-fu sagas set in premodern China, preferably starring Jet Li, poured out month after month: *Once upon a Time in China III* (5 February), *Fong Sai-yuk* (4 March), *Last Hero in China* and *Master Wong versus Master Wong* (two parodies released on 1 April), *Once upon a Time in China IV* (10 June), *Fong Sai-yuk 2* (30 July), and *Iron Monkey* (3 September). The dominance of cycles may have made younger filmmakers aware that packaging could suggest that disparate films formed a cycle. P. U. Productions, which specializes in horror, has tagged each film with a specific day of the year: *14 July* (1993, known in English as *Thou Shalt Not Swear*), which is the date of a ghost festival; *15 January* (1994, known in English as *Third Full Moon*), set on the Chinese equivalent of Valentine's Day; and *30 February* (1995, known in English as *The Day That Doesn't Exist*).

Cycles illustrate the need for any popular cinema to seek out innovation within a framework of familiarity. This process was evident when the New Wave generation found its entry point in the late 1970s. Most of the New Wave directors began with genre renovations, thrillers like Ann Hui's *The Secret* (1979) and Yim Ho's *The Happenings* (1980) and swordplay films like Tsui Hark's *The Butterfly Murders* (1979) and Patrick Tam's *The Sword* (1980). Even the comedies, like Tsui's *All the Wrong Clues (for the Right Solution)* (1981) and Yim Ho's *Wedding Bells, Wedding Belles* (1981), were somewhat out of the ordinary. "The strength of the new wave directors," Stephen Teo writes, "was forged in genre cinema where established conventions and forms were critically and stylistically reworked to suit the modern audiences of the 1980s."[11] Ann Hui moved from suspense drama (*The Secret*, 1979) to ghost comedy (*The Spooky Bunch*, 1980) to crime thriller (*The Story of Woo Viet*, 1981) to woman's melodrama (*Song of the Exile*, 1990), each time seeking to deepen the emotional resonance of the genre.

It is always tempting to explain genre development as a reflection of social trends, but we get more pertinent and proximate explanations if we also consider the filmmaking practice and the genre's specific tradition. Take the female-cop movies that earn local critics' scorn but captivate Western fanboys and fangirls.[12] We might posit that *Yes, Madam!* (1985), *Royal Warriors* (1986), *Angel* (1987), *The Inspector Wears a Skirt* (1988), *She Shoots Straight* (1990), and other girls-and-guns movies reflect the growing importance of women in the local economy. But there are more proximate explanations. First is the variorum nature of popular entertainment. Once a genre gains prominence, a host of possibilities opens up. Horror filmmakers are likely to float the possibility of demonic children, if only because the competition has already shown demonic teenagers, rednecks, cars, and pets. Similarly, once the male-cop genre is going strong, someone is likely to explore the possibility of a tough woman cop. Local traditions could sustain the innovation: swordplay and kung-fu films had celebrated the woman warrior, and in many 1970s erotic movies a raped woman takes violent revenge. Moreover, energetic heroines might attract women viewers, who made up half the local audience, even for action pictures.[13] The studio that launched the heroines cycle was D & B, an independent company anxious to establish itself in the market. Sammo Hung suggested the female variant on the cop-buddy formula, and Dickson Poon, D & B's owner, found an actress ready for stardom, the former Miss Malaysia Michelle Yeoh (Fig. 6.2). When Yeoh retired after marrying Poon, D & B launched other female fighters.[14]

Although genre pictures bear the traces of the cultural conversation, they are also talking among themselves. A form of "intertextuality" spontaneously emerges, as with the iconography of gangsters smoking Salems or red-box Marlboros, or as in *Mongkok Story* (1996), when the aspiring teenage triads eagerly discuss *A Better Tomorrow* (1986) and its ethics of brotherhood. These annotations can accumulate, building into a rewriting of the genre tradition. Whereas *A Better Tomorrow* was homosocial and homoerotic, *Mongkok Story* is explicitly homosexual, with the young waiter, Leung, becoming attracted to the triad leader, Ching (meeting him the nub: "Fung [Yam] turns the little girl into a bonfire while her father [Kent Cheng] is forced to watch the incineration. This repulsive scene accelerates into excruciating bad taste as Fung takes the charred corpse and puts it at Fatty's feet, all the while imitating the girl's voice: 'Daddy, I'm all dark. Don't you recognize me?'"[16]

In Hollywood, no actors as famous as Lee and Yam would appear in such fare. But Lee followed up with *Twist* (1995), a police procedural on the lines of *The Untold Story* in which Simon Yam commits brutal murders and then is even more brutally tortured into a confession. Like a lot of exploitation cinema, many entries in the cycle are based on actual cases, but they are presented with a mixture of sensationalism and cinematic flair that renders them deeply disturbing. Somewhat milder was a run of psychokiller films spun off by Herman Yau, featuring Anthony Wong (*Taxi Hunter*, 1993; *Underground Banker*, 1994), and one directed by Wong himself (*The New Tenant*, 1995).

By the end of the gore cycle, many Category III items were going straight to video. Still, the label was not completely disreputable. Derek Yee and Law Chi Leung parodied and celebrated the erotic film in *Viva Erotica* (1996), which traced the problems of making a Category III movie. For her portrayal of a porn star in *Viva Erotica,* former porn star Shu Qi earned two Hong Kong Film Awards in 1997. Even the Category III phenomenon relied upon an interplay of familiarity and novelty, operating within the boundaries of craft and industrial pressures.

The same dialectic makes stars perennial fixtures of any popular cinema. In Hong Kong, the public is unusually loyal. Japanese and American audiences are fickle, says Leslie Cheung, "But in Hong Kong, once the audiences love you, they go on loving you for a very long time."[17] Josephine Siao Fong-fong, who began acting in films as a child, is revered throughout the territory. At the 1997 Hong Kong Film Awards Shek Kin, a martial-arts actor of great longevity, received a standing ovation. Stars are not merely local celebrities; they have been crucial to the foreign markets, particularly during the boom of the 1980s and 1990s. Stephen Chiau was popular not only in Hong Kong but also in Taiwan, while Jet Li and Michele Yeoh were huge draws in Korea.[18] Some female action stars like Moon Lee and Oshima Yukari had little appeal in Hong Kong but did good business overseas. Stars who could command large regional audiences won big salaries, up to HK$12 million for Chiau and Li.

"If you want to create a film industry," notes one Hollywood producer, "then you've consciously got to encourage stars to emerge."[19] Hong Kong had several breeding grounds. The long-established stars of Cantopop music—Jacky Cheung, Leslie Cheung, Aaron Kwok, and Leon Lai—all launched robust film careers, while Ekin Chan, Sammi Cheng, and others

6.4 Anita Mui in *Saviour of the Soul* (1991).

of the new generation also began as singers. Another source of stars was television, the proving ground for the Hui brothers, Andy Lau, Chow Yun-fat, Simon Yam, Carol "Dodo" Cheng, Tony Leung Chiu-wai, and Stephen Chiau (who hosted a children's show). The martial-arts world brought to fame not only Bruce Lee and Jackie Chan but also Cynthia Rothrock, Jet Li, and Donnie Yen. Beauty contests, particularly the Miss Hong Kong pageant, revealed Maggie Cheung, Anita Yuen, and many other female stars.

Virtually no Hong Kong movies generate income from toys, games, and other merchandise, so stars become the most exploitable element. Stars are sold through fan magazines, fashion shoots, postcards, posters, calendars, games, puzzles, tote bags, and albums. They are kept before the public eye in TV guest appearances, charity shows, tours, premieres, and photo spreads in general-interest magazines.[20] By endorsing products and working in TV, film stars maintain their following throughout Southeast Asia. The biggest ones, like Jackie Chan and Jet Li, have the power to launch projects, hire directors, and oversee production. After Li's success in the first three *Once upon a Time in China* films, he was able to break with Tsui Hark and form his own company to produce *Fong Sai-yuk* (1993), for which he chose the director and composers, even managing to hire Ann Hui as production designer.

How do stars' familiar faces, voices, and bodies shape the art of entertainment? Most broadly, genres demand character types, so stars must to some degree match fixed roles: the ingenue, the middle-aged lothario, the "sour beauty" incarnated in heavy-lipped Anita Mui (Fig. 6.4).[21] The comedies often trade on types like the randy husband, the ditzy girl, the stingy wife, the butch biker girl. But part of the fun of a star system is that there is no inevitable match-up between traditional roles and star images. In Hong Kong many mid-range stars can play heroes, villains, or clowns (for example, Waise Lee, Ng Man-tat). Although the biggest stars like Jet Li, Stephen Chiau, Maggie Cheung, and Michele Yeoh are guaranteed to play positive roles, those parts can be shaded in a great many ways.

One thing that makes stars resist univocal typing is that they are seldom

FORMULA, FORM, AND NORM

just vacantly beautiful. They have marked, often exaggerated physical features. Leslie Cheung's delicate overbite gives him a slight pout; Tony Leung Kar-fai is remarkably tall and possesses a jawline that could plane a plank; Maggie Cheung's wide-spaced eyes make her seem perpetually alert. Compare Stephen Chiau's goofy, slightly impudent grin with Chow Yun-fat's blinding smile; the one is mischievous-childish, the other debonair-boyish. Films may build in references to the star's uniqueness, as when somebody is likely to comment on Anita Yuen's small breasts or Lau Ching-wan's dark complexion.

The star's distinctiveness would seem to dictate that we get the same character in every film. Doesn't John Wayne always play himself? Actually, no; there is a great distance between the awkward youth of *Stagecoach* (1939) and the driven racist of *The Searchers* (1956). Danny Lee, who loves to play a cop, can invest the role with jaunty amorality (*The Untold Story*, 1993), tortured conscience (*The Law with Two Phases*, 1984), or canny self-restraint (*The Killer*, 1989). Stephen Chiau often plays a bungler who has one outstanding skill, so each film must come up with a new area of expertise: kung-fu in *Fight Back to School* (1991), courtroom disputation in *Justice My Foot!* (1992), cooking in *God of Cookery* (1996). Different aspects of the star's physical presence can be brought out for particular roles. Leslie Cheung and Tony Leung Kar-fai have played both womanizers and gay men, each role activating slightly different aspects of their faces, bodies, and voices.

Popular filmmaking constantly remakes its stars from project to project, if only to differentiate the product. Give your star a new hairstyle or wardrobe or role, shoot some publicity photos, and your audience may get curious. *Tristar* (1996) puts Leslie Cheung in a priest's outfit and an Elvis costume, gives Lau Ching-wan a beard and a cigar, and makes the virginal Anita Yuen a cigarette-smoking hooker. *Don't Give a Damn* (1995) gives Sammo Hung a ponytail and Yuen Biao a goatee. To enjoy *The East Is Red* (1993) or *The Eagle-Shooting Heroes* (1993) fully one must savor the prospect of big stars promenading in ever more outrageous costumes (Fig. 6.5). Part of the pleasure of a new film lies in the new look it assigns a favorite actor.

Apart from the masquerade element, a popular cinema achieves variety by exploiting star personas in myriad ways. Stars can yield fast, barely noticeable exposition: the very presence of a star in an early scene signals us that this character is important, even if he or she is quite inconspicuous. Reading a novel offers no equivalent for the way that we intuitively expect that Rosamund Kwan, who is initially just one reporter in a crowd, will be a major character in *Undeclared War* (1990). But because we probably know who is in the film before we see it, exposition can also be somewhat reticent, exploiting what might be called "star ellipsis." In Peter Chan's *Comrades, Almost a Love Story* (1996), the first two scenes introduce the triad chieftain, played by Eric Tsang, in very brief shots. Prolonged shots of

6.5 *The Eagle-Shooting Heroes:* Campy costumes for Joey Wang (left), Maggie Cheung (center), and Tony Leung Chiu-wai (right foreground)

6.6 *Comrades:* Eric Tsang as the sympathetic triad, with Maggie Cheung.

Tsang, a veteran comedian, might have elicited automatic laughs from the audience, so cutting and framing keep the emphasis on other characters to sustain a serious tone.[22] More positively, we can fill out Tsang's portrayal thanks to our knowledge of his star persona. Since Tsang seldom plays a villain, we are ready to take the gangster for a fairly nice guy, an impression reinforced when he becomes more visible in his third scene (Fig. 6.6).

A film's plot may also manipulate the star's image in unpredictable ways. The obvious route is casting against type, which usually means casting to a different type. This alone can pique audiences' anticipation. What will happen when Dodo Cheng, known for playing cute, slightly sharp-edged romantic heroines, dowdies herself up to play a puritanical Mainland policewoman loose in Hong Kong (*Her Fatal Ways*, 1990)? What if demure Maggie Cheung becomes a foul-mouthed biker (*The Heroic Trio*, 1993)? The performance can become a charade, letting the audience glimpse a private party in which Dodo and Maggie cut loose. The gender-bending in Hong Kong cinema has sources in traditional theater—men playing female parts in Peking Opera, women playing male parts in southern and Shanghai theater—but when in *Swordsman II* (1992) and *The East Is Red* the female movie star Brigitte Lin plays Asia the Invincible, the man who has become a woman, there is the bonus of the star who develops two dimensions of skill.[23]

There are less obvious ways to let the plot revise the star persona. Jet Li is known as a rather impassive actor, specializing in parts that require stoic heroism mixed with a boyish awkwardness around women. The first scenes of *The Bodyguard from Beijing* (1994) present him as a ruthless warrior. Quite late, when the woman he is guarding falls in love with him, the plot begins to evoke the shy side of his star image, treating it now as a nervous hesitation about emotions he has never known. In such ways the star image can foreshadow character change. In *Days of Tomorrow* (1993) the Andy Lau character develops, quite late, into Andy Lau proper, the tormented and self-centered but sincere youth.

One can distribute aspects of the star persona among parts of the plot.

FORMULA, FORM, AND NORM

ema of the same era, but the films remain solid, sometimes stolid, pieces of continuity craft, showcasing their stories and performances.

As Hong Kong films won regional markets in the late 1950s, budgets and production values rose, so studio settings could be more elaborate. Filmmakers also began to go on location more frequently, yielding the relaxed, open-air look of *June Bride* (1960) and *Father Takes a Bride* (1961). Directors loosened up, perhaps partly as a result of exposure to the "new cinemas" of the West. The swordplay films of the late 1960s often displayed bravura style, and other genres became more technique-conscious. Lung Kong's *Story of a Discharged Prisoner* (1967) flaunts handheld shots and rapid cutting, particularly in fight scenes. Shu Shuen's *The Arch* (1970) is full of stylistic flourishes, including ambitious depth staging. Location shooting increased in the 1970s, since kung-fu films and crime dramas could be made cheaply outdoors. Michael Hui's comedies exploited actual exteriors, and his typical opening showed the city's streets at rush hour, crowded with people hustling to make a living.

Throughout the world filmmakers have sought to give classical continuity a greater expressive charge, and an easy way to do so is to vary the editing pace. While many 1960s Hong Kong films, particularly the opera movies, continued to hold shots for several seconds, some moved more quickly. *The Story of a Discharged Prisoner* has an average shot length of only five seconds, quite quick for any 1960s film from any country. Action pictures became rapidly cut, with Zhang Che and King Hu in the vanguard of the reforms. Throughout the 1970s the Cantonese *gang-chan-pian* (Hong Kong–made films) were designed to hold their midnight viewers, and Shu Kei has suggested that this purpose encouraged fast editing. Since all scenes were shot silent, filmmakers could cut the film for dynamic visual effect and then add bits of dialogue in the mixing stage. Certain exhibition customs also picked up the pace. In order to squeeze in more screenings, theaters often projected films faster than the standard, at twenty-six or even twenty-eight frames per second![30]

So the 1970s begins that era of breathlessly accelerated tempo—whirlwind action scenes, conversations ever on the move, rapidly changing angles, constantly mobile camera—that we associate with modern Hong Kong film. In these movies virtually nobody stays still unless he or she is dying. (And even then . . .) Just a frame entrance can pick up the tempo, since quite often we get a close-up of a head popping in, most exhilaratingly from the bottom edge. Zooms enliven not only kung-fu combats but also the simplest expository scenes. By the 1980s, the low-angle wide-angle shot became commonplace. Slow motion, a staple of action scenes, could mark emotionally significant flashbacks, and directors experimented with different rates of fast motion.

Color was being handled expressively too. As early as 1979, Alex Cheung's *Cops and Robbers* presented Hong Kong's characteristic nighttime palette, blue-steeped streets dotted with glowing reds. The final reel of *Peking Opera Blues* exploits the clash of brilliant reds, pinks, and blues onstage with the ominous blacks and browns of the police on the benches watching. As Hollywood became ever more drab and desaturated in its color schemes, assuming that realism required pale earth tones, Hong Kong filmmakers used blazing color.

Cutting got even faster. By the early 1990s, an average of four to six seconds per shot was normal in all genres. Michael Hui's 1981 comedy *Security Unlimited* averaged nearly seven seconds per shot; his 1990 film *The Front Page* ran closer to four. Action scenes, which could hardly get faster, did. The climactic fight between Bruce Lee and the Japanese villain in *Fist of Fury* (1972) rattles along at 2.7 seconds per shot, but the parallel scene in the quasi-remake *Fist of Legend* (1994) not only lasts three times as long but has an average shot length of merely 1.6 seconds. Over the same years, editing on shape and movement became refined to a degree not seen in other national cinemas. Look only at the concluding warehouse shootout of *Pom Pom and Hot Hot* (1992), and you will see cutting that is as imaginative yet rigorous (mirror compositions matched to symmetrical tracking shots) as anything in the 1920s European avant-garde. Mature Hong Kong film teaches a central lesson about popular film: scintillating style can override jerry-built plots.

Over the years that Hong Kong editing became rapid-fire, Hollywood movies were accelerating too, but with dire results. Music videos and digital editing technology encouraged filmmakers to cut fast without much regard for how compositions would flow together. To sell a song or a fight, a vague sense of busy excitement sufficed. The result was the pointlessly nervous cutting of the 1990s James Bond films and Michael Bay's *The Rock* (1996) and *Armageddon* (1998).[31] It would be a mistake, though, to deplore fast cutting because of Hollywood abuses; the skill of Hong Kong editing reminds us that in the right hands any film technique can be vivid and captivating.

Throughout the 1980s, Hong Kong directors pushed the premises of continuity filmmaking toward a pulsating expressive intensity. The films correlate gesture, composition, color, and music more exactly than we expect in Western live-action cinema (though it's common enough in our cartoons). An actor turns, and holds the pose. Now comes a blast of sound, a cut to a dynamic composition, even a flash of color to create a kind of visual vibrato. In *He's a Woman, She's a Man* (1994), Wing scuffles with her roommate, Yu Lo, shoving him through the window toward us; for an instant, his white shirt flares yellow from a street light (Figs. 6.7, 6.8). The shot moves from noisy dialogue to thrusting movement, capped by an unexpected color burst.

A more elaborate example occurs in *Saviour of the Soul* (1991). Maykwan (Anita Mui) has just seen her friend Koo killed and knows that she,

6.7 *He's a Woman, She's a Man:* Yu Lo scoffs at Wing's adulation of Rose . . .

6.8 . . . and she forces him out the window toward us.

her friend Chin (Andy Lau), and Koo's sister are the next targets. To draw away enemy fire she must abandon them. So she strides in as they wait in a corridor. Telling Chin that he has no claim on her love, she brusquely departs. The film is a futuristic fantasy, so directors Yuen Kuei and David Lai can coordinate complementary hues without regard for realism. The first stretch of the scene, when Chin and Koo's sister are mourning Koo's death, is dominated by pure, hard blues in lighting, walls, and Chin's costume, along with some pale greens in stretches of background; only some purplish reds, in the sister's baseball uniform, serve as accents. When May-kwan enters, she too presents a sharp-edged blue in her angular cape. She tells Chin she has no love for him and leaves him weeping as she strides out.

But as she passes through a pair of swinging doors, we cut to her coming to the camera. The image shifts to slow motion, and the color scheme explodes. Tightly framed, the door fills the screen with an intense mustard yellow, the shrieking complement to the blue-drenched scene we have just witnessed. As May-kwan walks toward us in close-up, unseen light sources turn her a brilliant orange. A surge of trumpets coincides rhythmically with this color burst and the pace of her walk, as does her voice-over monologue: "Sorry, Chin. Only this can get you out of danger." As a color echo, her hair suddenly glows with a streak of russet light, the same shade that had lit her hair earlier—when Chin was about to propose marriage and when she bowed over the dying Koo. Here imagery and sound cooperate to give tangible expression to Kwan's pang of guilt.

Such bold expressivity surely owes something to Cantonese Opera. In this dancelike theater virtually every gesture is matched by musical passages, particularly percussion, and a cascade of movement and music will be accented by a flash of color in the garments. Opera films occasionally underscore these synchronizations by means of rhythmic cuts and camera movements. Eisenstein spoke of the tendency in kabuki theater to "transfer" a feeling from one channel to another. When a quality reaches its maximum expressiveness in one domain, it leaps synesthetically to another:

"Whatever notes I can't take with my voice I'll show with my hands!"[32] His observation applies to Chinese opera and to Hong Kong cinema as well. In *Saviour of the Soul*, the somber mood materializes in rain, the sound of drizzle, and drenched blues and greens; then May-kwan's sorrow at departing "leaps" from Mui's performance to the music, the movement, and the dazzling color shift. No wonder local filmmakers admired Leone, a director who syncs up twitching eyes with screeches and yowls.

This expressive intensity can be coordinated with swift cutting and elaborate staging. In *A Chinese Ghost Story* (1987) the tax collector Ning Caichen falls in love with the ghost woman Nie Xiaoqian. But Xiaoqian has been condemned to serve the hermaphroditic tree spirit Lao Lao, who feeds on men's souls (thanks to a yards-long tongue). Caichen visits Xiaoqian unexpectedly. Hearing Qing, her ghost sister, coming, Caichen ducks underwater in a bathtub. Qing is soon followed by Lao Lao, who whips Xiaoqian and tells her that she must marry the Master of the Black Mountain. The rest of the scene is devoted to Xiaoqian's attempts to keep Qing and Lao Lao from finding Caichen in the bathtub. She blocks Qing's path to the tub, tosses a towel on the water, rips her dress when Lao Lao approaches, and falls forward into the tub in order to conceal Caichen (and to give him a boost of air in an underwater kiss). Eventually she manages to steer Qing and Lao Lao out, haul Caichen up, and help him escape.

An effortless pleasure to watch, the scene in Xiaoqian's boudoir is casually virtuosic. (We should expect no less from director of record Ching Siu-tung, though perhaps producer Tsui Hark had a hand in things.) The passage runs only a little over five minutes, but it consumes 170 shots. With the average shot less than two seconds long, the scene risks becoming choppy in the Michael Bay manner. The filmmakers make continuity harder for themselves by using only a couple of establishing shots, relying almost completely on medium shots and close-ups. Add to this the fact that the scene employs segment shooting, in which almost every shot is taken from a camera position not seen before, so we are constantly readjusting to a new slice of space. Finally, several of the shots are canted, creating off-kilter compositions that probably take a bit longer to grasp. Nearly everything proceeds according to the rules of the continuity system, but the filmmakers have set themselves some difficult problems of clarity and expressivity.

Which they solve triumphantly. The action is broken into cogently composed bits, with most shots highlighting the direction of a gaze or movement and some images presenting two elements in dynamic but well-designed depth (Fig. 6.9). The sequence relies on mastery of shot/reverse shot and eyeline matching; even without establishing shots we know exactly who is looking at whom and, more important, who is looking at the tub. The control of instant-by-instant legibility is admirable. When Xiaoqian opens her dress before dropping into the tub, the shot's first phase empha-

FORMULA, FORM, AND NORM   165

6.9 *A Chinese Ghost Story.*

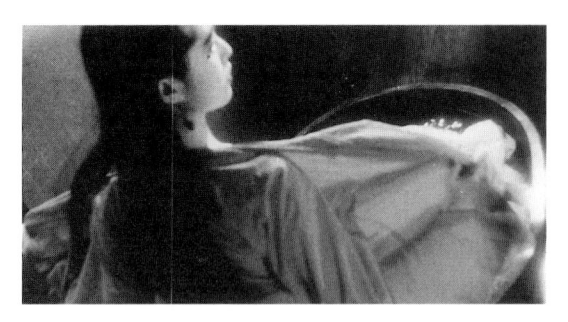

6.10 *A Chinese Ghost Story.*

6.11 *A Chinese Ghost Story.*

sizes her gesture, then clears a spot in the composition for Caichen, who pops up from underwater and stares (Figs. 6.10–6.11).

The filmmakers give the scene a firm flow by letting gestures echo one another. As Qing glances suspiciously toward the tub, there is a suite of rocking, symmetrical movements when the two women slightly turn their heads toward and away from it (Figs. 6.12–6.15). At one point, Lao Lao swings toward the tub, and the sequence sacrifices perfect axis-of-action continuity in order to let her-his body's movement continue the swiveling eyelines of the previous shot.[33] Then the sisters rise, and a series of matches on action makes this an effortless surge of drapery. In a final canted angle, Qing lunges toward the tub, but Xiaoqian delicately deflects her, the two sisters pivoting in unison (Figs. 6.16–6.17). I do not believe any Hollywood filmmaker, in 1987 or today, could mount movement with this degree of rhythmic exactness. American directors never learned the sort of discipline enforced by the Hong Kong martial-arts film, which transformed the way local filmmakers conceived cinematic action.

An Eisensteinian "transfer" of expressive elements resonates through the *Chinese Ghost Story* scene. The main quality here is liquidity, manifested not only in the tub water but in the rippling veils and robes associated with Nie Xiaoqian throughout the film. The fluidity of fabric becomes explicit first when Xiaoqian floats the towel on the water, then when Lao Lao snaps a long robe toward the camera like a crashing crimson wave.

166 PLANET HONG KONG

6.12 *A Chinese Ghost Story.*

6.13 *A Chinese Ghost Story.*

6.14 *A Chinese Ghost Story.*

6.15 *A Chinese Ghost Story.*

6.16 *A Chinese Ghost Story.*

6.17 *A Chinese Ghost Story.*

Xiaoqian slips the dress on, a moment accentuated by a leap on the musical track (a burst of her theme) and in the images (sudden close-ups of her hands gliding into the sleeves and knotting the sash). Soon, however, this robe is cast off, and Xiaoqian arcs gracefully into the tub for the kiss. Likewise, Qing coasts toward the tub as if borne by a current—a suitable gait for a ghost but still a pretty mundane counterpart to Xiaoqian's soaring and swooping. All this fluidity is counterpointed by an earthier instance of transfer. Offscreen Lao Lao snarls, and the noise is synchronized with a shot of Qing sneering. In the West only cartoon directors (and Eisenstein) would so exactly match one character's expressive sound to another character's expressive movement, palpably doubling the note of disdain.

Full of movement but never seeming rushed or confused, this sequence

FORMULA, FORM, AND NORM

from *A Chinese Ghost Story* displays a patterned precision typical of 1980s Hong Kong cinema. *The Story of a Discharged Prisoner,* despite its rapid pace, has rather awkward staging and cutting; in 1967 most local filmmakers had not yet learned how to make brief images instantly legible and integrated into vivid patterns. Twenty years later, filmmakers had mastered a smooth, dynamic variant of the continuity system. So sure were they of their skill that they set themselves technical challenges which could be overcome with brisk panache.

The craft pride underlying this technical skill never withered, but some filmmakers explored other options. They avoided the crisp, functional look and cultivated a softer image, blurred slow motion, and self-consciously abstract shots. The most famous exponent of this style is Wong Kar-wai, but early examples include Patrick Tam's fine underworld movies *The Final Victory* (1987) and *My Heart Is That Eternal Rose* (1989). Since Wong's *Chungking Express* (1994), this moody "software" technique has cropped up in several genres.

Another alternative was a less slick style. Filmmakers began to explore direct sound (that is, recording dialogue on the set), which by the end of the 1990s had become a mark of the "quality" movie. When Li Xiaojun (Leon Lai) fastens shut Li Qiao (Maggie Cheung)'s jacket in *Comrades,* the scratch of buttons comes forward over ambient traffic noise. In addition, some directors cultivated longer takes, letting the editing do less of the work. In some genres filmmakers began to build the entire film out of sustained shots of the actors' performances. Peter Chan's shots in *He's a Woman, She's a Man* and its sequel *Who's the Woman, Who's the Man?* (1996) average between ten and eleven seconds. As usual, economic imperatives have exerted some pressure too. With declining production budgets, direct sound and long-take filming have proved to save time in postproduction. Forced to shoot *Love Amoeba Style* (1997) very fast, Shu Kei deliberately used lengthy shots (averaging about thirteen seconds).

The most impressive example of this approach I know is Jacob Cheung's *Cageman* (1992). Most of the action takes place in a large hostel where homeless men live in stacked cages. The film celebrates communal spirit; the men would rather live here than be dispersed to state housing. Given such a cramped set, the easiest option is to build the film out of short, repeated setups. But Cheung boldly goes in the opposite direction. The average shot lasts an astonishing forty-two seconds, and each scene averages only six shots. Some takes go on for several minutes and involve elaborate camera movements snaking through the hostel's aisles. (The film was one of the first Hong Kong productions to utilize a Steadicam.) Cheung's long-take images jam the frame with faces, bodies, wire grids, and the clutter of each man's possessions. Because the story is about the group as a whole, the action almost never centers on any character. Cheung adroitly uses depth, figure movement, and camera movement to trace out the fluctuating dramatic tensions in this cramped space (Figs. 6.18–6.24).

6.18 Part of a nearly four-minute shot in *Cageman*: The cop Lam has come into the hostel looking for a petition. As he interrogates the young Mao, the landlord, Fatso, slips the papers to Koo.

6.19 Track in with Koo as he tries to pass through the ring of cops in the background while Fatso steps out right to quarrel with Lam.

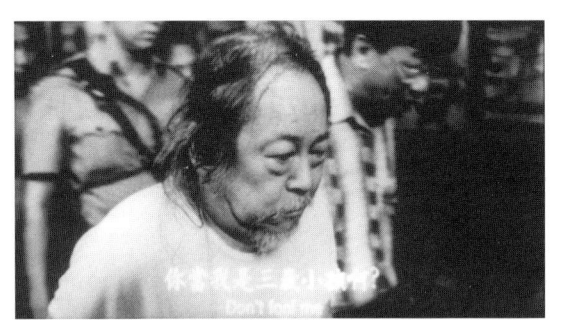

6.20 Turning, Koo comes past the camera . . .

6.21 . . . and circles around Fatso . . .

6.22 . . . before he's blocked by another cop in the background.

6.23 While Lam continues to lecture Mao offscreen, Koo starts back around Fatso.

6.24 The camera tracks back to show all of them, now opposite to the angle from which it started (Fig. 6.18).

169

This tactic yields one last contrast with Hollywood. I can find no Hollywood film from the last twenty years with an average shot length of more than nine seconds. Because of this bias toward fast cutting, most American directors have never learned how to choreograph a moderately complex ensemble performance within a sustained shot. True, De Palma takes pride in the marathon camera movement opening *Snake Eyes* (1998), and Scorsese tries to catch us up in the exhilaration of a mobster swaggering into a restaurant in *GoodFellas* (1990); but these are virtuoso following shots, a convention that became prominent in early talkies (*The Threepenny Opera*, 1931; *Scarface*, 1932), and they demand a talent more logistical than pictorial. Could any American director today sustain for minutes a shot in depth within such a constricted set—let alone a shot with the dozen characters and deft timing of *Cageman*? Despite Hong Kong cinema's commitment to fast cutting, some directors have preserved the skills of staging complex action, and not only in the action genre. The results show once more that the continuity system offers a stable yet flexible framework for popular filmmaking. It assures a minimal clarity and economy, and it permits innovation—if filmmakers cultivate a solid craft tradition.

R. G. Collingwood famously criticized mass art's reliance on formulas, claiming that a genuine work of art is one of a kind, irreducibly singular. Noël Carroll has vigorously questioned this claim, pointing out that art of all sorts often depends upon "generic forms inherited from a tradition."[34] The composers of Tin Pan Alley worked with unusually confining forms, but they were no different in principle from Renaissance painters conforming to a patron's program or a classical composer writing a minuet. All art, high or low, operates in complex relation to norms—complex because each work will mingle familiarity and novelty.

In popular art, novelty may also spring from the sheer demands of craft. When an artist begins reworking a received device, matters of workmanship impose themselves. The artist, at least the alert and ambitious one, gets caught up in intricacies of elaboration. New opportunities are flushed out. Here is a chance for a symmetry or an echo; there I can counterbalance something earlier; over there I can create a new expressive nuance. In passages like those from *Saviour of the Soul* and *A Chinese Ghost Story*, elaboration of this sort comes to the fore. The convention is still there, like the melody in an ornamented passage of music, but the treatment claims our attention too. Entertainment has an ornate, even mannerist side, and Hong Kong popular cinema displays it again and again.

WHATEVER YOU WANT: WONG JING

When he is not playing video games, the round-faced Wong Jing produces a dozen films a year under the auspices of two companies, Wong Jing's Workshop and BoB (Best of the Best), a partnership with director Andrew Lau and writer-producer Manfred Wong. Hong Kong remains Wong's most important market, but he is one of the few local producers still able to presell projects around Asia. Taiwan is his prime offshore target. He builds his packages around stars who are popular there, and he visits regularly to study market conditions. A keen believer in promotion, Wong focuses audience interest from the moment he announces a project. He starts publicizing a film before shooting and invites the press to visit locations and interview actors—uncommon in Hong Kong, where the buzz has usually started just before the midnight screening. The theatrical trailer for *God of Gamblers' Return* (1994), which marked the reappearance of Chow Yun-fat in the series, teased the audience with just one shot of the star. For the prequel *God of Gamblers 3: The Early Stage* (1996), Wong wrote a novella that was serialized in a newspaper, and he gave the story to a comic-book publisher so that a series could be launched before the film appeared. Star Leon Lai's hairstyle and clothing were kept secret until a few days before release.[1]

Wong Jing directs infrequently these days, preferring to write scripts and farm them out. His units are shooting several films at once, and he may tour two or three locations in the course of a day. When he does direct, he works very fast. Adopting a sort of second-unit system—the fights and chases are entrusted wholly to the action choreographer—Wong devotes himself to the dialogue scenes, which he can polish off in ten days. The scenes he most enjoys filming, he says, are the poker duels that climax many of his gambling films. These depend on dozens of close-ups of cards, hands, and shifting glances, all of which can be shot simply and quickly. He allows a week for editing and dubbing. Wong's streamlined system enabled him to affix his directorial signature to five films in 1991, five in 1992, nine in 1993, and six in 1994.

He held the decade's winning hand. From cheap program-fillers and Category III sensationalism to "event films" starring Chow Yun-fat, Jackie Chan, Stephen Chiau, and Jet Li, Wong's work has proved amazingly popular. In 1993 his productions accounted for 15 percent of all box-office receipts for local films. In 1996 he participated in fifteen films, which commanded 30 percent of local receipts. In the teeth of massive video piracy, BoB's *StormRiders* (1998) beat every U.S. movie except *Titanic* at the domestic box office. In the same year he was rumored to be in line to head a new studio facility to be built on government-allotted land.

In keeping with Kirk Wong's injunction to please everybody at every moment, Wong Jing's films string together bits of comedy, action, and pathos. They are the ideal example of script-by-brainstorming; each scene is stuffed with gimmicks. The opening is likely to be breathless. Within the first sixty seconds there will be a gag, a chase, or a suspenseful encounter. The curtain-raiser of *God of Gamblers* (1989) is low-key but gripping, introducing the hero first at a Las Vegas poker table and then in a prolonged gambling duel with a Japanese. *Last Hero in China* (1993), a mock-heroic version of Tsui Hark's *Once upon a Time in China* series, opens with a gigantic floating lantern pursuing women through a forest and seizing them with grappling hooks. After the unavoidable pause of the opening credits, Wong hurls us into a fight at a ferry station. Fourteen seconds into *High Risk* (1995) a gang of thugs mounts an incendiary assault on a schoolyard.

Thereafter the busyness does not cease. There is seldom pure drama; there is seldom pure anything. The Wong Jing comedy consists largely of farcical interludes based on pranks, disguise, mistaken identity, amnesia, and the splendors of human excretory processes. He has done interesting work with sweat, spittle, and nose mucus, but he excels in the rituals of the water closet. *Tricky Brains* (1991) strikes its dominant note early when "tricks expert" Stephen Chiau traps his victim on the toilet seat. The walls start to close in on the man, squirting him with water. Suddenly the back wall flies open, and both man and commode are rocketed into the center of a shopping mall. Later an office worker (played by Wong Jing) tricks Chiau into using the women's bathroom. Learning fast, Chiau tricks a woman into the men's room. At one point Chiau offers his father a piece of toilet paper as a tissue, explaining as the father wipes his face, "It was used, but I cleaned it off." This is vulgar cinema at its most gleefully appalling.

Wong Jing's Hollywood predecessors would be Bob Hope, Jerry Lewis, and Jim Abrahams and the Zucker brothers (*Airplane!* and *The Naked Gun!*). Yet even these farceurs look somewhat Racinean alongside Wong Jing's determined efforts to shred plausibility, character consistency, and good taste. Once tricked into the women's restroom, Stephen Chiau takes out lipstick and calmly applies it. *City Hunter* (1993) stages a Jackie Chan fight scene as a video game and periodically interrupts scenes with a lounge-girls' chorus breathing "Citeee Hun-*ter*" as Jackie pauses to smooth his hair and beam roguishly at the camera. In *Last Hero in China* as Jet Li performs a lion dance he is challenged by a giant cockroach brandishing power-saw legs. At the end of the film Li wins out by learning the "chicken style" of kung-fu—which he executes in a chicken suit.

Nothing adolescent is off limits: we get love potions in Cokes, itching powder in shorts, scenes centering on drool and superglue. *Royal Tramp* (1992) endlessly mocks the male member and includes a penis point-of-view shot. In *Whatever You Want* (1994) a horny clerk begs a genie to give him a penis that touches the floor. The genie obliges by shortening the man's legs. *Boys Are Easy* (1993) presents a Triad Olympics, complete with cheerleaders and execution by javelin; the starting pistol becomes an AK-47. Traditions are tossed. Characters burst into rhyming song and deliver dialogue while performing Chinese opera footwork; a lion dance ends when the lions indulge in a passionate kiss.

When he casts off the antic mood, Wong Jing can provide lively storytelling. *God of Gamblers*, modeled on Wong's straight drama *Casino Raiders* (1989), works out a fairly coherent plot, although it does resort to giving supergamester Ko Chun (Chow Yun-fat) a bout of amnesia that delivers him into the hands of scam artist Dagger (Andy Lau). The crisp fight scenes are punctuated by humor: after Lone Ng dispatches the thugs who attack Ko Chun on the subway, Ko Chun points out that they are Vietnamese like Lone. Lone Ng replies: "They're from North Vietnam." The disparity between gambler Ko Chun, with his dazzling smile and hair like black ice cream, and infantile Ko Chun provides broad comedy (Fig. WYW.1). When Ko Chun recovers his identity during a gunfight he becomes the blazing hero of the John Woo films (Figs. WYW.2). The gambling showdowns are kung-fu combats with cards and dice, spiced with adroitly timed close-ups and showy depth effects (Fig. WYW.3).

Wong Jing soon swerved the series toward crazy comedy, largely, it seems, because another company parodied his hit. *All for the Winner* (*Saint of Gamblers*, 1990) stars Stephen Chiau as Sing, an emigrant from China gifted with X-ray vision and the ability to alter cards' faces by concentrating on them. Sing's uncle introduces him to gambling by dressing him in a black suit, soaking gel into his hair, and making him watch a video of *God of Gamblers*, studying the scene in which Ko Chun enters the gaming room in slow motion. Sing obligingly strides into the gambling hall in slow motion, while everyone around him walks normally. The film ends with the triumphant ex-Mainlander strolling in, slow-motioned once more, dazzling in a white Mao jacket.

In a gesture of Hong Kong intertextuality, Wong Jing paid his plagiarists back by ripping off *All for the Winner*. In *God of Gamblers II* (lit. *Knight of Gamblers*, 1990), Dagger (Andy Lau) is introduced in a curtain-raiser proving that he is Knight of Gamblers, successor to his retired *sifu*, Ko Chun. But then Sing (Stephen Chiau) and his uncle arrive on the scene and dem-

WYW.1 *God of Gamblers:* Apparently the victim of amnesia, Ko Chun cowers.

WYW.2 Later, Ko Chun becomes a Woo-like hero. (Compare Fig. EM.3.)

WYW.3 A Wong Jing trademark: the gambling showdown, audaciously filmed.

onstrate Sing's magical winning techniques. To combat Sing, Dagger's opponent brings another supernaturally gifted master from China. The two wrestle psychokinetically to rearrange dice and alter each other's cards. In an epilogue, both Sing and Dagger wave to Ko Chun, glimpsed in an outtake from the first film. In reworking *All for the Winner* Wong Jing hit upon his most successful formula; fittingly, Wong Jing may have swiped the Wong Jing style itself.

So the franchise went on, expanding into wilder comedy and more grandiose drama. In *God of Gamblers III: Back to Shanghai* (*Knight of Gamblers II: The Gambling Saint of Shanghai Beach*, 1991) Sing is carried back to 1937, where he continues to battle the Chinese master. To forget his lovesickness he opens a McDonald's, which occasions a musical number in praise of pork buns. With *God of Gamblers' Return* Ko Chun is forced out of retirement by the murder of his wife; now his gambling skills include hypnosis. The prequel *God of Gamblers 3: The Early Stage* is uncharacteristically sentimental, but the direction is sharp and restrained, using superb camerawork in the final fifteen-minute poker combat.

Central to all these films is the idea of trickery. The most extended comic example is *Tricky Brains,* a Jonsonian exercise in pranks and petty spite, in which virtually everybody is fooling everybody. The same impulse finds dramatic expression in the gambling tales. The series format allows Wong Jing to build ever more elaborate patterns of deceit, double bluff, and tit-for-tat. Each *God of Gamblers* film demands that the viewer recall how the trick was played last time, and instead of simply recycling an old maneuver, the next film spins it in a fresh direction. If in one film Sing can change cards through telepathy, in the sequel his waning powers can change only the top half of a card. In the follow-up Ko Chun can therefore hypnotize his opponent into *believing* he is using the split-card device; it is as if he has been inspired by watching Sing in the series' previous entry. Here again, "collective creation" proves its usefulness. A roomful of screenwriters wracking their brains can come up with ever more intricate twists.

Cross-referencing is a constant in Wong Jing's scavenger movies. Their in-jokes are too opportunistic to count as homages. In *God of Gamblers*, Wong Jing himself appears as a man whom Chow Yun-fat threatens with castration. In *Tricky Brains*, the character played by Wong tries to pick up a woman by inviting her to a midnight show of *God of Gamblers II*. When Sing recognizes the Mainland gambling master, the music from the *Swordsman* series is heard; then Sing forces the master to hallucinate playing a role in the kung-fu film *Fong Sai-yuk* (1993), but as a woman. In *Boys Are Easy*, at a male bordello, women order men to enact famous movie scenes; Tony Leung Kar-fai bursts in reprising Chow Yun-fat's role in *A Better Tomorrow*, striding in slow motion, pistols extended. Silliness becomes brutally tasteless when, after Tony's client responds by firing upon him, his cry of protest—"I'm playing Mark, not Bruce Lee's son!"—alludes to the on-set death of Brandon Lee.

Wong Jing manages to make even a Category III film seem jolly. *Naked Killer* (1992; directed by Clarence Fok), a cult favorite in the West, is an elaborate penis movie. The female assassins shoot or stab men in the privates, there are recurring jokes with sausage, and the policeman hero has become impotent since accidentally shooting his brother. At one point, when characters discuss the male member, the offending word is bleeped out, mocking a ploy filmmakers use to dodge a Category III rating. At the end, the hero kisses the heroine and fires his gun convulsively; the shot triggers a gas explosion in which both die.

Whatever You Want (1994) is a bacchanalian celebration of pop connoisseurship and vulgar entertainment. Wong Jing steals the audition montage from *He's a Woman, She's a Man* (1994) and throws in a pastiche of 1950s Cantonese cinema. In an echo of *Speed* (1994), Anita Yuen dreams of steering a runaway bus across a gap in the highway. Anita has such fantasies because she watches videos all night; she once watched eight, she says, but they were by Wong Jing, so she ran them fast forward. She meets a genie who has the power of a VCR's remote control: he can pause scenes, freezing people in place while he leaves for a moment, and he can rewind an event so as to try a different course of action.

Through *Whatever You Want* drifts film director "Wong Jing-wai," a poseur sporting sunglasses and a painfully sensitive expression. Anita Yuen bumps into him while he is filming *Chungking Expect* (sic) with a man dressed as a woman in a trenchcoat and blonde bouffant wig; when Anita snatches her autograph book away from Wong, he shouts after her, "You have no personal style!" Later she goes to a screening of a film featuring the same actor stretched languidly out on a cow (mocking Wong Kar-wai's *Ashes of Time*, 1994). When a critic praises the movie as very symbolic, the bored audience starts to beat him. He protests: "You know nothing about postmodernism!" This is not light satire, but the shameless overplaying makes it quite funny. Earlier, as Anita runs through the streets while everyone around her is floating in slow motion, Wong Jing creates a trim parody of Wong Kar-wai's visual signature.

Unable to let a good idea alone, Wong belabored Wong Kar-wai at full length in *Those Were the Days* (1997). Arty Wong Jing-wai is now so louche he pirates VCDS and declares that he hates old Cantonese movies. He is mysteriously transported back to the 1960s. In order to return to 1997 he must make a successful film for a mogul suspiciously resembling Run Run Shaw. Wong tries to cater to public tastes, even inventing wire-work, but instead of a hit he can turn out only Ur-versions of *Days of Being Wild* and *Ashes of Time.* Yet Wong Jing-wai's artistic integrity attracts the admiration of a round geeky boy named . . . Wong Jing. Little Wong pesters big Wong endlessly, declaring he wants to make art movies when he grows up. Wong Jing-wai tells him to stick to gambling and sex farces, and asks him to throw in lots of urine and feces. "Making your movies lousy makes my movies first class."

Referentiality is played out more wrenchingly in *High Risk,* a big-budget action comedy that becomes a patchwork of Hollywood and Hong Kong movies. The curtain-raiser, in which schoolchildren are locked in a bus that is wired to detonate, milks another motif from *Speed;* the difference is that the bomb specialist Jet Li accidentally triggers the explosion, killing his own wife and child. This grim prologue contrasts with the next scene introducing Frankie Lone (Jacky Cheung), an egomaniacal action-movie star who purports to do all his own stunts but who actually uses Li as a double. Frankie is at once Jackie Chan (goofy mugging, dependence on his manager), Bruce Lee (fighting style, nunchaku sticks, yellow jumpsuit and *kiai* cries, as well as music from *Enter the Dragon*), and Jet Li himself (occasionally the music links Frankie to Huang Feihong).

All the characters converge on a jewelry show, which the archcriminal Doctor aims to rob. Soon the film becomes a Hong Kong *Die Hard,* with character roles and even musical themes copied literally. In his cowardly clumsiness Frankie becomes an antiheroic Bruce Willis skittering through the mêlée, except that instead of losing his shoes Frankie loses his pants. In the process the Hong Kong martial arts tradition is mercilessly travestied. The climactic punch-up lets Frankie parody Bruce Lee's cockiness, and it guys Jackie Chan's comic kung-fu, featuring prominent crotch jokes and the villain's explanation of where he got his nunchakus: "Bought from your shop—10 percent discount." Jet Li's own angular combat skills, which include driving a minicar through a hotel lobby and onto an elevator, play as fierce counterpoint to Frankie's ineffectuality—which he eventually overcomes with a cartoonish burst of energy reminiscent of *Young Master* (1980).

High Risk is smorgasboard à la Wong Jing. There are jokes on urination and potency. There are fights staged by Yuen Kuei with great brio. There are comically speeded-up scenes, obligatory references to China (the villains are veterans of the People's Liberation Army and the Vietnam border war), and outrageous shifts of tone. As the hotel staff are slaughtered in the lobby, one wounded man crawls up to where Frankie is hiding and begs for help, seizing the frantic Frankie's genitals in a death grip. There are wholly unprepared surprises, as when a woman hiding (in a lavatory stall, needless to say) thinks that she is safe until the chuckling villain empties a bag of poisonous snakes at her feet.

A rhapsodic critic in a vulgar-modernist mood could praise Wong Jing's as a naive cinema that, in its frenzy to fling together too much of everything, inevitably winds up creating perverse novelty: pop postmodernism. But Wong Jing is better understood as one edge of mainstream norms. His comedies carry to a noisy extreme long-standing conventions of episodic construction. As with the Hope-Crosby *Road* pictures, his swipings, parodies, and retoolings rejuvenate popular traditions in a wholly traditional way. In celebrating games of skill and misdirection, Wong Jing reveals himself as less a freewheeling naïf than a canny craftsman.

At the end of *High Risk*, Frankie takes public credit, offering to give all proceeds of the film to victims of the carnage—at the same time announcing that his next film will be based on the siege. No less guiltlessly self-promoting than Frankie, Wong Jing has built his career on a mixture of cheerful coarseness, zestful silliness, and assured technique. In *Whatever You Want*, Anita's rutting boss, who watches Category III videos at work, defends himself. "Vulgarity is the basic instinct of human beings. Humans misinterpret vulgarity. I change vulgarity into art so as to let you enjoy it." It is hard not to see this the Wong Jing credo.

7

PLOTS, SLACK AND STRETCHED

By the standards of festival cinema, Hong Kong's approach to narrative seems obstinately naive. While the West was watching Angelopoulos' *The Traveling Players* (1975), Ruiz's *La vocation suspendue* (1977), Kieślowski's *Blind Chance* (1981), Greenaway's *The Draughtsman's Contract* (1982), Carax's *Boy Meets Girl* (1983), von Trier's *The Element of Crime* (1984), and Varda's *Sans toit ni loi* (*Vagabonde,* 1985), this popular cinema clung to embarrassingly straightforward, even slapdash storytelling. The typical Hong Kong movie, as Geoffrey O'Brien puts it, proceeds by an "accretion of incidents" that yields an "improvisatory messiness."[1] The chronic weakness of Hong Kong film, says critic Li Cheuk-to, is "its inability to handle plot effectively."[2]

Which may make this tradition all the more appealing to those film scholars who argue that any mass-entertainment movie is a grab bag of appeals. In place of overarching coherence, they suggest, we should look for a tension between "spectacle" and "narrative." If we think of a story as a chain of causes and effects, actions and reactions, then what do we do with those moments when the story seems to halt and we are forced simply to watch and listen? The musical serves as a prototype: the plot becomes a clothesline to which brightly colored song-and-dance numbers are pinned. Once you start to distinguish between narrative and spectacle in this way, all movies start to look like musicals. Isn't a fight or a chase, a string of gags, a vast set, or a breathtaking landscape spectacle? What about those lingering close-ups of stars, or credits sequences with engaging music? At the limit, all popular film becomes a "cinema of attractions," to invoke Tom Gunning's influential term, and the plot becomes simply a pretext for the real *raison d'être,* the parade of splendors.[3]

Sensuous appeals are surely part of popular cinema, but the narrative/spectacle dichotomy is probably not the best way to understand them. For one thing, the split presupposes a fairly austere conception of narrative. In fact, storytelling is going on constantly in a popular film, and moments of spectacle are usually integral parts of the plot. Lovers express their attraction in "Dancing in the Dark" no less than in a rapid-fire banter; a lengthy close-up of Marlene Dietrich is a narrative event, marking her as a character inclined toward sultry contemplation. Car chases, gunfights, and explosions—all frequently invoked as signs of pure spectacle—develop the action, test the heroes, complicate the villain's plans, often kill off minor characters. Even if some parts of a film seem detachable, such as a string of gags that goes nowhere in particular, we should recall that stories also need padding and stretching. A folktale incorporates three brothers or three wishes or three tests of the hero, even though not much of the point would be lost if there were only two or one. The literary theorist Viktor Shklovsky called this a "stepped" structure, or "deceleration."[4] Any storyteller must fill out the story to the proper length, and so assorted materials—repetitions, gags, digressions, delays—are stitched in, more or less tightly. Instead of relying on the spectacle/narrative duality, we might better presuppose a continuum running between tightly woven plots and looser, more episodic ones.

Akin to the idea that popular cinema bounces between narrative and spectacle is the belief that in "postclassical" Hollywood (that is, since the 1960s or so) coherent storytelling has collapsed. Critics of a postmodernist stripe like this view because it coincides with what they take to be the rise of merchandising, distracted and interruptive viewing habits, and a general breakdown in our understanding of the modern world. To fragmentation of the audience and fragmentation of experience corresponds a fragmentation of the text.[5] One might then argue for Hong Kong cinema as exemplary of this postmodern chaos.

As so often, though, a close look at the films raises problems. Usually what the postmodernist critic takes as a fragmented film is just an episodic one, and there is nothing new about episodic narratives. Further, not all of today's film stories are particularly episodic. Many recent films, like *The Silence of the Lambs* (1991) and *Groundhog Day* (1993), display the sort of structural felicities to be found in *The General* (1927), *His Girl Friday* (1940), and *The Pajama Game* (1957). For some time, Hollywood movies have possessed more unity than they seem to need. It is as if filmmakers set up subtle echoes, balances, and refrains not to enhance thematic meaning (often the film's significance is not deepened by the patterning) but for the pleasure of creating an intricate design, the challenge of slipping in one more detail, and the desire to display skill, if only to peers. It may be that Hollywood, largely middle-class in its orientation, has absorbed enough canons of high art to prize the unities celebrated in eighteenth- and nineteenth-century aesthetics.

Granted, most Hong Kong cinema has yet to achieve Hollywood's degree of craft cleverness at the level of plotting. Yet it isn't useful to insist on these films as casual assemblages of narrative-spectacle or postmodern fragments. Their approach to storytelling, simple and insouciant as it may look, rests upon some powerful and long-standing principles of construction.

Since form often follows format, size limitations can govern structure. The short story is built differently from the serialized novel. Hong Kong filmmakers standardized film length at 90 to 100 minutes, or nine to ten reels. This maximized theater turnover, allowing audiences to be hustled in and out at two-hour intervals across a day. As we've seen, filmmakers took the nine reels as units of plot construction, so that the first reel would grab the audience's interest, the fourth reel would start a significant line of action, the sixth or seventh would provide another major turning point, and the last two or three reels would yield a protracted climax and conclusion, leaving the audience with a strong final impression. Sometimes the template was conceived of as a four-part structure, with beginning (reels 1–3, all major characters established), development (4–6, main story gets going and reaches a crisis about an hour in), and climax (7–9, the final half-hour).[6] These principles of construction also govern "art movies" like *Boat People* (1982) and *Rouge* (1988). Although some filmmakers claim not to follow the reel-by-reel formula, many still do. Kirk Wong, for instance, asks his screenwriters to prepare a nine-paragraph plot breakdown, each paragraph devoted to a ten-minute reel.[7]

Conventional plot anatomy is quite visible in Jackie Chan's *Project A* (1982). The first reel introduces Jackie as a cheerful coast guard officer and sets up the main problem: pirates are roaming the seas around Hong Kong, and the British rulers are wringing their hands while the coast guard and the police squabble over jurisdiction. The reel ends with a comic barroom brawl, establishing Jackie's quarrel with Yuen Biao, the police chief's son. Reel two offers lower-key exposition, showing the pirates' Hong Kong collaborator hiding in the British private club and introducing Sammo Hung, the shifty conman. Reel three: more comedy, with Jackie assigned to the police force and doing all he can to make parade-ground life miserable for Yuen.

Not until reel four does the main action kick into gear, when Jackie and Yuen join forces to invade the club and capture the collaborator. Jackie throws down his badge in disgust at police timidity and runs into Sammo, with whom he hatches a plot to capture the rest of the gang. In reels five and six, Jackie and Sammo try to swindle the gang. They botch the job, which leads to a sustained chase-and-fight sequence. Most viewers find this the most engaging stretch of the film (Fig. 7.1), but with respect to the main action it serves largely to fill out the format.

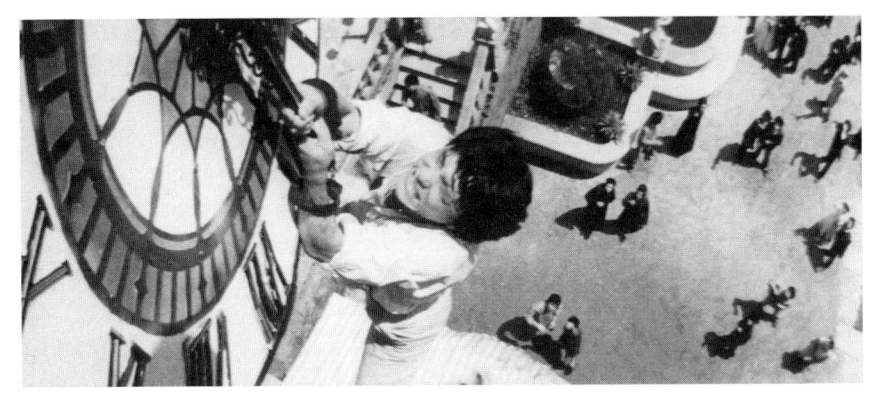

7.1 Jackie Chan dangles from a clock tower in *Project A*.

Project A's major twist comes on schedule in reel seven: the pirates seize a British ship and kidnap the governor, and Jackie is put in charge of the rescue mission. He disguises himself as the pirates' local contact and leads Sammo and Yuen to the pirates' island. Reels eight and nine present the siege on the lair, the final protracted battle with the pirate chieftain, and a quick epilogue showing Jackie and company on a raft, with the British captives paddling them back home.

Hong Kong's reel-by-reel template permits vivid curtain-raisers. *Aces Go Places* (1982), a prototype of modern construction, opens with the hero cheerfully pulling off a death-defying jewel heist that initiates the whole plot. Sometimes, however, the opening scene may have little relation to the action that follows. For example, at the start of *The Dead and the Deadly* (1982) a comic visitation from a ghost establishes the Sammo Hung character as good-hearted if meddlesome and sets up a key motif, but the ghost and the unfaithful wife he catches *in flagrante delicto* do not affect the main plot.

The nine-reel format also permits judicious padding. Any scriptwriter knows the problem of using up one's ideas too quickly and having the plot peter out in the second or third act. But if you treat minutes eleven through thirty as exposition and filler, you can insert the first major twist far enough along to build a solid story in the time remaining. In other words, padding is better placed sooner than later. So comic situations can be exploited at length, as in *The Dead and the Deadly*, when the entire third reel is devoted to Sammo Hung's antics with a corpse; the fourth reel gets the main plot going. In *Gun Men* (1988), the third reel consists of the aftermath of a fight, the mourning for a slain officer, and the administrative shake-up of the police force. Only in the fourth reel does Ding reunite with his army buddies, recruit them to the force, and launch his crusade against the opium dealers. The comedy *All's Well End's Well* (1992) sets up

PLOTS, SLACKED AND STRETCHED   ▪ ▪ ▪ ▪ ▪   181

its plotlines in the first three reels before the primary situations emerge: a husband installs his mistress in his house in order to defy his wife, while his brothers become involved with other women.

Very often, right after the fourth reel we find more filler. In *A Chinese Ghost Story* (1987) the fourth reel presents a major turning point. The demon controlling Nie Xiaoqian demands that she kill her lover Ning Caichen so that in three days she may marry the Master of the Black Mountain. By contrast, the fifth reel consists mostly of extended riffs: the old swordsman's frenzied rap in praise of Taoism and swordplay, followed by the demon Lao Lao's claiming another victim and a lyrical song montage recapitulating scenes we've already seen. The sixth reel recovers the story thread when Xiaoqian tells Caichen she's a ghost, mistaken identities are cleared up, and the swordsman proposes to use Caichen as bait to catch the demon. Alternatively, the middle reels can accumulate reversals and miniclimaxes. In the decisive fourth reel of *She Shoots Straight* (1990), the policewomen confront the main villain for the first time and kill his partner. This precipitates his act of vengeance in killing Tsung-pao in reel five, which also includes a poignant scene of the fallen cop's wife and sister concealing his death from his mother on her birthday.

Cinema City encouraged filmmakers to enliven each scene with special effects, fights, chases, and comedy bits, color-coding each on a reel-by-reel chart. If a scene did not have at least one colored bar, Clifton Ko recalls, it was punched up or dropped.[8] All of these factors, someone might suggest, involve breaking up "narrative" (the story line) with freestanding "spectacle." We get more exactness, though, by analyzing this practice as a formula for episodic construction. Screenwriters seem to have had no guidelines for motivating the middle climaxes or the attractions that pack each reel, so the plots tend not to develop long-running chains of action/reaction, with goals formed, blocked, recast, and fulfilled. Instead, as in *Project A* and *A Chinese Ghost Story*, the plot consists of short-range, fairly closed-off strings of scenes. As a result, complications get resolved seriatim rather than converging at a single climax. At the end of reel four of *Skinny Tiger and Fatty Dragon* (1990), the cop partners apparently solve a drug case. Reel five takes us through their vacation in Singapore, where they decide to quit the force and open a karaoke bar. But in reel six they run into the kingpin they captured earlier, and their pursuit simply resumes.

Because plot phases tend to halt and restart, they are often stitched together by coincidences. Chance meetings, that old favorite of popular narrative, are the principal linking devices. In *My Heart is that Eternal Rose* (1989), a woman becomes the mistress of a triad boss; unknown to her, her former boyfriend has become the boss's hitman. They meet again on the street just after he's fulfilled a contract. In *Hero* (1997), the man who is thrown off a bridge and left to drown is rescued by a passing fishing boat; his former lover happens to be living on the boat. Here, as so often in the adventure tradition, luck helps the hero. The bad guy is likely to run out of bullets at a fortunate moment.

Some Hong Kong critics would trace episodic plotting back to the moralistic Cantonese films of the postwar era,[9] but it may also be that such plots spontaneously revive much older strategies. Piecemeal plotting is characteristic of popular narrative, from oral epics to pulp adventure stories. Most kung-fu films resemble folktales, centering on barely motivated fights, near-repetitions of events, a hierarchy of subsidiary villains, and flagrantly patched-in comic interludes. Perhaps vernacular narrative in general tends toward episodic construction. For most audiences across history the intensity of strong moments has evidently counted for more than niceties of overall architecture. Madeleine Doran describes a tendency in Elizabethan drama to "organize events around several episodic centers, with the connections falling slack between them"—a good description of most Hong Kong movies.[10] Hollywood's concern for detailed motivation on many fronts probably makes it unusual among popular cinemas.

The popular origins of Hong Kong plotting also emerge in screenwriters' fondness for the disguises, cross-dressings, pranks, and foiled schemes beloved of many narrative traditions, from commedia dell'arte to silent cinema. Misunderstandings and mistakes of timing are put to both comic and dramatic uses. There are folkloric tests of ability, trials of strength and will, and challenges from strangers, not just in the martial-arts movies but also in the gambling cycle, where games of chance become dazzling set-pieces. Loose construction can set off a moment vividly, spring surprises through unprepared-for events, and even yield a peculiar sense of realism, in which life becomes just one damned thing after another. In *Lifeline* (1997), the daily routines of the firefighters are interrupted by abrupt accidents—a perilously hanging elevator, a car wreck—and by the personal problems plaguing each member of the team. There is a culminating moment in which all cooperate to conquer and survive a catastrophic fire, but the rescue effort is merely one more incident in their lives; it does not, as it might in a Hollywood film, solve their problems.

Accordingly, the central character may not trace out the "character arc" of the Hollywood hero. Whereas the march of events in *The Untouchables* teaches Elliot Ness to be more flexible and pragmatic, *Gun Men* simply assigns Ding to root out corruption and avenge his colleague's death. The breathless energy of *Speed* (1994) may recall Jackie Chan, but the plot sketches a psychological maturing rare in Hong Kong films: Jack (Keanu Reeves) must give up impulsive bravado and learn to outthink his adversary. The centrality of revenge to the Hong Kong action movie assures a rhythm of blow and counterblow that doesn't require character change. The hero, clinging to his mission, must fight for his pride (and sometimes his principles) without radically questioning himself. And the luck that attends the hero's efforts—the chance meetings, the empty pistol chamber—

becomes a kind of poetic justice, as if the accidents of the world naturally favored his unswerving refusal to change his personality.

Episodic construction favors tonal ruptures. Vulgar comedy can be slapped alongside pathos or suspense. The opening of Wong Jing's *God of Gamblers' Return* (1994) shows the murder of Ko Chun's wife and child, which sets him on the path of vengeance. But once he arrives in the People's Republic the situations become comic, with chases involving crotch jokes, garden shears, and inside references to the fact that Chow Yun-fat has gained weight since the first installment. The film's climactic poker game is a tense confrontation, but it is broken by two sidekicks' silly asides about Dragon Ball comics and AIDS. Similarly, Yuen Kuei's *Hero* is a serious gangster melodrama, but when the protagonist starts to spin lies about his pals, the film veers into anachronistic absurdities (such as making a 1930s triad leader into a pop star, complete with 1990s light show). Perhaps even stranger is *The Untold Story* (1992), which alternates the restaurateur's cruel murder spree with brazen gag scenes featuring the beautiful women in the chief investigator's life.

And endings? Episodic construction makes resolutions harder to predict than in most Hollywood films. Helen Soo, a U.S. importer of Hong Kong movies, has put her finger on it. "Anything goes in Hong Kong cinema. In American movies, the hero never dies. They never kill the child. Most Americans like a happy ending. In Hong Kong films you never know quite how the ending is going to be. It's very unpredictable, which makes it fun."[11] In many kung-fu films, such as *The Killer Wears White* (1980) and *The Bare-Footed Kid* (1993), the hero dies while eliminating the villain. The original version of *Righting Wrongs* (1986) includes a scene of a henchmen blowing up children, and at the end *both* protagonists die. No one is killed in the comedy *The Eighth Happiness* (1988), but after a happy ending in which every man gets the woman of his dreams, an epilogue shows the most hapless man losing his. Such surprises could be read as realism, or as simply a narrative artifice that elicits a broader range of emotions than American cinema has usually allowed.

The last example reminds us that like other popular cinemas Hong Kong has recourse to the double ending, which though defying plausibility allows a popular film to evoke a wide bandwidth of emotions. *Always on My Mind* (1993) centers on a harried TV newsman stricken with cancer. The film milks a long farewell scene and then indulges in a lachrymose montage to the title song. Suddenly, a final scene shows him recovered and living happily with his family. *The Iceman Cometh* (1989) goes even further. At the climax of this time-travel fantasy, the ancient swordsman (Yuen Biao) leaves the streetwalker (Maggie Cheung) to return to the Ming dynasty. But then an epilogue shows her having given up prostitution and working in a snack shop. With even less motivation than the second ending of *An Autumn's Tale*, a shy young student passes her: it is her warrior, apparently reincarnated, and the film ends as she seizes him in delight.

The double ending can work in reverse, promising an affirmative ending before going downbeat, as in the boxing drama *Somebody Up There Likes Me* (1996). By winning the climactic bout, the hero redeems himself in the eyes of his parents and is assured of his girlfriend's love. He immediately dies from the injuries of years of street fighting. The viewer can feel that he is vindicated and yet cheated of full happiness.

The films with epilogues are the exceptions. Many 1970s kung-fu dramas ended on an abrupt freeze-frame at the close of the final combat, leaving other plot elements dangling. One premise of reel-by-reel construction was that the finale should leave the viewer with a vivid impression, and perhaps the midnight screenings made filmmakers unwilling to tack on epilogues, when impatient spectators would begin chatting and heading for the exits. With the sudden freeze-frame, filmmakers could hold the viewer to the very last moment. Shu Kei suggests that filmmakers were influenced by the freeze-frame at the end of *Butch Cassidy and the Sundance Kid* (1969). In any event, the last shot of *Fist of Fury* (Fig. TD.3) proved so dramatic that the halted final image became a firm local convention.

During the 1980s, Gordon Chan recalls, screenwriters debated how to add epilogues conveying a thematic point. (The epilogue that Chan shot for *Fight Back to School*, 1991, was cut.)[12] When epilogues were used, they tended to provide a final plot twist, as in *The Iceman Cometh*, *Always on My Mind*, and *An Autumn's Tale*, rather than the brief celebration of the plot's achieved stable state we typically find in Hollywood. (Think of the epilogue of *Alien* [1979], when Ripley slips gravely back into her sleep capsule as the pod floats off into space.) The endings of Tsui Hark's *Shanghai Blues* (1984) and Woo's *The Killer* (1989) carefully avoided abruptness by dwelling on characters' reactions to the final turn of events. By the 1990s filmmakers were creating unhurried final moments, as in *Fong Sai-yuk* (1993), *In the Heat of Summer* (1994), *The Big Bullet* (1996), and *Task Force* (1997).[13]

Even a plot built out of discrete episodes can gain coherence by mobilizing two universal storytelling strategies: parallel situations and motivic associations. Neither is specific to episodic plotting, of course, but they stand out when a film lacks mechanisms of sustained cause and effect, and they can unify episodic action in surprisingly rich ways.

Parallels can govern entire plotlines, as in the double or triple courtships that wind through romantic comedies like *The Eighth Happiness* (1988) and *Boys are Easy* (1993). In *All's Well End's Well* (1992), three love affairs alternate in importance before all get resolved at the in-laws' eightieth birthday party. *The Banquet* (1991) oscillates between two rival property developers, each with an assistant and a romantic partner, hatching scams to swindle a mogul who wants to rebuild Kuwait after the Gulf War. Parallels can have a more folkloric quality too, as in *The Dead and the*

Deadly, which works variations on dead husbands returning to chastise randy widows.

Kung-fu films like *King Boxer* (1972) often play off parallels between competing schools, with the good son and his benevolent *sifu* set off against the heartless killer and his even more wicked master. In *policiers* the parallels between cop and crook constitute a genre convention, running from Fritz Lang's *M* (1931) through Clint Eastwood's *Tightrope* (1984) to *Gun Men* and Michael Mann's *Heat* (1995). John Woo's heroic triad sagas, obsessed with doubling their protagonist, underscore parallels by emphatic visual devices. Parallel characters or lines of action are time-honored ways to fill out any plot, and they can make loosely connected episodes seem rigorously related.

Parallel elements are often signaled by recurring motifs—lines of dialogue, lighting, costume, props, setting, bits of gesture, snatches of music, anything that can be highlighted and then repeated. Some motifs recur through all of popular cinema, such as the photo of the beloved that can be gazed at in moments of reverie or torn up in anger. Some are folkloric, such as the genie who grants three wishes (*Whatever you Want*, 1994), or the symmetrical wounding that one finds throughout Hong Kong action cinema. After the hero of *Casino Raiders* (1989) is hurt in his left hand, he demands that the villain bet his right arm and leg, while the villain counterbets on the heroine's right hand.

Sometimes the motifs are simple, localized, and strongly signaled. In *Moment of Romance* (1990), a feather-stuffed Macao pillow starts as a young man's gift to his girlfriend; when she fights off her parents at the hydrofoil station, she flails them with the pillow, which bursts open. The title of *Summer Snow* (1995) marks the central motif. At first the summer snow is the flutter of blossoms when the heroine leaves the clinic with her Alzheimer's-addled father-in-law. At the end, the two of them on the roof face the future reconciled, as pigeon feathers flutter down. Or the motif may be more oblique. In *Somebody Up There Likes Me,* the prizefighter and the woman meet when she brings water bottles to ringside for his opponent. Later, after he accidentally kills her brother in a bout, she bashes him with a water bottle. In *God of Gamblers* (1989), the wounded Ko Chun has a bandage wrapped around his head, with a single spot of blood in the center (Fig. 7.2). It resembles a *hachimaki* sweatband with the rising sun in the center, recalling that he has agreed to represent the Japanese in a gambling contest. Such visual motifs remind us how strongly popular cinema is weighted toward purely pictorial expression.

Music too gains a great deal of power through motivic organization. Since the 1980s, chiefly under the influence of New Wave directors, composers began to write through-composed film scores. The arrival of the synthesizer allowed them to turn out lots of music fast and cheaply, and so the sheer amount of music swelled. Only about five minutes of *The East Is*

7.2 *God of Gamblers:* Ko Chun's bandage.

Red (1993) are without musical accompaniment; no more than a minute goes unscored.

Ingenious directors began using music to pull story episodes together. The opening credits of Tsui Hark's *Peking Opera Blues* (1986) tell us that the music will be important: a painted-face actor rolls his eyes on the beat, and the title's three characters, *dao ma dan* ("Sword and Steed Woman"), flash onto the screen as they are belted out by the offscreen female singer. This pulse-pounding song immediately promises rapid action, an effect enhanced by Tsui's cutting the credits shots to match the musical phrases. Apart from generic accompaniment for suspense and chases, specific musical motifs play off the film's drama. The main theme, a wistful and languid melody, is first associated with the general's daughter, Cao Yun, but it quickly expands to denote the group of young people she befriends. Eventually the motif will serve as an all-purpose love theme, paralleling her affection for her brutish father with the attractions among her friends that never quite blossom into romances. By the end the theme has come to evoke Beijing itself, first when a whiff of the tune is heard as the three women study a globe, and later when the film bids farewell to the opera house.

Interwoven with this languid motif are two others. A lilting song ("Snowflakes Are Dancing") is first heard when the three heroines are cast out into the wintry night; later it underscores their subterfuges. The rousing title theme reappears quietly when the three women take refuge in the theater, then bursts out exuberantly in the epilogue as the five friends ride off in different directions. All three main motifs are also treated to different tempos and orchestrations. Perhaps most subtly, the languid theme is introduced in teasing bits, each occurrence adding a bar or two before it blossoms in its full form when Cao Yun becomes anguished at her betrayal of her father's trust. *Peking Opera Blues'* score helps bind together a fairly episodic intrigue.

This example also shows how any motif, auditory or pictorial, can heighten emotion. It can be invested with feelings on its first appearance, and when it returns those feelings can be enriched, qualified, or undercut. In *He Ain't Heavy, He's My Father* the son has a locket given to him by his elderly parents, a token of sacrifices of which he is largely unaware. After he is mysteriously flung back to the past, he meets his parents in their youth. He comes to respect his father as a leader of their tenement neighborhood and his mother as a woman who has left her wealthy family for love. He gives the locket to them as a token of his more mature appreciation of their struggles. What pleases us is not only the young couple's naive puzzlement at his gesture but our knowledge that at some point later in their lives they will spontaneously give the locket (back) to him, and he will now treasure it.

Or take the rather different emotional circuit hooked up in *God of Gamblers*. The master gambler Ko Chun is introduced through two motifs, his jade ring and his love of gold-wrapped slices of chocolate. The motifs suggest his upscale tastes and his adherence to Chinese tradition (jade and gold connote royalty), and they balance his maturity (the ring) against an incipient childishness (a passion for chocolate). The film goes on to expand each motif into a large-scale plot phase. The childish side of Ko Chun emerges in extreme form when a blow on the head gives him amnesia. He reverts to an infantile dependence on those around him, and his panic attacks can be calmed only by chocolate. The jade-ring motif gets developed in a more roundabout way. We know that Ko Chun has a habit of touching the ring when he is anxious about the cards he holds, and his opponents, having studied videotapes of his games, notice it too. But after the climactic game it is revealed that he knew they knew, and he deliberately stroked the ring to make them bet in error. The audience enjoys seeing a familiar element given a new significance: the grown man's idiosyncratic taste becomes a boy's demand for chocolate; the tic we have noticed is noticed by Ko-chun's adversaries too, but he proves to have been one jump ahead of them, and us.

This interplay of motif, implication, and emotion can extend beyond the single film, thanks to sequelitis. Critics normally deplore follow-ups as crass efforts to cash in on hits, but sequels and prequels can rework motifs we know, enriching them through new associations. *God of Gamblers 3: The Early Stage* (1997) reveals the origins of Ko-chun's slicked-down hair (Alain Delon) and jade ring (a woman he loved in his youth). More ambitiously, Tsui Hark's *A Better Tomorrow III* (1989) inverts the macho ethic of Woo's first two films, showing Mark's trademarks—flapping duster, smoky glasses, two-fisted shooting—to be derived from a woman who trained him in combat. It is not so much that such prequels, understood as prologues, make us rethink previous installments. Rather, we bring knowledge of the first entries to the prequel and watch how that knowledge is stretched or qualified by a new context. We know that Ko Chun will touch his ring, but in the prequel the gesture is more than a tic or stratagem, becoming a reminder of the dead woman he loved. We know that Mark is a resourceful warrior, but in the prequel a new range of feeling is invoked when his style is traced to a strong, clever woman. Since audiences are unwilling to give up characters they love, making a good sequel involves coaxing new shades of feeling out of the emotions already invested in familiar iconography.

The emotional resonance of motifs becomes particularly noticeable in two unusual strategies of Hong Kong storytelling. The momentary flashback not only reminds us of earlier scenes but also intensifies the emotion. The device goes back to the silent era and was gradually pruned out of Western cinema, but it is alive and well in Hong Kong. At the climax of *Feel 100%* (1996), Cherrie strums an old song on the guitar, and while she sings we see dissolving views of earlier scenes with Jerry, the young man she's not sure she loves. John Woo's *The Killer* (1989) likewise makes lyrical use of the fragmentary flashback. A second strategy is also anachronistic by Western standards. Many Hong Kong films reprise shots from the film while the final credits roll. These images replay enjoyable moments and may also recapitulate motifs that have bound the film together. At the limit, the credit sequence can provide a "rereading" of the film's action. The reprise in *She Shoots Straight* gathers scenes emphasizing male foolhardiness and female bonding, stressing the traumatic moment of loss, the death of the son/husband/brother. The end of *Shanghai Blues* (1984) cites an earlier scene, and the credits montage then replays that scene, as if the film were caught in an endless loop.

One artistic strength of Hong Kong cinema, then, is its use of parallels and motifs—musical, visual, or verbal—to bind together episodically plotted films. Zhang Che, King Hu, John Woo, Tsui Hark, Patrick Leung, and other outstanding filmmakers have understood how these craft traditions can also enhance a movie's emotional dimensions. The devices can be just as useful when the action is more tightly constructed. Thanks largely to the early 1990s generation, a finer-grained plotting is emerging in Hong Kong cinema.

Take again the hoary device of the flashback, but not the brief one showing a character overcome by a traumatic memory or a kung-fu hero suddenly recalling a technique that will defeat his opponent. Instead, some recent movies build their plots around extensive flashbacks, some of which take surprising turns. Jeff Lau's *Days of Tomorrow* (1993) centers on a film company seeking to remake an old movie. A young woman working on the set meets people who tell her about her mysterious father, the star Shing, and the brief flashbacks are mixed with her voice-over monologue. So far, so ordinary. Gradually the frame story is forgotten as the plot unwinds a long flashback that culminates in Shing's suicide attempt. At this point we get, for the first time in the film, his inner monologue; the shift in point of view occurs when the daughter understands the reasons for her father's suicide.

More viscerally, the key flashback in Herman Yau and Danny Lee's *The*

Untold Story (1993) catches the viewer between sympathy and loathing. The film intercuts the exploits of the cannibalistic killer with the police squad's casual investigation. It is hard to attach feelings to anyone in this carnival of sadism and petty ineptitude. But when the killer is captured and the police extract a confession under torture, we can hardly withhold some sympathy from a demented man who is suffering so much. Then comes the flashback to the crime we have not seen—the killer's relentless butchering of a family. We are left with no one to feel for; the killer commits suicide, his crimes disturbingly unexplained and unexcused.

Other recent films shrewdly refine parallels and motifs. One of the best examples is *He's a Woman, She's a Man* (1994). Wing worships her singing idol, Rose, and idealizes Rose's long-running affair with her composer and record producer, Sam Koo. To get closer to Rose and Sam, Wing disguises herself as a boy and answers an audition for aspiring singers. She is utterly untalented, but to show that he can make a star out of anybody, Sam picks Wing. Thanks to careful packaging, she (as a he) becomes a teen idol. All of Sam's team assumes that the androgynous Wing is gay. When Wing moves in with the energetically heterosexual Sam, Sam finds himself disturbingly attracted to his protégé. Sam is worried that he is becoming gay and so breaks off with Rose and flees from Wing. Having destroyed the love between her two idols, Wing returns crushed to her platonic roommate, Yu Lo. He convinces her to return to Sam, revealing herself as a woman. When Sam sees her all he can say is: "I don't care if you're a woman or a man, I love you."

Although director Peter Chan and screenwriter James Yuen were rewriting the script throughout shooting, the plot is satisfyingly trim.[14] The film begins with Rose winning the televised Music Awards, and she uses the occasion to thank Sam. The film ends a year later, with the next awards broadcast, in which the winning Rose announces that she and Sam are finished. Two celebratory parties, one after each award ceremony, measure the distance the story travels: the first party hints at Sam's dissatisfaction with Rose, while the second shows him pining for the lost Wing. Yu Lo teaches Wing to walk like a man; at the climax he shows her how to run like a woman (Figs. 7.3, 7.4). There is also a strong character arc, with Sam moving from annoyance at Wing's naïveté to friendly interest and then to anguished desire. At the same time, Wing gradually sheds her fangirl illusions and ungainly androgyny, becoming in the final scene a young woman. Even Rose, who could have been a comic harridan, is given a mature dignity in accepting her loss. During the first party Rose gives Sam a comically sexy T-shirt, but in the final one she gives him a plane ticket to Africa—where he had always wanted to go for inspiration ("like Paul Simon," as the script caustically has him say).

Objects are marked for plot functions: Rose's roses, to which Sam is growing allergic; Wing's Sesame Street puppets, with which she carries on imaginary dialogues; the piano at which Sam composes Wing's song, "My

7.3 He's a Woman, She's a Man: Wing learns to walk like a man . . .

7.4 . . . and run like a woman.

Life's Search"; and above all the green-glowing wands that fans wave during concerts. Wing naturally has plenty, and in her disguise she straps a bundle together to give her trousers a plausible bulge. When she and Sam get trapped in his jammed lift, she whips out one to calm his claustrophobia. At the end, Wing and Sam embrace in the lift, and in good Hollywood tradition it jams again; but now his voice comes out of the darkness: "Who cares?"

As an upscale, self-consciously sophisticated UFO production, *He's a Woman* locates its charms firmly in plot geometry. Chan and his collaborators understand that the rhymes and echoes, the foreshadowings and twists, the interanimating parallels can all serve emotion. Audiences laugh delightedly when Wing brings out her glowing wands to brighten Sam's elevator. Your skin prickles when, as Wing runs through the streets to find Sam, up surges the music of his song to her: "Search for all the moments in life." At the party, Sam dejectedly watches Rose working the room; cut to Wing running through the streets to find him (Figs. 7.5–7.7). The three shots draw a contrast (worldly Rose, simple Wing), arouse hope of a last-minute meeting (the crosscutting convention), and suggest Sam's wish that Rose be replaced by Wing. A dynamically shaped plot can map out emotional buildup and intense release, while salting in surprises that retrospectively feel inevitable. This design provides a different sort of pleasure from the abrupt oscillations and sharp contrasts of episodic storytelling. Critics whose tastes run to postmodern fragmentation often ignore tight plotting, but even in a tradition favoring slackness it can be a powerful part of the art of entertainment.

Martial-arts films display many of Hong Kong's storytelling principles with particular vividness. These unpretentious movies illustrate how a popular cinema can draw on indigenous subject matter to create distinctive, strongly profiled plots.

The history and legends surrounding China's martial arts provide a trea-

7.5 Sam looks . . .

7.6 . . . and sees Rose.

7.7 Cut to Wing, also in white, running to Sam.

sure house of stories, akin to Arthurian romance or tales of the U.S. frontier. Warlords promoted combat techniques well before 300 B.C., but the most important development occurred when the Bodhidharma carried martial arts to China along with Ch'an Buddhism (known in Japanese as Zen). Around 500 A.D., tradition has it, the Bodhidharma installed himself at the Shaolin Temple at the foot of the Songshan Mountains and taught monks meditation, breathing exercises, and fighting skills.

The Shaolin Temple is the emblem of Chinese martial arts, and its legends have been recycled in film after film. The temple is said to have housed about 1,500 monks, 500 of them trained fighters. Over the centuries the martial monks were occasionally called to help emperors with military campaigns, and Shaolin fighting techniques spread throughout East Asia. In 1674 the Qing ruler razed the temple. According to legend, the five monks who survived became the "Five Ancestors" who founded the secret societies known generically as triads. In fact many monks survived the fire and became street performers and Peking Opera actors. Later the Shaolin Temple was rebuilt, but in 1928 it was burned again in a battle among local warlords.[15]

Whereas martial arts were quickly integrated into Japan's warrior society, in China they survived in the shadows. The Qing dynasty (1644–1911) outlawed them as a threat to security. Some martial artists became entertainers, putting on harmless public demonstrations, lion dances, and

Peking Opera plays. The more devoted students of fighting went underground, developing batteries of secret techniques. Kung-fu plots often draw upon this tradition: the rivalry between schools, the duty to avenge a master or punish a disciple who has misused the master's teaching, and the pupil's need to learn a devastating style.

Popular literature drew extensively on martial-arts lore. Chivalric tales had circulated for centuries before coalescing in folk epics like *The Water Margin* (1644), which in turn became the basis of a flourishing family of genres during the Qing dynasty. There were tales of martial exploits, love stories with a chivalric element, and fantasies of supernatural swordsmen. These formed a central part of China's pulp fiction during the nineteenth and early twentieth centuries.

The 1920s saw a boom in Shanghai *wuxia* (heroic chivalry) novels. Some of these were highly nationalistic tales about Chinese striking back at Western imperialists. Others featured warriors with the power to fling swords great distances, emit death rays, ride on giant birds, and slay monsters. In one novel a giant serpent confronts the hero. He turns his sword into a ray of light and rides it up to a cliff edge, where he joins the heroine Ling-yun. The serpent spews a ball of fire at the humans, but Ling-yun flings her secret weapon, Heavenly Yellow Pearl, into the fireball, blowing up the serpent.[16] Admittedly, this sounds like a Tsui Hark scene, but even less fantastic tales present heroes vaulting great distances and developing ironlike palms, feats that some martial-arts schools claim are attainable through arduous training.[17] (The Boxers, who imagined themselves invulnerable to Westerners' bullets, were in the grip of such beliefs.) In any martial-arts film, there will be a thin line between what might be barely possible physically and what seems to outsiders pure fancy.

Martial-arts fiction continued to flourish after World War II in Hong Kong and Taiwan. There emerged a new-style *wuxia* novel centering on independent heroes who gradually matured, both as fighters and as men. The tone was somewhat antiheroic, displaying suspicion of authority and criticizing the hero's egotism and greed. The Taiwanese writer Gu Long published a series celebrating aggressive, ascetic heroes, and these spawned many films, such as Chor Yuan's *Killer Clans* (1976) and *Magic Blade* (1976).[18] The most famous exponent of the new *wuxia* novel was the Hong Kong writer Jin Yong, also known as Louis Cha. Jin developed the idea of a disabled hero, prototypically the one-armed swordsman. Many 1970s films were based on episodes in Jin's stupendously popular works, and more recently Wong Kar-wai's somber *Ashes of Time* (1994) and Jeff Lau's spoof *The Eagle-Shooting Heroes* (1993) derive from Jin tales.[19]

The *wuxia* novels and films created a heroic, mythicized past that was also on display in another story form. Early in the nineteenth century the Peking Opera emerged as a distinct entertainment. It seized audiences through vigorous music, gorgeous costumes and makeup, and above all the virtuosity of the actor, who was obliged to sing, dance, mime, perform acrobatics, and recite dialogue. Peking Opera created a set of stock types to be recycled in play after play. The actor's skill lay in the flawless execution of set-pieces and in subtle changes in formulas. Like filmmakers later, the troupe worked without a script, stringing together routines to suit new plots and devising fresh lyrics for traditional melodies. Cantonese Opera, the sweeter and less refined variant of Peking Opera that settled into Hong Kong, adapted the same premises.

In fiction, onstage, and in movies, martial arts came to saturate Hong Kong's popular culture. Legendary swordsmen and kung-fu masters are recycled through television series, and flying heroes fill comic books. One can't accuse it all of being boys' schoolyard games either, if only because women play a heroic role in these sagas to an extent without parallel in European or Anglo-American adventure yarns. From the swordswomen of silent Shanghai films through Xu Feng of the King Hu films and Angela Mao to Michele Yeoh in *Yes, Madam!* (1985) and Anita Mui in *Saviour of the Soul* (1991), Hong Kong action cinema has celebrated women warriors.

What brings audiences back to these tales? To some extent, they represent a China made for exiles. Roger Garcia has called martial-arts films a form of "mythic remembrance" for the diaspora, a legitimating fantasy.[20] However unhappy Chinese history has really been, one can imagine belonging to a country of stable traditions—not of law or government, but of honorable personal conduct. The *wuxia* tales make honor a matter of family, school, and ultimately the individual.

As each generation reworks these myths, Hong Kong critics often note, there emerges a recurring heroic plot. The *wuxia* hero is a gifted exponent of the fighting arts, and however bloody his or her deeds, the hero possesses righteousness *(yi)*. The hero's loyalty is to kin, friend, or teacher, all of whom must be defended against socially sanctioned violence. In the American western, the hero may bring civilized justice or right the wrongs that have evaded authority. But China has no strong traditions of impersonal, objective law. "The most striking characteristic in our political life as a nation," wrote Lin Yu-tang, "is the absence of a constitution and of the idea of civil rights."[21] The hero must exercise *yi* because the larger community offers no legal recourse; indeed, often the villains rule. Violence becomes the only solution.[22] The tradition continues in Hong Kong *policiers,* where the rogue cop, male or female, pursues illegal investigation, intimidation, torture, and vendetta punishment.[23]

By duty the hero is pledged to avenge any harm done family, friend, or teacher. The basic motive, in most martial-arts and gunplay films, is revenge. Often there is little psychological backstory about why the villain is cruel or how the hero came to possess *yi*. There is seldom any scruple about the morality of taking revenge, any sense that it taints the avenger. It is a rare film, such as Lau Kar-leung's *Eight-Diagram Pole Fighter* (1984), that shows revenge leading to obsessiveness, madness, and the slaughter of innocents. Usually the only price of revenge is that you may be obliged to kill a treacherous friend or relative. In Woo's *The Killer* (1989), John's drama revolves around the replacement of a betraying friend (Sidney the go-between) by an admiring adversary (detective Li). John's suffering springs partly from his wounding of an innocent woman, partly from his reluctance to punish Sidney for disloyalty.

Revenge can govern the whole action. As in Jacobean tragedy, the villain's initial act of aggression or betrayal may force the hero to spend the entire plot getting payback. Alternatively, things may be set in motion by competition in a tournament, or business rivalry among gangs, or (less often) competition for a woman. Typically someone dear to the hero will be hurt, or the hero will lose face through public humiliation. Thereafter action is fueled by vengeance. This can yield an escalating rhythm, since truly satisfying retaliation must raise the stakes. And whereas American films tend to let the vengeful hero off the hook at the end, allowing destiny to do the dirty work, Hong Kong heroes tend to be pitiless. Near the climax of *Lethal Weapon* (1987), Danny Glover allows the accidentally trapped villain to blow up. But at the start of *Righting Wrongs* (1986), Yuen Biao punishes the trapped assassins by firing the shot that sends their car into flames.

Granted, this conception of masculine honor is playground morality. Yet it is powerful for this very reason. If one had to pick dramatic motivations that would be understood around the world, regardless of the civil society in which one lived, revenge would be high on the list. One cross-cultural appeal of Hong Kong storytelling, particularly for male audiences, is clearly the central role it assigns to vengeance. The films' power is probably intensified for viewers who live in cultures in which civil justice is as untrustworthy as in classic Chinese society.

Vengeance as a driving force can yield intricate plots, as in Webster's *Duchess of Malfi*, but in Hong Kong movies it usually serves to enhance episodic tendencies. A film's *raison d'être* is the action, laid out in semi-detachable set-pieces. The stretches between the fights are filled out with delaying devices—episodes of scheming between rival schools or gangs, displays of combat techniques, the sufferings of the hero's sidekick, the arrival of secondary villains (each of whom must be dealt with in a separate fight). Regardless of the genre, the delaying devices—a series of torments or slayings—may serve to make the villains ever more worthy of punishment. The tone need not be consistent. Kung-fu films have a weakness for low-comedy digressions, a feature that carries over into cop-and-gangster films of the 1980s.

Whereas the 1960s swordplay films often developed some complexity of intrigue, the 1970s kung-fu films stripped the plot down to its essentials: a string of fights. Either the hero works his way through a host of enemies (the Bruce Lee variant), or the hero undergoes training, *then* works his way through a host of enemies (the Wang Yu/Jackie Chan variant). In any case the climax is a lengthy duel between the hero and the principal villain. Often the hero is put at a momentary disadvantage before he wins by superior skill or a secret tactic, or with the help of allies.[24] (Ganging up on a powerful antagonist is perfectly acceptable.) The modern *policiers* are not so different, with plot modules devoted to the discovery of traitors, the death of innocent witnesses, and the hero's public disgrace, wrapping things up in a culminating fight that can last as long as two reels.

Screenwriters of the 1960s may not have realized that by highlighting impressive fights they weakened plot structure. One recalls: "We wanted to emulate what Kurosawa had achieved. For instance, when we saw the ending of *Sanjuro* and *Yojimbo*, we'd say, 'That's the effect we want!' I think we were preoccupied with dramatic effects, and didn't think enough about the narrative as a whole, character development and relationships."[25] The same holds true for most Hong Kong action films today. Yet the very simplicity of the plotlines has helped the films travel well, and sometimes intriguing variations emerge. You can have several heroes, even five as in *Shaolin Avengers* (1976). You can proceed by a sort of "numerical exhaustion" principle. *Invincible Armour* (1977) centers on a villain whose body seems impregnable, so the hero must discover that this "armor" actually has five weak points, each of which he tries to penetrate in turn (and each of which is signaled by a flashing red dot). You can also multiply revenge plots. As we've already seen, one virtue of episodic plotting is the possibility of developing vivid contrasts of tone among parallel lines of action. In *Ninja in the Dragon's Den* (1982) a ninja comes to China bent on avenging the death of his father, and his target is Li, an old master who was once a member of a ninja society. This is a serious revenge plot. Running alongside it is another one involving a young martial artist who, when Li is killed by the avenging ninja, sets out to avenge *his* death. Eventually, in a comic version of the father-son motif, the youngster and the ninja join forces to defeat a magician who pursues them because they humiliated his son. Like many popular traditions, martial-arts plots often reveal a surprising formal ingenuity.

Modern urban action pictures have found another way to knit episodes together—by taking the spotlight off a single protagonist and interweaving various characters' stories. This can suggest a measure of realism, and it encourages the filmmaker to develop parallels and recurring motifs. *The Log* (1996), a police procedural directed by Derek Chiu Sung-kai, presents a cross-section of cops' personal problems—the overzealousness of a tough inspector, the sick fear felt by a rookie who accidentally shoots a thug, and the inarticulate pain of a dogged veteran who discovers that his wife is having an affair with his superior. The Chinese title, which translates as *Three Injured Policemen*, underscores the parallels. Although energetic action scenes trigger each man's crisis, there are moments of reflection and irony, as when the inspector is put in a cell with the suspect he has beaten and is abashed when the suspect forgives him "because I have accepted Jesus." Like other police procedurals, *The Log* pressurizes its action by setting all three plotlines within a brief span—ominously, the New Year's Eve that brings in 1997. The three working stiffs, all of whom plan to stay in Hong Kong after the handover to China, are counterposed to the colonialist top brass, who have comfortable bolt-holes abroad.

The same sort of compressed time scheme accentuates ironic parallels in another triple-strand crime plot, that of Cha Chuen-yee's *Once upon a Time in Triad Society 2* (1996). Dagger is a nervous pimp who would rather play mahjong than cut up rough. Dinosaur is a triad rascal who idolizes his mentor, an invincible fighter known as the God of the Sword. Dummy is a young, subdued plainclothes cop who wants to do his job without fuss. Through alternating editing, the film's first third contrasts Dagger's cowardice, Dinosaur's exhilaration in inflated heroics, and Dummy's dutiful, somewhat dull prudence. Each young man has a woman: Dagger's impudent whore, J.J.; Dinosaur's teenybopper girlfriend, Deda; and Dummy's pregnant wife, Crystal. The couples' lives intersect when rival triad chiefs call for a confrontation in Mongkok. Dagger and Dinosaur, who are friends, face each other on opposite sides of a crowd's shouting match, while Dummy and other cops race through the streets to prevent a gang riot.

Inadvertently, Dagger and Dinosaur trigger the fight, and the central stretch of the film shows, in an utterly unromanticized way, the gangs laying waste to the neighborhood. Dagger tries his best to hide but has to come out to protect J.J. After hacking up attackers on all sides, Dinosaur finds his gang wiped out. He is gushing blood. At the same time Dummy, who thinks his wife has been wounded, hunts for her. Each plotline is resolved in a vivid climax. Dummy finds his wife unharmed; Dinosaur dies listening to a romantic ballad on Deda's Walkman; and in a sequence of grotesque comedy Dagger is sent out to assassinate his boss's rival. The film concludes with a trick ending and a grimly comic wrapup.

Once upon a Time in Triad Society 2 blends genre-based suspense and fights with a carefully measured range of tone. Here Hong Kong's inclination toward episodic narrative creates a tissue of parallel scenes, and the tendency to mingle physical agony, sadness, and humor is controlled by confining each emotional register to a distinct line of action. Hong Kong critics saw Cha's film as debunking the hip glorification of twentysomething triads. Through its contrasting plotlines the film dismantles the conventions of loyalty and chivalry that defined the "heroes" movies and the *Young and Dangerous* cycle.

Interwoven plotting permits a nice balance between severity and slackness. In Patrick Leung's *Task Force* (1997), each detective-centered plotline has its share of pathos and humor, incidents accrue in a somewhat open-ended way, and the film teases us with romantic rivalries that never quite crystallize. Fruit Chan's *Made in Hong Kong* (1997) presents two main sets of characters: the young debt collector Chung Chiu along with his parents and friends, and the young girl Susan Hui, with her family and friends. The plot centers on Chung's efforts to make peace with his mother, protect his retarded friend, Sylvester, carry on a romance with his girlfriend, and avoid becoming too deeply involved with the triads. Sylvester witnesses Susan Hui's suicidal jump from a building, and he brings Chung two bloodsoaked letters. Chung's efforts to deliver them lead him to explore Susan's reasons for killing herself. After Sylvester and Chung's girlfriend, Wing, also die needlessly, Chung faces the same despair Susan had felt. Adding his own codicil to her note and delivering it to her parents, Chung kills himself. *Made in Hong Kong*'s adolescent anguish is sharpened by its hero's gradual discovery that a stranger shares his disillusionment with the adult world.

Slack or tightly woven, Hong Kong films reveal principles of popular plotting as if under an X ray. These principles may seem simple, but the tempo of production forces filmmakers to deploy them in novel ways. And sometimes the sheer familiarity of a device can arouse the thrill of circumstances clicking neatly into place. In *Casino Raiders* (1989) Sam (Andy Lau), who has failed his wife and friend, must redeem himself in a crucial card game. He takes off his wedding ring to be able to play more nimbly. Cut to a close-up of him slipping the ring off in the foreground, with his wife looking on apprehensively behind him. A straightforward scene like this provides an occasion for the audience to recall earlier events, to speculate on the characters' emotional states, to dwell on the loss, risk, and hope that the moment bears. In order to save his marriage Sam must take off his ring; he becomes worthy of winning only by momentarily relinquishing his pledge of commitment. Thanks to norms of storytelling and performance, style and genre, the moment takes on a vivid coloring, becoming at once fresh and deeply traditional. The forms and formulas of popular entertainment need not be subverted in order to command our interest. They have proved themselves over time and can, often with very little revamping, authentically engage an audience's eyes and ears and feelings.

8

MOTION EMOTION: THE ART OF THE ACTION MOVIE

Hong Kong popular cinema will be remembered chiefly for its preposterously exciting physical action. Without benefit of film schools or postmodern referentiality, three generations of directors spontaneously recaptured the visual dynamism of Chaplin, Keaton, Lloyd, and Fairbanks. Just as intuitively, they put into practice ideas articulated by the 1920s Soviet montage masters. The result is exhilarating entertainment. Many of these fights, stunts, and chases remain gems of audacious invention, and the best action films from Hong Kong are among the glories of popular art.[1]

Making a case for entertainment often requires us to take despised genres seriously, but perhaps you don't want to go as far as *The Smiling Swordsman* (1968), *Kung-Fu from beyond the Grave* (1982), and *Hong Kong Godfather* (1991). Yet even if you find the Hong Kong action movie nasty, brutish, and long, looking closely at the genre repays us in other ways. These films have managed to grip audiences throughout the world, and they help us understand how cinema can achieve kinesthetic artistry.

"The public loves action," Run Run Shaw observed, "all sorts of action."[2] Films showcasing chases, fights, stunts, and gunplay have found international popularity since the 1910s, when European "sensation films" of detection and espionage were widely exported. Douglas Fairbanks and William S. Hart opened up world markets for Hollywood. Later peplum and spaghetti Westerns helped revitalize Italy's film industry. Action films can be cheap to make, and there has long been a niche market for them in Third World countries and lower-end theaters in the West. Today, they are top-renting video fare. When you step off the Moscow subway, faded pink Stallones and Schwarzeneggers glower at you from the video kiosks.

During the late 1960s Hong Kong filmmaking distinguished itself through its bravura physical action. This helped make it a dominant industry in East Asia and gave it access to Europe and North America. Export success encouraged makers of swordplay and kung-fu films to borrow techniques from Hollywood. The rise of the Hollywood action-adventure genre in the early 1980s spurred Hong Kong filmmakers to push their distinctive approach still further, mixing gunplay with martial arts and acrobatics. Soon audiences around the world intuitively recognized the uniqueness of the Hong Kong action movie.

One can argue that this tradition attracts notice chiefly because it shows things that lie outside Hollywood's range of tolerance: torture, dismemberment, disembowelings, gouged-out eyes, jets of blood. Following the precedent of Japan (which since the 1920s has offered up the most gruesome films in the world), Hong Kong filmmakers have pushed the boundaries of taste. The prizefights in *Raging Bull* (1980) are hard to watch, but Patrick Leung's *Somebody Up There Likes Me* (1996) shows what a really rough boxing movie can be. There seem to be no limits. A kung-fu duel may go on for a dozen minutes, and a 1980s cop film may feature a car chase or gunfight in every reel. *In the Line of Duty IV* (1989) runs ninety-two minutes, forty-two minutes of that consisting of vigorous physical action.

Yet if exciting cinema were no more than Grand Guignol shock and a flurry of motion, Hong Kong films would not stand out from their competition in the international market. Their success owes a great deal to their command of the film medium. They are just better made than most other action movies. They adhere to principles of design and execution that we can only call formal, and these principles are intriguing and far from obvious. They spring from a controlled dynamic of standardization and innovation, that interplay of norm and novelty we have already seen at work in genres, stars, style, and storytelling. Like the Cantopop song which mixes Eastern scales with American four-bar structure and Latin instrumentation, the action movie has creatively reworked international conventions of film style.

> *I used to think that an American action choreographer must be the best in the world or an American director must be the best. But now I know we are the best when it comes to action. They learn from us. If you ask any American director to come and make an action movie our way, they can't.*
>
> JACKIE CHAN

The kinetic precision of these martial-arts films arises partly from the stringent codes governing Asian fighting traditions. The Chinese martial arts, which include both armed and unarmed combat, are known in Mandarin as *wushu* ("crafts of combat"), with the colloquial Cantonese *kung-fu*, a more recent term, indicating combat based on hitting and kicking. Any martial-arts style will have its distinctive weaponry, from swords and halberds to jointed staffs and the Okinawan nanchaku, but the basis of any style remains the control of the body. Combat arts are divided into "internal," or passive, ones and "external" ones, based on strong, penetrating attacks. The external approach in turn splits into "soft" arts and "hard" arts. The adept of the soft arts turns the attacking force against itself, employing a low center of breathing, circular movements, and a knowledge of vital points. The most famous soft approach is *t'ai chi*. In the hard approach, force meets force, and a high center of breathing sustains an explosive release of energy. The fighter attacks in straight lines, using not only arms and legs but also knees, shoulders, and head. Most kung-fu films display the hard approach.

Films also exploit a subdivision of the hard arts, known to all Chinese as "Northern Leg, Southern Fist." Asian legwork has a solid physical rationale. The legs have a longer reach than the arms, and their muscles are more thickly knit, so proper kicking can deliver devastating impact. Kicks are used in all variants of the hard arts, but in dry northern China, where people ride horses and walk great distances, legwork formed the basis of *wushu* styles. Northern schools, and particularly northern Shaolin kung-fu, use the arms to defend the torso while the fighter is jumping, twisting, spinning, and kicking. The graceful northern techniques were probably the basis for the acrobatics of Peking Opera, and the flying kick (which may have originated as a technique for unseating horsemen) has become the indelible image of kung-fu movie fighting.[3]

The southern hard styles, also known as southern Shaolin kung-fu, rely more on the upper body, supposedly because southern Chinese, rowing and poling along waterways, built up powerful shoulders and arms. Southern styles present solid stances and intricate arm and hand techniques. When kicks are used, they tend to be low. Several historical heroes of Hong Kong martial arts movies are identified with southern styles. The legendary Huang Feihong, for example, is known as an exponent of the Hung Gar style, a close-quarter tactic that is one of the five original forms of Shaolin kung-fu. Bruce Lee began as a student of Wing Chun, a short-range punching style. There is scarcely a style that has not been showcased in one film or another, such as *Choi Li Fat* (1970) and *Mad Monkey Kung-Fu* (1979). Many styles are modeled on animal movements, so a kung-fu film may show the hero discovering a technique by observing an animal's attack. The most famous example is probably Jackie Chan in *Snake in the Eagle's Shadow* (1978), in which he gets inspiration from a cobra's attack on a cat.

The distinction between Northern Leg and Southern Fist is not absolute, since many schools merged aspects of each. Thus the Praying Mantis system combines balanced footwork with lightning grabbing and clawing techniques. This pluralistic approach quickly carried over into cinema, which demanded the showiest forms of each style. Bruce Lee deplored the inconsistency of movie martial arts, but even he incorporated the flashy northern flying kick. Although a character may claim allegiance to one style or another, the performer may mix styles freely. A northern tech-

8.1 In maneuvers reminiscent of Peking Opera, Jackie Chan evades spears in *Fearless Hyena*.

nique will be followed by something southern or an acrobatic trick. "In films you can't play just one style," remarks Yuen Wah, an outstanding actor and choreographer. "It often depends on the camera angle or your distance from the camera as to what looks good."[4]

Conceptions of what looks good are derived as much from theatrical spectacle as from combat traditions. As a presentational mode, Peking Opera correlated each role with a set of correct movements, which were in turn broken down into precise gestures. A song's lyrics were treated as "time-movement units" like the patterns to be memorized in martial-arts training. Opera's combat forms were stylized elaborations of *wushu* movements, spiced with acrobatic displays.[5] In addition, opera plays could be very violent. In a plot that could fit a 1960s swordplay film, the play *Wu Song's Revenge* incorporates both swordfighting and unarmed combat: a tiger hunter tosses servants into a wine vat and hacks off conspirators' heads before slathering a message on the wall in their blood. Significantly, many Hong Kong action filmmakers came from Peking Opera academies. The most famous academy, Yu Jim Yuen's Opera School, produced the "Seven Little Fortunes," a boys' troupe that included Jackie Chan, Sammo Hung, Yuen Biao, Yuen Kuei, and Yuen Wah—supreme acrobats who have been fighting onscreen for decades.[6] *Painted Faces* (1988) presents a warm, idealized version of Master Yu's training; a striking result of the regimen, complete with poses and a rhythmic spear fight, can be seen in Jackie Chan's *Fearless Hyena* (1979; Fig. 8.1).

Because of the films' origins in literary, theatrical and martial traditions, Hong Kong critics usually see a profound continuity among the action genres. The gunplay films of the 1980s are indebted to the martial-arts movies of previous decades, where John Woo, Yuen Kuei, and many stars of crime movies began their careers.[7] In order to grasp the action aesthetic, it's worth sketching some lines of historical development.

The first martial-arts films were silent-era productions of Shanghai stu-

8.2 Palm power on display in *Burning of the Red Lotus Monastery*.

dios. Films like *The Nameless Hero* (1926) and *The Hero of Guandong* (1928) centered on the adventures of swordsmen and swordswomen. They came to be known as *wuxia pian*, "films of chivalrous combat." Stylized fighting, derived from the opera tradition, is said to have been introduced in *Li Feifei, the Heroine* (1925).[8] The eighteen-part serial *Burning of the Red Lotus Monastery* (1928) was the prototype of the fantasy swordplay movie; already there were flying daggers, weightless leaps, and palm power, the ability to shoot bursts of energy from one's hands (Fig. 8.2).[9] Many of the cinematic tricks that present superheroic feats were developed in this era, including wirework, double exposures, and animation. *Heroine of the Wild River: Big Trouble at Deer Horn Gulch* (1931) features fast-motion swordfights, a huge bird that carries off a little boy, animated silhouettes of eagles, and a woman warrior who tosses around gigantic barbells.

Fearing that the martial-arts films would harm children, the Chinese government suppressed them, but when Shanghai directors emigrated to Hong Kong in the late 1930s they revived the genre. Hong Kong films dropped many of the fantasy elements and based themselves more closely on Chinese opera and acrobatic stunts. One famous series centered on Fong Sai-yuk, the Cantonese hero trained by his mother. As the Hong Kong industry revived after the war, several companies devoted themselves to action pictures, which had strong export potential throughout Asia. Some firms relaunched fantasy swordplay, creating plots based on superheroes, stylized fighting, and magical effects, while others relied upon more realistic manual combat.[10]

Of the more authentic efforts the most popular was the series of seventy-six films devoted to the great Cantonese martial artist Huang Feihong (1847–1924), who performed and taught in southern China. Because little was known of his real life, a mythology grew up around his devotion to the Hung Gar school of martial arts, his powerful punches and "shadowless kick," and his skills as a physician. (Students get hurt while sparring, so masters traditionally know anatomy and herbal medicine.) Soon after World War II, newspaper articles and radio broadcasts revived interest in Huang and Shaolin kung-fu.[11] Writer Ng Yat-siu and director Wu Pang launched a film series with *The Story of Huang Feihong*, released in two parts in 1949. The series snowballed, becoming a major part of Cantonese production. In 1956 twenty-five Huang Feihong films were released. Kwan Tak-hing, a beloved theater performer, portrayed Huang as a peace-loving Confucian who used kung-fu as a last resort (Fig. 8.3). The villain was often played by Shek Kin, who became as familiar and revered as Kwan, not least because he usually reformed after Huang Feihong trounced him. (Shek is best known in the West as Han, the Doctor No figure of *Enter the Dragon*.) Often awkward in their staging and shooting, the Huang Feihong films were significant in showcasing genuine kung-fu. "Before," said Kwan, "everything was swordplay and magic!"[12] The series halted in 1970 (although Golden Harvest brought Kwan back as Huang in *The Skyhawk*, 1974). It served as a training ground for many of the leaders of kung-fu filmmaking in the decades to follow.

While Kwan Tak-hing regaled audiences, other Cantonese companies continued to make *wuxia pian*, mostly fantasy swordplays. These stabilized a repertoire of conventions that would never leave Hong Kong cinema: reverse motion, fast motion, hidden trampolines, and whirs and whooshes to emphasize colossal leaps. These technical devices demanded time and money; preparing a swordsman's leap on guy wires took five or six hours, and flying swords were usually produced through color effects or drawing on the film (Fig. 8.4). But when Shaws and MP & GI entered the market in a major way in the 1960s, the Cantonese martial fantasy lost ground before the rise of more violent and realistic Mandarin swordplay.

The Mandarin films marked a new sophistication in Hong Kong martial arts. Xu Zhenghong's *Temple of the Red Lotus* (1965), King Hu's *Come Drink with Me* (1966) and his Taiwan-made *Dragon Gate Inn* (1967), and Zhang Che's *Golden Swallow* (1967) and *One-Armed Swordsman* (1967) displayed a freshness, compactness, and brutal intensity. Color and widescreen began to be used. The biggest studios had sophisticated cameras like

8.3 Kwan Tak-hing wields a broom in this lobby card for *Huang Feihong and the Courtesan's Boat Argument* (1956).

8.4 A publicity still from *The Sword from the Sea (Part I)* (1964). Compare Figs. 6.1 and 8.2.

MOTION EMOTION 205

the lightweight Arriflex, which enabled filmmakers to employ handheld shots. Cutting became more rapid, particularly to hide wirework and other trick effects. The 1950s kung-fu films had simply allowed actors to improvise their fights, but now the martial-arts instructor became an important crew member. Many directors simply let the choreographer and cameraman supervise the action scenes. Choreography was staged very cinematically, using camera movements to exploit the widescreen format. Shooting a martial-arts film now consumed a month or more, and filming the fight sequences could take up to two-thirds of production time.[13]

The Mandarin swordplay films shrewdly absorbed lessons from the Italian Westerns and, as we would expect, from the Japanese *jidai-geki* (historical films). Kurosawa and his colleagues featured lightning swordplay, bodies crashing through screens, amputations, and geysers of blood. Hong Kong filmmakers had ample opportunity to study the films featuring the blind masseur-swordsman Zatoichi, a series that Shaws distributed locally. Shaws sent staff members to Japan to study production methods and began to hire Japanese directors and cameramen.[14] Run Run Shaw and his manager Raymond Chow would screen a Japanese film for directors and decide how to borrow its plot.

Hong Kong's "new *wuxia pian*," as they were called, drew material from the martial-arts novels being devoured by readers in Hong Kong and Taiwan: plots of vengeance, competition for the highest rank in the martial world, the search for treasure or a combat manual.[15] King Hu's intricate political intrigues and Zhang Che's blood-sodden, masochistic treatment of the martial tradition were far removed from the simpler, sunnier virtues on view in the Cantonese films. The Mandarin swordplay dramas trounced American imports at the local box office. They also played the major role in expunging Cantonese-language films; Shaws and Cathay held so many theaters that Cantonese action films were consigned to peripheral houses. But within a few years the Mandarin swordplay films were themselves overtaken in popularity by the return of unarmed fighting arts.

Shaw's *Chinese Boxer* (1970) is usually credited with reviving the kung-fu film. Assimilating the sword films' brutal violence and heroic suffering, the new kung-fu film reached its apogee in the early 1970s—still in Mandarin, but with a strong emphasis on southern Chinese fighting styles like Wing Chun. The genre's very name had a local flavor. In Cantonese *kung-fu* basically means skill in any domain, from cooking to teaching, but with the popularity of the Bruce Lee films it came to indicate manual fighting skills. In the 1970s, when local audiences were sensitive to Hong Kong's cultural uniqueness, kung-fu, a southern martial art with demonstrable historical origins, seemed strikingly modern compared to the northern *wushu*, which was rooted in myth and associated with fantasy and the supernatural.[16]

Kung-fu thrust Hong Kong films into Japan, South Korea, the United States, Europe, Latin America, and Africa. Major American studios were briefly buying kung-fu movies, and bottom-feeding distributors lived off them well into the 1980s. A kung-fu piece, with its simple costumes and props and a vague turn-of-the-century period setting—a village, a clearing or two—could be filmed more cheaply than a sword movie. Dozens of independent companies sprang up, many turning out films solely for overseas audiences. "Chop-socky" the cruder ones were called, and for many viewers the Hong Kong film is still synonymous with the quickies' disjointed plots, grotesque acting, and otherworldly dubbing, a mixture of snarling delivery, vernacular American vocabulary, and erratically fractured phrasing. (A favorite fan example: Your kung-fu has . . . gotten real . . . ly good.)

Kung-fu became the leading edge of Hong Kong cinema. Jimmy Wang Yu, originally a star swimmer, played in sword films before starring in *The Chinese Boxer* and other kung-fu classics, some of which he directed. Zhang Che smoothly switched from swordplay to kung-fu, eventually creating a crew of superb martial artists who became known in the West as the Five Venoms (from their 1978 film of the same name). To save money producers began to hire martial-arts choreographers to direct entire films. Martial-arts directors incorporated more fight scenes, filled expository passages with action and physical comedy, and gave up on sustaining even a moderately complex story line. The genre also passed to television, which revived the legendary figures Fong Sai-yuk and Huang Feihong.

Stephen Teo has plausibly argued that the kung-fu cycle hastened the end of the didactic, tradition-laden Cantonese cinema. Kung-fu established a more vernacular realism, laying the foundations for the New Wave and the slicker films of the 1980s.[17] Yet in other respects kung-fu set back production standards. Most filmmakers lost interest in the period detail and sumptuous decor of the swordplay epics. Endless zoom shots and slow motion gave the films a low-end reputation, and producers shamelessly recycled Western film scores, from James Bond tunes to *The Sting* and *Once upon a Time in the West*. Comic players had crossed eyes, buck teeth, mountainous pimples, and hairy warts. A hero might sport sequined aqua vests worthy of Liberace. Like Italian peplum and Mexican masked-wrestler movies, kung-fu screamed kitsch.

Nonetheless, the finest of the choreographers-turned-directors took kung-fu in fresh directions. Lau Kar-leung went beyond the genre's superficial interest in rival fighting styles and paid homage to what he saw as a rich, complex tradition. Yuen Woo-ping (*Snake in the Eagle's Shadow*, 1978) and Sammo Hung (*Magnificent Butcher*, 1979) developed the kung-fu comedy. Yuen went on to revise the Huang Feihong saga in the Jackie Chan vehicle *Drunken Master* (1978).

The late 1970s generation of choreographers-turned-directors soon recast the kung-fu film as the contemporary action-adventure movie. Films like Jackie Chan's *Project A* (1982) and Sammo Hung's *Winners and Sinners* (1983) and *My Lucky Stars* (1984) seamlessly integrate martial arts, modern stunt work, chases, and pyrotechnics. Yet old-fashioned kung-fu could still attract local audiences; lush Mainland-shot productions starring a fresh-faced Jet Li and many superb martial artists won big box office during the same years.

In the mid-1980s crime films became the dominant action genre, largely through the success of Woo's *A Better Tomorrow* (1986). The somewhat grubby look of much 1970s film was cast off for a hard-edged style that compared favorably with Hollywood. What the 1960s *wuxia pian* had owed to Japan, the 1980s *policiers* owed to *Road Warrior* (1981), *Raiders of the Lost Ark* (1981), and *48 HRS* (1982). Fight scenes were shot from a wide variety of angles and were cut to mere flashes. All over the territory buildings exploded and cars burst into picturesque fireballs. As Peter Chan remarks, Hong Kong films became "more Hollywood than Hollywood."[18]

A revealing detail is the new look of slow motion. Since the late 1960s Hollywood had employed it for action scenes, and it was a staple of the kung-fu films. By the mid-1980s, both American and Hong Kong action films relied heavily on the technique. Usually Hong Kong directors controlled speed of motion not during filming but during printing, which was cheaper and allowed some fashionable blurring of contour. Using slow motion to show characters simply walking or reacting, as Scorsese had in *Taxi Driver* (1976), became an index of quality, and so the films were padded out with achingly slow strutting and head-turning and ominously billowing trenchcoats. Slow motion could also smooth out bumpy camera moves, becoming, Herman Yau notes, "a way of making handheld shots that don't look too cheap."[19]

Martial-arts stars and directors eased into the new urban thrillers. Philip Kwok Chun-fung (Kuo Chui), for example, found fame as one of the "Five Venoms," then became an action director and actor (*The Big Heat*, 1988; *Hard Boiled*, 1992). After some lost years Ti Lung, star of many Shaw Brothers sagas in the 1970s, relaunched his career in *A Better Tomorrow* (1986). At about the same time, martial-arts experts could also practice their trade in the new cycle of *wuxia* fantasies initiated by Tsui Hark. Ching Siu-tung, who had choreographed Shaw martial-arts films and directed the sword film *Duel to the Death* (1983), took on *A Chinese Ghost Story* (1987) and its successors, as well as Tsui's *Swordsman* trilogy (1990–1993). Other masters of martial-arts filming helped supernatural sword-fighting tales become sure-fire exports.

Also popular overseas was another Tsui update, the old-fashioned kung-fu film bulked up with modern production values. The prototype was his version of the Huang Feihong tale, the *Once upon a Time in China* saga (1991–1997). Tsui's competitors scrambled to find vehicles for Jet Li, Donnie Yen, and other martial stars. Yuen Kuei shifted from directing modern-day actioners like *Top Bet* (1991) to costume kung-fu sagas like *Fong Sai-yuk* (1993), and Yuen Woo-ping was called in to choreograph Gordon Chan's *Fist of Legend* (1994), a loose remake of Bruce Lee's *Fist of Fury*.

Like the flying swordsman movies, the new kung-fu films had a short

8.5 *God of Gamblers:* As the tile lands . . .

8.6 . . . the camera zooms back to reveal Ko Chun smoothly swinging it around . . .

8.7 . . . to his smiling face.

heyday, and purists complained that Jet Li's northern *wushu* style hardly prepared him to portray Cantonese kung-fu heroes like Huang Feihong and Fong Sai-yuk. Yet these cycles served to keep the action movie varied throughout the 1990s. Filmmakers streamlined camera tricks like speeded-up motion, becoming very skillful at judging the subtly different rhythms yielded at twenty-two, twenty-three, and twenty-four frames per second. Cinematographers cunningly concealed wirework by shooting straight into the sun or by the "Charlie bar," which blocks the light beam so that the edge of the wire is not visible.[20]

Directors seemed to compete in finding flashy uses of old techniques like reverse motion. We see a ninja run and leap to a rooftop; in the filming he dropped from the roof and ran backward. If a dagger is to fly in and strike a doorjamb inches from the hero's eye, it can be filmed already in the jamb, then jerked away on a wire. During the 1980s reverse motion appears in dozens of guises. At the start of *God of Gamblers* (1989), gamblers compete in raking up mahjong tiles to make a high score. Ko Chun's rival knocks a tile away from him, the tile flies into the air, and the two men parry for it. Thanks to reverse motion, Ko Chun miraculously catches it on the edge of his wand (Figs. 8.5–8.7). During filming Chow Yun-fat started by holding the wand and smiling (Fig. 8.7), then waved the wand away (Fig. 8.6); as the

MOTION EMOTION

camera zoomed in on the tile, he flipped it up (Fig. 8.5). This piece of technical effrontery is indiscernible on the screen.

Hong Kong action cinema, then, developed by pulling foreign techniques—age-old photographic tricks, samurai swordplay, New Hollywood gloss—into a dynamic genre tradition. Hong Kong has never stopped swiping. As an earlier generation had studied Japanese imports in Shaws' screening room, 1980s directors rented laserdiscs of Hollywood action pictures. From *Die Hard* (1988) Lau Kar-leung's *Tiger on the Beat 2* (1990) lifts the idea of heroes fighting on shards of broken glass and the use of a firehose as a whip and escape rope. *Saviour of the Soul* (1991) owes more than a little to *Highlander* (1986).

This borrowing reached down to the very texture of the action films. As we've already seen, one reason Hong Kong cinema travels well is that at the level of style—the moment-by-moment unfolding of the story in shots and scenes—it is conservative. It obeys international norms of popular cinema. Filmmakers employ simple, legible compositions and combine them by means of continuity editing. Just as Hollywood musicals and Bombay song sequences use lengthy shots to fasten attention on the performers during dance numbers, in the 1970s some swordplay and kung-fu bouts are shot like musical numbers. Long takes and a panning camera allow us to see the flow of the choreography. This smoothness is difficult to provide on location, but in a studio one can carefully rehearse an extended combat sequence. Many of the Shaw films use the long take to display delicate choreography within the CinemaScope frame (Figs. 8.8–8.12).

Many action scenes, however, also rely on a tactic of continuity cinema called constructive editing. This technique builds up a sense of the entire action by showing only parts of it. Whereas an analytical breakdown gives us an establishing shot before showing the details, constructive editing de-

8.8 Intricate choreography in *The New One-Armed Swordsman* (1971): Lung with his jointed staff lunges rightward . . .

8.9 ... to clash with Feng as the camera tracks back.

8.10 Feng sinks to the lower left, pauses ...

8.11 ... and attacks again, spinning Lung around.

8.12 Feng moves to the lower right and pauses while Lung holds his stance.

nies us any overall view. With constructive editing we infer the entire action by mentally assembling the portions of the action seen in separate shots. The filmmaker must stage the shots carefully so that, cut together, they convey the action unambiguously.

Since the 1910s filmmakers have realized that constructive editing can make scenes of violent physical action very simple to follow. The first shot shows a cowboy firing his pistol; the next shows another cowboy ducking away. In the absence of an establishing shot showing both men, we infer that the first cowboy fired at the second. The technique is in every filmmaker's toolkit, and it was well-known to Chinese directors of the silent era. Soviet directors pushed this technique further in their pulsating action scenes. Here the pieces of action might consist only of brief, close shots of gestures and facial expressions, as in Eisenstein's Odessa Steps sequence in *Potemkin* (1925).

The constructive editing principle is not, of course, restricted to martial-arts combats, but it became central to Hong Kong action films. It was ideal for scenes demanding fantastic or supernatural feats, such as flying through the air or destroying an enemy from a distance through palm power. Feats of skill could be faked by inserting shots of doubles or by cutting together, say, a shot of a man leaping up, then a shot of the man very high in the air (launched by a trampoline or springboard). For example, *The First Sword* (1967), a fantasy swordplay film, opens with the hero plunging down from the rafters, somersaulting over the villain, and landing, striking a stance preparatory to fighting. This would be very difficult to execute in a single establishing shot, but four shots take care of it easily (Figs. 8.13–8.16). The closer views fasten the spectator's attention on the main action, while the rapid changes of shot maintain visual interest. There is an additional payoff: at the film's end the villain will be pinned to the ceiling in an image that echoes the first shot of this passage (Fig. 8.17).

But can't constructive editing make any actor look like a good fighter? Yes, and for this reason many aficionados consider it fakery. They prefer the long-take approach, which displays the the fighters' genuine skills more honestly. Bruce Lee insisted on longer takes and more distant views

8.13 The opening of *The First Sword:* The hero leaps from the rafters.

8.14 He somersaults down . . .

8.15 . . . and over the villain . . .

8.16 . . . before landing.

8.17 The villain punished at the end of *The First Sword*.

8.18 At the climax of *Enter the Dragon* (1973), Lee starts to kick Han.

8.19 A sudden cut allows a dummy to be substituted in the foreground, and Lee kicks it violently out of the shot.

to assure viewers that his feats were real, although he did have recourse to deceptive editing (Figs. 8.18, 8.19). There is a virtuosity in staging extended combats in single shots, yet partly because of the importance of acrobatic attractions like the weightless leap, constructive editing has been a mainstay of Hong Kong action cinema.

Some directors have used constructive cutting to set a rhythm or to create a percussive interplay among shot compositions, while King Hu stretched it to the breaking point. Even a fairly routine film shows how constructive editing can be fine-tuned. Chang Chang Ho's *King Boxer* (1972) presents a climactic tournament bout between the hero, Chih Hao, and his arrogant opponent, Meng. The decisive air battle is handled in seven shots. A brisk symmetry is immediately established between the fighters' parallel leaps (Figs. 8.20, 8.21), followed by a third shot mapping out their impending clash (Fig. 8.22). Then a pair of reverse shots of the fighters in midair gives us the essential information, one blow per shot: Chih Hao's kick that doubles Meng over (Fig. 8.23), then Chih Hao's punch (Fig. 8.24). Meng spins head over heels (Fig. 8.25) and crashes to earth (Fig. 8.26).

8.20 *King Boxer:* Meng leaps up, frontally (9 frames).

8.21 In a mirror-image shot, Chih Hao leaps up (8 frames).

8.22 The two fighters sail toward each other (10 frames).

8.23 Chih Hao kicks Meng in the chest, bending him over (11 frames).

8.24 Chin Hao punches Meng (7 frames).

8.25 Meng spins over in the air (12 frames).

8.26 Meng lands hard.

A single establishing shot could not so rivet our attention to the core events—the leaps, the clash, the loser's fall. The editing also creates a piece of Hong Kong physics: in midair a kick to the chest somehow drives a man's head down so that a downward punch can launch a midair somersault. In an earlier bout, each combatant was given parallel shots throughout, so that at the end we got a shot of Chih Hao landing, then one of Meng

216   *PLANET HONG KONG*

landing. Here, however, devoting two shots to Meng's fall breaks with the even-handed coverage at the scene's outset, underscoring Meng's defeat; no need to see Chih Hao land. The hero is privileged in another way. Although every shot is brief (the longest lasts only half a second), the hero always gets shorter shots than his adversary. There is a neat disproportion in the decisive instant: the key punch is given in the scene's shortest shot (seven frames; Fig. 8.24), but Meng tumbles over in nearly twice that time (twelve frames; Fig. 8.25). The blow must have been powerful if its effects last so long.

King Boxer's director is a journeyman, but he has mastered his craft. The force of the clash, the tactic that wins Chih Hao victory, and the insistence on Meng's shame are projected forcefully by the constructive editing. The impossibility of presenting this fight in a long shot has been turned to advantage: obligatory artifice has yielded artistic emphasis.

Constructive editing can stand as an index of how Hong Kong's action genres mastered the international cinematic idiom. Without such techniques, the films would not travel as well as they do, nor achieve their particular force. But Hong Kong filmmakers have not only borrowed. They have innovated.

What makes Hong Kong action scenes so thrilling? The spurting blood and gruesome details, sustained by a mastery of international film language, can't wholly account for the sense shared by hardcore fans and first-time viewers that these action films are radically different from those on offer elsewhere. They elate us. And calling them cartoonish, eye-popping, or over-the-top doesn't get us very far in understanding how they work, and work us up.

There is, most obviously, pure daring. Even though many stunts are faked through constructive editing and wirework, Hong Kong filmmakers put risk on the screen to an extraordinary degree. This is one premise of Jackie Chan's charm, executing harrowing stunts with a desperate eagerness to please and then under the credits rerunning the bone-crushing outtakes. Part of the adrenaline rush of these films comes from the camera's recording of real danger. I recall a friend telling me that I would like the firefighting movie *Lifeline* (1997). "It uses Hong Kong special effects," she said. "That is, no special effects." The firefighters are swallowed in flames and knocked down like tenpins by lumbering spools of burning fabric. Just shooting it was a job for daredevils (Fig. 8.27).

Along with the display of danger, these films put at their center sheer physical extravagance. By blending martial-arts techniques with the Chinese acrobatic and theatrical traditions, choreographers have created flamboyantly stylized combat. Heroes fight by turning cartwheels. A man thwacked by a spear doesn't just go down; he spins forward in a somersault (Fig. 8.28). A perforated gunman flies up and back in a parody of loss of bal-

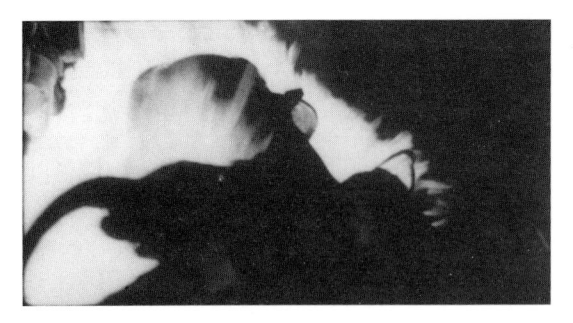

8.27 Flames engulf a fireman in *Lifeline*.

8.28 *Crippled Avengers* (Zhang Che, 1978).

8.29 *Once a Thief* (John Woo, 1991).

ance—while his partner ducks under him to fire in retaliation (Fig. 8.29). Even graceless falls look perfectly timed. In *Police Story* (1985), thugs bounce down escalators and smash their spines into glass cases. The tradition of showy combat makes Hong Kong physics pretty flexible. Swordfighters soar (Fig. 8.30). Warriors can fight on any surface: a cliff face, the tips of fence poles, even the heads of a crowd (Figs. 8.31, 8.32).

Fighting in films, Westerners seem to believe, ought to be realistically messy, its impetus dissipated by awkwardness and fatigue. Watch Harrison Ford, the current master of reluctant, logy combat, in *The Fugitive* (1993) as he wearily grapples with the murderer of his wife, and wonder why Hollywood heroes don't study a little acrobatic kung-fu. Why not learn to

8.30 *Duel to the Death* (Ching Siu-tung, 1983).

8.31 *Redress* (1969).

8.32 Fighting on heads in *Fong Sai-yuk* (Yuen Kuei, 1993).

8.33 *The Iceman Cometh* (Clarence Fok, 1991).

8.34 A bus stunt from *Aces Go Places II* (1983).

dodge blows, to hit the ground rolling, to leap over your adversary? Instead of a telegraphed uppercut, why not use a back flip to kick your opponent in the jaw (Fig. 8.33)?

We evidently think that effortless grace and geometrical precision belong to the circus. Hong Kong cinema frankly embraces a circus aesthetic, mixing amusement, astonishment, and a delight in farfetched feats. In *Dance of the Drunk Mantis* (aka *Dance of the Drunken Master*, 1979), an old master and his callow pupil defeat a skillful fighter by locking themselves into a cartwheel formation. Grinning cheerfully, a thief rides his motorcycle off a bridge, onto the top of a bus, and bounces safely down to speed off (Fig. 8.34). An attacker falls; a woman jams a pole into his chest, using him as a brace for vaulting up to a brick wall, where she perches like a spider (Fig. 8.35).

Any account of the Hong Kong action style must start with the sheer audacity of hundreds of stunts, all outlandish by Hollywood canons of plausibility. Perhaps, as Noël Carroll has suggested, the fascination of these scenes springs from imagining an escape from gravity and "the reality of flesh."[21] If so, this universal fantasy is one source of the films' power. The Hong Kong tradition challenges filmmakers to come up with ever more inventive ways of displaying the human body's efforts to burst its earthly bonds.

But this is not the whole story. Starting from astonishing movements of the body, filmmakers amplify them through the materials of cinema—movement, cutting, image composition, color, and sound. Hong Kong's commitment to rigorous patterning shows that a popular cinema can be as formally stringent as rhyming iambic pentameter or the rules of sonata form.

In any combat scene, each fighter's movement carves a clean path through the image, outlining a well-defined trajectory. Long ago the Soviet filmmaker Lev Kuleshov told his students that the most efficient movement looks best on the screen. "Only organized work comes out well in cinema."[22] Hong Kong filmmakers realize that sharp, easily read fighting

8.35 *Yes, Madam!* (Yuen Kuei, 1985).

gestures are necessary for a forceful effect. The director then enhances this legibility by well-chosen camera positions. As we've seen, the swordplay and kung-fu films perfected the segment-shooting method. Before filming, the instructor would decide on each character's school and combat style, but the fights would not be prepared in advance. Each fight was worked out on the set, with the shooting proceeding in continuity. Thus each camera position was adjusted to the exact bit of business that the shot would highlight. This is unlike the Hollywood "sandwich" style (Figs. 1.10–1.14).

The clarity of the action is furthered by one paradoxical quality. These scenes seem fast because they make calculated use of fixity. They seem constantly in movement because they incorporate stasis.

Very often the performers' movements aren't continuous. First there is a rapid thrust and parry, or a string of blows, or the whirl of a sword or spear. There follows a slight pause, often at the moment a blow is blocked, and the fighters are immobile, perhaps only for a fraction of a second. Then comes another burst of activity. The result onscreen is an overall flow that harbors a percussive rhythm. The short pauses articulate stages of action, giving them staccato efficiency. The static instants also make the movements seem more rapid by contrast. And each section of the pause/burst/pause pattern can be adjusted to different rates of movement.

Take a moment from Bruce Lee's *Way of the Dragon* (1972). Lee is in Rome helping some friends protect themselves from gangsters. He is about to return to Hong Kong when he must intervene in an alley fight. Armed with a pole, he knocks the knife from one man's hand (Fig. 8.36), pauses a split second, then jabs the pole into the attacker's groin. As the man slowly doubles over in the foreground, Lee, open-mouthed, holds his stance (Fig. 8.37). Then he uses the pole to press the man down (Fig. 8.38). When the thug has collapsed below the frameline, Lee pauses again (Fig. 8.39) before deliberately raising his hand to pluck his air ticket from his pocket (Fig. 8.40) and lift it over his head (Fig. 8.41). Then he throws it down furiously onto his victim's body (Fig. 8.42).

Print fails to capture this moment's fluidity, and it takes more time to tell it than to see it. Lee's movements engage us through a drum-tap micro-

8.36 *The Way of the Dragon.*

8.37 *The Way of the Dragon.*

8.38 *The Way of the Dragon.*

rhythm of pause/burst/pause. "Move like sound and echo," he advised his pupils.[23] Each gesture, itself Euclidean in its economy, is bracketed by instants of stillness, and these lend a subtly decelerating pulse to the scene. The first attacking stroke is followed by a pause of about an eighth of a second, the second thrust is followed by a quarter-second pause, and there is a pause of nearly half a second as Lee looks down at his victim. Finally, his

8.39 *The Way of the Dragon.*

8.40 *The Way of the Dragon.*

8.41 *The Way of the Dragon.*

8.42 *The Way of the Dragon.*

resolve to stay with his friends and fight on is conveyed in a single gesture, itself rhythmic: he takes about a second to retrieve his ticket and raise it over his head, but only a quarter of a second to snick it down contemptuously. He discards the ticket as curtly as he thrusts the pole.

The alternation of swift attack and abrupt rest is characteristic of the Asian martial arts. The hard styles of northern and southern kung-fu emphasize force meeting force, and the result is a visual snap. In these styles, blocking or deflecting a blow is as important as delivering one; each kick or punch is an explosive release of energy, synchronized with the release of a single deep breath. Moreover, kung-fu students learn that every technique consists of patterns, each one a specific configuration of arms, legs, and torso. During training the student learns to combine dozens of these patterns into "sets," sequences that have proved effective in combat. Each set is a series of rapid movements broken by poses.[24] Many kung-fu credit sequences feature the main actors performing sets, not only announcing to connoisseurs what styles will be showcased in the story but also laying down the pause/burst/pause scheme that will be seen throughout the film.

Another source of the scheme is Peking Opera, which is at bottom a rhythmic theater. The orchestra is led by the percussion, songs are molded to the metrics of accented syllables, the ensemble leader beats out a rhythm on clappers and drums, and gongs and cymbals mark a song's climax, a passage of combat, or a fixed posture.[25] Battle scenes are a blend of martial arts and acrobatics, with actors leaping and tumbling. They punctuate their movements with moments of pure stasis, the technique of *liang hsiang* ("displaying"), often underlined by a cymbal crash.

On film the confluence of these rich traditions brings us extraordinary combat. In a Hollywood fistfight, people punch for a while, usually rather slowly and seldom with the geometrical efficiency of kung-fu. The fighters seldom stop moving, even when they pause for breath, and they never freeze as abruptly as do Hong Kong performers. In *Die Hard* John McClane fights the towering blond thief Karl in the skyscraper's boiler room. Karl kicks McClane back against a flight of concrete stairs (Fig. 8.43). As Karl bends forward, McClane seizes his neck in a hammerlock and drags him

8.43 *Die Hard*.

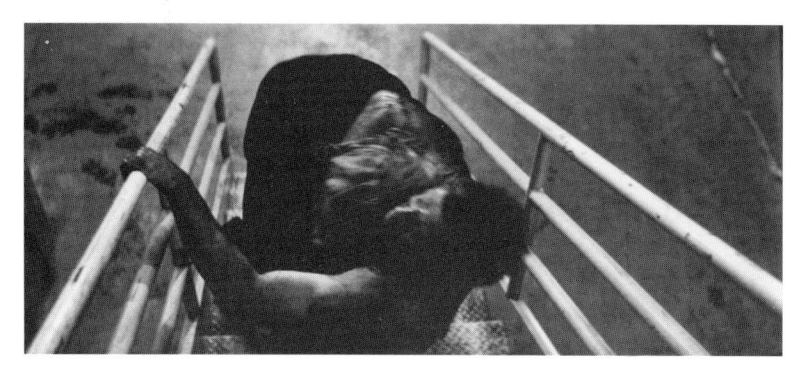

8.44 *Die Hard.*

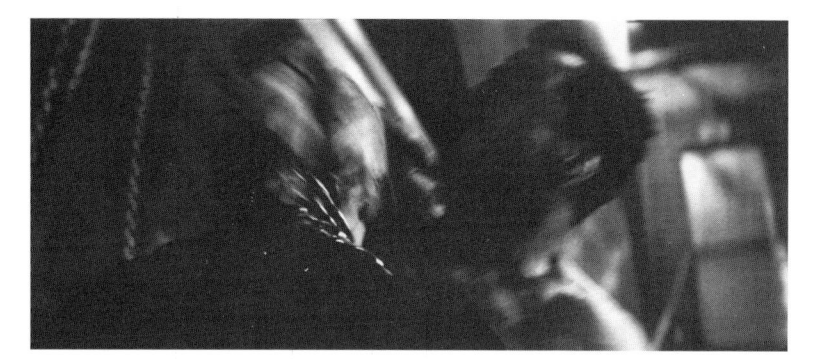

8.45 *Die Hard.*

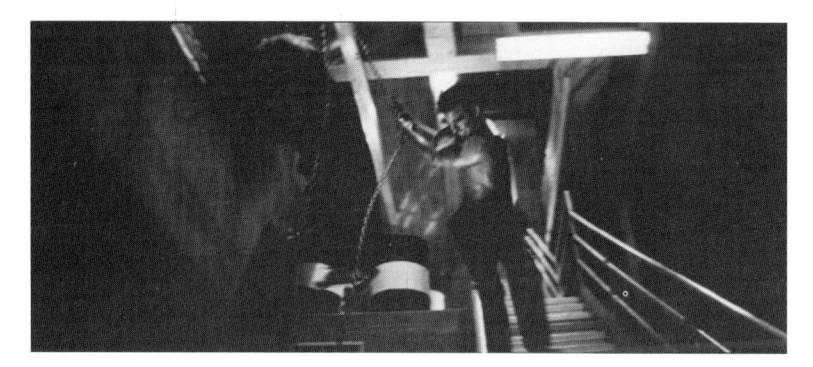

8.46 *Die Hard.*

8.47 *Die Hard.*

225

8.48 *Hard Boiled:* The killer fires from the floor.

8.49 Tequila rolls rightward through the flour.

8.50 A match-on-action cut continues Tequila's movement as he twists and launches himself off the table.

8.51 Another match cut carries Tequila across the floor toward the killer.

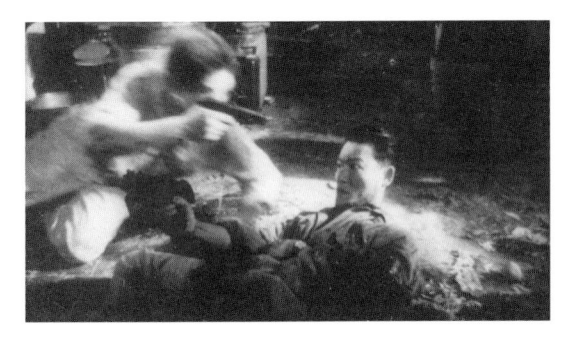

8.52 He glides into the shot . . .

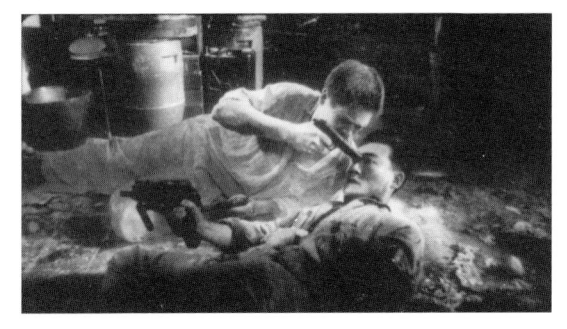

8.53 . . . and in the very last frame of the shot freezes in place before the killer.

up the steps, punching and cursing him (Fig. 8.44). The two men grapple against the railing. McClane twists a hanging chain around Karl's neck (Fig. 8.45) and shoves him off, leaving Karl hanging from the rigging. McClane then slides down the rail (Fig. 8.46), pulling the rigging across the room and slamming Karl into the opposite wall (Fig. 8.47). Throughout, the actors' movements are ill-defined, and some get concealed by parts of the set; there are no pauses to bracket phases of the fight. The movements lack efficiency, let alone clean-limbed attack and counter. This is a tussle.

Compare another scene in which a hero dispatches an adversary at close range. In the gun battle that opens *Hard Boiled* (1992), Tequila has raced

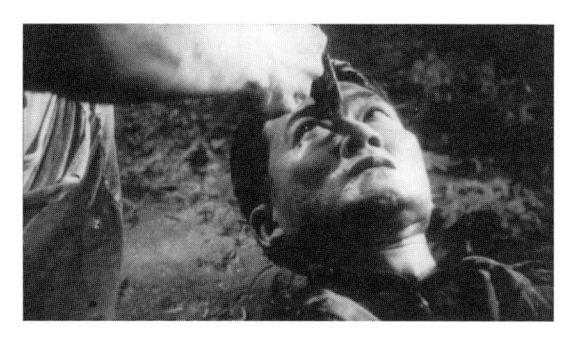

8.54 A close-up shows the killer transfixed.

8.55 A close-up of Tequila establishes his face as a white mask.

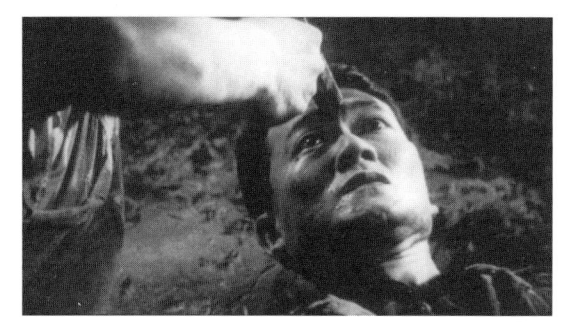

8.56 A return to the killer.

8.57 Tequila blows out the toothpick that has miraculously stayed in his mouth during the entire gun battle.

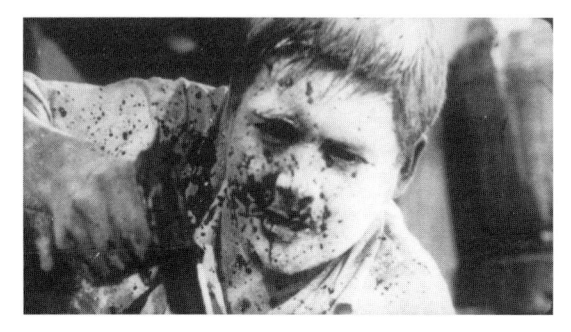

8.58 The killer's blood spatters Tequila.

into a kitchen in pursuit of a gangster who has shot his partner. The gunman lies on his back on the floor, firing (Fig. 8.48). Tequila dives onto a tabletop, rolls across it through a cloud of flour, and leaps off. Four shots map his rightward and downward trajectory (Figs. 8.49–8.52). In the last of these, he glides across the frame to come to a sudden halt, the pistol to the gunman's head (Fig. 8.53). There follow three close-ups in which the killer and Tequila stare at each other, motionless and silent (Figs. 8.54–8.56).

Tequila's dive consumes a second and a half; the unmoving exchange of looks lasts nearly as long. This comparatively long pause accentuates the next two movements, executed in quick succession: Tequila contemptuously spits out his toothpick (Fig. 8.57) and executes the killer, spattering blood across his own bleached face (Fig. 8.58). This is the lengthiest shot in the sequence, taking nearly three seconds.

There would be more to say about this passage—the fact that the shots of Tequila in movement are all about the same length (19 frames, 17 frames, 17 frames, and 20 frames), the way the flour mask turns Tequila into a ghostly avenger out of Chinese opera. What is relevant for us now is the way that Tequila's roll and dive form a virtually abstract surge of rightward energy before braking to an instant halt, hitting a pose of diagrammatic clarity: two men, one with the advantage. The poses are prolonged in order to throw the decisive acts—spat-out toothpick, bloody execution—into relief. John McClane has no time to reflect on killing Karl and no remorse for doing so, but Tequila's hesitation reminds us that by taking his revenge he will violate his duty as a policeman.

Hollywood filmmakers, once the world's leaders in portraying the dynamism of the human body, today seldom achieve rhythmic vitality. American action films substitute massive carnage and incessant bustle for well-calibrated views of precise, staccato movement. Hong Kong's closest

8.59 *Sanjuro:* The confrontation.

8.60 *Sanjuro:* The resolution.

8.61 *Legendary Weapons of China.*

8.62 *Legendary Weapons of China.*

affinity is with the Japanese *jidai-geki* movies, which display the same pause/burst/pause structure. But there is an instructive difference. As the *Way of the Dragon* example indicates, a Hong Kong fight scene consists of many small bursts and rests. The pause in the *Hard Boiled* passage, though only a second and a half, serves as the fraught conclusion of a shootout that lasts nearly five minutes. Postwar Japanese action films shift the balance. They tend to minimize the burst of movement and dwell on the moments of stasis. The typical Japanese fight scene is mostly buildup and aftermath. The near-parodic extreme occurs in the finale of Kurosawa's *Sanjuro* (1964), which consists of a two-and-a-half-minute, virtually immobile confrontation between Sanjuro and his adversary—broken by one slash (Figs. 8.59, 8.60). The waiting game is also quite common in the Zatoichi series, a major inspiration for Hong Kong filmmakers, and today in the action films of "Beat" Takeshi Kitano.

The pause/burst/pause pattern is so deeply characteristic of Hong Kong cinema that we can find it in noncombat scenes as well. It can accentuate the most minute bits of business. We have seen several examples already, notably in *A Chinese Ghost Story* (Figs. 6.9–6.17). Directors rhythmicize any scene they can. In *Legendary Weapons of China* (1982), a spy looking

MOTION EMOTION

8.63 *Legendary Weapons of China.*

8.64 *Legendary Weapons of China:* The warrior doll with spear.

8.65 *Legendary Weapons of China.*

8.66 *Legendary Weapons of China:* The warrior with spear.

8.67 *Bodyguard from Beijing:* To prevent his enemy from reaching the faucet, the hero (played by Jet Li) uses a towel...

8.68 ...to snap the faucet out of his reach.

for a mysterious stranger is distracted by a doll salesman in the foreground (Fig. 8.61). After a cut in, the hero takes one step forward; pause (Fig. 8.62). Then he takes another step; pause (Fig. 8.63). Then the doll pops into the foreground, in focus, creating a new pause (Fig. 8.64). But the doll salesman is merely a decoy. A cut reveals the stranger sitting elsewhere in the inn (Fig. 8.65). He continues the rhythmic pulse by grabbing his spear and standing up, pausing for another beat (Fig. 8.66). A pulse in the action, the cutting, and even lens focus have linked the unwitting hero to his target.

As these examples indicate, hand props can set off the performer's skills and accentuate the rhythm of the action. In *Bodyguard from Beijing* (1994), nearly every item in a modernistic living room and kitchen—sofas, flashlights, drawers, knives, Venetian blinds, dishtowels, even a TV remote and a dripping faucet—becomes a weapon as it is swept into the rhythm of the fight (Figs. 8.67–8.68). No Hong Kong filmmaker has better understood the action-enhancing possibilities of props and setting than Jackie Chan. The final battle of *Mr. Canton and Lady Rose* (aka *Miracles,* 1989) is set in a rope factory, where ropes become weapons, traps, and entangling webs. *Young Master* (1980) employs an ingenious skirt motif (Figs. 8.69, 8.70).

Clarity and precision in articulating movement carry an expressive charge: Kuleshov's "organized work" projects a dynamic, streamlined efficiency. John McClane's throttling of Karl is realistically clumsy, but it carries little affective thrust. Tequila's acrobatic roll and dive and his glide across the floor are implausibly graceful, yet here the emotion emerges more strongly than in *Die Hard.* Tequila is driven to avenge his partner, and his arrowlike thrust to the killer powerfully expresses hard-focused rage. In our example from *The Way of the Dragon,* Lee's disgust at his bungling attacker mingles with his sense of obligation to his friends, and both feelings are concisely expressed in the scornful flinging down of his air ticket.

The clarity and rhythmic regularity of the Hong Kong style fulfill one goal of popular cinema—arousing and channeling emotion. Instead of an impassive, restrained realism, filmmakers present a caricatural version of

8.69 *Young Master:* The old official's daughter flashes her skirt to distract and confuse Jackie, but later . . .

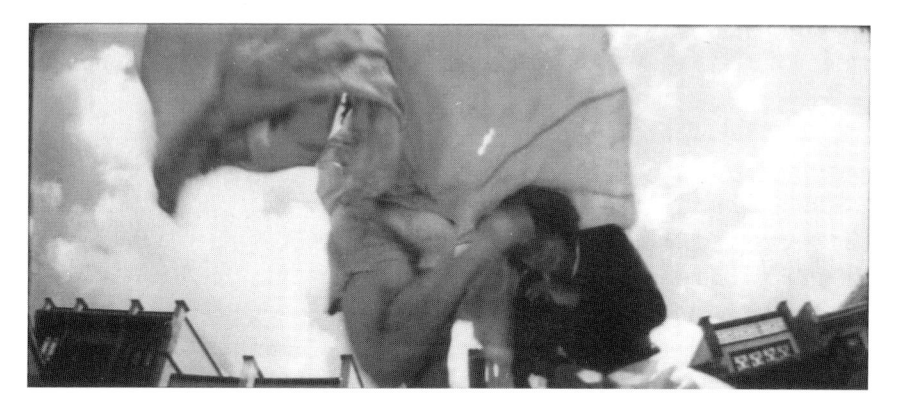

8.70 . . . Jackie snatches a piece of fabric from a shop and turns it into a Spanish dress that confounds his opponents.

the action that aims to carry away the spectator. A fight or chase is given a distinct, vivid emotional profile—ferocity, panic, evasiveness, meticulousness—or some combination of such qualities, as in Tequila's mixture of resourcefulness, poise, and fury.

Call it a strategy of expressive amplification. This means, first, that we must be able to read the performer at a glance. In our prime examples, Bruce Lee's fierce concentration and Tequila's icy deliberation are transparently evident. Jackie Chan, mugger that he is, presents angular postures and facial gymnastics just to exhibit the strain of executing a stunt. The "overplaying" we find in Hong Kong films stems from the desire to make manifest the expressive qualities inherent in each moment of the action.

Expressive amplification also emerges when film style magnifies the emotional dynamics of the performance. The most obvious tool here is shot scale. Hollywood habitually gives us more of the locale than we really need to see, usually through extreme long shots that show off big sets or the scenery around a car chase. Hong Kong directors judge their scale more exactly, using moderate long shots for acrobatic long takes (as in Figs. 8.8–

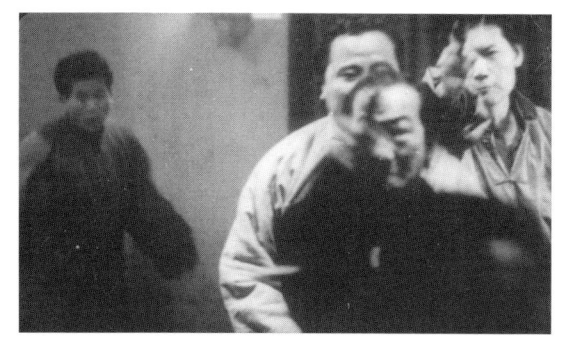

8.71 *Gun Men.*

8.72 *Gun Men.*

8.73 *Gun Men.*

8.74 *Gun Men.*

8.12) and tight medium shots and close-ups for the high points, as in Lee's pole maneuverings and Tequila's flour attack. A Hong Kong director would prefer not to send off a major villain in the distant long shot that (apparently) finishes Karl in *Die Hard* (Fig. 8.47).

The commitment to closer views opens several creative doors. First, all the resources of constructive editing are available to link these fragments of action. Second, the viewer's attention is always riveted on the key elements: the moving bodies. The carnal Hong Kong cinema puts the shots on a human scale. Third, a medium shot of the hero keeps some figures in the scene offscreen, so enemies can pop into the frame unexpectedly. In addition, filming the close view with a wide-angle lens can increase the perceived speed of movement coming at the lens, as in our *Way of the Dragon* shot.

Not least, close views allow even the slightest actions to become full-bodied attacks and counterthrusts. Tequila's spitting out of his toothpick is an instance, but an even finer-grained moment appears in Kirk Wong's *Gun Men* (1988). Members of a Shanghai gang invade another gang's headquarters and run wildly to the camera (Fig. 8.71). They are met by their rivals in an astonishing close-up: an empty frame (pause) into which pistols and the main villain thrust (burst) before halting (pause) (Figs. 8.72–8.73). Synchronized with the entry of the guns is the tiniest of movements: the

8.75 *Eastern Condors* (1987): Sammo Hung launches a lethal broadleaf in slow motion.

villain's eyes shift sharply from left to right! Cut back to a another static, angular composition in which the villain's gaze now slides left at the moment his minions start blasting (Fig. 8.74). The close shots let the movement of an eye herald a barrage.

All the technical tricks associated with Hong Kong action serve to enhance clarity, underscore rhythm, and amplify expressive force. Shooting in slight fast motion (kung-fu is often filmed at twenty-one to twenty-three frames per second) quickens the tempo and makes the fighters seem more efficient and precise. Conversely, slow motion can highlight information that would pass too quickly at normal speed. The two heroes of *Iron Monkey* (1993) attack the villain while balanced on fiery posts, and slow motion enables us to see through the flames and smoke to their precarious maneuvers. Certain stunts can be executed only in slow motion. Slow motion can make a strip of a broadleaf behave like a flexible blade (Fig. 8.75). Slow motion can also be highly expressive, displaying the difficulty of a stunt or the danger in a situation. A slow-motion shot can imbue the performer with strength and adroitness. Even in straight dramatic scenes, Woo and Tsui Hark are famous for using slow motion to evoke grave self-possession (when a hero strides to the camera) or ominousness (when a villain does). At the end of *Lifeline* the firefighters plunge back into the building, loping in slow motion: the technique makes palpable their dogged commitment to duty.

Most commonly, slow motion stretches out suspenseful moments. In *The Big Heat* (1988), the hero must fire at the villain who is about to blast him, but his hand is paralyzed. His girlfriend (now killed by the gangsters) earlier gave him a crucifix on a necklace. He loops it around his pistol's trigger and yanks it, squeezing off shots at the villain—all in agonizing slow motion. Like many Hong Kong sequences, this passage accretes expressive impact from variations in speed of movement. As the hero fires, the chain snaps and flies up in a slow-motion close-up, the crucifix twinkling. In an opposed slow-motion arc, the villain topples over stiffly. We never see the chain descend, but in a third shot the villain's face hits the ground fast. Variations in camera speed have not only prolonged the suspense but have created a sensuous metaphor: the murdered woman's tiny cross floats through the night, but the man drops as dead weight. Hong Kong cinema gives the smallest objects and gestures a kinetic thrust.

Now the much-maligned zoom shot makes sense. The zoom's primary role—enlarging a portion of a scene rapidly, or demagnifying part in order to show the entire context—is to provide information. In swordfight and kung-fu films, however, that aim is often secondary to matters of rhythm and expressivity. A fast zoom often plays out the pause/burst/pause pattern: fixed view, whip in to a detail, hold on it. The zoom often establishes a fight scene's tempo. Typically one shot ends with a zoom in to a fighter's face or arms or legs. Then we cut to a close view of the opponent before immediately and rapidly zooming out. The zoom can be timed around a blow as well, underscoring its force, or singling it out as the decisive one, or even reinforcing a pulse linking one punch to another (Figs. 8.76–8.78). In Yuen Woo-ping's *Dance of the Drunk Mantis*, the old master and his pupil are cartwheeling around a banker. He tries unsuccessfully to punch them, and the zoom singles out a punch as the one to which the old master responds (with a kick through the spread legs of the pupil). Such effects are hardly subtle, but the choreography and camerawork that create them are.

The same bold expressivity can be found on the soundtrack. Since Hong Kong action cinema is predominantly visual, creators have not been concerned to develop musical resources very much. They seem content with employing music to highlight emotional qualities, whatever the risk of cliché. In the kung-fu films a sting introduces the villain, a cowboy theme is often associated with the protagonist, and the final bout is filled with loud orchestral thrashings. Original scoring was often unimaginative: many directors believed that no car chase was complete without the bland jazz associated with television. Yet as we have seen, some filmmakers strove for more nuanced scores. *Peking Opera Blues'* pulse-pounding credits promise rapid action, and the rooftop climax makes telling use of an ostinato highlighted by abrupt stings.

In the action film sound effects are no less formulaically aggressive. Whooshes, slaps, thuds, and explosions are heard close up, even when shown in long shots. They signal the precision and force of each blow or gunshot, and the utter silence between them accentuates the pauses. Because every move is sold so vehemently, the decisive blow must often be oversold: the end of a fight is signaled by extremities of acting plus slow motion plus a cavernously echoing smash. The aggressiveness of kung-fu sounds is taken to a crazed limit in the draining climax of Donnie Yen's *Legend of the Wolf* (1997), when an endless flurry of fast-motion punches is accompanied by bass-heavy thuds. At the end, having employed virtually every filmic resource for accentuating the fight, the director re-

8.76 *Invincible Armour* (1977): The first beat, both visual and auditory: During a combat the hero falls back against a shield, striking it like a gong.

8.77 The second beat is provided by a fast zoom out as the master comes sailing in to attack.

8.78 Third beat: As the hero dodges the kick, the master strikes the shield, yielding another resounding clang.

sorts to a simple device: the frame goes black, over which we hear the villain scream.

Patrick Leung's *Task Force* (1997) presents a more nuanced weave of music and effects, voices and silence. The prostitute Fanny first encounters the dashing killer when he assassinates a gangster and blasts his way out of a restaurant. The entire scene plays as a deflating homage to John Woo gun battles. The soundtrack is constructed in layers: a quickly ticking drumbeat overlaid with pistol shots, an occasional harpsichord sting, and selected noises like the crash of saucepans. The killer tries to shield Fanny and then (in an homage to *Face/Off*) tenderly wraps her headphones around her ears. Suddenly all sound drops out except for "Oranges and Lemons Say the Bells of St. Clement's" sung by a warbling boy. As the carnage proceeds, only gunfire disrupts the placid music. The end of the fight is signaled when we abruptly hear one of the killer's victims crashing to the floor; the killer then discovers that Fanny is gone, her Walkman abandoned. The song stops. In a later scene the drumbeat signals the killer's return, and when he fires at his main target, the boy's song recurs during the battle. As the killer strides away the song becomes a hollow requiem: ". . . And chop off your head and laugh," with the final word repeated mockingly. The song reiterates the childish innocence of Fanny while also commenting on the killer's pitiless dedication to violence—an attitude that *Task Force* repudiates in the name of a policeman's devotion to keeping peace.

Editing has the task of expressively amplifying all these visual and auditory effects still further. Hong Kong filmmakers have become masters of matches on action and cuts on frame-edge activity, not least because these help create illusory stunts. More positively, the cutting preserves the clarity and force of the action from shot to shot. Outside Hong Kong, the normal rule is that close-ups should be cut shorter than long shots, but Hong Kong filmmakers show that if the long shots are well organized, they can be read in an instant. The dazzling climactic battle between spears and poles in *The Eight-Diagram Pole Fighter* (1983) consists mostly of long shots, but the average shot lasts only two seconds. Recall as well the rapid constructive cutting in *King Boxer*, which highlights symmetrical actions and emphasizes key blows (Figs. 8.20–8.24). Cuts may cooperate with zooms in signaling phases of the fight: a shot may end with a zoom in to a detail, with the next shot starting on a corresponding detail and then zooming back, expanding the arena for the next skirmish.

Editing can also enhance the tempo of the combat. Sometimes a cut to a static shot can interrupt a burst of action, providing a caesura. Or a scene will intercut slow motion and normal motion, providing a syncopated rhythm. Sometimes we will get a string of shots, each with its own pause/burst/pause pattern, as in the *Gun Men* sequence (Figs. 8.71–8.74). Or the cuts give continuous flow to a burst of action before interrupting it with

8.79 *Righting Wrongs* (1986): Hsia kicks with one foot, and his attacker falls rightward, but . . .

8.80 . . . in the very next shot Hsia is already kicking with the other foot, and the attacker falls to the left. The clashing diagonals of the kicks, physically impossible, produce a visual clatter.

stasis. In our *Hard Boiled* example, Woo's editing creates a smooth surge of action as Tequila rolls across the table to the floor, but the cut at the end of the fifth shot accentuates the instant when the action halts (Fig. 8.53). At the limit, the cuts may mark a beat with graphically clashing images—even at the risk of presenting action that is physically impossible (Figs. 8.79–8.80).

During the 1980s many American filmmakers began to "give the scene energy" just by increasing the number of cuts in it. This tendency was encouraged by digital editing equipment, which makes it easy to throw in dozens of extra shots. The result has been action sequences that lack physical and pictorial coherence.[26] It is a pleasure to turn to the Hong Kong cinema, where each shot aims at immediate legibility and maximum force. Here cuts intensify the drama and coordinate the rhythm of the sequence. For versatility and inventiveness of cutting, these filmmakers have no peers in recent popular cinema. One example from one of the finest action directors, Yuen Kuei, must stand for many marvelous passages. The sequence comes from *Righting Wrongs* (1986).

The policewoman Cindy Si is in a mahjong parlor to arrest a suspect. He resists, and some of his pals attack her. In the course of the fight, she flips a spittoon into one man's face, sends another bouncing off a gaming table (Fig. 8.81), and generally mops up the place. This exuberantly expansive action is prelude to some fine close-quarters work. With one leg Cindy pins a man to a table and digs out a pair of handcuffs to subdue him. But the other men attack again, and Cindy must fight them off. As she does, she manages to capture all four men with the single pair of handcuffs (Figs. 8.82–8.109).

The handcuffing phase of the scene gives us eighteen shots in only twenty-four seconds, making this passage as rapid-fire as any edit-happy Hollywood director might wish. Yet each shot is absolutely legible. The color scheme, which dresses the blonde Cindy in a bright yellow blouse

8.81 *Righting Wrongs:* Acrobatic fighting.

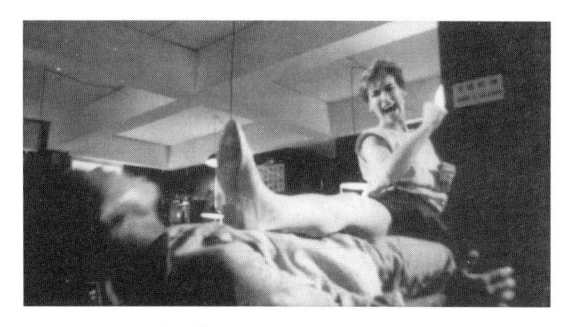

8.82 The handcuff sequence, shot 1: Cindy has one man pinned. The wide-angle lens exaggerates the length of her leg.

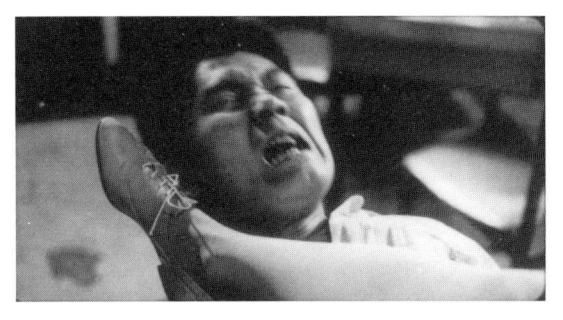

8.83 Shot 2: He grimaces.

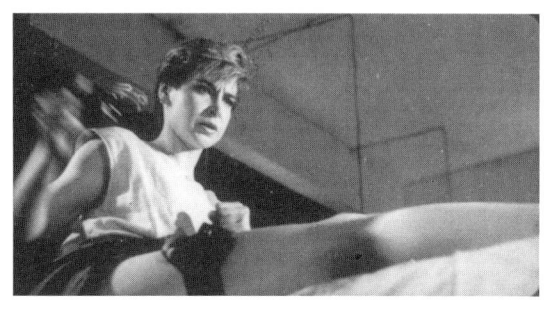

8.84 Shot 3: She snaps up her handcuffs . . .

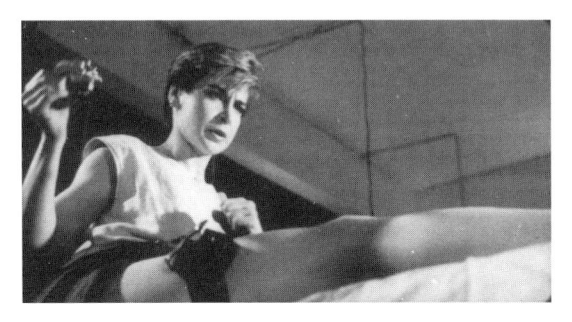

8.85 . . . and holds them poised in the shot's final frame.

8.86 Shot 4: After one frame of pause, the cuffs come in and are snapped onto the suspect's wrists.

and blue skirt, makes her stand out, as do her makeup and her butch-flip hairdo. The pivot points—clapping one cuff on the first man (Fig. 8.86), clapping the other on the fourth attacker (Fig. 8.105)—are presented in simple, quickly grasped close-ups. The medium shots serve to show the geometry of intersecting body parts, as well as to allow for surprise entrances from people offscreen (Fig. 8.97). Each image includes no more of the parlor than we need to see at that instant.

In the "sandwich" method typical of Hollywood, a fight scene is often

MOTION EMOTION

8.87 Shot 5: After one frame of pause, the suspect, now brandishing a knife, pops up from the bottom frameline. He pauses.

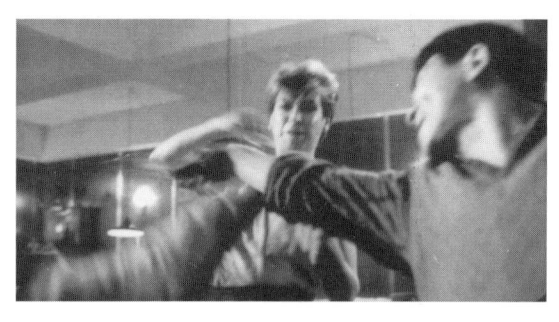

8.88 Shot 6: He thrusts into the frame and Cindy starts to wrap the handcuff chain around his wrist.

8.89 Shot 7: Match on action: She completes the movement, now firmly centered, and yanks down . . .

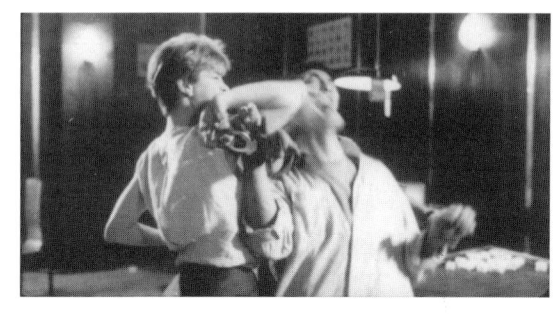

8.90 . . . before slamming her elbow up to knock the two men's heads together.

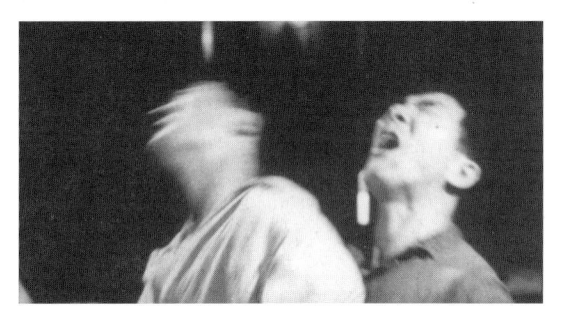

8.91 Shot 8: Their heads fly back . . .

8.92 . . . and Cindy springs into the gap to yank their heads down.

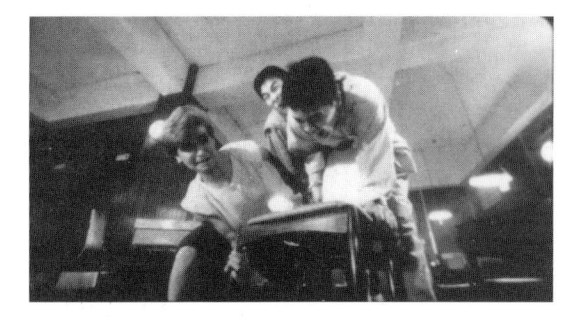

8.93 Shot 9: She pulls the men down to the chair, dragging them to a pause . . .

8.94 . . . then flips the chair up to pin them. Pause.

8.95 Shot 10: She pulls their arms through the chair legs, pausing . . .

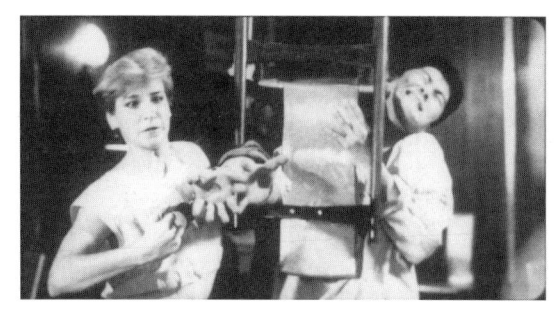

8.96 . . . before she turns . . .

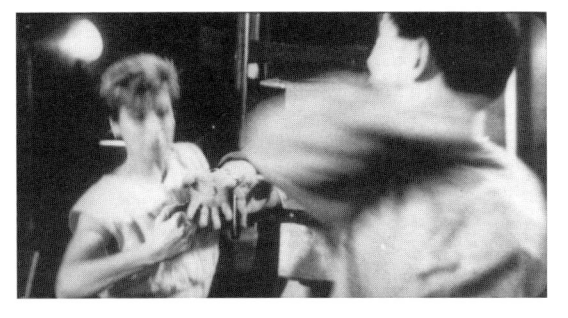

8.97 . . . and another man bursts in from frame right.

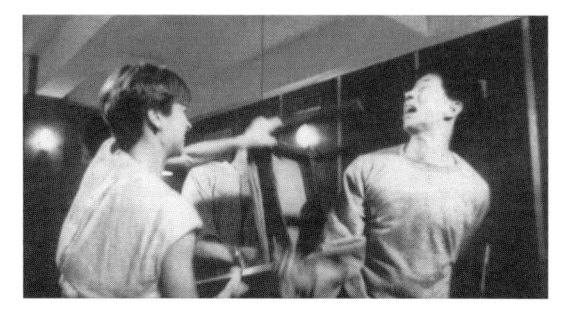

8.98 Shot 11: Cindy uses the chair legs to knock his arm down . . .

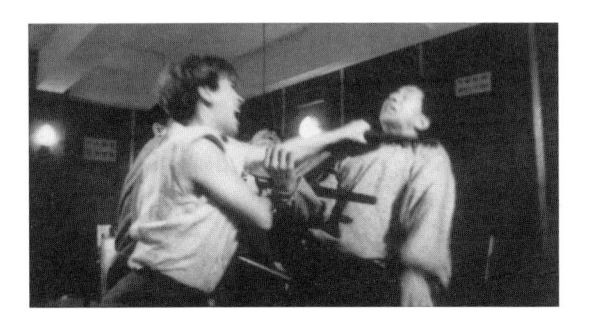

8.99 . . . then jams him against the wall.

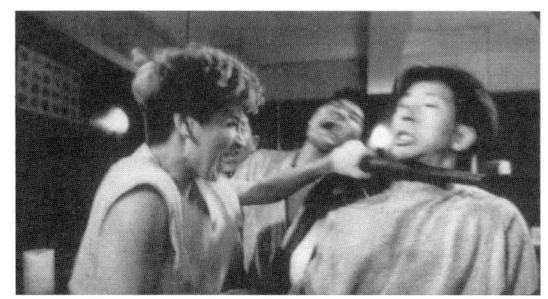

8.100 Shot 12: She holds all three men locked. But then . . .

8.101 . . . she looks left . . .

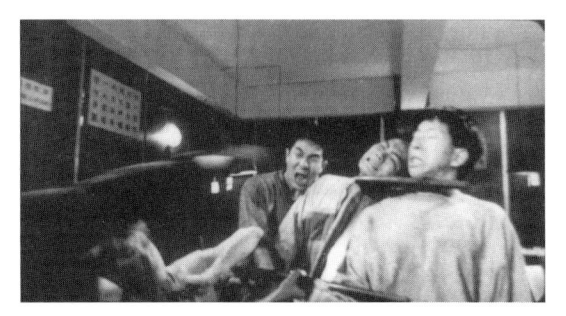

8.102 . . . and dodges to avoid a high kick as the camera tracks back . . .

241

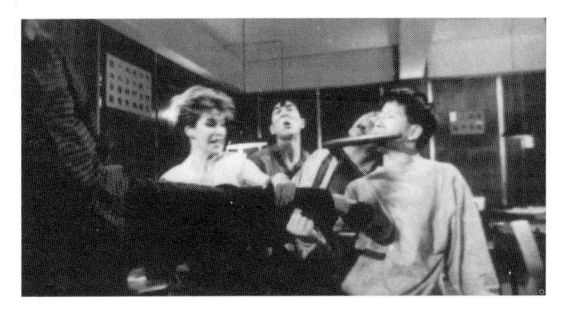

8.103 . . . and the foot strikes the first man; Cindy springs up.

8.104 Shot 13: She grabs the attacker's ankle.

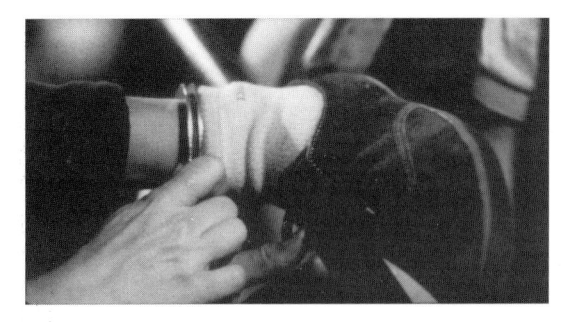

8.105 Shot 14: She cuffs it, an answer to shot 4 (Fig. 8.86).

8.106 Shot 15: A reaction shot, like that of shot 2 (Fig. 8.83), underscores what has happened.

8.107 Shot 16: The comic climax: A lady, four men, a chair, and a pair of cuffs.

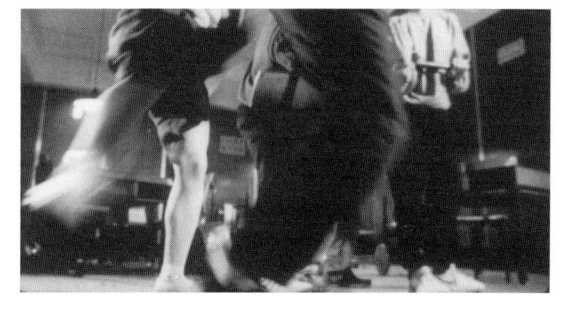

8.108 Shot 17: A final fillip: Cindy kicks behind the knee of the last attacker, and he crumples.

8.109 Shot 18: Match on action: The fulcrum collapses, and all four drop ignominiously to their knees.

shot with several cameras, with the cameramen catching the key gestures as best they can. Eventually the director will assemble the scene by alternating long-shot setups with a few closer ones. In the *Righting Wrongs* passage, by contrast, no camera position is repeated. Yuen Kuei has composed each image around a specific action, and other actions will require other setups. Two men's heads bounce off each other so as to allow Cindy to pop into a gap between them and yank their heads down (Fig. 8.92). Similarly, once Cindy has locked three men to the chair, she halts. This pause lasts only an eighth of a second, but it's long enough to demarcate the next phase of the shot, when she ducks away from the fourth thug's kick, and the camera swiftly tracks back to set up a new composition showing his attack landing on his ally (Figs. 8.101–8.103). The final shot of the four men cuffed (Fig. 8.107) gains its comic force from the fact that each one has been subdued in a string of close shots; this is our first view of their full humiliation. Abandoning Hollywood "coverage" (compare Figs. 1.10–1.16), the scene is a triumph of constructive editing and segment shooting.

The sequence also shows how the pause/burst/pause pattern can be modulated by the pace of editing. Often the cuts link movement smoothly across shots (for instance, Figs. 8.88–8.89), but a shot can also highlight a marked beat, from the most vivid action (Cindy slamming the suspect to the table with her leg) to lesser ones (the way she reaches smartly down for her handcuffs and snaps them up into the frame, Figs. 8.84–8.85). Cindy yanks an assailant's wrist down (Fig. 8.89), drags two men down with the chair (Fig. 8.93), pins a third man (Fig. 8.99), and finally locks them all up as a package (Fig. 8.107). At each stage the editing provides a distinct pause to allow us to see the result of her maneuver. The scene has two resolutions, each underscored by a pause. The first is a comic shot of the four men cuffed (Fig. 8.107). The second, which tops this, occurs when Cindy kicks behind the knee of the man supporting the whole contrivance and all collapse together to the floor, the final pause of the sequence underscored by a thump (Fig. 8.109).

A charming diversion in a film filled with set-pieces, the mahjong-parlor scene of *Righting Wrongs* exudes offhand mastery. To conceive the premise—a woman subduing four men with one pair of cuffs—and then to work it out in incisive detail requires imagination, a modest sense of the absurd, and an awareness of those mechanics of forceful, legible filmmaking pointed out by Kuleshov, Pudovkin, and Eisenstein in the 1920s. The construction is all the more admirable for the fact that it was developed on the set in a single day, with the director quickly deciding on each shot as each bit of action was conceived. This twenty-four seconds of cinema puts to shame the storyboarded fights in big-budget Schwarzenegger films, where firepower substitutes for briskness and finesse.

The best Hong Kong filmmakers understand that movie action is not a scattershot cataclysm. Energy will look more energetic when it is organized. Then the viewer, in the words of director Yuen Woo-ping, can *"feel the blow."*[27] This carnal cinema has discovered in the simplest film techniques ways to seize our senses. Granted, violent action is inherently exciting. "Nothing in life," remarked Winston Churchill, "is so exhilarating as to be shot at without result." Yet physical action demands artistic structuring if it is to thrill us. Strict patterning makes the action more intelligible, forceful, expressive.

How to explain this? Surely, art forms employing marked rhythms will be accessible to many audiences. We need no special training to grasp vigorous, well-structured movement. More exactly, it's not so much that we grasp it as that it grabs us; we respond kinesthetically, as when we tap our toes to music or hammer the air at a basketball game. These films literally grip us; we can watch ourselves tense and relax, twitch or flinch. By arousing us through highly legible motion and staccato rhythms, and by intensifying that arousal through composition and editing and sound, the films seem to ask our bodies to recall elemental and universal events like striking, swinging, twisting, leaping, rolling.[28]

Although Sergei Eisenstein is usually remembered as a theorist of montage, he claimed that the cornerstone of his conception of theater and cinema was expressive movement. By manipulating his or her body, the actor could impel the audience to imitate the movement, though in weakened form. The Hong Kong cinema may offer a better illustration of Eisenstein's theories than his own films do; at the least, the pause/burst/pause pattern seems to confirm his claim that maximal excitation arises when the actor frames each movement within static "points of excitation."[29] Eisenstein also speculated that by shaping the viewer's bodily rhythms, the actor's expressive movement could trigger emotional states. From this standpoint, we might ask whether the sheerly kinetic transport achieved by the Hong Kong action style makes us more susceptible to those feelings laid out for us by the drama. Devices that might seem mere stylistic embellishment, as we saw in *Saviour of the Soul*'s use of color, are central to expressive amplification, and our response to them may be heightened by our body's engagement with the primary action. By impelling us to invest ourselves physically, the movies prepare us to emote.

But even this speculation carries us only so far. For the films seem to do more than stir our senses and intensify our feelings. They offer us the illusion of mastering the action. Why do we leave these films not only tired but jubilant? Why do we think we can do anything? Partly because the kinetics have stamped the action's rhythm onto our senses; but also, I think, because the very cogency of the presentation has invited us to feel something of what supreme physical control might be like. Part of the pleasure of the *Righting Wrongs* sequence, for example, arises from its tidy simplicity. The whipcrack pulse, the crisp detailing, the effortless integration of props, the poise of Cindy Si, and the exactness of every camera position and cut—all combine to present the maximum compression and the maximum

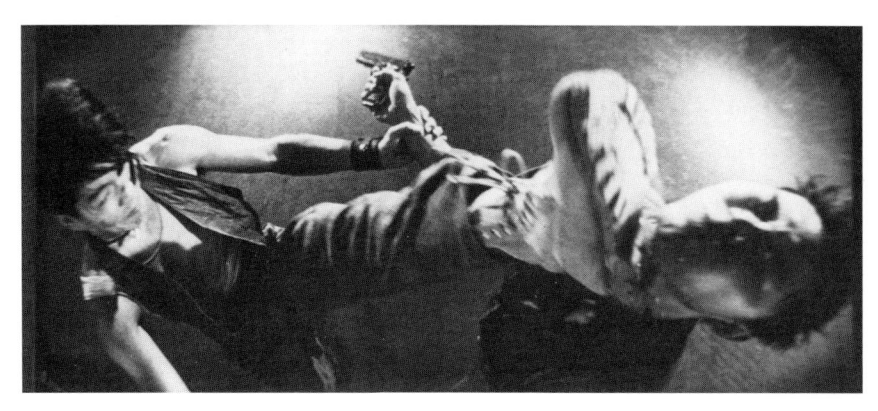

8.110 *Eastern Condors:* Sammo Hung uses camera position, the widescreen frame, and a distorting wide-angle lens to give Yuen Biao a comic-book kick.

precision. The result is an elation in efficiency. The policewoman's resourcefulness is conveyed through the unruffled neatness of the director's craft. In the best Hong Kong sequences, we rejoice in cinema's power over the physical world.

More detailed analysis could differentiate among action styles and trace their historical development. The long shots and fairly long takes of 1960s and 1970s swordplay and kung-fu films seem to have been elaborated by Sammo Hung and others in the late 1970s and refined in such mid-1980s achievements as Hung's *Wheels on Meals* (1984) and Jackie Chan's directorial masterpiece *Police Story* (1985). Over the same years there emerged a rough, handheld-camera approach visible in Lo Lieh's *Devil and Angel* (1973) and in the first modern *policier,* Leung Po-chi and Josephine Siao's *Jumping Ash* (1976), then extended in Alex Cheung's *Cops and Robbers* (1979) and the work of Kirk Wong (*The Club,* 1981; *Health Warning,* 1983; *Rock n' Roll Cop,* 1994).

As budgets swelled in the early 1980s, filmmakers were able to incorporate Hollywood filming techniques (extreme wide-angle and telephoto lenses, rack focus, faster cutting, more-varied slow motion). A fairly cosmopolitan style is evident in the trend-setting *Aces Go Places* (1982) and in Jackie Chan's *Project A* (1983). In *Ninja in the Dragon's Den* (1982) Yuen Kuei developed a "precisionist" approach that elaborated the action in depth and in unusual widescreen compositions. Soon a great many films cultivated a polished visual style, seen perhaps most triumphantly in Tsui Hark's *Peking Opera Blues* (1986). This was easily adopted to the revived genres of kung-fu and swordplay fantasy; it is the look that won fans around the world; it is Hong Kong's version of glossy American technique, although it surpasses Hollywood in vigor and brazen inventiveness (Fig. 8.110).

By the mid-1990s this style was looking old-fashioned. Young directors

8.111 *Task Force:* The Woo-inspired killer in action; compare Fig. EM.22.

8.112 *Task Force:* As a police official, John Woo faces down a young triad; soon he will congratulate the hero for defusing the fight: "Well done!"

put it in skeptical quotation marks, as in the fantasy of the God of the Sword in *Once upon a Time in Triad Society 2* (1996). In *Task Force* Patrick Leung paid his tribute to tradition by assigning a different style to each action scene: "The first is the gunfights that John Woo is famous for [see Fig. 8.111]. The second is swordfights, like in martial arts movies. The third is the fight between Eric Tsang and Orlando To, like those in kung-fu comedies. All three are unique to Hong Kong."[30] Leung cited these traditions partly, it seems, to criticize their view that violence could solve problems that are finally matters of law. His hero wins through refusing to kill, and when he carries the wounded killer to his superior, the officer (played by John Woo) congratulates him (and perhaps the filmmaker too, who used to be Woo's assistant; Fig. 8.112).

Some directors, often through financial constraints, moved toward a loose, improvisatory naturalism. The graceless gang fights shot with a handheld camera in Andrew Lau's *Young and Dangerous* films look realistically rowdy. More radically, other directors gave up coherence and clarity for sheer expressive intensity. Sammo Hung staged the combats for *Ashes of Time* (1994) in clean-cut moves, but Wong Kar-wai's step-printing and fish-eye lenses turn them into a blurry maelstrom (Fig. 8.113). Perhaps out of a desire to look up-to-date, some directors have even turned to the bustling incoherence of Hollywood action methods. As usual, though, several styles coexist. *Lifeline* and *Legend of the Wolf* build their excitement out of many of the principles that governed the films of the 1970s and 1980s. Patrick Yau's remarkable 1998 thrillers *The Longest Nite* (sic) and *Expect the Unexpected* mobilize rigorous cutting and dynamic movement not in order to project the exuberance of sheer movement but to give punishing force to a blunt, bleak nihilism. Many films of the 1990s demonstrate that the expressive resources of Hong Kong's action style are far from depleted.

Meanwhile, as if in rebuke to Hong Kong's brash sensationalism, Asian festival cinema slips steadily toward fixity and silence. Scenes of violence

8.113 Swordplay from the opening of the "international version" of *Ashes of Time*.

8.114 *City of Sadness:* The death of Wen-leung.

become awkward or opaque. The Korean film *Green Fish* (1997) pushes fistfights off into the distance. In Hou Hsiao-Hsien's *City of Sadness* (1989) the shooting of Wen-leung is barely visible; shadows and foreground figures conceal the action (Fig. 8.114). Such Asian "art films" have their own agendas, and they remind us of the limits of a popular aesthetic: there is no Hong Kong *Sonatine* (1991) or *Goodbye South Goodbye* (1996). Popular cinema probes a bounded range of options. Still, it does *probe* that range, revealing depths and shadings and unexpected nuance within what is too quickly dismissed as cliché.

The action picture, thriving on vulgarity, carnality, and sensuous appeal, is a paradigm case of popular film. It is also manifestly an instance of craft. If we want to understand the full range of what movies can do, we do well to pause over even a despised genre like the chop-socky or the gunfest. Creating spellbinding excitement out of dozens of well-judged niceties is no small undertaking. The artisans of Hong Kong have entertained multitudes by making motion yield emotion. Their work can still teach us a lot about how cinema works.

THREE MARTIAL MASTERS: ZHANG CHE, LAU KAR-LEUNG, KING HU

From the mid-1960s to the early 1980s, three directors rang remarkably diverse variations on Hong Kong's martial-arts traditions. All worked at some point for Shaws, all found fresh ways to treat the episodic structure and combat conventions of swordplay and kung-fu movies, and all have been unfairly neglected by Western critics.[1]

The oldest, Zhang Che (1923–), was an emblem of Chinese disasporan filmmaking. Soon after World War II he began writing screenplays in Shanghai. He fled the Communist revolution to Taiwan, where he made the island's first Mandarin-language film and worked on Kuomintang propaganda. In 1957 he settled in Hong Kong. There he began a prolific career, directing more than sixty films before retiring in the late 1980s. Zhang was among the earliest to produce updated *wuxia pian* (*Tiger Boy*, 1966) and kung-fu films (*Duel of Fists*, 1971). Many of his movies are insignificant, but at his best Zhang built a masochistic heroism out of vigorous, often brutal action.

Zhang cranked out martial-arts movies for Shaw Brothers from the mid-1960s to the late 1970s. He gave the *wuxia pian* a new technical sophistication—rapid cutting, handheld combat shots, careful compositions (Figs. 8.8–8.12)—while ratcheting up the violence. He packed each reel with fights, and he cultivated a Grand Guignol approach to swordplay. Cantonese swordplay films had been relatively sanitized, but under the influence of samurai cinema Zhang reveled in sensational effects. He was not averse to blindings and disembowelings, but he had a special fondness for vagrant body parts. In *The One-Armed Swordsman* (1967) a master chooses the young Fang Kang to head his school and marry his daughter. Fang refuses the post and leaves. The daughter, distraught, challenges Fang to a duel, and when she loses, she angrily chops off Fang's arm. Thereafter he is thrashed and humiliated until he learns to fight again.

Zhang's films, usually prepared with scriptwriter Ni Kuang, find the

TMM.1 *Crippled Avengers:* The death blow.

hero's mutilation echoed everywhere. Throughout *The One-Armed Swordsman*, Fang's father's broken swordblade becomes a totem of his own debility, and the combat manual from which he teaches himself swordsmanship is, like Fang himself, torn in half. Zhang's revenge plots set up a grimly playful exchange of appendages: not so much an eye for an eye as an eye for an ear. *Crippled Avengers* (aka *Mortal Combat*, 1978) presents a catalogue of sadistic mutilations. In an opening attack on a kung-fu master's family, swordsmen slice off his wife's legs and his son's arms. The master fits his son with steel arms, and, unsurprisingly, the boy grows up to be a bully. One day he casually blinds a street peddler, deafens a blacksmith, chops the legs off a passerby, and reduces a fourth man to infantilism by pressure on his skull. The victims of his depredations learn kung-fu and return to wreak revenge in a series of astonishing combat scenes, each tailored to the avengers' deficits. At the end, the villainous father is strung up like a side of beef as the blind, deaf, and legless fighters attack; the death blow is delivered by the legless one, now fitted out with steel legs like the son's arms (Fig. TMM.1).

Incomplete, the original Chinese title of *Crippled Avengers*, is not a bad name for many of Zhang's films. *The New One-Armed Swordsman* (1971) creates another weird variant of payback. In the opening scene, the cocky young swordsman Lei Li (using *one* sword) is defeated by master Ho, expert with the jointed staff (consisting of *three* rods). As punishment for losing, Lei must hack off his own right arm. Later, his friend Feng fights Ho with *two* swords and is defeated; Ho then chops Feng's body in *half*. In the final battle, shouting, "What you did to Feng Chun I shall do to you!" Lei eventually uses *three* swords in quick succession to counter Ho's three-sectioned staff. Vengeance is intensified: Ho ends up impaled by three swords (in retaliation for Feng's death) but also minus an arm (vengeance for Lei's own loss). One outrageous shot supplies the final reckoning (Fig. TMM.2).

THREE MARTIAL MASTERS

TMM.2 *The New One-Armed Swordsman:* Two one-armed swordsmen, with an unclaimed arm pinned between them.

TMM.3 *The New One-Armed Swordsman.*

Tit-for-tat sadism is accompanied by themes of compulsive male honor. Even though Zhang's early swordplay film *Golden Swallow* (1967) is named after a woman warrior, the plot centers on Silver Roc, the tragic hero. The one-armed swordsman Fang is the object of two women's love, but the crucial action centers on his learning to fight again. If Zhang Che brings in a female love interest, she usually offers support from the sidelines while the oblivious hero pursues his obsessions. More often Zhang replaces romance with male bonding, producing a series of smoldering masculine couples (Jimmy Wang Yu and Lo Lieh, Ti Lung and David Chiang, Alexander Fu Sheng and Chi Kuan Chun). In *The New One-Armed Swordsman*, David Chiang is Lei, the brooding and anxious James Dean figure, while Ti Lung plays Feng, the bluff, openhearted, not overbright adventurer. The two pledge brotherhood as Lei's girlfriend Pa Chiao looks on, then set off together, ignoring her (Fig. TMM.3). Later Lei and Feng lounge on a rope like schoolboys, and Feng predicts that soon Lei will be happily married to Pa Chiao. Feng then goes off unwitting to his death. All that remains for Lei is bloody revenge.

In his kung-fu films, Zhang replaces two partners with the superb ensemble known to Western fans as the Five Venoms, multiplying male affinities and leaving no room for women at all. Films like *Avenging Warriors* (1979) are filled with the Venoms' horseplay. An entire reel of *Crippled Avengers* is devoted to the blinded man and the deafened man; adding up to one complete warrior, they fight arm in arm. John Woo, who assisted Zhang on several films, inherits this homoerotic romanticism, and the parallel injuries in his films (*The Killer*'s double blinding of John and Jenny, the spiraling cycles of Russian roulette of *Bullet in the Head*, the villains' wounded eyes in *Hard Boiled*) may owe something to Zhang's ruthlessly geometrical settling of accounts.

Lau Kar-leung (in Mandarin, Liu Jia-liang) was Zhang Che's premier martial-arts instructor. Born in Guangdong Province in 1935, Lau entered the Hong Kong film industry very young. His father, a martial artist for the Huang Feihong series, gave him stuntwork and small parts. Lau started work at Shaws as an action choreographer and then in 1975 as director. The films Lau made over the next decade, connoisseurs agree, represent the high-water mark of the kung-fu genre. The kung-fu films known to most Americans resemble B westerns; a Lau film is often the equivalent of a rough, stubborn Raoul Walsh, say *Manpower* (1941) or *White Heat* (1949), with Keatonesque comic touches thrown in and some elegiac moments recalling John Ford.

Lau took as his subject the world of martial arts. Trained in the southern Shaolin styles, he focused so single-mindedly on the lore, rituals, and disciplines of kung-fu that he seems to reverse the industry's priorities: instead of using kung-fu to keep local cinema going, he used cinema to document and preserve the traditions he venerated. Characters define and express themselves through their fighting styles. Lau's favored player, his bald, scowling brother Lau Kar-fai, serves less as a character than as an abstract exemplar of the single-minded dedication demanded by the martial arts.

In *The 36th Chamber of Shaolin* (aka *Master Killer*, 1978), a young man's father and friends are murdered by the Manchus and he flees to the Shaolin Temple. He begs the abbot to teach him kung-fu so that he may seek vengeance. Reluctantly the abbot agrees. The training is stupendously rigorous: there are thirty-five test chambers, each devoted to perfecting a single technique. The bulk of the film charts the sheer obstinacy the young man displays in his training. He must learn to run across a stream on floating bundles of twigs; he must learn to shift his eyes rapidly while keeping his chin absolutely still; he must learn to bash sandbags with his forehead. Throughout, the Shaolin monastery is presented in loving detail, and Lau delights in showing how training exercises spring from homely chores of washing dishes and hauling water. A perfunctory climax presents the

TMM.4 Marital discord in *Shaolin Challenges Ninja.*

youth retaliating against his adversaries; the film's real conclusion shows him as the master of a new, thirty-sixth chamber devoted to training commoners to fight the Manchus.

Lau Kar-leung could celebrate the Shaolin tradition in a comic vein too, as in the delightful *Dirty Ho* (1979), *Mad Monkey Kung Fu* (1979), and *My Young Auntie* (1981). In *Shaolin Challenges Ninja* (1978), a sort of Cantonese *Taming of the Shrew*, a young Chinese lord marries a proud Japanese woman. Every day the newlyweds quarrel over which nation's martial artistry is superior, and the dispute always ends in an all-out battle—over the breakfast table, in the parlor, in the courtyard. Every day the wife loses, and in pique she returns to Japan. Her father recruits several ninja from his school, and she brings them back to fight her husband. After he has defeated each one, she becomes a docile wife. Each character is little more than a repertoire of fighting techniques capped by a patriotic attitude, but Lau's one-joke situation showcases a range of weapons and stratagems, creating an entertaining textbook of Chinese and Japanese fighting traditions (Fig. TMM.4).

Lau mixed drama and humor to vivid effect. *Legendary Weapons of China* (1982) opens with a shocking scene. The Yi Ho Boxer society, convinced that their training allows them to resist Western bullets, line up for a test; all are shot down by their comrades. In despair a branch leader dissolves his cadre, but the main group sends three spies to track him down. The film starts as a charade of disguises, with the spies prowling around one another (Fig. TMM.5), but it quickly modulates into broad comedy, including a parody of Zhang Che in which a mock-warrior pretends to be disemboweled and then stuffs his intestines back in to fight on. There is also droll voodoolike magic, in which a master makes a distant fighter do his bidding by twisting the arms and legs of a doll. The film concludes with an all-out duel incorporating no fewer than eighteen exotic weapons.

Martial-arts experts declare Lau's to be the most authentic combats ever

TMM.5 Intrigue in *Legendary Weapons of China*.

staged for film, displaying fighting styles at their most dazzling. But thanks to the resources of Movietown he developed a robust cinematic sense as well. In *Legendary Weapons*, two rival spies are hiding in an attic. They alternate between trying to spear the suspect in the bedroom below and trying to stab each other with flying daggers. The scene plays out in a rocking, give-and-take rhythm, marked by swift thrusts, sudden stillness, and soft thunks as blades sink into wood or sacks of grain. The cutting and framing here announce the pulsating dynamism of the 1980s action style.

Lau's cinematic skill fused with his fascination with martial traditions to yield one of the most impressive of his last Shaw works. *The Eight-Diagram Pole Fighter* (1984) is a somber dissection of the revenge motif. The film opens on a battlefield that owes more to proscenium theater than to realism; out of a black void two color-coded armies emerge and slaughter each other. Two brothers survive. One returns to his mother and goes mad; the other retires to a monastery, where he learns pole-fighting. The final mêlée in the headquarters of the traitor is one of the high points of Hong Kong cinema, and in its whirlwind energy it puts to shame the contemporaneous "action cinema" of Spielberg and Walter Hill. The hero's pole flails his enemies like grain; he leaps and lunges from a pyramid of coffins; he rescues his sister by lashing her to his back. As he is about to be overwhelmed, he is rescued by the monks, who whack their poles into the jaws of their adversaries and yank out the men's teeth.

The Eight-Diagram Pole Fighter insists on the price of revenge. Innocent people are dragged into the second son's vendetta, and he becomes an antisocial obsessive. Once revenge is accomplished, he cannot return to his family. Like Ethan Edwards in *The Searchers* he simply strides out, too consumed with hatred to live among civilized people. Lau's sympathy seems largely with the monks who insist, in film after film, that revenge debases the martial arts and that perfecting one's skill while extinguishing worldly vanity is the mark of the master.

A consummate studio filmmaker, Lau Kar-leung started directing just as the martial-arts movie was giving ground to Cantonese comedy and cop action. While Jackie Chan, Sammo Hung, and the New Wavers were updating kung-fu, he patiently refined its classic forms. When Shaws stopped producing films, Lau made a Mainland coproduction (*Martial Arts of Shaolin*, 1986) and then moved into the urban action genre (most notably with *Tiger on Beat*, 1988, and its frantic shotgun-machete-and-chainsaw duel). Working sporadically in the 1990s, he was dismissed from directing Jackie Chan's *Drunken Master II* (1994) because he demanded that Chan execute the drunken kung-fu style accurately.[2] It is hard not to see *The Eight-Diagram Pole Fighter* as Lau's valedictory for an entire local tradition.

King Hu (1931–1997) worked in Hong Kong but was not fully of it. He was born in Peking and died in Taipei. He spent the last several years of his life in Los Angeles, trying to get backing for *The Battle of Ono*, a tale of Chinese immigrants caught up in the California gold rush. After emigrating to Hong Kong in 1949 he worked in several studios, first in art departments, then at Shaws as an actor, then as an assistant director on costume dramas, and finally as a director of two films, the war drama *Sons of the Good Earth* (1965) and the swordplay film *Come Drink with Me* (1966). When the latter proved successful, he left Shaws and began making films in Taiwan, while keeping some ties to Hong Kong companies. While Zhang Che and Lau Kar-leung settled snugly into studio routine, Hu's grandiose aims led him to costly one-off productions. (*A Touch of Zen*, 1971, took years to complete.) None of his five 1970s films found success in Hong Kong, and by the early 1980s his projects could not get backing. He started directing the Tsui Hark production *The Swordsman* (1990), but after disagreements with Tsui, Hu left the project. His last film, *Painted Skin* (1993), was a Hong Kong–China coproduction. He died as John Woo, Terence Chang, and other Hollywood newcomers were gathering funding for *The Battle of Ono*.

In thirty years King Hu made just eleven features, and his fame rests upon six features and two shorts, all swordplay tales. His first two outings in the genre were triumphs: *Come Drink with Me* helped establish the new *wuxia pian*, and *Dragon Gate Inn* (1967) was one of the biggest box-office successes in Southeast Asia. Yet King Hu was uninterested in combat techniques, and he credited his films' excellent fights to the choreography of Han Yingjie (best known in the West as the title villain of Bruce Lee's *The Big Boss*, 1971).

Despite his slender output King Hu was probably Hong Kong's finest director of the 1960s and 1970s. As much a scholar as a filmmaker, he researched costumes and settings in detail. He planned his films fastidiously, handing out each scene's storyboards to cast and crew—a process unheard-of in catch-as-catch-can Hong Kong production. By filming in Taiwan,

South Korea, and Hong Kong's offshore islands he could take advantage of spectacular locations, avoiding the slightly stifling studio air that pervades even the best films of Zhang Che and Lau Kar-leung. He brought an offhand humor to scenes of outrageous action; after snagging an arrow in a wine bottle or flipping backward across an inn, his poker-faced fighters remain as unflappable as Budd Boetticher heroes. In a tradition that already favored women warriors, Hu gave them not only awesome powers but cheerful dignity, mysterious reserve, and sardonic humor. One of the great pleasures of Hu's cinema is the growing importance of Xu Feng, his main swordswoman; Xu plays both villains and heroines with an intent, unruffled frown.[3]

Hu used the Mandarin movie as an occasion to explore China's tragic history of state corruption. In a genre that spun out plots of private revenge and family loyalty, he elaborated political intrigues, complete with bluffing, disguise, and shifting alliances. He gravitated to the Ming dynasty, a period in which venal cliques plotted against one another and cooperated only to oppress the people. He tried to capture China's confrontation with external invaders, like the Mongols and the Japanese, and portrayed the Ming as a period when Confucianism, Taoism, and Buddhism jostled one another (*A Touch of Zen; Raining in the Mountain*, 1979).[4]

Steeped in historical atmosphere, Hu's films draw upon Ming traditions of knight-errantry to provide an image of idealistic heroism that is rare in Hong Kong cinema. If Zhang Che's heroes are defined by male friendship and Lau Kar-leung's by their dedication to the Shaolin heritage, King Hu's heroes fight for a cause—most often, patriotic loyalty—and they protect the weak and innocent. His selfless heroes and heroines have an aloof severity far removed from the sweaty anguish of Zhang's mutilated swordsmen and the hard-won discipline of Lau's kung-fu masters. Their psychology is rudimentary at best, and in *The Valiant Ones* (1975) they are mere ciphers, but this only gives them a grave purity, turning them into emblems of the tranquillity earned by mastery of fighting arts. For Hu, this conception of chivalry, a natural nobility and a solemn dedication to justice, is the most shining heritage to emerge from centuries of sordid Chinese history.

Take *Dragon Gate Inn*. At the start a voice-over narration dates the action precisely: 1457, when the palace eunuch Cao Shaoqin controls two military agencies, under the command of officers Pi and Mao. Cao executes Minister of Defense Yu, and by decree Yu's children are sent into exile. But Cao is determined to kill them before they reach freedom. In a roadside skirmish they are saved by Zhu Hui, a passing swordsman. Cao vows to hurry to Dragon Gate Inn and kill them there. But when the forces of Pi and Mao arrive they encounter another mysterious swordsman, Xiao. In a series of escalating challenges reminiscent of Leone saloon encounters, Xiao resists bullying and eventually kills an officer. Only gradually does it emerge that Xiao has been summoned by the innkeeper, who is actually an old general loyal to the executed Yu. And even more slowly does it emerge that Zhu Hui and his sister (posing as a boy) have also come to join the fight. Games of deceit, poisoned wine, eavesdropping, and sudden death spice up the evening at the inn before the conflict finally surfaces and the long battle to protect the children can begin. The film relies on subsidiary antagonists who exist chiefly to delay the fight with the principal villain, but it treats the convention with historical specificity, sustained suspense, and subterfuges that keep the audience guessing along with the characters.

Zhang's and Lau's fighters use swordplay and kung-fu to express their feelings and communicate with their opponents. King Hu's warriors deploy an unfussy, impersonal technique; their fights chiefly manifest their intensity of purpose. No need for spartan training sessions in a King Hu film. His heroes and heroines arrive completely adequate, utterly self-possessed, gliding through the commotion with a calm concentration that provokes jubilation in the spectator. Only in a climactic battle will the strain start to tell, and even then the heroes seldom succumb to anger; they simply exchange sharp glances, as if transmitting their next tactic telepathically. When a warrior starts to lose poise, another enters to take things in hand. The most characteristic moment occurs in *A Touch of Zen*, when after Gu and Shi are about to succumb to the villain Xu Xianchun, the monk Hui Yuan floats in, arcing gently through the air, landing softly, trying to reason with Xu before he deals him a few regretful, devastating blows. He incarnates that touch of zen that, perhaps under the influence of Japanese cinema, all of Hu's heroes and heroines possess.

Hu's choreographer, Han Yingjie, had trained in Peking Opera, and Hu frankly acknowledged that he designed combat scenes as ballets, not as plausible fights. Chases through forests and among inn tables are accompanied by opera percussion, particularly the clapper *(ban)*. Hu underscores characters' entrances not only by the *ban*'s stinging crack but also by a sharp rolling of the eyes or an abrupt cut.[5] Western art, King Hu claimed, is torn between imitation and expressivity, but Chinese art always offers both, using real materials to present something unreal.[6] Hu's heroes and heroines increase their stature by fighting in ways that are neither strictly realistic nor obviously fantastic. Their combats become visual metaphors of propulsion, grace, power.

Critics commonly divide Hu's principal films into two batches. *Come Drink with Me*, *Dragon Gate Inn*, the short *Anger* (1970), and *The Fate of Lee Khan* (1973) all center on inns. The isolated inn, King Hu felt, was "the most dramatic of locations. Few places can squeeze time and space together like them, where all kinds of conflicts can occur."[7] Here intrigues converge, warriors can appear disguised as musicians or harmless travelers, military leaders can set up headquarters, secret messages can be exchanged and conspiracies hatched. A drunkard's innocent song can distract authori-

TMM.6 *The Fate of Lee Khan:* Utilizing the widescreen.

TMM.7 *Raining in the Mountain:* Chases become games of hide-and-seek in the mazelike monastery.

ties or convey a coded order. The inn's central area also provides a multi-level set for chases and fights. Dining tables are excellent launching pads, and a staircase landing allows waitresses to dive-bomb churlish guests. The clutter of his inns coaxed King Hu into designing clever widescreen images of combat (Fig. TMM.6).

Even the inn films do not confine themselves wholly to interiors; by the end conflicts spill outdoors. A second set of films is built around exteriors, unfolding across a series of breathtaking landscapes. *A Touch of Zen* is the prototype. It begins in a village and concludes its first part with one of Hu's greatest scenes, an aerial combat in a bamboo grove (Fig. 1.1). The second half expands further, carrying its fighters through forests and mountains to a seascape transformed into a vista of Buddhist transcendence. *The Valiant Ones*, a virtual anthology of combat scenes, is a journey from coastline through forests back to rocky coast, with a rest stop in the pirates' ostentatiously formal headquarters. *Raining in the Mountain* offers a kind of spatial synthesis. The Buddhist monastery becomes at once a vast arena and a honeycomb of corridors, rooftops, and passageways (Fig. TMM.7). In the end, though, even this porous space proves too confining, and the two vil-

THREE MARTIAL MASTERS   257

TMM.8 *Raining in the Mountain.*

lains flee into the mountains, where they encounter a torrent of fighting women swathed in yellow and crimson (Fig. TMM.8).

Along with their heroic idealism and visual splendor, the films display an engaging eccentricity. King Hu was perfectly capable of shooting and cutting a straightforward fight, but he often sought to convey the otherworldly speed and agility of his fighters through stylistic choices that we can only call experimental. Densely crowded settings partially conceal a thrust or leap. Swordfighters swing in and out of the shot, starting to slash as they exit; we must wait for the target to spring back in, showing the wound. Hu's jumpers flit through the frame, as if the camera cannot catch them. He uses doubles to create visual sleight-of-hand. In *The Valiant Ones*, a "whirlwind" technique lets a warrior come at an opponent from all sides (Figs. TMM.9–TMM.12).

Above all, Hu took pride in rapid cutting, claiming that he was the first Hong Kong director to use eight-frame shots.[8] He calls on constructive editing, which is supposed to lay out the action clearly, and then does all he can to sabotage it. He likes to shave frames off the launch/leap/land cycle, or eliminate one or two phases altogether, so that the heroes' maneuvers become as abrupt and disconcerting to the viewer as they are to their adversaries. In *The Valiant Ones* Xu Lian runs and delivers a flying kick at his opponent, then trots back to run forward and kick again; he does this *ten times*. King Hu gives us each bone-rattling assault in a flurry of cuts, but he presents a different combination of shots each time, nearly always eliminating some phase of the action, fanning out a set of variations on how constructive editing can create ellipsis. Hu also accelerates attacks through flagrant jump cuts (Figs. TMM.13–TMM.14). Instead of floating endlessly like the Hong Kong swordsmen of the 1990s, Hu's fighters are usually up and down in an instant. Did Cao Shaoquin really leap over trees at the climax of *Dragon Gate Inn*? When the heroes do stay aloft, they're still rendered in bursts of cinematic shorthand; the elliptical cutting,

TMM.9 *The Valiant Ones:* Madam Wu dodges the Japanese pirate . . .

TMM.10 . . . and, using the "whirlwind" technique, materializes in the foreground (by means of a double).

TMM.11 As the pirate turns toward her, the double dives under the frameline, and he is struck from behind . . .

TMM.12 . . . by Madam Wu, who finishes him off.

TMM.13 In *A Touch of Zen* the villain (played by choreographer Han Jingyie) leaps up . . .

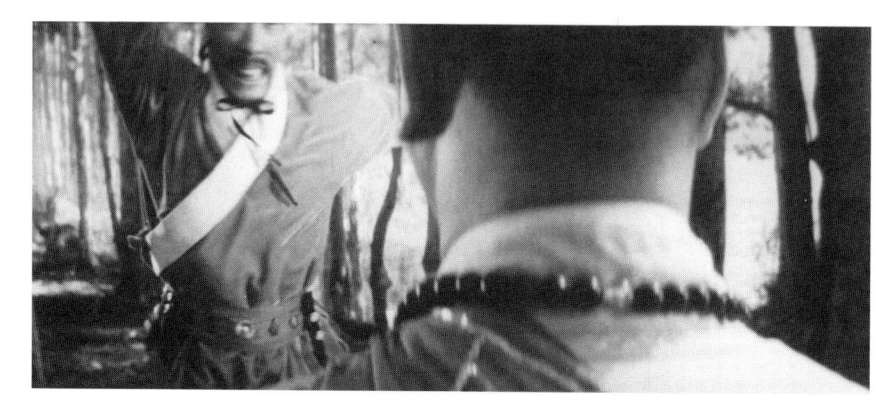

TMM.14 . . . and the very next frame shows him landing.

granting us only glimpses of their trajectory, makes their prowess seem half-miraculous.

Before Wong Kar-wai's *Happy Together* (1997), *A Touch of Zen* was the only Hong Kong film to win a prize at Cannes, and appropriately it received a special award for "superior technique." The award sparked some Western interest in Hu's films, but they are still generally unknown, playing in the occasional retrospective and almost completely unavailable on video. (The Japanese, who have always appreciated him, have produced fine widescreen video versions, as well as the first full-length book on him.) From 1966 to 1979, Hu was one of the finest directors working anywhere, and he was certainly the most boldly experimental filmmaker attached to the Hong Kong industry. His achievement lay in his enrichment of the traditions of popular cinema.

9

AVANT-POP CINEMA

Over ominous drum tattoos the opening credits of Daniel Lee's *What Price Survival?* (1994) present a fusillade of puzzling images. In whirlwinds of snow and dirty leaves, swordsmen in black greatcoats slash at each other. A woman looks mysteriously on. Couples walk through a bleak orchard. We glimpse a gravesite and a Japanese temple. Then the story begins. Recognizing an image here and there, we gradually realize that the opening has sampled the film to come. The effect is to alert us to ritualistic repetitions: elaborate duels set in a no-man's-land that is nominally 1930s Japan; the pervasive and otherworldly color scheme of black, gray, and white, broken only by spurts of dark blood; the uncannily similar clothes worn by all characters; the equation of the protagonist's two fathers. The credits of *What Price Survival?* present a phantasmagoria of instants out of which a story will precipitate.

In a European film such a tactic would look fairly experimental, akin to the thematic overtures of Bergman's *Persona* (1966) and Resnais's *Mon oncle d'Amérique* (1980). Yet in this genre movie, the sequence is so ferociously exciting that no ordinary viewer could object to its obscurity. In fact the audience has often seen something like it. You could take it as a variant of those TV episodes that open with teasing glimpses of high points to come, or those reprises that many Hong Kong films run under the *final* credits; you could even take it as a coming-attractions trailer. You could say that the film shifts its final credits montage forward, or that it simply swallows its own preview. Either way, it turns a commercial convention into a fresh formal device.

Entertainment builds novelty into its basic demands, and some genres, such as science fiction and detective stories, welcome innovative storytelling. Entertainment is also playful, and we ought to expect that the very devices that lure in audiences may be occasions for open-ended experiment. The fan-aesthete often assumes that Hong Kong's disorienting originality arises when haste, poverty, low (or no) taste, and a dash of nuttiness spontaneously fuse. Usually the situation is more mundane. In commercial film, experimentation is usually not anarchic messing about but self-conscious craftsmanship. It is hard to argue that the devious use of point of view in Hitchcock, the stylistic surprises in Yasujiro Ozu, and the flamboyant montage opening *What Price Survival?* come straight from the id. These innovations are the result of patient care. Driven by competition, contrariness, or just the urge not to repeat oneself, the ambitious artisan presses against tradition, testing how far one can go while still playing by the rules of the game.

In 1996 the Hong Kong Arts Development Council set aside the equivalent of several hundred thousand U.S. dollars to fund film and video shorts.[1] At the center of this effort was the Zeman Media Centre, founded at the Hong Kong Arts Centre in 1993 to give local independent filmmakers access to production and postproduction facilities. The Arts Centre also worked with the Urban Council to create an annual video and film competition.

Out of the Zeman Centre came a call for a new cinema. A group named "[ying e chi]" (complete with brackets), which means "the will to create cinema," declared a crisis in Hong Kong production and Asian culture as a whole. The 16mm and 35mm projects made by members of [ying e chi]'s would be more radical: "1997, the handover year, [ying e chi] first retrospective of works; independent, hand-crafted and tailor-made with shoestring budgets, outside of the establishment, new tendencies, experimentation, alternative, non-categorizable, neither in nor out, avant-garde, beyond boundaries, very good and not too good, everything altogether . . . all because we have chosen to make films, to create cinema."[2] By the spring of 1999 [ying e chi] was distributing several 35mm shorts and features, and Hong Kong seemed to have laid the foundations for a lively sector of independent filmmaking.

Old hands would recall that they had tried something similar long before. In 1968 the student newspaper *University Life* created a ciné-club to screen members' 16mm films. The still cheaper gauge of super-8mm opened up production to many more people, and new film clubs emerged. While a few members of the New Wave were involved with the independent sector, the Hong Kong industry never made room for anything like independent film production as it developed in the United States, Europe, or Japan. Experimental work was relegated to annual festivals.

The difficulties of bringing a fresh attitude into the 1970s industry are epitomized in the case of Shu Shuen, Hong Kong's first significant woman director and a harbinger of the New Wave. Born in China in 1941, Shu Shuen (also known as Tang Shuxuan or Cecille Tang Shu Shuen) moved to Hong Kong and then attended film school at the University of Southern California. Her first film, *The Arch* (1970), was an early independent production, funded by American backers, shot in Hong Kong and Taiwan, and completed in the United States. *The Arch* performed weakly in Hong Kong, but it had successful runs in North America and Europe and became something of a festival item. Shu Shuen's next film was *China Behind*, a story of five Mainlanders fleeing Mao's Cultural Revolution; finished in 1974, it was not commercially released until 1987. She made two satiric comedies before withdrawing from filmmaking and moving to the United States.

Shot in Taiwan, *China Behind* was a daring criticism of political conditions in the people's Republic. The first half uses newsreel technique to capture Red Guard mayhem, and even static scenes become filled with tension when background loudspeakers blare out political slogans. When the five fugitives take flight, their ideals collapse. In one shocking scene, a pregnant, half-starving refugee hides in a farmhouse and begins wolfing down rice; a little boy discovers her, and the distraught woman nearly kills him before her lover intervenes. As the woman staggers out through the farmyard, color drains from the shot, as if confirming her moral degradation. The refugees arrive in Hong Kong, where they find menial jobs or turn to religion. Remaining at a cool distance from its characters, *China Behind* is an exercise in piercing realism far different from the kung-fu movies and sex comedies that ruled the local scene.

Hong Kong critics consider Shu Shuen's earlier film, *The Arch*, to be a forerunner of the New Wave, and it is remarkably sophisticated for a filmmaker in her twenties. Derived from a Lin Yutang adaptation of a folktale, *The Arch* tells of a widow whom her village is about to honor for her chastity. But Madam Dong is attracted to Captain Yang. At great effort she holds herself back, so he seduces her daughter. As Yang and the daughter marry, the arch honoring Madam Dong is completed; but by then she is nearly mad with frustration. Perhaps influenced by the Western feminist movement, Shu Shuen turns the film into a parable of the repression of women's sexuality. (The Freudianism is quite flagrant: the eager daughter caresses an ear of corn, and at the pitch of desire, Madam Dong chops off a rooster's head.) Pictorially as well *The Arch* remains impressive. Hong Kong critics have pointed out its adaptation of methods from Chinese poetry and painting.[3] Shu Shuen makes inventive use of the pan-and-zoom style so common internationally, and her superimpositions and freeze-frames look forward to Wong Kar-wai's (Figs. 9.1–9.2).

The experimental élan of *The Arch*, reminiscent of the "young cinemas" of Europe and Latin America, seems all the more daring in light of the New Wave films that followed. The internationally famous ones, such as Allen Fong's *Father and Son* (1981), Ann Hui's *Boat People* (1982), and Yim Ho's *Homecoming* (1984), were solid realist exercises. In Hong Kong, a naturalistic cinema shot in neighborhoods, using local dialects and unknown actors was a bold gesture, but by world standards most of these films seemed unadventurous. Still, a few directors tried more unusual things. The initial version of Tsui Hark's *Dangerous Encounter—First Kind* (1980) examined

9.1 *The Arch:* Madam Dong runs to the camera and halts at an angle in the right foreground, leading us to think that the frame is frozen.

9.2 After a beat, Yang steps forward in the background; then he "freezes" too.

class differences and political violence through a cynical story of well-off schoolboys who plant bombs for the fun of it until they're blackmailed by a policeman's sadistic sister. But censors, fearing a rash of copycat bombings, forced Tsui to shoot new scenes, making the schoolboys guilty of a hit-and-run accident and expanding a sketchy subplot about U.S. Vietnam veterans turned gunrunners. Tsui's style is ragged and grating, and he fills the film with Buñuelesque imagery—a cat impaled on a spike, boys gunned down in a cemetery. The final massacre has some of the disturbingly rousing nihilism of Arrabal's *Viva la muerte* (1971).

Patrick Tam's *Nomad* (1982) offers another cross-class intrigue, interweaving romance with the machinations of Japanese Red Guard terrorists. This time the production company recut the film, and Tam disowned it. Tam became known as the most radical of New Wavers; his debut, *The Sword* (1980), had a quasi-Japanese elegance (arcing tracks, artful silhouettes, elliptical editing), while *Love Massacre* (1981) was an exercise in yuppie Guignol. Perhaps most imaginative of the New Wave countercanon is Kirk Wong's *Health Warning* (1983), scripted by Jerry Liu. In the early twenty-first century a traditional kickboxing school clashes with a vaguely punkish neo-Nazi club. The atmosphere of solemn brutality is mesmerizing, enhanced by ceaseless synthesizer throbbing. Nearly devoid of dialogue, unfolding in perpetual night and cavernous, misty interiors, *Health Warning* is something of a Hong Kong *Blade Runner*.[4]

These films conveyed their social criticism with vigor and brashness, but alongside the Taiwanese "New Cinema" of Edward Yang and Hou Hsiao-hsien, which emerged at the same time, even the most untraditional Hong Kong New Wave films come down firmly on the side of Hollywood. Tsui Hark suggests as much: "We never got into what's behind, the soul or spirit behind the New Wave. And what do we have that makes us so different from the past filmmakers . . . in the industry? There's not much difference."[5] Certainly, however, the New Wave succeeded in clearing a small space for art cinema.

9.4 *Centre Stage:* Maggie Cheung reenacting her performance.

9.3 *Centre Stage:* Ruan Lingyu in her original film.

Whatever success they find in festivals or foreign markets, Hong Kong's more recent art films remain strongly rooted in the conventions of local entertainment. A revealing moment occurs at the climax of Stanley Kwan's *Rouge*. In 1930s Shanghai a courtesan (Anita Mui) dies in a suicide pact. As a ghost she returns to 1980s Hong Kong searching for the lover who failed to join her (Leslie Cheung). She finds him working as an extra at a film studio. As she advances upon the decrepit old man, Kwan juxtaposes her with a swooping warrior being filmed outside. The effect is to contrast cinematic artifice with genuine suffering; but it also invests Fleur's sorrow with the scourging fury of a swordswoman. Even while debunking the artifice of wirework and sword stunts, Kwan relies on genre traditions to intensify the contrasts among modern Hong Kong, where no one would die for love; Shanghai of the 1930s, licentious but still bound by hierarchy; and an ancient China of martial honor. Kwan's very title refers back to the first feature-length film made in Hong Kong, *Rouge* (1925).

While festival filmmaking keeps in touch with entertainment, the mainstream gives some room to play. The craft tradition encouraged King Hu, Tsui Hark, John Woo, and other filmmakers to explore various stylistic options, often for the sake of vividness and expressive force. With the production surge of the early 1990s, new opportunities for renovation arose. Since a star-laden movie would probably not lose money in regional markets, some directors were able to experiment in fairly daring ways.

One of the most prestigious instances is Stanley Kwan's *Centre Stage* (aka *Actress*, 1992), an ambitious biopic treating the 1930s Shanghai film star Ruan Lingyu. Kwan intercuts original footage from Ruan's films, footage of Maggie Cheung enacting episodes from Ruan's private life, and documentary interviews with Cheung and Kwan about the project (Figs. 9.3, 9.4). The interplay among levels of fiction, though somewhat tame by Western standards, was virtually unprecedented in Hong Kong cinema.

AVANT-POP CINEMA   265

Less well-known is *To Liv(e)* (1992), by the critic Evans Chan. The story, centering on two couples debating emigrating from Hong Kong, is broken up by a series of letters the heroine considers writing to Liv Ullmann, who criticized Hong Kong's treatment of Vietnamese immigrants. The film has a tendentious air furthered by 1969-style Godardian monologues that pin talking heads against abstract backgrounds, but the schematic message is softened by lyrical montages and passionate voice-over commentary.

The most famous director to benefit from the production boom was Wong Kar-wai. Thanks to the Taiwanese success of his star-laden first film, *As Tears Go By* (1988), he was able to make *Days of Being Wild* (1990), a breakthrough for the new generation. Despite its three Cantopop superstars (Leslie Cheung, Andy Lau, Jacky Cheung) and the top-line actresses Maggie Cheung and Carina Lau, Wong's languid character study was a financial disaster. But it earned enthusiastic critical support, winning five of the annual Hong Kong Film Awards. Wong returned to screenwriting until he found Taiwanese financing for the swordplay epic *Ashes of Time* (1994). *Chungking Express* (1994) and *Fallen Angels* (1995) showcased young stars in offhand plots and fleeting images that evoked both fashion photography and MTV. Unsuccessful with general audiences, Wong's films were felt to have captured the tastes of the "software generation."

All Hong Kong filmmakers have had to come to terms with Wong's prominence. Jeff Lau, Wong's partner in Jet Tone Films, seems to shadow him closely. Lau's triad romance *Love and the City* (1994) parallels *As Tears Go By*; *Days of Tomorrow* (1993) is somewhat comparable to *Days of Being Wild*; and the spoof *The Eagle-Shooting Heroes* (1993) uses the same cast and the same source novel as *Ashes of Time*. *Love and the City* is particularly interesting for its domestication of Wong-style voice-overs and the way ricocheting pager messages inform us of the characters' progress. Even Tsui Hark, a powerful innovator himself, may have felt Wong's influence; *The Blade* (1995), with its meditative voice-over commentary and nuanced shifts of filming speeds, can be read as a savage, deromanticized reply to *Ashes of Time*.

Wong's success has reshaped the look and sound of local cinema, with many of today's thrillers and romances adopting his interior monologues, grotesque angles, and scrambled time schemes. A generation of "Wong wannabes" has been inspired to push still further. In the short films *Out of the Blue* (1995) and *Out of the Blur* (1996) Jan Lamb offered vignettes in the *Chungking Express* vein. Lamb, who has been a graphic designer and disc jockey, veered Wong's style still closer to TV commercials. (*Out of the Blur* was produced by Commercial Radio and financed by Fuji Film and Polygram.) Lamb and two other directors contributed episodes to the portmanteau feature *Four Faces of Eve* (1996), a showcase of post-Wong pyrotechnics. The end credits are put at the beginning and then run in reverse order, with video-degraded imagery over a scratch-and-mix soundtrack. The four stories, each starring Sandra Ng, purport to display different aspects of Woman, but mostly they are exercises in bobbing camerawork, candy colors, and *Fallen Angels* pastiche.

Another director represented in *Four Faces of Eve* is Eric Kot, former disc-jockey partner to Jan Lamb and now a fixture of twentysomething comedies like *Feel 100%* (1996). Kot's debut feature, *First Love: The Litter on the Breeze* (1997), is by Western standards probably the most experimental mainstream film yet made in Hong Kong. In dark glasses and fright wig, Kot explains that in January 1996 Wong Kar-wai contacted him to make the film. One can only wonder what Wong (let alone the Japanese investors) thought when confronted with this farrago of sketchy imagery, machine-gun cuts, and willfully constipated storytelling. Kot outlines some possible stories of first love, launches two or three, discards them after a few scenes, and after nearly half an hour settles on a sketch about a mentally retarded garbage man who every night runs into a sleepwalking girl. This tale ends (though bits of it will recur later) and another starts up, the story of a grocer who flees from marriage to one woman, marries another, and then finds his first love haunting him at his grocery. At the end, Kot returns to tell us, "I don't know how to make this film. What should I do?" He apologizes to Wong Kar-wai.

Kot's reputation as a comedian helps motivate the jumpy digressions and saves the film from pure pretentiousness. The duplex plot is modeled on *Chungking Express*, a fact elaborately pointed out by Kot's commentary, and the style is a frantic collection of fish-eye distortions, antiphonal voice-overs, variable-speed movement, splashes of color, and parodic inserts. Whenever a scene seems to be building, it falls to bits, interrupted by foggy frames or a new bit of action elsewhere. *First Love* is indeed litter on the breeze, but it does dramatize the avant-pop potential of Hong Kong cinema: in few nations would such an offhand exercise employ big stars and wind up screened in multiplexes.

In all these films and many more, directors are telling stories with a fresh freedom. Meandering, casually converging plotlines have become a premise of ambitious local cinema. One of the earliest results of Arts Development Council investment was Chang Wai-hung's feature *After the Crescent* (1997). Centering on a girl who has learned she is pregnant, the film traces the intersecting paths of several young people across a night of the full moon. Yu Lik-wai's *Love Will Tear Us Apart* (1999), another ADC project, also presents crisscrossed character destinies. The films' antidramatic sobriety and static staging link them to the Taiwanese tradition of Hou Hsiao-Hsien, but structurally they loop and knot stories in the Wong Kar-wai manner.

Under the influence of Wong, Tarantino, and Kieślowski, some genre films have also devised more complex narrative structures. The least disruptive tactic is to weave together parallel tales, as in policiers like *The Log* (1996) and absurdist gangster pictures like *Once upon a Time in Triad Society 2* (1996). Interwoven plots have also become common in youth comedies: show a batch of roommates, each one facing a crisis in love or work. An early example is the yuppie romance *The New Age of Living Together* (aka *In Between*, 1994). Clarence Fok's *Passion 1995* (1995) starts out with one couple, explores their relationship for a bit, then lets them pass a man on the street; we follow him and slowly pick up his story. Eventually the two stories connect.

Rarer than the interwoven plot is the spliced one, which presents two or more complete stories, one after the other, linking them through a character or a motif or just spatial contiguity. The prototype of this is Wong Kar-wai's *Chungking Express*, but one refreshing horror film exploits the same device. *February 30* (1995), known in English as *The Day That Doesn't Exist*, starts with a story about a young woman whose fiancé becomes a zombie after an auto crash. After invading her life, he accepts death. In the second tale a negligent father is killed in another traffic accident. He returns to life in the body of a rich voluptuary who achieves sexual gratification through murder. The link between the tales is provided by a bumbling young policeman who courts the zombie's girlfriend and who meets the reincarnated truck driver in the hospital. Both protagonists are reborn as monsters preying on innocence, but the second tale becomes morally complex by punishing the truck driver for his selfish disregard of his family. The policeman adds a counterpoint of lascivious comedy to the first story's melodrama of lost love and to the second tale's seriosatiric edge. If the interwoven plot is becoming a staple of the comedy and the policier, the spliced plot has emerged as a convenient format for horror films (e.g., *01:00 a.m.*, 1995; the *Troublesome Night* series, 1997 onward).

The most intricate model of plotting depends on forking-path patterns, like those in Kieślowski's *Blind Chance* (1981) and Resnais's *Smoking/No Smoking* (1994). Here the plot presents one string of events, hops back to a nodal point, and traces out an alternative set of consequences. In Cha Chuen-yee's *Once upon a Time in Triad Society 1* (1996) the sadistic gangster Kwan is wounded by a mysterious assassin and is taken to the hospital. His voice-over monologue introduces a flashback tracing his career and presenting him as more victim than villain. Once he achieves a measure of sympathy, we return to the present as he lies on the operating table, and Kwan's voice admits he's been lying. There follows another long flashback that corrects the autobiography we have already seen. "I was born to be a triad." Instead of being bullied by older boys, he is the bully. Instead of being betrayed by a friend, he is the traitor. While the structure has a whiff of overcleverness, it is venturesome in steering the viewer from loathing to sympathy and finally to a more detached contempt for Kwan's irredeem-

gels: Wong intercuts shots of Killer and Agent passing through the same locales at different times, so that they seem simultaneously to accompany and to miss one another. Wong's voice-over technique is particularly useful in binding the film together. It is initiated in a fairly orthodox way in *As Tears Go By*, where Ngor recites a letter she has left for Wah. By *Days of Being Wild*, though, the monologues are purely confessional, issuing from some parallel realm, pouring out across sequences to create links and symmetries, recollections and prefigurations.

Disparate plotlines meet. In *Days of Being Wild*, it is one character, the intense but cold Yuddy, who brings everyone together; even though he dies at the end, Wong envisioned a second film in which Yuddy's spell would still grip the others. In *Fallen Angels* the link between the two plots is initially spatial: Agent lives in the guest house of Chungking Mansions managed by Ho Chi Mo's father, and some of Killer's murders are committed there. As events unfold, both stories turn out to center on aggression—the murders for hire engineered by Agent and Killer, Ho's nonstop harassing of passersby, and Charlie Young's vindictive hysteria at Blondie, who has stolen Charlie's boyfriend.

Wayward as they look, Wong's films are well organized, with each character or couple becoming the focus of a string of scenes. *Days of Being Wild* assigns one reel to Lizhen and another to Mimi, each section tracing the woman's obsessive reaction to losing Yuddy. The first two reels of *Fallen Angels* are spent on Killer and Agent, the third on Ho Chi Mo, the fourth again on Killer and Agent. Then the plotlines mix across several reels until they separate again: the eighth reel shows Killer's last job and his death; the last reel follows Ho after his father's death to his final encounter with Agent. In *Ashes of Time*, reel one establishes Ouyang Feng's inn and Huang Yaoshi's visits, reels two and three are devoted to the story of the Murong siblings Yin and Yang, reels four and five to the Blind Swordsman, reels six and seven to Hong Qi and the fulfillment of the Egg Girl's vengeance, and reels eight and nine to Huang Yaoshi, Ouyang Feng, and the woman they both love. (*Ashes'* brief, disconcerting flashbacks fret this arrangement somewhat, creating a distressed surface that puzzles first-time viewers.) Wong Kar-wai has taken up the reel-by-reel scheme that has ruled Hong Kong scenario writing and used it as both a way of organizing footage (handy if you don't script much in advance) and a means of shifting the spotlight across characters whose destinies are interwoven.

Within and across these large chunks, the films trace repetitive loops, both big and small. Characters return to the same places and replay actions and lines of dialogue. Huang Yaoshi visits Ouyang Feng every spring, and the Egg Girl begs passing swordsmen to take up her cause. In *Happy Together* Yiu-fai's job as doorman at the tango bar builds up a rhythm of routine varied by Po-wing's brazen paradings of new johns. Wong ingeniously

AVANT-POP CINEMA   275

explores cyclical patterns of plotting—usually to show his apparently free-floating characters locked in work habits and ill-starred loves and friendships. Our last view of Po-wing shows him slumping drunkenly against the doorway in which Yiu-fai crouched throughout earlier scenes. In *As Tears Go By,* Wah is forever obliged to go out to rescue Fly, constantly forced to pass between Hong Kong and Lantau Island, again and again laying siege to the restaurant over which his rival, Tony, presides. The triads take turns playing victim and bully in ever more dangerous games of bravado.

Wong often clusters these cyclical scenes in ways that highlight the repetitions. *Days of Being Wild* opens with abrupt, very similar sequences of Yuddy visiting the snack bar and gradually seducing Lizhen. Later the beat cop (Andy Lau) encounters Lizhen searching for Yuddy over several evenings, and the scenes, played out side by side, melt into virtually one long night. The same effect obtains in *Ashes of Time* when the rapidly alternating visits of Yin and Yang to Ouyang Feng's inn create a roundabout quarrel between brother and sister, with Ouyang Feng as the relay. A kind of limit is reached in *Chungking Express*'s second tale, when Officer 633 visits the Midnight Express snack bar in four successive scenes, each registering a fluctuation in his love life while setting the terms of his and Faye's out-of-synch courtship.

Although time is presented as evanescent, then, the Wong Kar-wai film is built out of moments which replay something that has gone before. An instant becomes a curiously static point condensing both past and future, as when Officer 223 bumps against the blonde woman in Chungking Mansions, and his voice-over declares: "Fifty-seven hours later I fell in love with this woman." Again, Wong turns a Hong Kong tradition to his advantage; instead of abandoning episodic construction in favor of a tighter Hollywood dramaturgy, he loosens his plots still more and then gives them formal and thematic density through cross-referenced motifs.

"Each film has to be 'different,'" notes cinematographer Doyle. "In narrative style, in structure. In its so-called 'look.'"[21] Wong is proudly polystylistic. *As Tears Go By* is filmed in hard blocks of red, ultramarine, and orange, all pierced by solid black shadows; silhouettes and unexpected angles are linked by restless cutting. *Days of Being Wild* has a more languid rhythm, with softer lighting and much longer takes. *Ashes of Time,* shuffling back and forth in time, charts the changes in the desert from brilliant ochre to thick, shadowy brown. *Chungking Express* is all high-key available-light shooting, while *Happy Together* presents grimy, bleached colors. *Fallen Angels* indulges in an almost unprecedented visual grotesquerie in performance and camerawork: not only are the characters always shrieking or brooding, but the outrageous wide-angle shooting turns them into gargoyles (Fig. 9.9).[22]

And each film is hardly of a piece, for Wong delights in trying out technical alternatives in different scenes. *Fallen Angels* mixes frenetic editing

9.9 *Fallen Angels:* Agent pines and smokes in a wide-angle shot.

9.10 *Chungking Express:* 633 drinks in slow motion while the crowds surge around him in fast motion and Faye stares at him as if in a freeze-frame.

with a few complexly orchestrated ensemble takes. *Days of Being Wild* was planned in four movements, each corresponding to a different set of stylistic options (Bressonian close-ups, B-film long takes, vigorous depth of field, and a return to the long take).[23] *Ashes of Time* is virtually a compilation of different ways to present a swordfight. Yin/Yang is filmed in the flying swordsman manner, the Blind Swordsman fights in the "Japanese style" of Zatoichi, and Hong Qi's breathless step-printed battles are, we might say, pure Wong Kar-wai.[24]

Despite a pluralism verging on eclecticism, Wong leaves authorial fingerprints. There is his urge to travesty star images. He dirties up pop idols, luring them into twitching and chainsmoking, and generally turns staggeringly attractive men and women into masks or freaks—a tactic in keeping with post-Punk conceptions of beauty. (One critic has suggested that *Ashes of Time* is Hong Kong's first grunge movie.)[25] Then there is Wong's slow motion. In *As Tears Go By* he devised the technique of shooting action at only eight, ten, or twelve frames per second and then "stretch-printing" the result to the normal twenty-four frames. The comparatively long exposure during filming makes movement blur, while the printing process, repeating each frame two or three times, produces a jerky pulsation.[26] Wong shifts visual accents by using different rates of stretch-printing, adding or deleting frames at different points.

He goes on to stage his shots so that actions in different zones unfold at different rates. The most famous, and most parodied, example is the shot in *Chungking Express* in which Officer 633 is slowly drinking coffee at the snack bar as crowds flash by (Fig. 9.10). In *Happy Together,* Yiu-fai smokes and ruminates with normal fluidity in the foreground, while behind him out-of-focus soccer players float in ghostly slow motion. In *Fallen Angels,* Ho Chi Mo's mooning over Charlie is given a dreamy tentativeness by a more marionettish treatment, enhanced by dripping distortion (Fig. 9.11). For a director interested in memory and ephemerality, variable-speed

9.11. Dissolving melancholy in *Fallen Angels*: The camera filmed through the bar window while water sprayed onto the window's edges; the actors moved very slowly, the extras in the background moved very fast, and the whole scene was shot at four frames per second. The shot lasts two minutes onscreen, but it took twelve to shoot.

9.12. *All the Wrong Clues (For the Right Solution)* (1981): A femme fatale asks for a chair, and she stands waiting in the foreground while men behind her scramble in fast motion to find one.

movement provides an ideal expressive vehicle. Still, the experiment is facilitated by a popular tradition that has routinely slowed or speeded up filming and printing in order to make combat scenes clearer and more forceful. By varying the speed of action, often from shot to shot, Sammo Hung, John Woo, and others (Fig. 9.12) provided a norm that Wong could revise for his own ends.

Like his colleagues, Wong has exploited the resources of music. There is probably some influence from music videos, seen most clearly in his tendency to give over nearly an entire sequence to a pop-song accompaniment for the action. In *As Tears Go By*, stretches of "Take My Breath Away" weave in and out during Wah's visit to Lantau Island and his meeting, missing, and remeeting Ngor, while in *Chungking Express* Faye cleans Officer 633's apartment to the tune of "Dreams" (sung by the actress, Faye Wong). At other times a solemn single shot will be accompanied by a hypnotic musical passage, as in the gentle coasting through the Philippines forest *(Days of Being Wild)* and the slow rotation above the Iguaçu falls *(Happy Together)*. This Scopitone aesthetic, which recalls *A Hard Day's Night* (1964) and *A Man and a Woman* (1966), becomes overt when a character activates a jukebox or even, as in *Fallen Angels*, curls herself over one. The jukebox may pump out the song that will accompany the next action; or it may not, as in the California Café scenes of *Chungking Express*: just before Officer 633 inserts his coin, a haunting jazz theme drifts through the stretch-printed shot.

The debt to music video again connects Wong to popular entertainment, but his style transforms the formula. Instead of selling the song, he makes the song part of the expressive atmosphere bathing his characters. He has

278   PLANET HONG KONG

said that he would like people hearing the song in everyday life to recall the moment in his film.[27] It is a bold bid: the tune triggers a reverie that includes your memory of the film's own scenes of reverie. Moreover, Wong's visual style has a precision and patterning untypical of MTV. Consider the "Take My Breath Away" music montage in *As Tears Go By*. Wah pursues Ngor, then he leaves her, and then she races to catch up with him. Wong introduces a series of devices one by one—rhythmic cutting, figure movement paced to the beat, bursts of color (an orange-and-yellow bus shearing across the image), conflicting lateral movements through the frame, and stretch-printing when Wah springs into the shot, grabs Ngor, and jogs her into the bus shelter for some desperate kissing. Wong caps it by slowly scalding color out of the image as the couple clutch each other. Unlike most music videos, this sequence holds each image long enough to permit expressive elements to accumulate and step up the lyrical intensity. It is flashy and ingratiating but also rigorous.[28]

Wong, like von Sternberg, shifts between a nearly hypnotic stare and a teasing glimpse. The landscape shots, the lengthy close-ups of the characters (*Days of Being Wild* lingers on Yuddy's pout), and the long tracking shots following a figure through a crowd or up a staircase invite the spectator to study a slowly unfolding spectacle. By contrast, the film will reward us with a perversely blocked view—a nearly subliminal shot of Yin leaving the inn *(Ashes of Time)*, hair straggling in front of a face, slits in curtains, semiopaque plastic curtains, and narrow alleys and stairways. The freeze-frame is demanded partly because without it we could not see the essential moment, but the freeze-frame can also tantalize us by coming a little too late (Fig. 9.13). Elliptical cutting can achieve the same end, as when the Blind Swordsman abruptly kisses the Egg Girl before setting out to die for her. However important the music and voice-over monologues are, Wong remains faithful to the Hong Kong tradition of seizing the viewer's attention with an energetic image—even if we just miss seeing it completely.

The music, the slurred gestures, the sideswiping visuals all lend Wong's characters an unashamed romanticism. Nature echoes their passions. Lowering clouds always threaten rain, the formulaic climate of movie sadness. At moments of crisis people lift their eyes to the skies, as if seeking deliverance. Peggy Chiao Hsiung-ping points out that all the characters nurse visions of utopia (the tropical forest in *Days of Being Wild*, the California of *Chungking Express*, the waterfall of *Happy Together*).[29] They also love to exhibit their passions, if only to themselves. A young man's girlfriend gives him a drinking glass; when he thinks she's dumped him, he throws it into the ocean. A young man, convinced his girlfriend won't call, leaves his pager clipped to a fence. Gay lovers nurse each other through sickness and quarrel over cigarettes. The airhead Baby can run whooping through McDonald's just to sit beside Killer; in the modern world, this be-

9.13. The drug smuggler in *Chungking Express* tosses off her blonde wig in pulsing freeze-frames; by the time the stop-action seizes her, she is virtually out of the frame, a blur of black hair and dark glasses.

9.14. *Ashes of Time:* Ouyang Feng's sister-in-law dies remembering him.

comes a passionate declaration of love. People expire with the image of their loved one before them (Fig. 9.14). Yuddy dies on a train remembering the girl he met at three o'clock on April sixteenth, but then he asks his friend to tell her he didn't remember her—the better to confirm his reputation as a cad. Romantic gesture verges on tear-jerking cliché. Killer cannot bear to hear the song ("Losing You") that he used as a message to tell Agent he didn't love her. In *Ashes of Time* Yin wants Huang Yaoshi to die longing for her; another woman dies longing for Ouyang Feng, who in turn mourns her death by setting his inn afire. These characters pine flamboyantly.

To treat these lovelorn films as abstract allegories of Hong Kong's historical situation risks losing sight of Wong Kar-wai's naked appeal to our feelings about young romance, its characteristic dilemmas, moods, and moves. He dramatizes the sidelong eye-play of flirtation (Is she looking at me? Do I look cool smoking or eating in this booth? Am I willing to wait for him?) and takes seriously all youth's conceits (Will I forget this moment with my lover? Is my towel crying?). Some might find the whole package too self-consciously cute, too full of twentysomething attitudinizing. These youths—Wong has yet to make a film organized around an older person's perspective—are often living out childish fantasies. The men in *Chungking Express* decorate their apartments with toy airplanes and stuffed animals; the swordsmen of *Ashes of Time* are slackers. The women wait or tidy up the men's disheveled lives. Youthful exuberance can turn into infantile rage, as when Yuddy thrashes his mother's lover, or in *Fallen Angels* when Charlie and Ho beat up an inflatable sex doll. Cute kids can turn nasty. When Killer struts into lethal action, firing his pistol to the beat of a soundtrack rapping out, "'Cause I'm cool . . .," we are invited to take him at the song's word.

These are the faults of a deeply sentimental cinema. Almost devoid of irony, Wong's films, like classic rock and roll, take seriously all the crushes, the posturing, and the stubborn capriciousness of young angst. They rejoice in manic expenditures of energy. They celebrate the momentary heartbreak of glimpsing a stranger who might be interesting to love. The best comparison is surely not with Godard, whose romantic streak has a bitter edge. In Wong Kar-wai, Hong Kong may have its Truffaut, the director who in *Tirez sur le pianiste* and *Jules et Jim* concentrated on not-quite-grown-up characters brooding on eternally missed chances. In any case, Wong stands out from his peers by abandoning the kinetics of comedies and action movies in favor of more liquid atmospherics. He dissolves crisp emotions into vaporous moods. For all his sophistication, his unembarrassed effort to capture powerful, pleasantly adolescent feelings confirms his commitment to the popular Hong Kong tradition.

ROMANCE ON YOUR MENU:
CHUNGKING EXPRESS

Wong Kar-wai's *Chungking Express* (1994) might seem a paradigm of light cinema, beguiling but insubstantial. Compared to Edward Yang's somber *The Terrorizers* (1986), another disjointed tale of intersecting urban lives, it looks like pure fluff. Yet in *Chungking Express* entertainment fosters genuine experimental impulses. Analyzing the craft that shaped this insouciant exercise reveals how a play with popular forms can be at once diverting and innovative.

The film offers Hong Kong's best-known spliced plot. First comes the tale of Officer 223. On the eve of his twenty-fifth birthday, realizing that his girlfriend has left him for good, he strikes up a one-night acquaintance with a mysterious blonde woman, who is actually a drug smuggler and a murderer. There follows the story of Officer 633, who is dumped by his airline-hostess girlfriend. While he pines for her, he becomes the object of affection for fast-food countergirl Faye. She sneaks into his apartment and spruces it up with new towels, goldfish, clothes, and canned goods. When he finally asks her out for a date, she stands him up and leaves to become an air hostess herself.

The first story takes place chiefly in Tsimshatsui, in and around the decaying warren of Indian restaurants and guest houses known as Chungking Mansions. The second takes place in the Lan Kwai Fong neighborhood of Hong Kong island. The two plotlines converge at the Midnight Express fast-food counter in Central, which both policemen patronize. The hinge between the plots is a casual moment: 223 bumps into Faye, the frame freezes, and as "California Dreaming" rises on the soundtrack, 223's voice-over tells us, "Six hours later she fell in love with another man," and we see 633 strolling to the counter. Symmetrically, the film closes with an epilogue at the Midnight Express, when, after a year, Faye drops by to find that Officer 633 has bought the place.[1]

This split structure arose from the need to whip up a movie in short order. In early 1994 Wong Kar-wai's painfully slow production of *Ashes of Time* was interrupted for two months. Pressed to fulfill his contract for a second feature, Wong stitched together script ideas he had been considering for years. (A third story was to have been included, but as the shooting developed there was no room for it; it became the Killer plotline of *Fallen Angels*.) *Chungking Express* was filmed in sequence ("like a road movie," Wong says), with Wong writing each scene the night before or even the morning of the day it was to be shot.[2] Specific motifs, such as the canned goods, arose from the contingencies of shooting, which favored working in brightly lit convenience stores.[3]

Originally Wong wanted the stories to intersect fairly often; he envisioned an ending in which the four main characters would meet at the lounge in Taipei airport.[4] As the film stands, he says, "The two stories are quite independent. What puts them together is that they are both love stories. I think a lot of city people have a lot of emotions but sometimes they can't find the people to express them to."[5] Although most critics treat the film as an allegory of time and space in modern (or postmodern) Hong Kong,[6] taking it as an exercise in comparative romance accounts better for its formal finesse—its doubled motifs, its web of parallels, and its echoic time structures.

The film has a rough reel-by-reel plot outline,[7] and within each reel, Wong has coiled his modular cycles of routine: not only both officers' visits to Midnight Express but also the blonde woman's visits to the drug dealer's bar, 223's repeated efforts to phone May and other ex-girlfriends, and the constant alternation of scenes in which Faye sees 633 eating at a street stall and scenes in which she invades his apartment. Although *Chungking Express* feels loosely structured because it depends on coincidental encounters, the plot is built out of a daunting number of minutely varied repetitions of locales and routines. As these cycles compare characters and situations, cause and effect become less important than parallels among congruent or contrasting aspects of love.

The mere lineup of characters creates matching couples. In the first part, 223 and the blonde woman share a chaste night, far more innocent than the voracious clinches of the drug-lord bar owner and his Filipina paramour (who dons a blonde wig). In the second part, the loveplay between 633 and his stewardess girlfriend—her mimicking safety instructions before takeoff, his gliding a toy plane along her sweat-speckled back—offers yet a third version of romance, a cuddly sexiness midway between the two love affairs of the first story. As the blonde replaces May for the lonely 223, so Faye replaces 633's lover—first by becoming his clandestine cleaning lady, then by becoming a stewardess herself. Like the primary pair of the first story, Faye and 633 sleep together innocently, but both 633 and Faye have some of the childlike qualities of 223; neither is as world-weary as the blonde.

Among these four couples, cross-references abound. 223 bumps into the blonde as he will later brush against Faye, triggering the second plotline. The blonde announces that she can't sleep, but after several drinks with

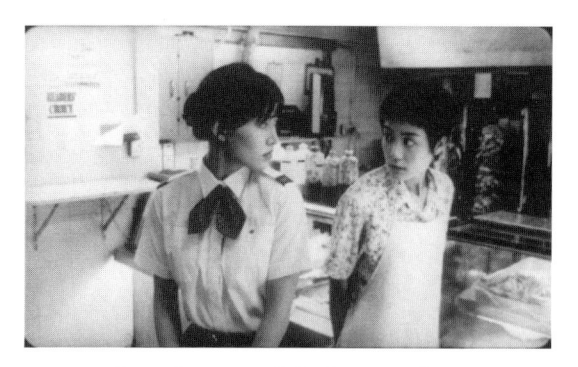

RYM.1 The air hostess and the future air hostess.

223 she passes out. 633 drinks lots of coffee and can't sleep, so Faye dissolves some sleeping pills in his bottled water to make sure he rests. Both stories invoke air travel: the blonde fails to load her drug-laden stooges onto the plane, 633 conducts an extended romance with a stewardess, and Faye becomes an air hostess at the end (Fig. RYM.1). Three of the four women are associated with music. The bargirl dances to sensuous reggae from the jukebox, Faye prefers the more innocent "California Dreaming," and the stewardess poses playfully to "What a Difference a Day Makes." Even shoes matter: Officer 223 scrubs the blonde's pumps, an image that prefigures our views of the stewardess' pumps when she rides past 223's apartment on the escalator and of Faye's pumps when, now a stewardess herself, she pauses before the Midnight Express in the film's last scene.

Most of these motifs hint at different attitudes toward love. Nearly all the characters are hopelessly romantic. In quest of a date, 223 dials up every girl he has ever met, while 633 locks himself up at home and imagines his apartment crying, his towel sobbing, and his soap wasting away, all in sympathy for him. When Faye is introduced at Midnight Express—significantly, cleaning up—she is presented as even more self-absorbed and otherworldly than the boyish cops. She listens endlessly to "California Dreaming," scrubs and sweeps to the wistful wail of a Cantopop version of the Cranberries' "Dreams," even apparently dreams that she is crashing 633's apartment.

If love is a soliloquy and a dream, it is also devotion: as Faye will spruce up 633's apartment, 223 dutifully wipes off the blonde's shoes while she sleeps. Love is loss but also hope. Both men will be abandoned once more, but each is rewarded with a teasing sign of affection. The blonde leaves a birthday message on 223's pager, while Faye dodges a date with 633 but a year later gives him hope by filling out a new boarding pass on a fresh napkin.

Above all, love is food. "It's heaven when you / find romance on your menu," sings Dinah Washington as 633 and the air hostess nuzzle in his apartment. 223 waits a month for May to take him back, marking it not on a calendar but by the expiration dates on cans of pineapple—her favorite

RYM.2 When 223 bumps into Faye, a freeze-frame initiates the second main plot.

food, on which he will gorge the final night. While the blonde sleeps beside him, 223 eats four chef's salads. Officer 633 is introduced ordering chef's salads to take home to his stewardess girlfriend. The night he changes his order marks the moment their affair wanes, because, he claims, she now realizes that she has a choice. The avuncular owner of the Midnight Express urges the forlorn 223 to date his countergirl (another woman named May) and then her replacement, Faye; later he will urge 633 to forget Faye and take up May. The owner grants that each love, like each dish, is different, but one should broaden one's tastes. Try fish and chips, he urges, or pizza, or a hot dog.

The blonde woman states the point most baldly in her voice-over commentary on 223's mooning over May: "Knowing someone doesn't mean keeping them. People change. A person may like pineapple today and something else tomorrow." But each lovelorn cop treats his woman as irreplaceable. May is wrong, 223 suggests, to think of him as "no different from a can of pineapple." Officers 223 and 633, gulping down their canned fruit or sardines or chef's salads, are idealists. Each man is looking, in Wong's words, for the person to whom he can express his emotions, the one right dish on which he may dine indefinitely.

Love takes time too. As in all Wong Kar-wai films, the theme of time is prominent, but the romance angle enables *Chungking Express* to explore different ways in which time may be lived. A film centrally about flirtation is ideally suited for Wong's aesthetic of the glimpse. The principle is announced at the beginning, when the blonde woman flees a stalking camera and dodges behind a curtain just before the opening title interrupts our view. Faces are blocked by dark glasses or room clutter; compositions are fractured, or the camera pans away before we have fully registered an expression; cuts are jerky. Each main character in the second story is given one very brief shot in the first part. Intensifying this sense of ephemerality is the freeze-frame, capturing the elusive moments of affinity or revelation (Fig. RYM.2). More specific to this film is the use of slit-staging; at Midnight Express and various bars people are squeezed together to narrow and

RYM.3 Slit-staging at Bottoms Up as the drug dealer caresses his doxy.

RYM.4 Slit-staging at Midnight Express: Faye at work.

RYM.5 Faye lounging and pining at Midnight Express.

RYM.6 Faye mooning at California Café. (Compare Figs. 9.8, 9.9, and 9.14.)

impede our vision (Figs. RYM.3, RYM.4). Yet the film also bores in on lived duration, lingering pensively as the characters do (Figs. RYM.5, RYM.6), allowing us to stare at the objects that sustain the characters' reveries. A can of pineapple or a bottle of beer can evoke love's disappointments.

The split structure helps Wong show how time shapes the vicissitudes of romance. Part one, with all its expiration dates and ominous digital clocks, is ruled by a single deadline. By May 1, 223's twenty-fifth birthday, he vows to reconcile himself to losing his girlfriend May. The same day is the blonde's deadline for consummating the drug operation (assigned to her by the bartender in the form of tins of sardines); after the deal collapses, May 1 becomes her deadline for escaping Hong Kong. So the first story condenses its action into a few days, from April 28 to the morning of May 1. Part two stretches over several weeks before providing an epilogue a year after 633's and Faye's aborted date. Without clocks or expiration stamps, the second story makes flight its master metaphor: the toy jet in 633's apartment, the plane that soars overhead, the imagined escape to California, the jokey ways in which the argot of airline travel becomes the language of love, and finally the two boarding passes Faye prepares for 633—ambivalent Dear John letters. The only deadline presented in the second story is the rain-soaked boarding pass, promising travel somewhere a year later.

Surely the two parts' different senses of time have a topical significance for Hong Kong: the looming deadline of 1997, the more undefined options of staying or emigrating or floating in between, like an airline attendant or an astronaut businessman. But again, these two conceptions of time are subjected to a plot which insists that the search for romance must adjust to changes on the menu.

"What a difference a day makes," sings Dinah, "twenty-four little hours." Although the song is played in the second tale, it could serve as a title for the first part. Officer 223 wants love fast and sudden, like a snack in an OK store or Midnight Express. Once May is gone, any woman he brushes against could be the One. 223 tries so hard to make the future happen that he invests each day with fateful significance. Will May finally accept him? Will he find romance with the blonde woman? The clock is ticking. By the end, when he gets the blonde's birthday message, he has a typical Wong Kar-wai epiphany. Happily letting himself be drenched by a spring shower ("I think it will rain," the woman had said), he clutches his heart and looks up. His voice intones that he'll remember her all his life: "If memories could be canned, would they also have expiration dates? If so, I hope they last for centuries." The future has become an open-ended vista, thanks to a moment's kindness and the pleasures of reverie and recollection.

Officer 633's love life has none of the fraught urgency of 223's. 633 lives an apparently solid affair with his stewardess. Romance is always on his menu, a predictable round of sex charades and chef's salads. Then his woman leaves him. 633 will have to learn the lesson proclaimed in Dennis Brown's reggae song, "Things in Life," played in the first part: "It's not every day we're gonna be the same way / There must be a change somehow." Or, if 633 really listened to Faye's pick hit, the Mamas and the Papas' tale of abandoning brown leaves and gray skies for California, he would learn that a change is also a chance.

Both men linger over lost love. Officer 223 tries for a return to the status quo (recovering May), then an instant change (a date for the night, a new romance with the mysterious blonde). Officer 633, cut loose from his girlfriend, just drifts—hence the loose, episodic cycles of the film's second story. As his life spins slowly around his routines—pounding his beat, sipping strong coffee at the same food stall—Faye introduces tiny changes: new toothbrush mug, new bedspread, new sandals, new goldfish, and a snapshot of herself stuck to his mirror. All at once he notices them, and when he finally catches her remaking his apartment—that is, the texture of his life—her devotion to the enterprise seems to make him realize that he might change. Packing up the stewardess's clothes, putting on the shirt Faye has left for him, he goes out to meet her and start fresh.

RYM.7 California Café: As 633 inserts his coin, crowds hurry past him. (Compare Fig. 9.10.)

RYM.8 At the track, 223 reacts to his pager message.

RYM.9 At the fast-food shop, 633 reads Faye's note.

By now, though, their rhythms no longer mesh. Faye can be seen as a condensed version of the film's other women. She works to canned music as the bargirl does, she wears dark glasses and puts her hand to her chin like the blonde, and she becomes the new flight attendant in 633's life. Like the last two women, she is also committed to varying the menu and moving on. Her signature tunes are "California Dreaming" and "Dreams," in which the singer announces that her life is changing in "every possible way." Like the air hostess, Faye leaves 633—for the real California, as her song always promised she would. He sits in the California Café talking to his beer bottle and wondering if Faye, in her California, will remember their date. A year later, Faye belatedly keeps the appointment, waiting for him: "I wonder if he ever read my letter." Their out-of-synch affinities are marked by Wong's typical slurred, biplanar rates of motion (Fig. RYM.7).

Still, 633 has budged. He would not read the first hostess's letter to him, but after discarding Faye's message he rescues it from the rain. Drying it in a fast-food oven, he finds that she has picked up his flight metaphors, promising him another chance by leaving a boarding pass. His epiphany, like 223's, comes in the rain and is highlighted by parallel compositions (Figs. RYM.8, RYM.9).

The epilogue of the second story wistfully balances the end of the first. As 223 loosened up, cherishing his memories and accepting an indeterminate future, 633 embraces change. Earlier Faye invited him to come to California with her, but he preferred "to stay in one place." When Faye returns a year later, she finds him running the Midnight Express (the previous owner "needed a change"), and he's renovating it.[8] 633 is even listening to "California Dreaming," at the volume she had preferred. He explains, "It takes time to get used to things." He's ready for her: as she fills out the boarding pass he volunteers to go "wherever you want to take me."

So Wong Kar-wai's characteristic preoccupation with time finds concrete embodiment in different attitudes to romance. Brutal sexuality, incarnated in the drug smuggler and his lusty bargirl, is sterile and ends in death. By contrast, four women show two rather innocent and obtuse men the need to accept the changes brought on by love. You can relax impetuous demands (Officer 223) and break out of mundane routines (Officer 633). Like the popular cinema out of which it comes, *Chungking Express* focuses on boys meeting, losing, and getting, or not quite getting, girls. But Wong revivifies the formula. Instead of tightening up the plot, he slackens it beyond even Hong Kong's episodic norm, letting a fine network of parallels and recurring motifs come forward. Deeply indebted to popular tradition, committed to a conception of light cinema, his confection nourishes all filmmakers who dream of movies that are at once experimental and irresistibly enjoyable.

FURTHER READING

The most important English-language sources on Hong Kong film are those published jointly each year by the Hong Kong International Film Festival (hereafter HKIFF) and the Hong Kong Urban Council, listed chronologically below.

Lin Nien-tung and Paul Yeung, eds. *Cantonese Cinema Retrospective (1950–1959).* 1978.
Lin Nien-tung, ed. *Hong Kong Cinema Survey (1946–1968).* 1979.
Lau Shing-hon, ed. *A Study of the Hong Kong Martial Arts Film.* 1980.
——— *A Study of the Hong Kong Swordplay Film (1945–1980).* 1981; rev. ed. 1996.
Shu Kei, ed. *Cantonese Cinema Retrospective (1960–1969).* 1982; rev. ed. 1996.
——— *A Comparative Study of Post-War Mandarin and Cantonese Cinema: The Films of Zhu Shilin, Qin Jian, and Other Directors.* 1983.
Li Cheuk-to, ed. *A Study of Hong Kong Cinema in the Seventies (1970–1979).* 1984.
——— *The Traditions of Hong Kong Comedy.* 1985.
——— *Cantonese Melodrama (1950–1969).* 1986; rev. ed. 1997.
——— *Cantonese Opera Film Retrospective.* 1987; rev. ed. 1996.
——— *Changes in Hong Kong Society through Cinema.* 1988; rev. ed. 1998.
——— *Phantoms of the Hong Kong Cinema.* 1989.
——— *The China Factor in the Hong Kong Cinema.* 1990; rev. ed. 1997.
Law Kar, ed. *Hong Kong Cinema in the Eighties.* 1991.
——— *Overseas Chinese Figures in Cinema.* 1992.
——— *Mandarin Films and Popular Songs: 40's–60's.* 1993.
——— *Cinema of Two Cities: Hong Kong—Shanghai.* 1994.
——— *Early Images of Hong Kong and China.* 1995.
——— *The Restless Breed: Cantonese Stars of the Sixties.* 1996.
——— *Fifty Years of Electric Shadows.* 1997.
——— *Transcending the Times: King Hu and Eileen Chan.* 1998.
——— *The Hong Kong New Wave: Twenty Years After.* 1999.

Four more publications from this prodigious Festival deserve mention: the retrospective volume edited by Emily Lo, *20th Anniversary of the Hong Kong Interna-*

tional Film Festival, 1977–1996 (Hong Kong: Urban Council, 1996); the exhibition catalogue published by the Hong Kong Film Archive, *50 Years of the Hong Kong Film Production and Distribution Industries: An Exhibition* (Hong Kong: Urban Council, 1997); the parallel publication of conference proceedings edited by Law Kar, *Fifty Years of Electric Shadows: Report of Conference on Hong Kong Cinema 10–12 Apr 1997* (Hong Kong: Urban Council, 1997); and another exhibition catalogue, *The Making of Martial Arts Movies—As Told by Filmmakers and Stars* (Hong Kong: Provisional Urban Council, 1999).

Another indispensable reference work is *1969–1989 Shou Lun Ying Pian Piao Fang Ji Lu* (Box-office records of first-run films, 1969–1989) (Hong Kong: Film Biweekly, 1990). This list has been updated and corrected in an online resource, Ryan Law's Hong Kong Movie DataBase (http://www.hkmdb.com/office/index-en.shtml). Several of the Festival publications above provide listings of releases before 1969. For the years since 1989 the Hong Kong, Kowloon, and New Territories Motion Picture Industry Association Ltd. has published annual lists of releases, with plot synopses, credits, and reported earnings. These volumes are *Hong Kong Films 1989–1990, Hong Kong Films 1991, Hong Kong Films 1992, Hong Kong Films 1993, Hong Kong Films 1994–1995,* and *Hong Kong Films 1996.* A team of researchers is at work documenting the territory's entire cinematic output. The first fruits of the project are *Hong Kong Filmography: Vol. I (1913–1941)* (Hong Kong: Hong Kong Film Archive/Urban Council, 1997) and *Hong Kong Filmography: Vol II: 1942–1949* (Hong Kong: Hong Kong Film Archive/Provisional Urban Council, 1998).

Fan guides provide a lot of information, and most are fun to read (although it is always best to verify dates, titles, and names of personnel in the sources listed above.) In English the following are helpful: Rick Baker and Toby Russell, *The Essential Guide to Hong Kong Movies* (London: Eastern Heroes, 1994); Fredric Dannen and Barry Long, *Hong Kong Babylon: An Insider's Guide to the Hollywood of the East* (New York: Hyperion/ Miramax, 1997); Stefan Hammond and Mike Wilkins, *Sex and Zen & A Bullet in the Head* (New York: Fireside, 1996); Bill Palmer, Karen Palmer, and Ric Meyers, *The Encyclopedia of Martial Arts Movies* (Metuchen, N.J.: Scarecrow Press, 1995); and Thomas Weisser, *Asian Cult Cinema* (New York: Boulevard Books, 1997). Simone Bedetti and Massimo Mazzoni's *La Hollywood d'Oriente: Il cinema di Hong Kong dalle origini a John Woo* (Bologna: PuntoZero, 1996) includes a floppy disk housing a useful filmography. The most extensive study in Italian is Alberto Pezzotta's *Tutto il cinema di Hong Kong: Stili, caratteri, autori* (Milan: Baldini and Castoldi, 1999).

On the Web, there are many Hong Kong–related sites. The best database is Ryan Law's http://www.hkmdb.com, which allows the inquirer to search through more than 8,000 movie titles and 2,500 capsule reviews. One can search by director, writer, star, genre, distribution circuit, production company, language, and year. The same site offers weekly coverage of the industry. For links to other sites, try also Joseph Fierro's Hong Kong Cinema, at http://egret0.stanford.edu/hk/index.html.

Stephen Teo's *Hong Kong Cinema: The Extra Dimensions* (London: British Film Institute, 1997) is a magisterial synoptic history, surveying directors, genres, and social context. Complementing Teo is Paul Fonoroff's handsome *Silver Light: A Pictorial History of Hong Kong Cinema, 1920–1970* (Hong Kong: Joint Publishing, 1997). Miles Wood's collection of interviews, *Cine East: Hong Kong Cinema through the Looking Glass* (Guildford, Surrey: FAB Press, 1998) provides insights into filmmaking in the 1990s. Other important studies are Bey Logan's lively and authoritative *Hong Kong Action Cinema* (London: Titan, 1995) and Ralph Umard's *Film Ohne Gretzen: Das Neue Hongkong Kino* (Lappersdorf: Kerschensteiner, 1996), a mighty collection of interviews, essays, and filmographies. See also three books that appeared while this book was in press: Lisa Odham Stokes and Michael Hoover, *City on Fire: Hong Kong Cinema* (London: Verso, 1999); Bérénice Reynaud, *Nouvelles Chines, nouveaux cinémas* (Paris: Cahiers du cinéma, 1999); and Stefan Hammond, *Hollywood East* (New York: Contemporary, 2000).

NOTES

1 ····· ALL TOO EXTRAVAGANT, TOO GRATUITOUSLY WILD

1. Roger Greenspan, "*Five Fingers of Death*," *New York Times*, 22 March 1973, p. 54.
2. Virgil Thomson, *The State of Music* (New York: Vintage, 1962), p. 90.
3. In Europe subsidized films characteristically return less than half the money sunk into them. See "Hollywood's Fading Charms," *The Economist*, 22 March 1997, p. 72.
4. Leonard Klady, "Overcrowded Fest Circuit Fills Niche Pix Functions," *Variety*, 1–7 September 1997, pp. 7, 14.
5. I try to outline some of these in *Narration in the Fiction Film* (Madison: University of Wisconsin Press, 1985), pp. 205–233. See also Kristin Thompson and David Bordwell, *Film History: An Introduction* (New York: McGraw-Hill, 1994), pp. 406–458, 492–516.
6. Rolanda Chu, "On the Lam: An Interview with Ringo," *Hong Kong Film Magazine* no. 4 (1995): 19.
7. See, for example, David Bordwell, "Modernism, Minimalism, Melancholy: Angelopoulos and Visual Style," in *The Last Modernist: The Films of Theo Angelopoulos*, ed. Andrew Horton (New York: Praeger, 1997), pp. 11–26.
8. Quoted in Stephen Teo, "The *Dao* of King Hu," in *A Study of Hong Kong Cinema in the Seventies*, ed. Li Cheuk-to (Hong Kong: HKIFF/Urban Council, 1984), p. 34.
9. The philosopher Noël Carroll calls these "garden-variety" emotions in his enlightening *A Philosophy of Mass Art* (Oxford: Clarendon Press, 1998), pp. 276–282.
10. Bruce Thomas, *Bruce Lee: Fighting Spirit* (London: Sidgwick and Jackson, 1994), p. 74.
11. Quoted in "*An Autumn's Tale*," *New Hong Kong Films 1987/88* (Hong Kong: Urban Council, 1988), p. 21.
12. Richard Dyer and Ginette Vincendeau call this a "patchwork" aesthetic in their introduction to *Popular European Cinema* (London: Routledge, 1992), p. 12.
13. Edward Gross, "Tales from the Script," *Cinescape* 4, no. 3 (July/August 1998): 27.

14. The *New York Times* noted of Keaton's *Our Hospitality:* "Here we find a well-defined plot, not just a series of gag incidents . . . About as logical a comedy as we have seen" (quoted in *Film Daily,* 2 December 1923, p. 15). For an analysis of the film's tight construction, see David Bordwell and Kristin Thompson, *Film Art: An Introduction,* 5th ed. (New York: McGraw-Hill, 1997), pp. 199–205. On the intricacies of *Groundhog Day,* see Kristin Thompson, *Storytelling in the New Hollywood: Analyzing Classical Narrative Structure* (Cambridge, Mass.: Harvard University Press, 1999).

15. Sharon Kinsella analyzes this phenomenon in "Cuties in Japan," in *Women, Media, and Consumption in Japan,* ed. Lise Skov and Brian Moeran (Honolulu: University of Hawaii Press, 1995), pp. 220–254.

16. For insights into the issue of accessibility, see Carroll, *A Philosophy of Mass Art,* pp. 107–109.

17. Andrew Sarris, "Notes on the Auteur Theory in 1962," in *The Primal Scream: Essays on Film and Related Subjects* (New York: Simon and Schuster, 1973), p. 50.

18. So we should work as much as possible with film copies, not video versions. Video often degrades a film's visual quality. Video color does not match the original film's. Widescreen films are often cropped on video, so that part of the original image is eliminated. In Hong Kong, video copies are often cut down from the original release print. Video does not reproduce film frames one-for-one, so counting frames—an important part of analyzing cutting—is rendered merely approximate in video copies. And so on.

19. See Les Paul Robley, "Hot Set," *American Cinematographer* 77, no. 1 (January 1996): 50.

20. This idea is discussed in David Bordwell, Janet Staiger, and Kristin Thompson, *The Classical Hollywood Cinema: Film Style and Mode of Production to 1960* (New York: Columbia University Press, 1985), p. 83.

HONG KONG AND/AS/OR HOLLYWOOD

1. Law Kar, personal communication.
2. Quoted in Beth Accomando, "Terence Chang," *Giant Robot* no. 4 (1996): 67.
3. Quoted in Orson Welles and Peter Bogdanovich, *This Is Orson Welles,* ed. Jonathan Rosenbaum (New York: HarperCollins, 1992), p. 22.

2 ///// LOCAL HEROES

1. The term "triads" is a generic label for secret societies. The Triads, apparently named in the seventeenth century, constitute only one group.
2. Quoted in "Dialogue 1: Kirk Wong—Roger Garcia," in *Hong Kong Cinema '83,* ed. Jerry Liu (Hong Kong: Urban Council, 1984), p. 6.
3. "The Bottom Line," *Asiaweek,* 5 April 1996, p. 59; Ezra F. Vogel, *The Four Little Dragons: The Spread of Industrialization in East Asia* (Cambridge, Mass.: Harvard University Press, 1991), p. 68; Kevin Rafferty, *City on the Rocks: Hong Kong's Uncertain Future* (New York: Viking, 1989), p. 163; Michael Harris Bond, *Beyond the Chinese Face: Insights from Psychology* (Hong Kong: Oxford

University Press, 1991), p. 91. For general surveys of Hong Kong's history, problems, and accomplishments, other good sources are Felix Patrikeeff, *Mouldering Pearl: Hong Kong at the Crossroads* (London: George Philip, 1989); Marina Dyja and Dorian Malovic, *Hong Kong: Un destin chinois* (Paris: Bayard, 1997); and Stephen Vines, *Hong Kong: China's New Colony* (London: Aurum, 1998).

4. Philip Bowring, "Don't Forget That Some Things Should Change in Hong Kong," *International Herald Tribune,* 26 February 1997, p. 8; Christine Loh, "Closing the Gap of the Haves and Have-Nots," *South China Morning Post,* 7 April 1997, p. 20.

5. On Hong Kong's political structure, see Norman Miners, *The Government and Politics of Hong Kong,* 5th ed. (Hong Kong: Oxford University Press, 1995); Kathleen Cheek-Milby, *A Legislature Comes of Age: Hong Kong's Search for Influence and Identity* (Hong Kong: Oxford University Press, 1995); and Joseph Y. S. Cheng and Sonny S. H. Lo, eds., *From Colony to SAR: Hong Kong's Challenges Ahead* (Hong Kong: Chinese University Press, 1995).

6. Dick Wilson, *Hong Kong! Hong Kong!* (London: Unwin Hyman, 1990), p. 197.

7. Hong Kong's early years are traced in detail in G. B. Endicott, *A History of Hong Kong,* 2d ed. (Hong Kong: Oxford University Press, 1964). A lively synoptic view is Alan Birch, *Hong Kong: The Colony That Never Was* (Hong Kong: Odyssey, 1991).

8. Wilson, *Hong Kong!* pp. 11–20.

9. Quoted in Jim Rohwer, *Asia Rising: How History's Biggest Middle Class Will Change the World* (London: Brealey, 1996), p. 88.

10. Suzanne Berger and Richard K. Lester, *Made by Hong Kong* (New York: Oxford University Press, 1997), pp. 16–22; Rafferty, *City on the Rocks,* pp. 142–145.

11. Berger and Lester, *Made by Hong Kong,* pp. 21–24, 49–50; Rafferty, *City on the Rocks,* pp. 189, 207–241. For a survey of Hong Kong's business traditions, see Michael J. Enright, Edith E. Scott, and David Dodwell, *The Hong Kong Advantage* (New York: Oxford University Press, 1997).

12. For a detailed account of the process of negotiation and withdrawal, see Robert Cottrell, *The End of Hong Kong: The Secret Diplomacy of Imperial Retreat* (London: John Murray, 1993).

13. For a comprehensive account of the Tiananmen Square events, see Part I of Orville Schell's *Mandate of Heaven: A New Generation of Entrepreneurs, Dissidents, Bohemians, and Technocrats Lays Claim to China's Future* (New York: Simon and Schuster, 1994).

14. Of the many speculations on Hong Kong's prospects under Chinese rule, particularly useful are Michael Yahuda, *Hong Kong: China's Challenge* (New York: Routledge, 1996); and Bruce Bueno de Mesquita, David Newman, and Alvin Rabushka, *Red Flag over Hong Kong* (Chatham, N.J.: Chatham House, 1996).

15. Several scholars have begun to unearth signs of this process in the 1960s. See Poshek Fu, "The Turbulent Sixties: Modernity, Youth Culture, and Cantonese Film in Hong Kong," in *Fifty Years of Electric Shadows,* ed. Law Kar (Hong Kong: HKIFF/Urban Council, 1997), pp. 40–46; Linda Chiu-han Lai, "Nostalgia and Nonsense: Two Instances of Commemorative Practices in Hong Kong Cin-

57. Li Cheuk-to, "*Young and Dangerous* and the 1997 Deadline," in *Hong Kong Panorama 96–97*, ed. Jacob Wong (Hong Kong: HKIFF/Urban Council, 1997), p. 11.
58. Quoted in Havis, "A Better Today," p. 16.
59. Interview with Athena Tsui, 22 March 1997.

TWO DRAGONS

1. The best studies of Bruce Lee I know are Cheng Yu, "Anatomy of a Legend," in *A Study of Hong Kong Cinema in the Seventies (1970–1979)*, ed. Li Cheuk-to (Hong Kong: HKIFF/Urban Council, 1984), pp. 23–25; Tony Rayns, "Bruce Lee and Other Stories," in ibid., pp. 26–29; and Stephen Teo, *Hong Kong Cinema: The Extra Dimensions* (London: British Film Institute, 1997), pp. 110–121. Lee has of course been the object of a huge amount of popular writing and specialized study among martial arts experts. I have culled biographical information mostly from three volumes: Alex Ben Block, *The Legend of Bruce Lee* (New York: Dell, 1974); Linda Lee, *The Bruce Lee Story* (Santa Clarita, Calif.: Ohara, 1989); and the most probing of the lot, Bruce Thomas, *Bruce Lee: Fighting Spirit* (London: Sidgwick and Jackson, 1994). There are valuable memoirs in *The Legendary Bruce Lee*, edited from *Black Belt Magazine* (Santa Clarita, Calif.: Ohara, 1986), and interesting behind-the-scenes film material in two books by Robert Clouse, *The Making of "Enter the Dragon"* (Burbank: Unique, 1987) and *Bruce Lee: The Biography* (Burbank: Unique, 1988). Lee's own writings include *Chinese Gung Fu: The Philosophical Art of Self-Defense* (1963; reprint, Santa Clarita, Calif.: Ohara, 1996) and *Tao of Jeet Kune Do* (Santa Clarita, Calif.: Ohara, 1975). See also Nick Davidson's in-depth study of Lee's fighting style, "The Real Game Begins . . .," in the fanzine *Fists of Fury* no. 1 (1997): 7–23.
2. According to legend, the confusion in titles came when the labels on the cans got switched en route to the United States.
3. I have been unable to trace these films, but Mel Tobias refers to them in *Flashback: Hong Kong Cinema after Bruce Lee* (Hong Kong: Gulliver, 1979), p. 90.
4. Thomas, *Bruce Lee*, pp. 341–342.
5. Quoted in Block, *Legend of Bruce Lee*, p. 42.
6. Quoted in Thomas, *Bruce Lee*, p. 117.
7. Quoted in Block, "The Hong Kong Style: Part 1," *Esquire* 80, no. 2 (August 1973): 76.
8. Quoted in Maxwell Pollard, "In Kato's Kung Fu, Action Was Instant," in *Legendary Bruce Lee*, pp. 43–44.
9. Quoted in Linda Lee, *The Bruce Lee Story*, pp. 96–97.
10. Most of the biographical material on Jackie Chan in what follows is drawn from Jackie Chan and Jeff Yang, *I Am Jackie Chan: My Life in Action* (New York: Ballantine, 1998); Jeff Rovin and Kathy Tracy, *The Essential Jackie Chan Sourcebook* (New York: Pocket Books, 1997); Renée Witterstaetter, *Dying for Action: The Life and Times of Jackie Chan* (New York: Warner Books, 1997); and Clyde Gentry III, *Jackie Chan: Inside the Dragon* (Dallas: Taylor, 1997). See also the interviews collected in John R. Little and Curtis F. Wong, eds.,

Jackie Chan, (Chicago: Contemporary Books, 1998); and Teo, *Hong Kong Cinema,* pp. 122–134.
11. Quoted in Winterstaetter, *Dying for Action,* p. 21.
12. Quoted in Little and Wong, *Jackie Chan,* p. 40.
13. Quoted in Rovin and Tracy, *Essential Jackie Chan,* p. 90.
14. Colin Geddes and Jason Gray, "Jackie, eh," *Asian Eye* no. 2 (1995): 10.

3 ,,,,,, THE CHINESE CONNECTIONS

1. Kristin Thompson, *Exporting Entertainment: America in the World Film Market, 1907–1934* (London: British Film Institute, 1985), pp. 143–144.
2. Stephen Teo, *Hong Kong Cinema: The Extra Dimensions* (London: British Film Institute, 1997), pp. 3–39; Grace L. K. Leung and Joseph M. Chan, "The Hong Kong Cinema and Its Overseas Market: A Historical Review," in *Fifty Years of Electric Shadows,* ed. Law Kar (Hong Kong: HKIFF/Urban Council, 1997), p. 143; Paul Fonoroff, "Orientation," *Film Comment* 24, no. 3 (May–June 1988): 52–54.
3. Mac C. Shin, "Hongkong," in *Motion Picture Yearbook of Asia* (Tokyo: Far East Film News, 1956), p. 59.
4. Silas Lee, "An Interview with Luo Junxiong," in *A Comparative Study of Post-War Mandarin and Cantonese Cinema: The Films of Zhu Shilin, Qin Jian, and Other Directors,* ed. Shu Kei (Hong Kong: HKIFF/Urban Council, 1983), p. 121.
5. Weng Ling-wen, "The Dian Mou Film Company: Cantonese Film Group," in *Cantonese Cinema Retrospective* (Hong Kong: HKIFF/Urban Council, 1978), pp. 58–59.
6. Hubert Niogret, "J'étais à Hong-Kong, je n'ai pas vu de films karaté, mais j'ai dîné avec Run Run Shaw et chanté avec lui 'Happy birthday to Lisa Lu,'" *Positif* no. 169 (May 1975): 40.
7. Weng Ling-wen, "Shaw Brothers (Hong Kong) Ltd.: The Cantonese Film Group," in *Cantonese Cinema Retrospective,* pp. 59–60; Hong Kong Film Archive, *50 Years of the Hong Kong Film Production and Distribution Industries: An Exhibition* (Hong Kong: Urban Council, 1997), pp. 45–46; Herb A. Lightman, "Film in the Far East . . . and 'Down Under,'" *American Cinematographer* 51, no. 6 (June 1970): 548, 549, 554; Michael John Weber, "What Makes Run Run Run?" *American Film* 11, no. 8 (June 1986): 39; Alex Ben Block, *The Legend of Bruce Lee* (New York: Dell, 1974), p. 57; Niogret, "J'étais . . .," p. 40.
8. Ezra F. Vogel, *The Four Little Dragons: The Spread of Industrialization in East Asia* (Cambridge, Mass.: Harvard University Press, 1991), p. 66.
9. Leung and Chan, "Hong Kong Cinema," p. 144.
10. I. C. Jarvie, *Window on Hong Kong: A Sociological Study of the Hong Kong Film Industry and Its Audience* (Hong Kong: University of Hong Kong Centre of Asian Studies, 1977), p. 59.
11. Lynn Pan, *Sons of the Yellow Emperor: The Story of the Overseas Chinese* (London: Mandarin, 1991), p. 367.
12. Lin Nien-tung, "Foreword," in *Hong Kong Cinema Survey (1946–1968)* (Hong Kong: HKIFF/Urban Council, 1979), p. 4; Fonoroff, "Orientation," p. 54.
13. Stephen Teo, "Hong Kong's Electric Shadow Show: From Survival to Discov-

ery," in *Fifty Years of Electric Shadows*, ed. Law Kar (Hong Kong: HKIFF, 1997), p. 23.

14. "Kung Fu Films: The Second Coming," *Asiaweek*, 27 July 1979, p. 34.
15. "Cathay Organization: Asian Movie Legend Plays Catch-up on Exhibition Roots," *Variety Deal Memo*, 14 February 1995, pp. 10–11; Li Cheuk-to, "Popular Cinema in Hong Kong," in *The Oxford History of World Cinema*, ed. Geoffrey Nowell-Smith (London: Oxford University Press, 1996), p. 708.
16. John A. Lent, "Hong Kong," in *The Asian Film Industry*, ed. John A. Lent (London: Croom Helm, 1990), p. 100.
17. Block, *Legend of Bruce Lee*, p. 55; Ian Findlay, "Hong Kong's Cinema Survives, Despite Soaring Production Costs," *Far Eastern Economic Review*, 20 October 1983, p. 62; "Kung Fu Films," p. 36.
18. Steve Fore, "Golden Harvest Films and the Hong Kong Movie Industry in the Realm of Globalization," *Velvet Light Trap* no. 34 (Fall 1994): 44–45.
19. Interview with Tsui Hark, 4 April 1996; Law Kar, "The 'Shaolin Temple' of the New Hong Kong Cinema," in *A Study of Hong Kong Cinema in the Seventies (1970–1979)*, ed. Li Cheuk-to (Hong Kong: HKIFF/Urban Council, 1984), pp. 114–116; interview with Ann Hui, 12 February 1997; Li Cheuk-to, "The Return of the Father: Hong Kong New Wave and Its Chinese Context in the 1980s," in *New Chinese Cinemas*, ed. Nick Browne et al. (Cambridge: Cambridge University Press, 1994), p. 161.
20. Paul S. N. Lee, "The Absorption and Indigenization of Foreign Media Cultures: Hong Kong as a Cultural Meeting Point of East and West," in *Hong Kong Cinema in the Eighties*, ed. Law Kar (Hong Kong: HKIFF/Urban Council, 1991), p. 78; Law Kar, "Hongkong Film Market and Trends in the '80s," ibid., pp. 72–73.
21. Kar, "HongKong Film Market," p. 72.
22. Shaws returned to film production in a systematic way in the mid-1990s with a few midbudget films like *Out of the Dark* (1995) and *Loving You* (1996). Many of these were made by former Shaws employees such as Johnnie To, Wong Jing, and Stephen Chiau.
23. Interview with Wellington Fung, 28 November 1996.
24. Findlay, "Hong Kong's Cinema Survives," p. 62.
25. Interview with Wong Jing, 22 November 1996.
26. Law Kar, "Hongkong Film Market," p. 72.
27. See Daiwon Hyun, "Hong Kong Cinema in Korea: Its Prosperity and Decay," *Asian Cinema* 9, no. 2 (Spring 1998): 38–45.
28. Li Cheuk-to, "Popular Cinema," pp. 704–705.
29. For an excellent review of triad involvement and other matters discussed in this chapter, see Michael Curtin, "Industry on Fire: The Cultural Economy of Hong Kong Media," forthcoming in *Post Script*.
30. For this reason Stephen Teo has called them a "delayed" phase of the New Wave; *Hong Kong Cinema*, p. 184.
31. Clyde Gentry III, *Jackie Chan: Inside the Dragon* (Dallas: Taylor, 1997), p. 57.
32. Because the film was financed by a Taiwanese company, this seems to be the print that circulates internationally.
33. Pan, *Sons of the Yellow Emperor*, p. 370.

34. See Liu Hsien-chang, "Interacting Cinema Development between Taiwan and Hong Kong: The Past and the Future," in *A Perspective of Chinese Cinema of the 90's* (Taipei: Golden Horse Film Festival, 1994), pp. 55–56.
35. Interview with Shu Kei, 20 November 1997.
36. Interview with Peter Tsi, 26 November 1996.
37. Liang Hai-chiang, "Hong Kong Cinema's 'Taiwan Factor,'" in Law Kar, *Fifty Years of Electric Shadows*, p. 162. See also Liu, "Interacting Cinema Development," pp. 55–56.
38. Interview with Gordon Chan, 23 November 1996.
39. Interview with Shu Kei, 20 November 1997.
40. Wai Hin, "The Terracotta Warrior," *New Hong Kong Films 89/90* (Hong Kong: Urban Council, 1990), p. 45.
41. Interview with Peter Tsi, 26 November 1996.
42. Fiona Halligan, "Chow Still Keen," *Variety*, 29 January–4 February 1996, p. 48; Mark Woods, "Asia on Rise, Study Sez," *Variety*, 14–20 December 1998, p. 30.
43. Interview with Abe Kwong, 22 November 1996.
44. "Harvest Fails as Films Flop," *Variety Deal Memo*, 14 April 1997, p. 4. Hollywood films often command higher ticket prices than Hong Kong ones.
45. See, for example, international figures in *Hollywood Reporter*, 8 October 1996, I-7.
46. "Hollywood Prospers in HK as Local Box Office Suffers," *Variety Deal Memo*, 27 October 1997, p. 1.
47. Interview with Gordon Chan, 23 November 1996.
48. For background on UFO, see the interview with Peter Chan in Miles Wood, *Cine East: Hong Kong Cinema through the Looking Glass* (Guildford, Surrey: FAB Press, 1998), pp. 7–29.
49. Interview with Herman Yau, 27 November 1996.
50. For more on the *Feel 100%* series, see the interview with Joe Ma in Wood, *Cine East*, pp. 90–101.
51. I owe this suggestion to Athena Tsui.
52. Remarks at the conference "Fifty Years of Electric Shadows," sponsored by the Hong Kong International Film Festival, 10 April 1997. Interestingly, an "Anti-Piracy Midnight Show" was held for the U.S. film *The Corrupter* (1999) starring Chow Yun-fat; rumor has it that pirates attended, taped the film, and released VCDs soon afterward.
53. By 1994 there were more than 150,000 public video venues in the People's Republic, nearly all showing unlicensed product; Hu Ke, "The Influence of Hong Kong Cinema on Mainland China (1980–1996)," in Law Kar, *Fifty Years of Electric Shadows*, p. 171.
54. The top 10 percent of city dwellers have an average annual disposable income of only US$1,240 per person; "Not Quite a Billion," *The Economist*, 2 January 1999, p. 56.
55. Willy Wo-lap Lam, "'Cultural Invasion' Feared," *South China Morning Post*, 23 November 1996, p. 8; Willie Brent, "China Pic Prod'n Drops as Gov't Squeezes Biz," *Variety*, 23–29 September 1996, p. 30.
56. Shu Kei remarks at conference, "Fifty Years of Electric Shadows," 10 April 1997.

57. See Hu, "Influence," pp. 173–178.
58. Halligan, "Chow Still Keen," p. 48; Willie Brent, "China Opens but Film Supply Still Closed," *Variety*, 30 November–6 December 1998, p. 34.
59. See Willie Brent, "Foreign Operators Moving into China," *Variety*, 1–7 December 1997, p. 56; Don Grove, "Tough Going: Sino the Times," ibid., pp. 1, 86; Willie Brent, "Production Trail Leads to L.A.," *Variety*, 16–22 February 1998, p. 10.
60. For example, when the 1997 Cannes Film Festival screened the French-funded Chinese film *East Palace, West Palace*, a tale of homosexual life in Beijing, Chinese authorities pulled Zhang Yimou's *Stay Cool* from the festival.
61. In most European countries, Hollywood films attract 70–80 percent of local admissions; Angus Finney, *The State of European Cinema: A New Dose of Reality* (London: Cassell, 1996), p. 2. In France during the 1990s, Hollywood's share of the box office has fluctuated between 54 and 61 percent; "French Cinema Blossoms to $836 Million," *Variety Deal Memo* 6 July 1998, p. 7.
62. Bruce Einhorn, "What Hit Hong Kong's Film Industry?" *Business Week* international ed., 4 May 1998, p. 34; Maureen Sullivan, "HK Biz Gets Boost from Gov't," *Variety*, 1–7 December 1997, p. 52.
63. Mark Woods, "After the Fall: Asian Currency Squeezed," *Variety*, 13–19 October 1997, p. 18; Don Groves, "Crisis Region? Duration of Financial Woes Uncertain," *Variety*, 1–7 December 1997, pp. 49, 56; Mark Woods and Martin Peers, "Orient Express Brakes for Showbiz," *Variety*, 3–9 November 1997, p. 113; "Village Roadshow's Recipe for Asian Expansion," *Variety Deal Memo*, 16 March 1998, p. 12; Benedict Carver, "Asian $ Crisis Crunches O'seas Sales," *Variety*, 2–8 February 1998, pp. 5, 10; Don Groves, "Asian Flu Batters Healthy O'Seas B.O.," *Variety*, 10–16 August 1998, pp. 7, 12.
64. The consortium consisted of Media Asia, Era, Mei Ah, China Star, Shaw Bros., and Wong Jing's company. See "After '90s Decline, Film Industry Stabilizes, TV Expands amid Economic Woes," *Variety Deal Memo*, 14 September 1998, pp. 5–8.
65. Einhorn, "What Hit Hong Kong's Film Industry?"; "Sale Speculation Swirls around HK's Golden Harvest," *Variety Deal Memo*, 13 April 1998, p. 1; Maureen Sullivan, "Chow Spreads Words of Optimism on Biz," *Variety*, 29 June–12 July 1998, p. 10; interview with Wellington Fung, 4 April 1998; "Toei: Japan's Most Diversified Major Studio Aims at Asian Co-Prods to Boost Regional Income," *Variety Deal Memo*, 2 February 1998, pp. 6–7; Don Groves, "Village Reaps Golden Harvest with Accord," *Variety*, 10–16 August 1998, pp. 14–15; Maureen Sullivan, "Hong Kong Adds Screens," *Variety*, 30 November–6 December 1998, p. 38.
66. Neil Strauss, "Hong Kong Film: Exit the Dragon?" *New York Times*, 2 August 1998, sec. 2, pp. 1, 22. See also the dossier "Hong Kong fin de siècle," *Positif* no. 455 (January 1999): 72–102.

4 ,,,,, ONCE UPON A TIME IN THE WEST

1. The great exception to this generalization is India, which for decades housed a flourishing multilingual film industry and does not have an extensive export

market; but until recently the Indian industry was protected by government restrictions on imported films.
2. David Puttnam with Neil Watson, *The Undeclared War: The Struggle for Control of the World's Film Industry* (London: HarperCollins, 1997), p. 328.
3. The original figure is HK$1 billion. See Derek Elley, "Hong Kong," *Variety International Film Guide 1997*, ed. Peter Cowie (London: Tantivy, 1997), p. 155.
4. The cutoff point for entry is an annual revenue of US$500 million. See *Variety*, "The Creators" supplement, 26 August–1 September 1996, pp. 40–65. Billionaire Run Run Shaw is one of the wealthiest men in the region, but he shrewdly moved out of film production when television came to dominate Asia.
5. Daniel Sauvaget, "Made in Hongkong," *Image et son* no. 281 (February 1974): 48–50.
6. "U.S. Rage of Chop-Socky Films: Karate Breaks Out of Chinatown," *Variety*, 9 January 1974, p. 72; "$11,106,237 to Chop Socky Pics in U.S. Playoff," *Variety*, 8 May 1974, p. 68.
7. Quoted in Sauvaget, "Made in Hongkong," p. 64.
8. For a discussion of the two versions of *The Protector*, see Clyde Gentry III, *Jackie Chan: Inside the Dragon* (Dallas: Taylor, 1997), pp. 40–43.
9. Ray Greene, "Jackie Chan, Superstar," *Boxoffice* 132, no. 2 (February 1996): 12.
10. "New Line's Bottom Line: Red Alert," *Variety*, 11 November 1996, p. 73.
11. On the importance of the Asian market, see Wade Major, "Orientation," *Boxoffice*, February 1996, pp. 30–36.
12. Leonard Klady, "The Top 125," *Variety*, 9–15 February 1998, p. 31.
13. David Cohen, "Introducing Hong Kong's Talent to the World," *South China Morning Post*, 17 March 1997, p. 19.
14. Ibid.
15. See *Hong Kong Action Theater! Cinematic Action Role Playing Game* (Lawrence, Kans.: Event Horizon, 1996).
16. See Christopher Holmes Smith, "Method in the Madness: Exploring the Boundaries of Identity in Hip-Hop Performativity," *Social Identities* 3, no. 4 (1997): 345–374.
17. For discussions of *Can Dialectics Break Bricks?* see *Image et son* no. 273 (June–July 1973): 146–147; and *La saison cinématographique 73: Image et son* no. 276/277 (October 1973): 110–111. A U.S. tape produced by Keith Sanborn and Ediciones la Calavera presents a French-dubbed black-and-white version, subtitled in English.
18. Run Run is still a reporter's dream come true. In May 1997 at the age of eighty-nine he married his main producer, Mona Fong.
19. Vincent Canby, "'Have You Seen Shu Lately?' 'Shu Who?'" *New York Times*, 13 May 1973, sec. 2, p. 1.
20. Sauvaget, "Made in Hongkong," pp. 47–64.
21. His 1974 essay "Threads through the Labyrinth" remains a stimulating effort to understand Hong Kong cinema as popular art; Tony Rayns, "Threads through the Labyrinth: Hong Kong Movies," *Sight and Sound* 43, no. 3 (Summer 1974): 138–141.
22. Verina Glaessner, *Kung Fu: Cinema of Vengeance* (London: Bounty, 1974).
23. I. C. Jarvie, *Window on Hong Kong: A Sociological Study of the Hong Kong*

Film Industry and Its Audience (Hong Kong: University of Hong Kong Centre of Asian Studies, 1977).
24. Marco Müller, ed., *Cinemasia*, 2 vols. (Venice: Marsilio, 1983).
25. "Made in Hong Kong," *Film Comment* 24, no. 3 (May–June 1988): 33–56
26. Geoffrey O'Brien, "Blazing Passions," *New York Review of Books*, 24 September 1992, pp. 38–43.
27. Richard Meyers, Amy Harlib, and Bill and Karen Palmer, *Martial Arts Movies: From Bruce Lee to the Ninjas* (Secaucus, N.J.: Citadel, 1985), p. 11.
28. Interview with Roger Lee, 22 March 1997.
29. See *Movie Tour Guide* (Tokyo: BNN, 1995) and subsequent volumes.
30. For early issues of *Asian Trash Cinema* editor Tom Weisser compiled annotated filmographies, eventually publishing them in book form as *Asian Cult Cinema* (New York: Boulevard, 1997); *Eastern Heroes* brought out a comparable volume, Rick Baker and Toby Russell's *Essential Guide to Hong Kong Movies* (London: Eastern Heroes, 1994).
31. Quoted in Rick Baker and Toby Russell, *The Essential Guide to Deadly China Dolls* (London: Eastern Heroes, 1996), p. 7.
32. I have more than a dozen versions, forwarded by thoughtful friends. Please don't send me any more.
33. Quoted in David Chute, "Editor's Note," *Film Comment* 24, no. 3 (May–June 1988): 34.
34. Dave Kehr, "Chan Can Do," *Film Comment* 24, no. 3 (May–June 1988): 38–39.
35. Harry and Michael Medved, *The Golden Turkey Awards: The Worst Achievements in Hollywood History* (New York: Berkeley, 1980), p. xii.
36. O'Brien, "Blazing Passions," p. 39.
37. Stefan Hammond and Mike Wilkins, *Sex and Zen & A Bullet in the Head* (New York: Fireside, 1996), p. 95.
38. Roger Greenspan, "*Five Fingers of Death*," *New York Times*, 22 March 1973, p. 54.
39. Quoted in "The Men behind Kung-Fooey," *Time*, 11 June 1973, 75.
40. David Chute, who did a great deal to introduce Hong Kong cinema to North America, notes wryly: "I sat through too many screenings full of sneering slackers, gleefully hooting at films they supposedly considered classics, to retain much nostalgia for the 'cult' of Hong Kong cinema"; "New Maps of Hong Kong," *Film Comment* 34, no. 3 (May/June 1998): 85.
41. Gary Groth, "Daniel Clowes Revealed!" *Comics Journal* no. 154 (November 1992): 62.
42. Steve Fantone, "*Chinese Ghost Story II*," *Asian Eye* no. 1 (Spring 1993): 25.
43. Gere La Due, "F Stop," *Cineraider* no. 2 (1994): 42.
44. See "Best/Favorite," *Cineraider* no. 5 (1996), pp. 33–36.
45. *Days of Being Wild* does place high in the critics' poll compiled by Fredric Dannen and Barry Long, but comparatively few U.S. critics cite it. See *Hong Kong Babylon: An Insider's Guide to the Hollywood of the East* (New York: Hyperion/Miramax, 1997), pp. 328–412. A significant 1995 Hong Kong critics' poll is found in *1994 Xiang Gang Dian Ying Hui Gu* (1994 Hong Kong Film Retrospective) (Hong Kong: Hong Kong Film Critics Society, 1996), pp. 252–264.

46. Don E. May Jr., "Jackie Chan Stuntfest Spectacular [*Twin Dragons*]," *Film Threat* no. 16 (June 1994): 27.
47. Damon Foster, "Hong Kong Heroes," *Oriental Cinema* no. 11 (1996): 30; idem, "Chow Yun Fat and Other Hong Kong Heroes," *Oriental Cinema* no. 13 (1997): 41–42.
48. See "Killers and Dogs," *Asian Eye* no. 1 (Spring 1993): 15; David E. Williams, "Gone to the Dogs," *Film Threat* no. 17 (August 1994): 9–11; David Bourgeois, "Stalking the Dog," *Film Threat* no. 18 (October 1994): 18–23. Ringo Lam, who made *City on Fire,* remarked that *Reservoir Dogs* was no copy, but that he had not been above lifting the idea of *Witness* (1985) for *Wild Search* (1989); Rolanda Chu, "On the Lam: An Interview with Ringo," *Hong Kong Film Magazine* no. 4 (1995): 17.
49. Jayne Caeneddi, "Hong Kong Gender Benders: Drag and Transvestitism [sic] in Tsui Hark's Movies," *Asian Trash Cinema* no. 6 (1994): 37.
50. I'm grateful to Athena Tsui, who suggested several points developed in this paragraph.
51. Howard Hampton, "Once upon a Time in Hong Kong: Tsui Hark and Ching Siu-tung," *Film Comment* 33, no. 4 (July/August 1997): 18.
52. J. Hoberman, *Vulgar Modernism: Writing on Movies and Other Media* (Philadelphia: Temple University Press, 1991), pp. 32–40.
53. For a survey of this subcultural cinema, see Pete Tombs, *Mondo Macabro: Weird and Wonderful Cinema around the World* (New York: St. Martin's, 1998).
54. Richard Morgan, "The Internet is the New Jet Propeller," *Variety*, 20–26 July 1998, p. 4.
55. Hammond and Wilkins, *Sex and Zen*, p. 11.
56. See John Fiske, *Understanding Popular Culture* (Boston: Unwin Hyman, 1989), p. 25. For a critical discussion of this position, see Noël Carroll, *A Philosophy of Mass Art* (Oxford: Clarendon Press, 1998), pp. 236–241.

ENOUGH TO MAKE STRONG MEN WEEP

1. Bérénice Reynaud, "*The Killer* Insider," *Village Voice,* 12 May 1991, p. 60.
2. Quoted in Mel Tobias, *Flashbacks: Hong Kong Cinema after Bruce Lee* (Hong Kong: Gulliver, 1979), p. 177.
3. See Athena Tsui, "John Woo and *Bullet in the Head*" (manuscript), pp. 1–2.
4. Quoted in Rolanda Chu, "On the Lam: An Interview with Ringo," *Hong Kong Film magazine* no. 4 (1995): 23.
5. Law Kar, "Hero on Fire: A Comparative Study of Jon Woo's 'Hero' Series and Ringo Lam's 'On Fire' Series," in *Fifty Years of Electric Shadows* (Hong Kong: HKIFF/Urban Council, 1997), p. 72; Li Cheuk-to, "Tsui Hark and Western Interest in Hong Kong Cinema," *Cinemaya* no. 21 (Autumn 1993): 51. Stephen Teo speaks of *The Killer* as pushed "to the point of excess"; *Hong Kong Cinema: The Extra Dimensions* (London: British Film Institute, 1997), p. 178.
6. Interview with Peter Tsi, 8 April 1997.
7. Richard James Havis, "A Better Today: Hong Kong's John Woo Finally Does It His Way in Hollywood," *Cinemaya* nos. 39–40 (Winter–Spring 1998): 13.

8. Quoted in "John Woo on His Career," in *New Hong Kong Films '86/'87*, ed. Leong Mo-ling (Hong Kong: Urban Council, 1987), p. 35.
9. Martin Wong, "Number One with a Bullet," *Giant Robot* no. 5 (1996): 20.
10. Julien Fonfrede and Michael Gilson, "Biting the Bullet with John Woo," *Asian Eye* no. 1 (Spring 1993): 7; Wade Major, "Harder Target," *Boxoffice* 132, no. 2 (February 1996): 29.
11. Quoted in Aljean Harmetz, "Toning Down, John Woo Earns His Hollywood R," *New York Times*, 15 August 1993, p. H11.
12. Major, "Harder Target"; 29; "Woo's 'Hard' Introduction to Hollywood," *USA Today*, 20 August 1993, p. 5D.
13. Beth Accomando, "Terence Chang," *Giant Robot* no. 4 (1996): 65.
14. See Mary Hardesty, "Nike Woos the World Cup," *American Cinematographer* 79, no. 8 (August 1998): 82–87; "Mission Impossible: 2," *Cinescape* 4, no. 4 (September/October 1998): 70.
15. Bérénice Reynaud, "Woo in Interview," *Sight and Sound* 3, no. 5 (May 1993): 25.
16. See, for example, John Woo, "About John Woo," *Asian Cult Cinema* no. 20 (July 1998): 54.
17. Voice-over commentary for the Criterion laserdisc release of *The Killer*.
18. Reynaud, "Woo in Interview."
19. See Barbara Scharres, "The Hard Road to *Hard Target*," *American Cinematographer* 74, no. 9 (September 1993): 70. He would push this tendency to wild limits in *Face/Off*, which sometimes used more than ten cameras at once; Bérénice Reynaud, "Entretien avec John Woo," *Cahiers du cinéma* no. 516 (September 1997): 28.
20. Commentary for laserdisc edition of *The Killer*.
21. Ibid.
22. Ibid.
23. For a suggestive analysis of motifs clustered around character relationships, see Maitland McDonagh, "Action Painter: John Woo," *Film Comment* 29, no. 5 (September–October 1993): 46–49.
24. Teo, *Hong Kong Cinema*, pp. 176, 181.
25. Reynaud, "Entretien," 26–27; quoted in Antoine de Baecque, "Dans la peau de l'autre: *Face/Off* de John Woo," *Cahiers du cinéma* no. 516 (September 1997): 26.

5   MADE IN HONG KONG

1. Much of the information in this chapter comes from interviews with Shu Kei and Peter Tsi. I am grateful to them for their patient assistance.
2. The standard reference here is Robert C. Allen, *Vaudeville and Film, 1895–1915: A Study in Media Interaction* (New York: Arno Press, 1980).
3. The great exceptions are those countries that have vertically integrated systems but where censorship intervenes so stringently that politically suspect films are routinely shelved. The main instances are the former Soviet Union and the People's Republic of China.
4. Poshek Fu, "The Turbulent Sixties: Modernity, Youth Culture, and Cantonese

Film in Hong Kong," in *Fifty Years of Electric Shadows*, ed. Law Kar (Hong Kong: HKIFF/Urban Council, 1997), pp. 42–43. Only one major distributor-exhibitor did not have its own production company. When Newport took over the Golden Princess chain in 1988, it booked independent productions. (See Li Cheuk-to, "A Review of Hong Kong Cinema, 1988–1989," in *Ninth Hawaii International Film Festival: A Viewer's Guide* [Honolulu: East-West Center, 1989], pp. 36–37.) But as the output of independents fell, Newport followed other companies and began funding films to supply the chain.
5. I am grateful to Athena Tsui for explaining this system to me.
6. See Law Kar, "Hongkong Film Market and Trends in the '80s," in *Hong Kong Cinema in the Eighties*, ed. Law Kar (Hong Kong: HKIFF/Urban Council, 1991), p. 70.
7. I say "mainstream" in order to set aside the Category III softcore pornography. The surge in Hong Kong production of the early 1990s is largely attributable to the Category III boom, which fell off rapidly after 1993. Thus, of the total number of films released in 1992 (215), 1993 (242), 1994 (181), 1995 (150), and 1996 (104), the number of Category III films accounted for 109, 123, 59, 36, and 12, respectively. These figures come from the annual surveys by the Hong Kong, Kowloon, and New Territories Motion Picture Industry Association Ltd., *Hong Kong Films*.
8. Paul S. N. Lee, "The Absorption and Indigenization of Foreign Media Cultures: Hong Kong as Cultural Meeting Point of East and West," in Law Kar, *Hong Kong Cinema in the Eighties*, p. 79.
9. Interview with Tsui Hark, 4 April 1997.
10. Interview with Andrew Lau, 26 March 1997.
11. This excludes Chow Yun-fat, who departed for Hollywood in 1995, and the golden trio of Jackie Chan, Stephen Chiau, and Jet Li.
12. Interview with Tsui Hark, 4 April 1997.
13. The average negative cost for an American studio film is currently about US$50 million, but relatively few films actually hit that mark. The average is skewed by a few films upward of $80 million and a great number costing between $20 million and $30 million. See Martin Dale, *The Movie Game: The Film Business in Britain, Europe, and America* (London: Cassell, 1997), pp. 30–32, 176.
14. Interview with Wellington Fung, 4 April 1998.
15. Interview with Winnie Tsang, 28 November 1996.
16. Interview with Jerry Liu, 28 November 1996.
17. Ibid.
18. Quoted in David Cohen, "Introducing HK's Talent to the World," *South China Morning Post*, 17 March 1997, p. 19.
19. Interview with Andrew Lau, 26 March 1997.
20. Interview with Wong Jing, 22 November 1996.
21. Interview with Gordon Chan, 23 November 1996.
22. Interview with Shu Kei, 20 November 1996; interview with Sandy Shaw, 21 March 1997.
23. Interview with Sandy Shaw, 21 March 1997.
24. On weekdays Hong Kong theaters start the first show at noon or 12:30 P.M. and

then run four more shows (at 2:30, 5:30, 7:30, and 9:30). Weekends demand a sixth show at 4:00.

25. Some silent filmmakers, notably in Soviet Russia, plotted reel by reel. Since theaters had only one projector and had to pause when reels were changed, a division into "acts" could give the interruptions dramatic emphasis.
26. Panel discussion at the conference "Fifty Years of Electric Shadows," sponsored by the HKIFF, 10 April 1997.
27. Ibid.
28. Yuen Woo-ping, who began directing in 1978, says: "I've never held a complete script while shooting"; interview, 27 November 1996. Tsui Hark agrees: "I never have a mature script before production," interview, 4 April 1997.
29. Interview with Peter Chan, 28 November 1997.
30. Comment at panel discussion at the conference "Fifty Years of Electric Shadows," 11 April 1997.
31. Interview with Wellington Fung, 28 November 1996; interview with Raymond Lee, 22 March 1997.
32. Lin Nien-tung and Paul Yeung, eds., *Cantonese Cinema Retrospective (1950–1959)* (Hong Kong: Hong Kong Film Festival/Urban Council, 1978), p. 97.
33. Interview with Francis Ng, 8 April 1997.
34. Interview with Herman Yau, 27 November 1996.
35. Interview with Yuen Woo-ping, 27 November 1996; interview with Tsui Hark, 4 April 1997.
36. Interview with Herman Yau, 27 November 1996.
37. Interview with Gordon Chan, 23 November 1996.
38. Interview with Herman Yau, 27 November 1996.
39. "The Lucky One Becomes the Cop: Ringo Lam on *Full Alert*," in *Hong Kong Panorama 97–98*, ed. Jacob Wong (Hong Kong: HKIFF/Urban Council, 1998), p. 40.
40. Tim Greenwood, "Dragon Gate Fling," *Eastern Heroes* 2, no. 2 (1993): 23.
41. "Gere LaDue Replies," *Cineraider* no. 3 (1994): 6.
42. Colin Geddes and Jason Gray, "Smashing through the Looking Glass," *Asian Eye* no. 2 (1995): 16.
43. Interview with Shu Kei, 20 November 1996.
44. Interview with Shu Kei, 7 April 1997.
45. Rolanda Chu, "On the Lam: An Interview with Ringo," *Hong Kong Film Magazine* no. 4 (1995): 21; Jason Gray, "*Bullet in the Head*," *Asian Eye* no. 1 (Spring 1993): 14.
46. Li Cheuk-to, "Political Censorship: The Fatal Blow," *Cinemaya* no. 4 (Summer 1989): 42–44; "Hongkong's Swing to Blood and Guts," *Asiaweek*, 26 December 1980–7 January 1981, p. 43; Paul Fonoroff, "Decade Round-Up," in Law Kar, *Hong Kong Cinema in the Eighties*, p. 68.
47. Starting in November 1995, Category II was subdivided into Category IIA: Not Suitable for Children; and Category IIB: Not Suitable for Young Persons and Children.
48. Interview with Roger Lee, 22 March 1997; interview with Peter Tsi, 26 November 1996; interview with Peter Chan, 28 November 1996.

49. Interview with Wong Jing, 22 November 1997.
50. I thank Yuen Woo-ping for explaining this shooting routine to me in an interview (23 November 1996). As early as 1974 American producer Fred Weintraub complained: "They have no sense of the way we make pictures . . . They do their cuts in the camera . . . They don't bother to cover each scene from a lot of angles so the director has very little do do except string the film together" (quoted in Alex Ben Block, *The Legend of Bruce Lee* [New York: Dell, 1974], p. 103). James Glickenhaus, director of Jackie Chan's American picture *The Protector* (1985), was annoyed to discover that Hong Kong directors did not film master shots. "They shoot very short sections . . . I told them I wanted to shoot the fights in masters and then, if they didn't work, go back and cover them" (quoted in Bey Logan, *Hong Kong Action Cinema* [London: Titan, 1995], p. 70). When Ringo Lam, after his Hollywood project *Maximum Risk* (1996), began using the master-shot method on *Full Alert* (1997) it was a cause for comment (interview with Francis Ng, 14 April 1997).
51. For a discussion of how this worked elsewhere in another era, see Kristin Thompson, "Early Alternatives to the Hollywood Mode of Production: Implications for Europe's Avant-gardes," *Film History* 5 (1993): 386–404.
52. Tom Pollock, quoted in Paul Farhl and Sharon Waxman, "When 'Cut' Really Means Cut Back," *Washington Post National Weekly Edition*, 11 May 1998, p. 9.

A CHINESE FEAST

1. Tony Rayns, "Hard Boiled," *Sight and Sound* 2, no. 4 (August 1992): 20.
2. Li Cheuk-to, "Tsui Hark and Western Interest in Hongkong Cinema," *Cinemaya* no. 21 (Autumn 1993): 50.
3. For details of Tsui at work, see the dossier "'My Boss' Tsui Hark, *HK Orient Extreme Cinéma* no. 2 (April 1977): 62–63; and Tsui Hark, "Pour une nouvelle culture chinoise," ibid., no. 3 (July 1997): 68–72. On Tsui's Hollywood experiences see Steven de Souza, "*Knock Off,*" *Fade In* (Summer 1998): 80–85; and Tsui Hark, "Retour d'éxil," *Made in China, Cahiers du cinéma* special issue, 1999, pp. 32–35.
4. See Beth Accomando, "Army of Harkness," *Giant Robot* no. 8 (1997): 30.
5. Ibid., p. 29.
6. Tony Rayns, "*Die Bian* (*The Butterfly Murders*)," *Monthly Film Bulletin* no. 603 (April 1984): 114.
7. Lawrence Chua, "Separation Anxiety," *Village Voice*, 10 April 1990, p. 74.
8. Pat Aufderheide, "Dynamic Duo," *Film Comment* 24, no. 3 (May–June 1988): 44–45. See also Nansun Shi, "Profession: productrice," *Made in China, Cahiers du cinéma* special issue, 1999, p. 19.
9. Quoted in Accomando, "Army of Harkness," p. 29.
10. Interview with Gordon Chan, 23 November 1996.
11. Stephen Teo, *Hong Kong Cinema: The Extra Dimensions* (London: British Film Institute, 1997), p. 162.
12. See Ange Hwang, "The Irresistible: Hong Kong Movie *Once upon a Time in*

China Series," *Asian Cinema* 10, no. 1 (Fall 1998): 10–23; and Laurent Courtiad's interview, "Wong Fei-hung par Tsui Hark," *HK Orient Extrême Cinéma* no. 6 (March 1998): 40–47, 95.
13. Quoted in Accomando, "Army of Harkness," p. 29.
14. "Interview Tsui Hark," in Ralph Umard, *Film ohne Grenzen: Das Neue Hongkong Kino* (Lappersdorf: Kerschensteiner Verlag, 1996), p. 40.

6 ′′′′′ FORMULA, FORM, AND NORM

1. Angus Finney, *The State of European Cinema: A New Dose of Reality* (London: Cassell, 1996), p. 61.
2. Stephen Teo, "Li Hanxiang's Aesthetics of the Cynical," in *A Study of Hong Kong Cinema in the Seventies (1970–1979)*, ed. Li Cheuk-to (Hong Kong: HKIFF/Urban Council, 1984), p. 97.
3. Liu Damu, "Chinese Myth and Martial Arts Films: Some Initial Approaches," in *Hong Kong Cinema Survey (1946–1968)*, ed. Lin Nien-tung (Hong Kong: HKIFF/Urban Council, 1979), p. 43.
4. Mel Tobias, *Flashbacks: Hong Kong Cinema after Bruce Lee* (Hong Kong: Gulliver, 1979), p. 177.
5. Law Kar, "Hongkong Film Market and Trends in the '80s," in *Hong Kong Cinema in the Eighties*, ed. Law Kar (Hong Kong: HKIFF/Urban Council, 1991), pp. 72–73.
6. For a brief overview of Hong Kong horror, see Colin Geddes, "Black Dog's Blood and Moonbeams: Gyonshi in Hong Kong Cinema," *Asian Eye* no. 2 (1995): 21–26. More detailed coverage can be found in the essays in Li Cheuk-to, ed., *Phantoms of the Hong Kong Cinema*, (Hong Kong: HKIFF/Urban Council, 1989).
7. Ng Ho, "Abracadaver: Cross-Cultural Influences in Hongkong's Vampire Movies," in ibid., pp. 29–35.
8. Sek Kei, "Achievement and Crisis: Hongkong Cinema in the '80s," in Law Kar, *Hong Kong Cinema in the Eighties*, p. 52.
9. Softcore eroticism was a pan-Asian phenomenon. See "The Sex Surge," *Asiaweek*, 23 May 1980, pp. 20–22.
10. Li Cheuk-to, "The Rise of the Big-Timer," in *Sixteenth Hong Kong International Film Festival* catalogue (Hong Kong: HKIFF/Urban Council, 1992), pp. 108–112.
11. Stephen Teo, *Hong Kong Cinema: The Extra Dimensions* (London: British Film Institute, 1997), p. 149.
12. For a fan guide to this and related subgenres see Rick Baker and Toby Russell, *The Essential Guide to Deadly China Dolls* (London: Eastern Heroes, 1996).
13. Interview with Sandy Shaw, 21 March 1997. For a comparable U.S. view, see Catherine Clinch, "Women in Action," *Journal of the Writers Guild of America, West 9*, no. 5 (May 1996): 20–24.
14. Bey Logan, *Hong Kong Action Cinema* (London: Titan, 1995), pp. 156–161.
15. Interview with Peter Chan, 10 April 1997; interview with Shu Kei, 20 November 1997; Li Cheuk-to, "When the Going Gets Tough," in *Twentieth Hong*

Kong International Film Festival (Hong Kong: HKIFF/Urban Council, 1996) pp. 27–30.
16. Thomas Weisser, *Asian Cult Cinema* (New York: Boulevard, 1997), p. 173.
17. Quoted in Gerd Blake, *Hong Kong Voices* (Hong Kong: Longman, 1989), p. 26.
18. Grace L. K. Leung and Joseph M. Chen, "The Hong Kong Cinema and Its Overseas Market: A Historical Review, 1950–1995," in *Fifty Years of Electric Shadows*, ed. Law Kar (Hong Kong: HKIFF/Urban Council, 1997), p. 147.
19. Quoted in Finney, *State of European Cinema*, p. 54.
20. Joanna C. Lee, "Star Culture!" *Hong Kong Film Magazine* no. 3 (Spring 1995): 13–15.
21. On the "sour beauty" see Teo, *Hong Kong Cinema*, pp. 29–38.
22. Interview with Peter Chan, 6 February 1999.
23. For a deft celebration of Lin's charms, see Howard Hampton, "Venus, Armed," *Film Comment* 32, no. 5 (September/October 1996): 42–48.
24. A. C. Scott, "The Performance of Classical Theater," in *Chinese Theater: From Its Origins to the Present Day*, ed. Colin Mackerras (Honolulu: University of Hawaii Press, 1983), p. 142.
25. I am grateful to Anthony Wong for suggestions about the range of acting styles in Hong Kong cinema (interview, 26 March 1997).
26. See Paul Ekman, commentary in Charles Darwin, *The Expression of the Emotions in Man and Animals*, 3d ed. (New York: Oxford University Press, 1998), pp. xxx, 64.
27. See David Bordwell, Janet Staiger, and Kristin Thompson, *The Classical Hollywood Cinema: Film Style and Mode of Production to 1960* (New York: Columbia University Press, 1985), pp. 194–240; Kristin Thompson and David Bordwell, *Film History: An Introduction* (New York: McGraw-Hill, 1994), chaps. 2 and 3.
28. See David Bordwell, *On the History of Film Style* (Cambridge, Mass.: Harvard University Press, 1997), chaps. 5 and 6.
29. See David Bordwell, *Ozu and the Poetics of Cinema* (Princeton: Princeton University Press, 1988); and Bordwell, "A Cinema of Flourishes: Japanese Decorative Classicism of the Prewar Era," in *Reframing Japanese Cinema*, ed. David Desser and Arthur Noletti (Bloomington: Indiana University Press, 1992), pp. 327–345.
30. Interview with Shu Kei, 20 November 1997.
31. On *Armageddon* (average shot length, 2.3 seconds), see Todd McCarthy, "Noisy 'Armageddon' Plays 'Con' Game," *Variety*, 29 June–12 July 1998, p. 38.
32. Sergei Eisenstein, "The Unexpected," in *Film Form*, ed. and trans. Jay Leyda (New York: Harcourt, Brace, 1949), p. 23.
33. Tsui Hark remarks that Hollywood film editors found some of his cuts on figure action illogical. "In my films, the shot/reverse shots don't always follow the eyelines but rather the bodies, often tiny parts of them—an extended hand, a fist, a leg folded in an unnatural position . . . I know the 180-degree rule as well as the Americans, but for me it's a rule which belongs to the past"; "Retour d'éxil," *Made in China, Cahiers du cinéma* special issue, 1999, p. 33.
34. Noël Carroll, *A Philosophy of Mass Art* (Oxford: Clarendon Press, 1998), p. 67.

WHATEVER YOU WANT

1. Interview with Wong Jing, 22 November 1996.

7 ′′′′′ PLOTS, SLACK AND STRETCHED

1. Geoffrey O'Brien, "Blazing Passions," *New York Review of Books,* 24 September 1992, p. 41.
2. Li Cheuk-to in roundtable discussion, "A Review of the 1987 Hong Kong Cinema," in *New Hong Kong Films 87/88* (Hong Kong: Urban Council, 1988), p. 7.
3. See Tom Gunning, "The Cinema of Attractions: Early Film, Its Spectator, and the Avant-Garde," in *Early Cinema: Space, Frame, Narrative,* ed. Thomas Elsaesser (London: British Film Institute, 1990), pp. 56–60.
4. Viktor Shklovsky, "The Relationship between Devices of Plot Construction and General Devices of Style" (1919), in *Theory of Prose,* trans. Benjamin Sher (Elmwood Park, Ill.: Dalkey Archive Press, 1990), pp. 28–34.
5. For a discussion of this position, see Kristin Thompson, *Storytelling in the New Hollywood: Analyzing Classical Narrative Structure* (Cambridge, Mass.: Harvard University Press, 1999), pp. 344–352.
6. Gordon Chan interview, 23 November 1996; Clifton Ko, remarks in panel, "The Operations of the Hong Kong Film Industry: From 1984 to 1989," in *Fifty Years of Electric Shadows: Report of Conference on Hong Kong Cinema 10–12 April 1997,* ed. Law Kar (Hong Kong: Urban Council, 1997), pp. 16–17.
7. Interview with Abe Kwong, 22 November 1996; interview with Peter Tsi, 21 March 1997.
8. Clifton Ko, remark in panel discussion at the conference "Fifty Years of Electric Shadows," sponsored by the HKIFF, 10 April 1997.
9. Li Cheuk-to, "Thoughts on the Films of Qiu Jian and Zhu Shilin," in *A Comparative Study of Post-War Mandarin and Cantonese Cinema: The Films of Zhu Shilin, Qin Jian, and Other Directors,* ed. Shu Kei (Hong Kong: HKIFF/Urban Council, 1983), pp. 113–114.
10. Madeleine Doran, *Endeavors of Art: A Study of Form in Elizabethan Drama* (Madison: University of Wisconsin Press, 1954), p. 298.
11. Quoted in David Armstrong, "Video Village: South San Francisco Company Dominates Asian Film Distribution Market," *San Francisco Examiner,* 11 May 1998, p. B1.
12. Interview with Shu Kei, 20 November 1996; interview with Gordon Chan, 23 November 1996.
13. Thanks to Athena Tsui and Thomas Shin for suggestions on these points.
14. Interview with Peter Chan, 28 November 1996.
15. Howard Reid and Michael Croucher, *The Way of the Warrior: The Paradox of the Martial Arts* (London: Century, 1983), pp. 22–62.
16. James J. Y. Liu, *The Chinese Knight-Errant* (London: Routledge and Kegan Paul, 1967), pp. 131–133.
17. Instructions can be found in David Chow and Richard Spengler, *Kung Fu: History, Philosophy, and Technique* (Burbank: Unique, 1982), pp. 145–154.
18. Liu Damu, "From Chivalric Fiction to Martial Arts Film," in *A Study of the*

Hong Kong Swordplay Film (1945–1980), ed. Lau Shing-hon (Hong Kong: HKIFF/Urban Council, 1996), pp. 57–59.

19. For a detailed study of the connections between *Ashes of Time* and the novels of Jin Yong, see Juanita Huan Zhou, "*Ashes of Time:* The Tragedy and Salvation of the Chinese Intelligentsia," *Asian Cinema* 10, no. 1 (Fall 1998): 62–70.
20. Roger Garcia, "Alive and Kicking, the Kung Fu Film Is a Legend," *Far Eastern Economic Review*, 20 October 1985, p. 61.
21. Quoted in Michael Harris Bond, *Beyond the Chinese Face: Insights from Psychology* (Hong Kong: Oxford University Press, 1991), p. 58.
22. Ma Ka-fai, "Hero, Hong Kong Style: A Structural Study of Hero Films in Hong Kong" (M.A. thesis, University of Chicago, 1990), pp. 13–16.
23. I thank Peter Tsi for suggesting this idea to me.
24. For more on these schemas, see Daniel Sauvaget, "Made in Hongkong," *Image et son* no. 281 (February 1974): 53–57.
25. Quoted in Lau Shing-hon, "Qiu Gangjian," in Lau, *Hong Kong Swordplay Film (1945–1980)*, p. 209.

8   MOTION EMOTION

1. Some of the points made in this chapter are developed in slightly different directions in my essay "Aesthetics in Action: Kung-Fu, Gunplay, and Cinematic Expressivity," in *Fifty Years of Electric Shadows*, ed. Law Kar (HKIFF/Urban Council, 1997), pp. 81–89.
2. Quoted in Hubert Niogret, "J'étais à Hong-Kong, je n'ai pas vu de films karaté, mais j'ai dîné avec Run Run Shaw et chanté avec lui 'Happy Birthday to Lisa Lu,'" *Positif* no. 169 (May 1975): 39.
3. David Chow and Richard Spangler, *Kung Fu: History, Philosophy, and Technique* (Burbank: Unique, 1982), pp. 39–42; Howard Reid and Michael Croucher, *The Way of the Warrior: The Paradox of the Martial Arts* (London: Century, 1983), p. 70.
4. Mike Leader, "Yuen Wah Cometh," *Eastern Heroes* 2, no. 4 (1994): 12.
5. A. C. Scott, "The Performance of Classical Theater," in *Chinese Theater: From Its Origins to the Present Day*, ed. Colin Mackerras (Honolulu: Unviersity of Hawaii Press, 1983), pp. 118–133.
6. Bey Logan, *Hong Kong Action Cinema* (London: Titan, 1995), p. 11.
7. See, for example, Law Kar's "Huang Fei-hung's Family Tree," in *Wong Fei Hung: The Invincible Master*, ed. Yu Mo-wan (Hong Kong: Urban Council, 1996), unpaginated.
8. Yu Mo-wan, "Swords, Chivalry, and Palm Power: A Brief Survey of the Cantonese Martial Arts Cinema," in *A Study of the Hong Kong Swordplay Film (1945–1980)*, ed. Lau Shing-lian (Hong Kong: HKIFF/Urban Council, 1996), p. 102.
9. Lin Nien-tung, "The Martial Arts Hero," in ibid., p. 13.
10. Yu Mo-wan, "Swords, Chivalry, and Palm Power," pp. 99–102.
11. See Yu Mo-wan, "The Prodigious History of Wong Fei Hong," in *A Study of the Hong Kong Martial Arts Film*, ed. Lau Shing-hon (Hong Kong: Urban Council,

1980), pp. 79–86; and Ng Ho, "The Three Heroic Transformations of Huang Feihong," in Yu, *Wong Fei Hung*, n.p.
12. Logan, *Hong Kong Action Cinema*, p. 12.
13. Lau Shing-hon, "Han Yingjie," in Lau, *Study of the Hong Kong Swordplay Film*, pp. 214–215.
14. Lau Shing-hon, "Xu Zhenghong," ibid., p. 203; idem, "Qiu Gangjian," ibid., p. 207.
15. Yu Mo-wan, "Swords, Chivalry, and Palm Power," pp. 104–105.
16. Stephen Teo, *Hong Kong Cinema: The Extra Dimensions* (London: British Film Institute, 1997), pp. 98–99.
17. Ibid., pp. 97–108.
18. Interview with Peter Chan, 10 April 1997.
19. Interview with Herman Yau, 27 November 1996.
20. Ibid.
21. Noël Carroll, "Fists of Fury," *Soho Weekly News*, 7 September 1978, p. 68.
22. Lev Kuleshov, *Kuleshov on Film*, ed. and trans. Ron Levaco (Berkeley: University of California Press, 1974), p. 67.
23. Quoted in Linda Lee, *The Bruce Lee Story* (Santa Clarita, Calif.: Ohara, 1989), p. 65.
24. Wong Kiew Kit, *The Art of Shaolin Kung-Fu* (Shaftesbury, Dorset: Element, 1996), pp. 2–3.
25. Scott, "Performance of Classical Theater," pp. 125–127.
26. On this trend see Jane Hamsher, *Killer Instinct: How Two Young Producers Took on Hollywood and Made the Most Controversial Film of the Decade* (New York: Broadway, 1997), p. 146; and Ian Grey, *Sex, Stupidity, and Greed: Inside the American Movie Industry* (New York: Juno, 1997), p. 174.
27. Interview with Yuen Woo-ping, 23 November 1996.
28. After writing this chapter I was happy to find another student of action cinema taking note of "muscular sympathy" created when someone feels the strain and release of another person's movements. See Aaron Anderson, "Action in Motion: Kinesthesia in Martial Arts Films," *Jump Cut* no. 42 (1998): 1–11, 83.
29. See the extended discussion in Mikhail Iampolski, "*Rakurs* and Recoil," *Aura* 4, no. 1 (1998): 4–15. On expressive movement in Eisenstein generally see David Bordwell, *The Cinema of Eisenstein* (Cambridge, Mass.: Harvard University Press, 1993), pp. 115–120.
30. "Our Anti-Hero Is a Human Being: Interview with Director Patrick Leung and Scriptwriter Chan Hing-kar," in *Hong Kong Panorama 97–98*, ed. Jacob Wong (Hong Kong: HKIFF/Urban Council, 1998), p. 63.

THREE MARTIAL MASTERS

1. On Zhang Che, see Jerry Liu, "Chang Che: Aesthetics = Ideology?" in *A Study of the Hong Kong Swordplay Film (1945–1980)*, ed. Lau Shing-hon (Hong Kong: HKIFF/Urban Council, 1996), pp. 159–162; Lau Shing-hon, "The Tragic Romantic Trilogy of Chang Che," in *A Study of the Hong Kong Martial Arts Film*, ed. Lau Shing-hon (Hong Kong: HKIFF/Urban Council, 1980), pp. 91–96;

Tian Yan, "The Fallen Idol—Zhang Che in Retrospect," in *A Study of Hong Kong Cinema in the Seventies,* ed. Li Cheuk-to (Hong Kong: HKIFF/Urban Council, 1984), pp. 44–46; Stephen Teo, *Hong Kong Cinema: The Extra Dimensions* (London: British Film Institute, 1997), pp. 98–103.

On Lau Kar-leong, see Roger Garcia, "The Autarkic World of Liu Chia-liang," in Lau, *Hong Kong Martial Arts Film,* pp. 121–134; Tony Rayns, "Resilience: The Cinema and Liu Jialiang," in Li, *Hong Kong Cinema in the Seventies,* pp. 51–56; Bey Logan, *Hong Kong Action Cinema* (London: Titan, 1995), pp. 44–57; Teo, *Hong Kong Cinema,* pp. 104–108.

These directors are also discussed in François and Max Armanet, *Ciné Kung Fu* (Paris: Ramsay, 1988) and "Made in Hong Kong," *Cahiers du cinéma* no. 362–363 (September 1984).

There are many good studies of King Hu. The most complete roundup of information in English is in Law Kar, ed., *Transcending the Times: King Hu and Eileen Chang* (Hong Kong: HKIFF/Urban Council, 1998). See also Teo, *Hong Kong Cinema,* pp. 87–96; and Tony Rayns, "King Hu: Shall We Dance?" in *Hong Kong Martial Arts Film,* pp. 103–106. Tony Rayns's "Director: King Hu," *Sight and Sound* 45, no. 1 (Winter 1975/76): 8–13, offers an important interview. The only full-length study is King Hu, Yamada Koichi, and Udagawa Koyo, *King Hu buyo den'ei sappo: A Touch of King Hu* (Tokyo: Soshi-sha, 1997). For a more detailed exploration of the stylistic matters touched on here, see David Bordwell, "Richness through Imperfection: King Hu and the Glimpse," in Law Kar, *Transcending the Times,* pp. 19–24.

2. John R. Little and Curtis F. Wong, eds., *Jackie Chan* (Chicago: Contemporary Books, 1998), p. 106.
3. Xu later became one of Taiwan's most important film producers, responsible for *Farewell My Concubine* (1993) and *Temptress Moon* (1997).
4. See Michel Ciment, "Entretien avec King Hu," *Positif* no. 169 (May 1975): 32.
5. Peggy Chiao Hsiung-pi, "The Master of Swordplay," *Cinemaya* no. 39–40 (Winter–Spring 1998): 72–76.
6. Charles Tesson, "Calligraphie," *Cahiers du cinéma* no. 360–361 (September 1984): 21.
7. Quoted in Peggy Chiao Hsing-ping, "Master of Swordplay," p. 74.
8. He was not, but he used even shorter ones.

9   AVANT-POP CINEMA

1. Interview with Jimmy Choi, 12 April 1996; Cristina Hilsenrath, "Freedom of Expression," *Variety,* 22–28 June 1998, p. 38.
2. *Hong Kong Independent Film: A New Generation: Retrospective Screening* (Hong Kong: Hong Kong Arts Centre, 1998), unpaginated.
3. Two excellent analyses are Law Kar, "The Significance of *The Arch,*" in *A Comparative Study of Post-War Mandarin and Cantonese Cinema: The Films of Zhu Shilin, Qin Jian, and Other Directors,* ed. Shu Kei (Hong Kong: HKIFF, 1983), pp. 163–165, and Lau Shing-hon, "Shu Shuen: The Lone Rider in Hong Kong Cinema in the 1970s," in *Hong Kong Cinema in the 1970s,* ed. Li Cheuk-to (Hong Kong: HKIFF/Urban Council, 1984), pp. 106–109.

4. I am grateful to Tony Rayns for calling my attention to *Nomad* and *Health Warning* as important works in the "countercanon."
5. Quoted in Beth Accomando, "Army of Harkness," *Giant Robot* no. 8 (1997): 30.
6. "I don't think anyone has done what we did regarding heroes," remarks Cha. "I mean, Chow Yun-fat is always a cool dude, he just doesn't do drugs. I think if you are going to be a gangster, you must be really bad, bad enough to kill your own father." See Linda Iai and Kim Choi, "An Interview with Director Cha Chuen Yee on *Once upon a Time in Triad Society 2*," in *Hong Kong Film Panorama 96–97*, ed. Jacob Wong (Hong Kong: Urban Council, 1997), p. 18.
7. Michel Ciment, "Entretien avec Wong Kar-wai: Travailler comme dans une 'jam session,'" *Positif* no. 410 (April 1995): 39–40, 42–43; Bérénice Reynaud, "Entretien avec Wong Kar-wai," *Cahiers du cinéma* no. 490 (April 1995): 37.
8. For examples see Ackbar Abbas, *Hong Kong: Culture and the Politics of Disappearance* (Minneapolis: University of Minnesota Press, 1997), pp. 48–62, and Michael Hoover and Lisa Stokes, "A City on Fire: Hong Kong Cinema as Cultural Logic of Late Capitalism," *Asian Cinema* 10, no. 1 (Fall 1998): 25–41.
9. Quoted in Fredric Dannen and Barry Long, *Hong Kong Babylon: An Insider's Guide to the Hollywood of the East* (New York: Hyperion, 1997), p. 52.
10. Christopher Doyle, *Angel Talk* (Tokyo: Prénom H, 1996), p. 56.
11. Reynaud, "Entretien avec Wong Kar-wai," p. 38.
12. Christopher Doyle, *Buenos Aires* (Tokyo: Prénom H, 1997), pp. 144, 212.
13. Idem, "To the End of the World," *Sight and Sound* 7, no. 5 (May 1997): 17.
14. Derek Elley, "Hongkong," in *Variety International Film Guide 1992*, ed. Peter Cowie (London: Tantivy Press, 1991), p. 190.
15. According to Lau, he shot the Brigitte Lin story and the scenes at the Midnight Express café (interview with Lau, 26 March 1997). Then Lau was preparing to direct his own film and left the project. According to Wong Kar-wai, when he brought Doyle aboard they reshot some of Lau's footage (Tony Rayns, "Poet of Time," *Sight and Sound* 5, no. 9 [September 1995]: 13). "The style of the film was actually established between Lau Wai-keung and me when Lau was doing the cinematography for the first part; so when Chris came in, he just had to extend that style" (Jimmy Ngai, "A Dialogue with Wong Kar-wai," in Jean-Marie Lalanne et al., *Wong Kar-wai* [Paris: Dis Voir, 1998], p. 113). Both Lau and Doyle are credited on the film as cinematographers, although some English-language sources credit only Doyle.
16. Larry Gross, "Nonchalant Grace," *Sight and Sound* 6, no. 9 (September 1996): 9.
17. See Curtis Tsui, "Subjective Culture and History: The Ethnographic Cinema of Wong Kar-wai," *Asian Cinema* 7, no. 2 (Winter 1995): 93–124, for the most thorough discussion of this line of argument.
18. Ciment, "Entretien avec Wong Kar-wai," p. 44.
19. "For *Ashes of Time* my principal objective was to find a desert that could function as a symbol for the characters' emotional states"; quoted in Reynaud, "Entretien avec Wong Kar-wai," p. 39.
20. Doyle, *Angel Talk*, p. 28.
21. Ibid., p. 50.
22. For most shots Doyle used a lens attachment that yielded a focal length of

6.3mm, so wide that its area of view sometimes included Doyle's assistant standing alongside the camera. See Patricia Thomson, "A Jazz Session with *Fallen Angels,*" *American Cinematographer* 79, no. 2 (February 1998): 16–18; Hubert Niogret, "Entretien avec Christopher Doyle," *Positif* no. 442 (December 1997): 17.

23. Ciment, "Entretien avec Wong Kar-wai," p. 42.
24. Ibid., pp. 43–44.
25. Ngai, "Dialogue with Wong Kar-wai," p. 116.
26. I thank Andrew Lau and Herman Yau for explaining this process to me in detail. See Doyle, *Buenos Aires,* pp. 80, 104, 148, and 174, for information about these techniques.
27. Peter Bowen, "Time of Your Life," *Filmmaker* 4, no. 2 (Winter 1996): 32.
28. Contrast the use of the same pop song in *Top Gun* (1986).
29. Peggy Chaio Hsiung-ping, "*Happy Together:* Hong Kong's Absence," *Cinemaya* no. 36 (1997): 20.

ROMANCE ON YOUR MENU

1. There are at least two versions of *Chungking Express,* the Hong Kong release and an "international" version (the one circulating on film and video in Europe and North America). The latter runs nearly five minutes longer than the Hong Kong version, chiefly because of extra footage showing the blonde woman kidnapping the child of a friend of the Indians who have betrayed her. There are also differences on the music track, most strikingly during the scene in which Officer 633 drinks coffee at Midnight Express; in the Hong Kong version, we hear Faye Wong's cover version of "Dreams," but in the international version the shot is silent. My discussion of the film refers to the international version, since it is the one generally available.
2. Quoted in Michel Ciment, "Entretien avec Wong Kar-wai: Travailler comme dans une 'jam session,'" *Positif* no. 410 (April 1995): 45.
3. Bérénice Reynaud, "Entretien avec Wong Kar-wai," *Cahiers du cinéma* no. 490 (April 1995): 38.
4. Tony Rayns, "Poet of Time," *Sight and Sound* 5, no. 9 (September 1995): 15.
5. Quoted in "*Chungking Express,*" in *The Nineteenth Annual Hong Kong International Film Festival* (Hong Kong: HKIFF/Urban Council, 1995), p. 37.
6. For example, Akbar Abbas, *Hong Kong: Culture and the Politics of Disappearance* (Minneapolis: University of Minnesota Press, 1997), pp. 41–62. Wong discusses his attitude toward filming Hong Kong in "L'architecte et le vampire," *Made in China, Cahiers du cinéma* special issue, 1999, pp. 26–29 (1999): 26–29.
7. The first four reels are devoted to Officer 223 and the mysterious blonde woman; her murder of her bartender-boss ends the fourth reel. At the start of the next reel, after 223 has received the blonde woman's paged message, he drops in at the Midnight Express, where he bumps into Faye and launches the next plotline. This wends its way up to reel nine, when Officer 633 discovers the changes in his apartment, confronts Faye, makes the date, and is stood up at the California Café. The tenth reel shows the two reuniting a year later.
8. Ironically, the film made the Midnight Express stall so famous that the owner redecorated it.

ACKNOWLEDGMENTS

Research for this book was supported by the Wisconsin Alumni Research Fund as administered by the University of Wisconsin–Madison Graduate School. The University's Institute for Research in the Humanities kindly granted me a senior fellowship, which allowed me release time to travel and write. I am grateful for this support, as well as for the funding of a film series and symposium on Asian cinema, "Light in the East," held during the 1996–97 academic year and sponsored by the UW Anonymous Fund, the Humanistic Foundation, the Consortium for the Arts, and the International Institute.

No writing project has enriched my life more than this one. In 1995 Li Cheuk-to kindly took me out to lunch during the Hong Kong International Film Festival, and that was just the beginning. He encouraged me to write this book and offered me precise criticisms and corrections of every chapter. Through Cheuk-to I met others. Stephen Teo proved another great source of information, suggestions, and good fellowship. Stephen also read the entire manuscript and offered much advice. Athena Tsui has been my eyes and ears in Hong Kong. She kept me up-to-date, arranged interviews, and gave me access to a great deal of information. Shu Kei, polymathic director-producer-distributor-critic, and one of the most vital players in local film culture, patiently answered my questions for hours on end. *Planet Hong Kong* simply would not exist were it not for Cheuk-to, Stephen, Athena, and Shu Kei.

The energetic staff of the Hong Kong International Film Festival provided a cheerful atmosphere for my visits; I owe special thanks to Law Kar and Jacob Wong. I am very grateful to Peter Tsi, who met with me on several occasions and gave me unique insights into the film industry; and to the members of the Hong Kong Film Critics Society, who shared their ideas at an all-night dinner. The following people kindly gave interviews: Gordon Chan, Peter Chan, Jimmy Choi of the Hong Kong Arts Centre, Wellington Fung of Media Asia, Ann Hui, Michael Hui, Abe Kwong, Andrew Lau, Albert Lee of Golden Harvest, Roger Lee of Golden Harvest, Jerry Liu of Media Asia, Francis Ng, Sandy Shaw, Winnie Tsang of Golden Harvest, Tsui Hark, Anthony Wong, Wong Jing, Herman Yau, and Yuen Woo-ping.

Michael Campi has been immensely generous in offering rare material and in suggesting things to watch. Likewise Tony Rayns, Western doyen of Eastern cinema, has for years been keeping me updated on Asian cinema, while also prodding me to consider forgotten and unappreciated films. I first met Bérénice Reynaud at the Festival, and her energetic intelligence has steered me to important films and ideas; she also provided many detailed suggestions on this manuscript.

During several of my stays in the territory, Patricia Erens of Hong Kong University offered me hospitality. I have learned a lot from her perspective on the city she lives in. For sharing information I thank Sam Ho, Linda Lai, Ryan Law, Cynthia Liu of the Hong Kong Film Archive, Ma Ka-fai, Chen Mei, Hector Rodriguez, Thomas Shin, David Stratton, Eliza Walsh-Lau Man Yee, Norman Wang, and Esther Yau, with particular thanks to Till Brockman, Alberto Pezzotta, Peter Rist, and Miles Wood. Access to film prints was provided Mike Arnold of Rim Films, Peter Chow, Vivian Chow of Asian CineVision, Rolanda Chu, Ange Hwang of Asian Media Access, John Soo of Tai Seng, John Vasco, and Coco Wong of Golden Harvest Films. Special thanks go to Gabrielle Claes of the Royal Film Archive of Belgium, who invited me to attend a 1997 tribute to Hong Kong cinema; and to Ludo Bettens, who arranged for me to view several films held in the Archive's collection.

Thanks also to the Hong Kong Film Archive and to Winnie Fu, who helped me obtain Figs. 1.6, 3.1, 8.2, 8.3, and 8.4 from the Archive's collection.

At home, Hong Kong film has kept me in touch with many friends. My colleagues at the Institute for Research in the Humanities, particularly director Paul Boyer, were a continuing source of ideas and information. My editor at Harvard, Lindsay Waters, was exceptionally gracious in launching and sustaining this project, and Kim Steere carefully engineered its intact arrival at the Press. Thanks once again to Ann (Omit Needless Words) Hawthorne. Marianne Perlak and David Foss were keenly attentive in designing yet another of my books. Barbara Scharres, programmer extraordinaire at the Film Center of Chicago's Art Institute, has long supported Hong Kong cinema in the Midwest. Thanks also to those other Midwesterners David Desser and Fu Poshek for enjoyable discussions. Here at Madison I have been helped by Tino Balio, Sally Banes, Ben Brewster, Pu-kui Chan, Lisa Dombrowski, Nelson Ferreira, Maxine Fleckner-Ducey, Ed Friedman, Erik Gunneson, Kevin Heffernan, Jonathan Hertzberg, Scott Higgins, Lea Jacobs, Vance Kepley, Jim Kreul, Anita Mok, Jim Moy, J. J. Murphy, Paul Ramaeker, Doug Riblet, Sally Ross, Paddy Rourke, Rafe Vela, Mike Walsh, Sean Weitner, Juanita Zhou, and Pauline Zveiniks, with particular thanks to Hideaki Fujiki and Jim Udden. Warm appreciation goes to the Guardians of the Shaolin Temple—Mark Bendian, Joe Lindner, and Mike Pogorzelski—and to Nat Olson, master of the digital domain and full-time fan of Hong Kong cinema.

Noël Carroll and Kristin Thompson provided initial encouragement and detailed comments on early drafts. They know how much every project I undertake owes to them.

INDEX

Aces Go Places (1982), 4, 70, 71, 151, 181, 245
Aces Go Places II (1983), 220
Aces Go Places III: Our Man from Bond Street (1984), 138
Action films, 1–2, 11–12, 19–25, 49–60, 67, 98–113, 123–125, 127, 142, 150, 153–154, 162, 163, 183–184, 191–198, 199–247, 248–260, 316n28
After the Crescent (1997), 267
All for the Winner (1990), 40, 151, 173–174
All's Well End's Well (1992), 6–7, 18, 181–182, 185
All the Wrong Clues (For the Right Solution) (1981), 135, 137, 153, 278
Always on My Mind (1993), 127, 184, 185
Angel (1987), 90, 153
Arch, The (1970), 162, 262–263, 264
Art cinema: in the West, 6, 7, 17, 261; in Hong Kong, 6, 69, 93, 119, 180, 262–267
Ashes of Time (1994), 73, 74, 93, 176, 193, 246, 247, 266, 270, 272, 273, 274–275, 276, 277, 279, 280, 282, 318n19
As Tears Go By (1988), 72, 266, 270, 272, 273, 274, 275, 276, 277, 278, 279
Attendance at Hong Kong films, 34, 35, 66, 70, 72, 75, 76, 80
Autumn's Tale, An (1987), 10, 154, 184, 185
Avenging Warriors (1979), 42, 251

Banquet, The (1991), 11, 185
Better Tomorrow, A (1986), 5, 41, 71, 89, 93, 94, 99, 100, 101–105, 106, 108, 114, 131, 136, 153, 175, 208, 270
Better Tomorrow II, A (1987), 99, 100, 105–106, 111, 125
Better Tomorrow III, A (1989), 40, 188–189
Big Boss, The (1971), 49, 52, 67, 68, 254
Big Bullet, The (1996), 18, 42, 185
Big Heat, The (1988), 208, 234–235
Big-timer films, 152
Blade, The (1995), 143, 144–145, 266
Bodyguard from Beijing, The (1994), 159, 231
Boys Are Easy (1993), 10–11, 173, 175, 185
Broken Arrow (1996), 85, 101
Bullet in the Head (1990), 40, 85, 94, 99, 100, 109–110, 111, 251
Butterfly Murders, The (1979), 135, 137, 142, 143, 153

Cageman (1992), 168–170
Cantonese-language production, 3, 4, 32, 35, 61–62, 65, 66, 68–69, 72, 204
Cantonese Opera films, 62, 98, 162, 206
Carroll, Noël, 170, 220, 295n9
Casino Raiders (1989), 38, 173, 186, 198
Category III films, 128, 155–156, 175, 177, 309n7
Cathay Film Company (1965), 62, 66, 67–68, 98, 206
Censorship, 127–128, 310n47
Centre Stage (1992; aka *Actress*), 93, 265
C'est la vie, mon cheri (1993), 76
Cha Chuen-yee, 36, 123, 197, 268–269

323

Chan, Ekin, 27, 77, 156
Chan, Evans, 61, 266
Chan, Fruit, 198
Chan, Gordon, 47, 72, 74, 76, 81, 124, 185, 208
Chan, Jackie, 3, 4–5, 19, 36, 39, 42, 50, 55–60, 68, 71, 72, 73, 74, 75, 76, 79, 80, 83, 84–85, 88, 89, 90, 93, 118, 119, 124, 126, 128, 137, 154, 157, 160, 172, 173, 176, 177, 180–181, 183, 196, 200, 201, 202, 207, 217, 231, 232, 245, 254, 311n50
Chan, Jordan, 27, 191
Chan, Peter, 38, 62, 77, 122, 128, 158, 168, 190, 208
Chang, Terence, 19, 85–86, 120, 254
Chang Chang-Ho, 214
Chang Wai-hung, 267
Cheng, Carol "Dodo," 157, 159
Cheng, Sammi, 77, 156
Cheung, Alex, 162, 245
Cheung, Cherie, 10, 111
Cheung, Jacky, 117, 156, 176, 266
Cheung, Jacob, 168–170
Cheung, Leslie, 101, 111, 117, 156, 158, 266
Cheung, Mabel, 10, 72
Cheung, Maggie, 87, 157, 158, 159, 266
Chiao Hsiung-ping, Peggy, 280
Chiau, Stephen, 6, 18, 36, 40, 42, 44, 75, 76, 95, 119, 151, 156, 157, 158, 172, 173
China, 28–31, 40–41, 62, 64, 78–80, 127, 191–194, 255
China Behind (1974), 127, 263
Chinese Boxer, The (1970), 67, 83, 206, 207
Chinese Connection, The. See Fist of Fury
Chinese Feast, The (1995), 9, 11, 37, 117, 127, 145–148
Chinese Ghost Story, A (1987), 71, 135, 136, 138, 151, 165–168, 170, 182, 208, 229
Chinese Ghost Story II, A (1990), 93
Ching Siu-tung, 71, 74, 93, 165, 208
Chor Yuan, 100, 193
Chow, Raymond, 49, 68–69, 80–81, 83–85, 86, 116, 206
Chow Yun-fat, 10, 36, 42, 71, 73, 75, 86, 94, 99, 100, 101, 105, 111, 123, 127, 157, 158, 160, 172, 173, 175

Chungking Express (1994), 6, 12, 36, 73, 128, 168, 176, 266, 267, 268, 270, 271, 272, 273, 274, 276, 277, 278, 280, 282–289, 318n15
Cinema City & Films Co., 70, 72, 77, 99, 116, 119, 182
City Hunter (1993), 39, 50, 76, 172–173
City on Fire (1987), 86, 89, 94, 270
Color, 118, 124, 138, 162–165, 244, 277, 279
Come Drink with Me (1966), 67, 204, 254, 256
Comrades, Almost a Love Story (1996), 38, 39, 77, 128, 158, 168
Constructive editing, 210–217, 243
Continuity filmmaking, 161–170, 210–217, 311n13
Cops and Robbers (1979), 162–163, 245
Craft of filmmaking, 13–17, 93, 117, 129–134, 161–170, 189
Credit sequences, 134, 189, 224, 261
Crippled Avengers (1978), 42, 218, 249, 251
Critics: in Hong Kong, 44–48, 93; in the West, 95–96
Culture, local, 28–33, 44–48, 52, 54, 59–60, 69

Dance of the Drunk Mantis (1979), 220, 235
D & B Films, 77, 116, 153, 154
Dangerous Encounter—First Kind (1980), 46, 69, 127, 135, 137, 263–264
Days of Being Wild (1990), 38–39, 46, 72, 93, 176, 266, 270, 271–272, 274, 275, 276, 277, 278, 279
Days of Tomorrow (1993), 150, 159, 266
Day That Doesn't Exist, The (1995), 152, 268
Dead and the Deadly, The (1982), 42, 151, 181, 185–186
Die Hard (1988), 176, 210, 224–226, 231, 233
Don't Give a Damn (1995), 38, 158
Don't Stop My Crazy Love for You (1993), 93
Doyle, Christopher, 271, 274, 276, 318n15, 318n22
Dr. Lamb (1992), 155
Dragon Gate Inn (1967), 67, 204, 255–256, 258
Dragon Inn (1992), 124

Drunken Master (1978), 56, 207
Drunken Master II (1994), 58, 59, 254
Duel to the Death (1983), 208, 219

Eagle-Shooting Heroes, The (1993), 158–159, 193, 266
Eastern Condors (1987), 18, 234, 245
East Is Red, The (1993), 158, 159, 185–186, 271
Editing, 2, 13, 14–16, 24, 102–105, 108, 109, 110, 125–126, 134, 142–143, 161–170, 206, 210–217, 227–228, 237–245, 246, 253, 258, 260, 261, 277, 279, 311n50, 313n33
Eight-Diagram Pole Fighter, The (1984), 194–195, 237, 253, 254
Eighth Happiness, The (1988), 160, 184, 185
Emotion, 8–10, 187–189, 231–234, 244–245, 280–281
Enter the Dragon (1973), 49, 52
Exit the Dragon, Enter the Tiger (1976), 54, 55
Expect the Unexpected (1998), 246

Face/Off (1997), 85, 86, 100, 112–113, 237, 308n19
Fallen Angels (1995), 266, 267, 270, 271, 274, 275, 277, 278, 280, 283
Fan subcultures in the West, 87–97
Fast-motion imagery, 209, 235
Fate of Lee Khan, The (1973), 256, 257
Fearless Hyena (1979), 55, 56
Feel 100% (1996), 77, 189, 267
Fight Back to School (1991), 6, 19, 158, 185
Film Workshop, 71–72, 85, 119, 135–139
Final Option, The (1994), 42, 76, 124
First Love: Litter on the Breeze (1997), 267
First Option, The (1996), 47, 124
First Sword, The (1967), 212–213
Fist of Fury (1972), 49, 50–52, 53, 83, 163, 185, 208
Fist of Legend (1994), 50, 163, 208
Fists of Fury. See *The Big Boss*
Five Fingers of Death. See *King Boxer*
Flashbacks, 7, 189–190
Fong, Allen, 46, 69, 137, 263

Fong Sai-yuk (1993), 133, 152, 157, 175, 185, 203, 207, 208, 209, 219
Fonoroff, Paul, 81
Foster, Damon, 94
Four Faces of Eve (1996), 266–267
Front Page, The (1990), 40, 163

Game of Death (1978), 49–50, 53–54
Genres, 76, 149–156
Glaessner, Verina, 88
God of Cookery (1996), 37, 158
God of Gamblers (1989), 37, 89, 131, 172, 173, 175, 186, 187, 188, 209
God of Gamblers II (1990), 173, 175
God of Gamblers III (1991), 174
God of Gamblers 3: The Early Stage (1996), 171, 174, 188
God of Gamblers' Return (1994), 171, 174, 184
God of Gamblers series (1989–1996), 41, 131–132, 152, 173–175
Golden Harvest, 49, 56, 68–69, 70, 76, 80–81, 83–85, 98, 99, 116, 120, 128, 155, 204
Golden Swallow (1967), 204, 250
Gross, Larry, 272
Guangyi company, 64, 119
Gu Long, 100, 193
Gun Men (1988), 5, 19–25, 133, 136, 181, 183, 186, 233–234, 237

Han Yingjie, 254, 256
Happy Together (1997), 6, 260, 270, 271, 272, 273, 275–276, 277, 278, 279
Hard Boiled (1992), 37, 42, 74, 85, 94, 99, 100, 112, 127, 208, 226–228, 229, 232, 233, 238, 251
He Ain't Heavy, He's My Father (1993), 38, 77, 154, 188
Health Warning (1983), 245, 264
He and She (1994), 38
Heart to Hearts (1988), 76, 154
Heat (1995), 14–16, 129, 161, 186
Her Fatal Ways series (1990–1994), 40, 159
Hero (1997), 43, 182, 184
Heroes, 42–44, 194–196, 249–251, 255–256
"Heroes" crime cycle, 5, 18, 41, 48, 71, 89, 94, 99, 186, 197, 208
Heroic Trio (1993), 90, 159

He's a Woman, She's a Man (1994), 38, 77, 154, 163–164, 168, 175, 190–191
Heung, Charles, 41, 119
High Risk (1995), 39, 172, 176–177
Ho, Leonard, 68, 80
Hollywood: distribution, 1, 34–35, 64, 74–75, 76, 79–80, 82–83; aesthetics, 7–8, 10, 11, 18–25, 129, 161–170, 178–180, 221, 228, 239, 243
Hong Kong Arts Centre, 45, 262
Hong Kong Film Critics Society, 44–45
Hong Kong International Film Festival, 45, 69, 88
Horror films, 151, 268
Hou Hsiao-Hsien, 6, 74, 247, 264
House of 72 Tenants, The (1973), 68
Hu, King, 1–2, 13, 17, 67, 68, 73, 88, 133, 136, 162, 194, 204, 206, 214, 254–260, 265
Huang Feihong, 52, 176, 204, 205, 207, 208, 209, 251
Hui, Ann, 4, 6, 32, 36, 46, 69, 110, 137, 150, 152, 153, 157, 263
Hui, Michael, 3, 32, 36, 40, 68, 98, 157, 162, 163
Hui, Ricky, 69, 99
Hui, Sam, 32, 70
Hung, Sammo, 42, 56, 68, 70, 71, 73, 86, 93, 118, 120, 126, 151, 153, 158, 160, 181, 202, 207, 245, 246, 254, 278

Iceman Cometh, The (1989), 184, 185, 219
Independent film in Hong Kong, 262–267
Industry of film in Hong Kong, 34–36, 61–81, 82–86, 115–134, 203–207, 262–267
In the Heat of Summer (1994), 38, 185
Invincible Armour (1977), 196, 236
Iron Monkey (1993), 136, 152, 234

Japanese cinema, 64, 67, 72, 83, 88, 96, 100, 200, 206, 208, 229, 277
Jarvie, Ian, 64, 88
Jin Yong (aka Louis Cha), 120, 193
Jumping Ash (1976), 150, 245
Justice, My Foot! (1992), 158

Kehr, Dave, 91
Killer, The (aka *Sacred Knives of Vengeance*, 1972), 104
Killer, The (1989), 5, 8, 85, 92, 93, 99, 106–109, 110, 111, 112, 113, 127, 136, 158, 185, 189, 195, 251
King Boxer (1972), 83, 92, 186, 214–217, 237
Kitano, Takeshi, 17, 98, 229, 247
Ko, Clifton, 118, 120, 122, 182
Kot, Eric, 77–78, 267
Kung-fu films, 3, 35, 42, 49–60, 68, 72, 73, 74, 83–85, 89, 98, 129–130, 132, 145, 152, 162, 186, 194–196, 206–207, 208, 246
Kurosawa, Akira, 88, 100, 196, 206, 228, 229
Kwan, Stanley, 6, 46, 72, 119, 265
Kwan Tak-hing, 52, 204, 205

Lam, Ringo, 5, 7, 32, 40, 69, 85, 86, 99, 115, 119, 124, 127, 270, 311n50
Lamb, Jan, 266
Last Hero in China (1993), 172, 173
Last Hurrah for Chivalry (1979), 98
Lau, Andrew, 117, 129, 151, 246, 318n15
Lau, Andy, 36, 39, 73, 126, 157, 159, 173, 266, 270
Lau, Jeff, 72, 189, 193, 266
Lau Ching-wan, 158
Lau Kar-fai, 119, 251
Lau Kar-leung, 119, 132, 194–195, 207, 210, 251–254, 255, 256
Law, Clara, 6, 72, 127
Law Kar, 45, 99
Law with Two Phases (1984), 103, 158
Lee, Bruce, 3, 8, 49–55, 56, 58, 59, 60, 66, 67, 68, 76, 83–84, 86–87, 88, 121, 128, 157, 163, 176, 177, 196, 201, 206, 208, 221, 232, 254
Lee, Daniel, 137, 261
Lee, Danny, 103, 118, 127, 158, 189
Left-wing cinema, 46, 62
Legendary Weapons of China (1982), 229–231, 252, 253
Legend of the Wolf (1997), 43, 246
Leung, Patrick, 197, 200, 237
Leung Chiu-wai, Tony, 157, 159, 271
Leung Kar-fai, Tony, 158, 175
Li, Jet, 36, 72, 96, 119, 128, 152, 156, 157, 159, 172, 173, 176, 177, 208, 209
Li Cheuk-to, 44, 47, 72, 99, 135, 178
Li Hanxiang, 73, 150

Lifeline (1997), 43, 183, 217, 218, 234, 246
Lin, Brigitte, 72, 75, 159, 271
Log, The (1996), 42, 196–197, 268
Long Arm of the Law, The (1984), 103, 105
Longest Nite, The (1998), 246
Love Amoeba Style (1997), 77, 123, 168
Love and the City (1994), 266
Love in the Time of Twilight (1995), 144
Love Will Tear Us Apart (1998), 267
Lung Kong, 99, 162

Ma Ka-fai, 42
Made in Hong Kong (1997), 43
Mak, Johnny, 103
Mandarin-language production, 3, 35, 61–62, 65, 66, 73, 116, 204–206, 255
Martial arts, 50–53, 84, 191–196, 200–204, 224, 251, 256
Media Asia, 120
Midnight shows, 26–28, 33, 122
Money Crazy (1977), 98
Mongkok Story (1996), 153–154
Motifs, narrative, 108, 185–189, 275–276, 283–286, 288, 289
Motion Picture and General Investment Company (MP & GI), 62, 64, 65, 66, 116, 121, 204. *See also* Cathay Film Company (1965)
MP & GI. *See* Motion Picture and General Investment Company
Mr. Vampire (1985), 151
Mui, Anita, 157, 194
Music, 36, 70, 76, 77, 107, 126, 139, 143, 146, 163–165, 167, 186–187, 235–236, 256, 278–279
My Heart Is That Eternal Rose (1989), 168, 182

Naked Killer (1992), 93, 155, 175
New One-Armed Swordsman, The (1971), 42, 210–211, 249–250
New Wave, 4, 45, 46, 69–70, 72, 88, 152–153, 207, 254, 262, 263–264
Ng See-yuen, 55
Ngai, Jimmy, 44
92 Legendary La Rose Noire (1992), 76, 154
Ninja in the Dragon's Den (1982), 196, 245
Nomad (1982), 264

O'Brien, Geoffrey, 89, 92, 178
Once a Thief (1991), 85, 99, 100, 111–112, 218
Once upon a Time in China (1991), 5, 74, 88, 90, 123, 133, 135, 136, 138, 139, 143, 146, 152, 157, 172, 208
Once upon a Time in China II (1992), 128, 152
Once upon a Time in Triad Society 1 (1996), 39, 123, 268–269
Once upon a Time in Triad Society 2 (1996), 36, 39, 197, 246, 268
One-Armed Swordsman, The (1966), 67, 144, 204, 248, 249
Opera, Chinese, 55, 56, 62, 150, 160, 173, 192, 193, 194, 201, 202, 224, 256
Operation Condor (1991), 58
Organized Crime and Triad Bureau (1994), 121
Outlaw Brothers, The (1990), 93, 133
Overbey, David, 91

Painted Faces (1988), 202
Parallels, narrative, 102, 106, 107–108, 113, 185–186, 196, 268, 269, 274–276, 283–285, 286–289
Passion 1995 (1995), 268
Pause/burst/pause rhythm, 221–231, 243
Peking Opera Blues (1986), 2–3, 7, 16, 93, 118, 131, 136, 138, 140–142, 143, 147, 148, 187, 235, 245
Plain Jane to the Rescue (1982), 100, 114
Plotting, 19–22, 55–56, 122, 159–160, 178–198, 267–270, 272–276, 283–288
Police Story (1985), 5, 19, 58, 59, 90, 218, 245
Pom Pom and Hot Hot (1992), 19, 163
Poon, Dickson, 77, 116, 153, 154
Popular cinema as concept, 5–17, 149–150, 160–161, 178–180, 198, 220, 261–262, 289
Private Eye Blues (1994), 38
Private Eyes, The (1976), 32
Production process, 120–134, 171, 205–207, 221, 254–255, 271–272, 282–283
Project A (1983), 4–5, 58, 59, 71, 180–181, 182, 207, 245
Protector, The (1985), 84, 311n50

Raining in the Mountain (1979), 255, 257–258
Rayns, Tony, 88
Reel-by-reel plotting, 122, 180–182, 275, 283
Reflection, popular cinema as, 36–37, 47
"Relationship" movies, 76–77
Reservoir Dogs (1992), 86, 94
Return of the Dragon, The. See The Way of the Dragon
Reverse-motion imagery, 209–210
Righting Wrongs (1986), 39, 184, 195, 238–243
Rock n' Roll Cop (1994), 40, 123, 245
Rodriguez, Hector, 46
Ross, Jonathan, 90
Rothrock, Cynthia, 157
Rouge (1988), 72, 93, 180, 265
Royal Tramp (1992), 173
Run and Kill (1993), 155–156

Saviour of the Soul (1991), 163–164, 170, 194, 210, 244
Scorsese, Martin, 45, 100, 170, 208
Scriptwriting, 120–122, 172, 196
Secret, The (1979), 46, 69, 152, 153
Segment shooting, 129–131, 142–143, 165–167, 221, 243, 311n50
Sek Kei, 45, 48, 151
Sequels, 188–189
Sex and Zen (1991), 155
Shanghai Blues (1984), 5, 71, 93, 138, 139–141, 143, 147, 148, 185, 189
Shaolin Avengers (1976), 196
Shaolin Challenges Ninja (1978), 252
Shaw, Run Run, 4, 63, 64, 68, 82, 83, 84, 86, 87–88, 92, 117, 132, 199, 206
Shaw, Sandy, 121
Shaw Brothers, 3–4, 63, 64, 65, 66, 68–69, 98, 116, 119, 121, 126, 204, 206, 208, 248, 254
Shek Kin, 52, 156, 204
She Shoots Straight (1990), 153, 182, 189
Shi, Nansun, 40, 119, 138
Shu Kei, 39, 118, 120, 123, 126, 168
Shu Shuen, 45, 127, 162, 262–263
Siao Fong-fong, Josephine, 156, 245
Skinny Tiger and Fatty Dragon (1990), 182

Slow-motion imagery, 102–105, 107, 109, 162, 207, 208, 234–235, 277–278, 288
Snake in the Eagle's Shadow (1978), 55, 56, 201, 207
Somebody Up There Likes Me (1996), 185, 186, 200
Soo, Helen, 184
Speed (1994), 20, 75, 175, 176, 183
Stars, 149–150, 156–160
StormRiders (1998), 151, 172
Story of a Discharged Prisoner (1967), 99, 131, 162, 168
Style, 7–8, 23–25, 100, 102–105, 107, 108, 109, 111, 113, 118, 123–126, 129–131, 139, 142, 146–147, 160–170, 210–247, 276–280, 285–286, 288
Subtitles, 89, 91, 126–127
Summer Snow (1995), 36, 186
Supercop (Police Story 3) (1992), 59, 72, 125
Sword, The (1980), 153, 264
Swordplay films, 42, 62, 67, 68, 71, 74, 89, 120, 129–130, 136, 152, 162, 193–194, 203–206, 210–214, 246, 248–251, 254–260, 277
Swordsman (1990), 74, 136, 175, 208, 254, 271
Swordsman II (1992), 74, 159

Taiwan as Hong Kong market, 65, 66, 73–75, 120, 171
Tam, Patrick, 46, 69, 153, 168, 264, 270
Tarantino, Quentin, 45, 84, 86, 94, 267, 269, 270
Task Force (1997), 9, 10, 13, 43, 185, 197–198, 237, 246
Taxi Hunter (1993), 77, 156
Teo, Stephen, 40, 67, 207
Terracotta Warrior, The (1990), 74
Third Full Moon (1994), 152
36th Chamber of Shaolin, The (1978), 251–252
Those Were the Days (1997), 176
Thou Shalt Not Swear (1993), 38, 152
Thunderbolt (1995), 58, 72
Tiger on Beat (1988), 160, 254
Ti Lung, 99, 100, 101, 208, 250
To, Johnnie, 43, 133
To Be No. 1 (1996), 38
To Liv(e) (1992), 266

Tom, Dick, and Hairy (1993), 77, 154
Tong, Stanley, 85, 125
Too Many Ways to Be No. 1 (1997), 269
Top Banana Club (1996), 269
Touch of Zen, A (1971), 1–2, 7, 13, 88, 254, 255, 256, 257, 260
Triads, 41, 72
Tricky Brains (1991), 172, 174, 175
Tristar (1996), 139, 158
Tsang, Eric, 118, 158–159, 246
Tsi, Peter, 99–100
Tsui, Athena, 42, 48
Tsui Hark, 2–3, 5, 32, 40, 41, 46, 62, 69, 71, 72, 74, 85, 87, 88, 89, 90, 93, 94, 95, 100, 105, 117, 118, 119, 120, 127, 128, 133, 135–148, 150, 152, 153, 157, 165, 172, 185, 187, 188, 208, 234, 245, 263–264, 265, 266, 271, 278, 310n28, 313n33
Twist (1995), 156

UFO. *See* United Filmmakers Organization
Undeclared War (1990), 40, 158
United Filmmakers Organization (UFO), 77, 78, 154–155, 191
Untold Story, The (1993), 77, 78, 155, 158, 184, 189–190
Untouchables, The (1987), 19–25, 183

Valiant Ones, The (1975), 255, 257, 258–259
Video, 34, 73, 74, 78, 80, 84, 89–90, 129, 279, 296n18
Vulgarity, 6–7, 172–177

Wang, Joey, 71, 72, 271
Wang Yu, Jimmy, 67, 68, 196, 207, 250
Way of the Dragon, The (1972), 49, 51, 52–53, 58, 68, 221–224, 229, 231, 233
We're Going to Eat You (1980), 135, 137
Whatever You Want (1994), 173, 175–176, 177, 186
What Price Survival? (1994), 261, 262
Wheels on Meals (1984), 58, 245
Wicked City (1992), 136
Wild Search (1989), 18
Winners and Sinners (1983), 59, 71, 207
Win's Entertainment, 41, 119, 120
Wong, Anthony, 27, 36, 39, 77, 155–156, 269

Wong, Kirk, 5, 19–25, 28, 33, 40, 69, 85, 121, 172, 180, 233, 245, 264
Wong, Manfred, 78
Wong Fei-hung. *See* Huang Feihong
Wong Jing, 10–11, 39, 71, 120, 121, 128, 131, 155, 171–177, 184
Wong Kar-wai, 6, 36, 38, 46, 72, 119, 133, 143, 149, 168, 176, 193, 260, 266–267, 268, 269–281, 282–289, 318n15, 318n19
Woo, John, 5, 40, 41, 43, 71, 74, 85–86, 87, 89, 93, 94, 98–114, 118, 127, 136, 142, 185, 186, 189, 195, 202, 208, 218, 234, 246, 251, 254, 265, 278
Working Class (1985), 143–144

Xu Feng, 194, 255

Yam, Simon, 155–156
Yang, Edward, 6, 74, 264, 282
Yau, Herman, 77, 124, 155–156, 189, 208, 246
Yee, Derek, 72, 76
Yen, Donnie, 157, 208, 235, 237
Yeoh, Michelle, 72, 86, 153, 156, 194
Yes, Madam! (1985), 90, 153, 194, 221
Yim Ho, 46, 69, 119, 136, 152, 153, 263
Young and Dangerous 4 (1997), 26–28, 33, 34, 41, 43, 77, 78, 81, 125, 129–130, 197
Young and Dangerous series (1996–), 26–27, 38, 39, 40–41, 48, 73, 77, 78, 81, 117, 119, 120, 125, 154, 246
Young Master (1980), 57–58, 59, 177, 231, 232
Yu Lik-wai, 267
Yuen, Anita, 12, 157, 158, 175
Yuen Biao, 56, 158, 195, 202, 245
Yuen Kuei, 70, 177, 184, 202, 208, 238, 245
Yuen Wah, 202
Yuen Woo-ping, 56, 70, 207, 208, 244, 310n28, 311n50

Zhang Cheh, 67, 98, 100, 132, 162, 204, 206, 207, 210–211, 218, 248–251, 252, 254, 255, 256
Zoom shots, 162, 207, 235, 236, 237
Zu: Warriors from the Magic Mountain (1983), 71, 135, 137–138, 150